>> *ON THE MOVE*

>> *ON THE MOVE*

Women and Rural-to-Urban Migration
in Contemporary China

Edited by **ARIANNE M. GAETANO** *and* **TAMARA JACKA**

COLUMBIA UNIVERSITY PRESS   *New York*

Columbia University Press
Publishers Since 1893
New York Chichester, West Sussex
Copyright © 2004 Columbia University Press
All rights reserved

Library of Congress
Cataloging-in-Publication Data
   On the move : women and rural-to-urban migration in contemporary China
/ edited by Arianne M. Gaetano and Tamara Jacka.
     p.   cm.
     Includes bibliographical references and index.
     ISBN 0–231–12706–5 — ISBN 0–231–12707–3 (pbk.)
     1. Rural women—China—Social conditions. 2. Migration, Internal—
China. 3. China—Social conditions—1976– I. Title: Women and rural-to-
urban migration in contemporary China. II. Gaetano, Arianne M. III. Jacka,
Tamara.
HQ1767.O528 2004
307.2'4'0820951—dc21
        2003048900

Columbia University Press books are printed
on permanent and durable acid-free paper.
Printed in the United States of America
c 10 9 8 7 6 5 4 3 2 1
p 10 9 8 7 6 5 4 3 2 1

CONTENTS

8. The Impact of Labor Migration on the Well-Being
   and Agency of Rural Chinese Women: Cultural and
   Economic Contexts and the Life Course
   Rachel Murphy / 243

PART 4. WRITING LIVES

ACKNOWLEDGMENTS

We would like to extend heartfelt thanks to our contributors for their dedication to this project. It has truly been our good fortune to collaborate with these talented authors who facilitated the process of producing this volume with their unwavering enthusiasm, diligence, and goodwill. Our own scholarship has been greatly enriched through this collegial exchange of knowledge. We sincerely thank them for an enjoyable experience.

We are grateful to the Gender Relations Centre, Research School of Pacific and Asian Studies, Australian National University, for supporting Tamara's work on this project, and to Annegret Schemberg and Ria Van de Zandt for their excellent copyediting.

Special acknowledgment is due the many members and staff of the Migrant Women's Club in Beijing, who have offered their friendship and shared their lives with us over the past several years. We are indebted to them for invaluable assistance with our research and for our deepening understanding of migrant women's issues and experiences.

Our editors at Columbia University Press deserve much credit for bringing this book to fruition. Wendy Lochner provided unwavering support for this project from its inception; Suzanne Ryan nurtured it through the production process; and Leslie Kriesel provided meticulous copyediting.

Finally, we give thanks to our families and friends for their ongoing support.

>> ON THE MOVE

Tamara Jacka and Arianne M. Gaetano

Introduction: Focusing on Migrant Women

>> China today is undergoing a process of rapid and massive social and economic changes comparable to the industrial revolution that occurred in Europe, but squeezed into decades rather than spread over centuries. One of the most visible and significant manifestations of this process has been a huge increase in migration from the largely agricultural countryside and remote rural interior to the relatively industrialized urban areas, particularly the towns, cities, and Special Economic Zones of the coastal provinces, as well as the provincial-level cities. Most of these migrants are so-called unofficial, temporary, de facto, or non*hukou* migrants, belonging to what is commonly deemed the "floating population" (*liudong renkou*). This term refers to anyone who has moved, either temporarily or long-term, away from their registered place of residence without a corresponding transfer of official residence registration, or *hukou*.[1] Nonlocal registration (i.e., nonlocal *hukou*) thus distinguishes those we refer to as "migrants" in this volume from those known as official, permanent, or de jure migrants (*qianyi renkou*): people of primarily urban origin whose relocation to another city has been officially sanctioned or directed. Estimates of the size of the floating population[2] now range upwards of 100 million,[3] and the vast majority of migrants currently living in urban areas are peasants.[4] These rural migrants in particular are at the front line of both domestic and global capitalist development, working for

1

the lowest wages in poor and often unsafe conditions and in occupations that urbanites shun.[5] This book draws together important new research on the lives of "unofficial" rural-to-urban migrant women, presenting their experiences of migration and the context that shapes those experiences, and exploring the impact of migration on the identities, values, worldviews, and social positions of migrant women themselves, as well as on social relations, especially gender relations, and the discourses that inform them.

The recent surge in rural-to-urban migration has attracted a great deal of attention from scholars both in and outside China, but the scope of this attention has been fairly narrow. Most studies have been concerned primarily with the macro-level demographic, economic, and political effects of migration, and with how the influx of migrants into urban areas should be managed.[6] To date, relatively few scholars have sought to understand how rural-to-urban migration in China is experienced by migrants themselves,[7] and even fewer have focused on the circumstances of female rural-to-urban migrants or examined the impact of gender on the experience of migration.[8] Until recently, this lack of attention to gender was also a characteristic of studies of migration in other parts of the world.[9] Yet, given what we have learned about that migration, we can surmise that the experiences of rural-to-urban migrants in China will have a major impact on those individuals' worldviews, sense of identity, and relationships with others, and on social relations more generally.[10] This is likely to be particularly significant in the case of rural women's migration for a number of reasons.

First of all, it has been suggested that outmigration may provide an important avenue of escape for women suffering gender oppression or violence,[11] and may even help to reduce suicide rates among rural women. This is important because suicide rates in China are about three times the global average and, unlike in any other country in the world, most suicides are young rural women. Among rural women aged 15 to 35, suicide accounts for more than 20 percent of all deaths.[12]

Rural Chinese women, like many of their counterparts in other developing countries, may experience and be empowered[13] by a degree of autonomy from the patriarchal authority of parents or of in-laws and a broadening of horizons when they migrate to urban areas.[14] Certainly, the latter appears to be an important motivation for migration. In one survey of migrants in four Chinese cities, over half the women cited "more experience in life" as their main reason for migrating, while higher income was the chief motivation for male migrants.[15] Chapters in this volume suggest that rural women who migrate make more independent and informed decisions, from how to spend their hard-earned wages to when and whom they will marry, and in regard to issues of sexuality and reproduction. In addition, as elsewhere in the world, married women who accompany their husbands or families in migration may experience a shifting of power in their marital relationships, as the couple together negotiates the urban market and society.[16] Finally, rural women who do not themselves migrate are nonetheless influenced by the migration of their spouses or other household members, taking up new duties and responsibilities.

On the other hand, rural migrants of both genders suffer discrimination and exploitation as outsiders (*waidiren*) in the cities and as cheap and "flexible" labor. In the case of women, this oppression is often compounded by sexual exploitation, discrimination, and abuse. In addition, the inequalities of wealth and differences in lifestyle and environment that currently exist between rural and urban China, and the barriers placed in the way of rural migrants trying to integrate into urban society, are likely to make the transition from country to city (and back) very difficult. For a large proportion of migrants, the fact that migration occurs at a time when they are negotiating the shift from youth to adulthood complicates their situation. Finally, young rural women's migration may pose particular difficulties, both for the individuals involved and for their families and communities, because it conflicts with the usual expectation that women will marry in the countryside and take responsibility for the domestic sphere when they are in their early twenties. In addition, for married women migrants separated from their children, there may be a weakening of emotional ties and guilt, though their earnings may provide the children with an improved material life.[17]

Migrant women returning to the countryside may find that employment away from home gives them greater standing and authority in the community, or else it alienates them from fellow villagers. Returned migrant women may be able to use skills they have learned while away to improve their own economic situation and bring much-appreciated status and income to their family and fellow villagers. Or alternatively, they may feel themselves trapped once more in a life of backbreaking field work and monotonous domestic chores.

Finally, some scholars have suggested that, while rural women's migration to and from urban areas will play an important role in bringing "modern," progressive ideals and values to the countryside, it may be very difficult for individual rural women returning to the countryside to readjust to "traditional," patriarchal rural culture.[18] We should be wary, however, of an equation between "urban" and "progressive," or "less patriarchal" on the one hand and "rural" and "patriarchal" on the other. It may be that a significant proportion of migrant women suffer far greater gender (and other forms of) oppression and unhappiness while working away from home, and are greatly relieved to return to the countryside.

To date, there simply has not been enough published research on the experiences and agency of migrant women or the relationship between rural women's migration and sociocultural change in China. The aim of this book is to contribute to an improvement in our understanding of these issues. Through analyses based on in-depth research in different parts of China, the chapters provide insights into rural women's motivations for outmigration, their experiences of work and of life in the city, the strategies they employ to negotiate or overcome their inferior status in the eyes of urbanites, their social networks and ties to home, the ways they try to shape a future for themselves, and the long-term implications of migration for themselves, their families, and their village communities.

Unlike so many other studies of the floating population that are motivated by concern about the economic effects of rural-to-urban migration or its impact on urban society, this volume is primarily concerned with the impact of migration on migrants themselves. This book also differs from other studies in paying particular attention to the ways in which gender shapes both the experiences and the consequences of migration. Its central aim is to understand what rural-to-urban migration means to rural women, and from there, to gain insight into how rural women's migration to urban areas and back transforms social relations, identities, and gender ideologies both in urban areas and in the countryside.

As a whole, this book is framed by a focus on the experiences and voices of individuals and groups who are otherwise socially marginalized. On the one hand, as feminists have long recognized, such a focus can point out shortcomings and gaps in existing knowledge, and can call into question interpretations and analyses made without consideration of subaltern experiences. The chapters in this volume contribute to our understanding of sociocultural change in contemporary China by conveying insights from the perspective of rural migrant women, who have been left out of the majority of studies on migration to date. On the other hand, an approach that takes any individual's or group's understandings of their experiences as the singular foundation for knowledge will be limited by a failure to account for the ways in which subjectivities, experiences, and the communication of experience are shaped through discourses, institutions, and networks of power.[19] This book therefore takes care to relate migrant women's identities and practices with those discourses of contemporary Chinese society that are productive of gender, class, and rural/urban differences.

OUTLINE OF THE CHAPTERS

The contributors to this volume address our central aim from a variety of angles using different theories and methodologies, but with strong commonalities. Apart from this introductory essay, a chapter on the representation of migrant women in the media, and a collection of stories by migrant women themselves, the remainder of the chapters are based on qualitative fieldwork and attend carefully to what migrant women have to say about their experiences, their decisions, and their actions. Moreover, all of the chapters draw out and endeavor to understand the interconnections and interactions among migrant women's subjectivity, self-representation, and agency on the one hand, and broader structures, institutions, and sociopolitical discourses on the other.

Part 1 of the book is concerned with representations and identities of *dagongmei*, or "working sisters." This term refers to migrant women, most of whom are in their teens and twenties, who work in urban waged labor. The first two chapters examine the ways *dagongmei* negotiate dominant discourses and images relating to modernity, gender and sexuality, and rural/urban differences. Each seeks to contribute to our understanding of power and resistance by looking at the complex consequences of migrant women's negotiations of their identity.

In chapter 1, Arianne Gaetano discusses issues relating to the agencies, experiences, and subjectivities of young rural women working in domestic service in Beijing. These women's motivations and expectations for migration and their assessments of their experiences must be understood, she argues, in the context of multiple and competing discourses relating to the identity and role of the "modern urban woman" on the one hand and of the "filial rural daughter" on the other. Migrant women's agency, she suggests, lies in their ability to balance the contradictions between these discourses. In the first part of the chapter, Gaetano demonstrates that in their decisions to migrate to the city, young migrant women are often motivated by a desire conditioned by a powerful discourse of modernity, according to which staying in the countryside means being left behind in the march of progress. Rural gender and kinship roles, daughters' relatively marginal roles in rural production, and the loss of autonomy that will likely result from marriage further strengthen women's desire to "escape" the countryside, even for a brief period. However, expectations surrounding marriage, norms of gender propriety, and popular stereotypes associating women's mobility with immorality are also of concern to young women considering migration to the city.

In the remaining sections of her chapter, Gaetano demonstrates the numerous ways in which migrant women balance these desires and concerns. For example, through quotations from her conversations with women working in domestic service, she shows that this occupation is often chosen because it is considered "safe." Underlying this assumption is the belief that domestic service is appropriate work for women because of its location within the domestic sphere. In contrast, other work open to migrant women, such as in restaurants and clubs, is undesirable because these are mixed-sex venues where a woman's virtuous reputation might be compromised.

Domestic service, however, is less lucrative than many other jobs. Moreover, it is stigmatized by both urbanites and rural people, largely because of its historical associations with servility. The low prestige of domestic service together with the disrespect, exploitation, and abuse suffered by many domestic workers can both derail their quest for a modern urban identity and threaten to damage their own and their family's reputations in the village, affecting prospects for marriage. Yet against these challenges, Gaetano argues, domestic workers manage to fashion a new identity that is both filial and modern, deploying various tactics to minimize the negative effects of such work. In particular, Gaetano finds, consumption and tourism are significant means for young migrant women to partake of a modern urban identity they are denied in their role as domestic service workers. In addition, by using their widening social networks to facilitate the migration of fellow villagers and by acquiring skills and education, migrant women gain prestige for themselves and their families, and enhance their filial role. Still, Gaetano concludes, migration involves much compromise and exacts from young rural women both sacrifices and rewards.

Chapter 2, by Tiantian Zheng, is a case study of rural migrant women working as bar hostesses in the city of Dalian, performing services, including those related to sex, for mainly urban men. Women such as these are among the most socially stigmatized of all rural migrant women; they are the stereotypical immoral "other" from whom women such as the domestic workers in Gaetano's study struggle to distinguish themselves. Based on participant observation in ten karaoke bars, Zheng's study provides a detailed analysis of the daily strategies through which bar hostesses deploy their stigmatization and oppression in order to resignify their identities. Like the domestic workers in Gaetano's study, these women use consumption to try to shed their "country bumpkin" image in favor of a "modern urban" persona. At the same time, they are highly aware of, and adept at manipulating, the dual sexual stereotypes of the rural woman as both whore and virgin. Thus, they try to make themselves more attractive to male clients by using various techniques of ornamentation and body refashioning. In addition, with some male clients they play up the image of the rural woman as sexually promiscuous and available, using provocative performances, suggestive body language, and ribald songs. With others, however, they wipe off makeup, cast their eyes downward, and act demurely, imitating the stereotype of the shy, virginal, obedient young girl fresh from the countryside, who needs the "care" and "sympathy" of an urban man.

Clearly, these women are not just the passive objects or recipients of dominant discourses on rurality and sexuality. But should we celebrate their performances as ingenious and triumphant forms of resistance or see them as the acts of desperate victims? Zheng suggests neither, or perhaps both. By playing to urban men's stereotypes and sexual fantasies about rural women, hostesses earn incomes that are higher than those of most urbanites and well beyond the reach of the women working in domestic service discussed in chapter 1. This enables them to engage in forms of consumption that help them to overcome the stigma of being a peasant. Furthermore, some hostesses make important social connections through their clients and are able to start their own businesses, further their education, gain urban household registration, and establish enduring sexual and emotional relationships with urban men, things that other migrant women can only dream of. In this manner, hostesses are able to appropriate state-sanctioned discourses of consumption, sexuality, and identity for their own material and social advancement. However, as Zheng concludes, this very agency paradoxically reinscribes a discourse that legitimizes and naturalizes the dual stereotypes of young rural women as docile virgins and promiscuous whores, and consequently reinforces their marginality and low status.

In chapter 3, Wanning Sun focuses on issues of discursive construction and representation of rural migrant women. Sun builds upon the insight of Gaetano and Zheng that in order to understand migrant women's experiences and identities, it is necessary to first appreciate that contemporary Chinese culture is pervaded by powerful discourses that position rural migrant women as symbols of moral and social inferiority.

Sun's chapter focuses on representations of *dagongmei* from Anhui, comparing their images in the official Women's Federation media with those in the commercial press. The former, she argues, seek primarily to indoctrinate readers with an official understanding of the "ideal" rural woman who does not challenge patriarchal gender and sexual norms and who, if she migrates, nevertheless quickly returns to the countryside to serve her family and village. The commercial press, in contrast, strives for profit by providing entertainment and pleasure. Articles in commercial media attract a readership primarily by fetishizing the *dagongmei* and inviting voyeurism into their lives, which are depicted as mysterious, marginal, violent, and socially and sexually transgressive. They also include "compassionate journalism," which conveys to middle-class urban readers a sense of self-righteousness by providing the opportunity for them to sympathize with the less fortunate *dagongmei*.

Sun argues that for all the differences in ideological orientation, audience, and institutional context, the strategies that official and commercial media adopt in representing migrant women converge in important ways. In both cases, the migrant women are objects of a "controlling" gaze, although in the former it is the state's gaze at work, and in the latter the gaze comes from an urban readership seeking either voyeuristic pleasures or reaffirmation of humanistic, middle-class values. In neither medium are rural migrant women accorded a voice of their own. Sun, however, sees some cause for optimism in the fact that commercial media articles, especially compassionate journalism, promote a concern for human rights, social justice, and respect for the law, and thereby constitute a discursive space for the development of a cultural citizenship that may generate change in the direction of empowering *dagongmei*.

The two chapters in part 2 of the book shift our attention to the impact of migration on the life courses of rural women, and the strategies that these women employ to carve out a future for themselves. Both are concerned with marriage, a central issue in rural migrant women's lives. As Louise Beynon points out, for young rural women who have traditionally always married out of their own village, the question of marriage looms large on the horizon, and it is connected to fundamental issues relating to separation from their natal family and the search for a new place in society, their aspirations for the future, and their life trajectories. Both chapters argue against the conventional distinction made between women's labor migration and marriage migration. Significantly, they indicate that women's motives for migration often relate to both income generation and marriage, that work in the city can have a significant impact on women's aspirations and decisions with regard to marriage, and that some who migrate initially for economic reasons ultimately marry and settle away from their home village, in a town or city.

In chapter 4, Louise Beynon suggests that migration should be conceptualized as a "motive path" through life space as well as geographical space, whereby women migrate in search of work that will give them a sense of independence and accomplishment. Her chapter is based on fieldwork carried out with rural migrant women working in the city of Chengdu, in

Sichuan province. It examines the impact of working and living in the city on rural women's attitudes toward and aspirations for marriage, and the extent to which migrant women are able to exercise agency and control in deciding on a future partner and a future place.

For these women, Beynon suggests, the search for a future through marriage may be more anguished than for rural women who do not migrate. Having been influenced by urban ideas on love and marriage and having experienced a degree of autonomy in the city, they are unwilling to settle for a traditional rural husband, but there are enormous structural, practical, and cultural barriers to finding an urban partner. According to Beynon, the rural migrant women of Chengdu are caught in several dilemmas: they have left home to gain independence, but most cannot create a secure life in the city; they want to postpone marriage for as long as possible because they see it as a constraint on their freedom, but they know that this is a dangerous strategy as marriage is necessary to secure a future; and finally, their attitudes toward rural life and relationships and their own identities have undergone significant changes in the city, but new expectations are almost impossible to realize.

Chapter 5 shifts the focus of attention from migrant women's aspirations for the future to their actual experiences of marriage. Drawing on fieldwork conducted in Zhangjiagang, a county-level city with a Special Economic and Tax Waiver Zone in Jiangsu province, Lin Tan and Susan Short report important new findings about the lives of rural women who have migrated to the city from afar and settled there in marriage. Such women, they argue, marry differently because of their migration experience. First of all, their marriages are different because of differences between their own backgrounds and those of local women, and because of whom, how, and why they marry. Among the migrant women who have married into Zhangjiagang, most come from poorer rural areas, and they married at younger ages than local women. This is due partly to the fact that they come from places where women are expected to marry younger, and partly to the migrant women's eagerness to marry in order to gain a greater degree of stability and legitimacy than they could achieve as single *dagongmei* working in the city. In marriages involving migrant women, the age discrepancy between spouses is greater than in marriages involving local women. Furthermore, the men that migrant women marry are more likely to be poorer, both economically and educationally, than other men in the area, or to be in poor health. In many cases, migrant women marry men who have difficulty finding wives locally, and often neither these men nor their families perceive the women to be ideal marriage partners. These findings confirm some of the anxieties about marrying urban men expressed by the migrant women interviewed by Beynon.

Second, Tan and Short find that once married, migrant women in Zhangjiagang experience marriage differently from local women because they are outsiders in the community, often physically distant from networks of family and friends, and frequently perceived with suspicion or wariness within their new families because of this outsider status. However, migrant women who have married in Zhangjiagang deploy active strategies to negotiate their "double outsider" position. They strive particularly hard to avoid conflicts with their husbands and win the affections of their in-laws. They also cultivate friendships with other migrant women and try to build new support networks by encouraging other women from their home villages to migrate to Zhangjiagang for work or marriage. Despite the obstacles they faced, most of the migrant women whom Tan and Short met in Zhangjiagang were quick to emphasize that their lives were better than they might have been had they married in their home villages, and they rarely expressed regret. The authors conclude, therefore, that women who migrate and marry into a county-level city, despite being "double outsiders," can and do successfully make themselves "a place" that if at times is isolating, can also bring happiness.

The chapters thus far have focused on urban settings and featured urban research. Part 3 turns to the countryside, with three chapters that all draw upon fieldwork conducted in the village setting. Chapters 6 and 7 engage with data from surveys carried out in the provinces of Anhui and Sichuan. In chapter 6, C. Cindy Fan analyzes the records of interviews with migrants returning to their home villages for the annual Spring Festival (i.e., the Lunar New Year). Her chapter emphasizes four aspects of migrant women's experiences. First, she examines women's economic motivations for migration and the financial contributions their work makes to their households. She finds that women are as economically active as men during periods of migrant work, and that such work is an important means for women to be recognized by their families as active economic contributors, and for families to improve their material standing and well-being.

Second, Fan examines the role of migrant women in forging networks among fellow migrants and villagers. As others have documented, such networks are an important source of information for migrants and play an important role in channeling them toward particular destinations and certain occupations. Fan's chapter demonstrates that women's social networking activities play a central role in facilitating the migration of other rural women and providing a basis for companionship and support. Ironically, however, the gendering of these networks, whereby male migrants help their "brothers" and female migrants help their "sisters," reinforces gender segmentation in the work force and homogenizes the experiences of migrants.

Third, Fan argues that urban work experiences can empower women migrants and enable them to become potential agents of social change in rural areas. She shows that returning migrant women have gained a sense of independence. They seek to incorporate new views and lifestyles into village life and to engage in new forms of production and alternative gender divisions of labor. On the other hand, in the final part of her chapter, Fan argues that despite the many contributions that women migrants make to their families and villages, their agency and their ability to contribute to the village and foster social change are limited by deep-rooted traditions and institutional constraints. In particular, she argues that marriage is disempowering for rural women because it usually causes them to abort their wage work and thereby decreases their economic mobility, limiting their opportunities for autonomy and agency and forcing them to rely on their husband's wages for improving the household's well-being.

Chapter 7, by Binbin Lou, Zhenzhen Zheng, Rachel Connelly, and Kenneth Roberts, compares Anhui and Sichuan women's patterns of migration, discusses the ways in which returning migrant women reflect upon their experiences of urban life, and finally examines the effects of migration upon returned women's lives in the village. The chapter presents some findings on patterns of migration in the two provinces that contrast to most other studies to date, including that of Fan in the previous chapter. According to this study, in both Anhui and Sichuan, large numbers of women migrate after marriage. Indeed, in the Sichuan villages studied, the majority of migrant women first migrated *only* after marriage. The authors claim that, while it may have been more accurate in the 1980s, today "the sense that marriage ends migration for rural women is simply not correct." This statement is likely to have profound implications for our understanding of the impact of gender roles on migration, the place of migration in rural women's life courses, and changing social relations in the countryside.

Another major finding reported in this chapter is that migration by both unmarried and married rural women is becoming much more prevalent than previously, to the extent that, in Anhui especially, it is now difficult to find women in their late teens who have not migrated. This is having an important effect on the way villagers perceive rural women's outmigration. In Anhui, which has a longer history of women's outmigration than Sichuan, there is little stigma attached to it, whether the women are married or single, and villagers show relatively high levels of tolerance and understanding toward returning migrant women. In Sichuan, until the late 1990s, the outmigration of young unmarried women (but not married women accompanied by their husbands) was surrounded by the kinds of anxiety and stigma discussed by Gaetano in chapter 1. In addition, returning migrants who had adopted urban dress and customs continued to be met with relatively high levels of suspicion and antagonism. By the time of the study, however, the outmigration of both unmarried and married women was increasingly acceptable.

The authors of chapter 7 report that, contrary to expectation, there are few location-based differences in migrants' views of urban life. Similar to other chapter authors, they find that substantial rural/urban differences commonly faced by these migrants lead to highly ambivalent attitudes toward the migration experience. On the one hand, the women relay bitter memories of hard work, exploitation, and difficult living conditions. On the other hand, they express pride in their triumph over adversity, their increased autonomy and improved self-confidence, their independent income, and their new skills, values, and ideas.

In chapter 8, Rachel Murphy directs our attention to a previously neglected area of research: the impact of migration on the well-being and agency of women living in the countryside. Like Fan and Lou et al., Murphy discusses the situation of returned migrant women, but she also analyzes the impact of migration on "stayers," women who do not migrate themselves but who belong to a household in which one or more other members migrate. Her chapter, based on fieldwork in four villages in Jiangxi province, examines the impact of migration on rural women in terms of their workloads, the visibility and perceived value of their labor, their access to resources, and their perspectives on social norms, gender roles, and entitlements. She finds that these vary in complicated ways according to village, household, and individual factors.

The outmigration of family members, Murphy finds, increases the workload of rural women across all stages of the life course, but elderly women and girls from poverty-stricken households suffer the most. Elderly women are adversely affected because they are burdened both with raising grandchildren and with farming, yet they are not perceived as productive laborers. Girls in poor households are also pulled into child care and farming, which hurts their well-being because they are withdrawn from school.

Both unmarried and married women who have firsthand experience of working in the city appear to enjoy more of the positive effects of migration. These migrants and returnees benefit from the opportunity to earn independent income for their own use, the increased visibility of their economic contributions to their households, and the fact that with their knowledge of urban labor markets they are able to indicate to other household members that they have a "fallback position" as an alternative to farming. Finally, rural women who receive regular remittances from other household members also partake of the positive benefits of migration, in the form of improved material wealth and social status.

However, in common with other contributors to this book, Murphy also finds that returned migrant women who have been exposed to new values and lifestyles are frequently dissatisfied with their lives back in the countryside. The reality of village life, including conservative social norms and inadequate resources, sometimes prevents them from acting on their broadened perspectives and exercising agency. While for some women outmigration can be seen as an escape from unhappiness and even suicide, for others, a return from the city to "more of the same" in the village causes or exacerbates emotional difficulties. More research is required to get a clearer picture of the long-term impact of migration on the emotional well-being of rural women in China. Yet Murphy's chapter provides a framework for future research that must take into account individual, household, and community-level factors.

This book concludes with seven stories written by rural migrant women for a competition on the theme "my life as a migrant worker," which have been translated by Tamara Jacka and Song Xianlin. In a brief introduction to the prize-winning entries, Jacka suggests they are case studies illustrating many of the issues raised in the previous chapters, including how gender and kinship relations influence the timing and meaning of women's outmigration and in turn affect the status of returned migrant women. The stories vividly convey the discrimination, exploitation, and hardship faced by rural women in the city and the ambivalence and uncertainty that migrant women feel about their futures, and illuminate the sense of achievement that some migrant women gain from being able to determine the course of their own lives, overcoming the challenges involved in migration and work in the city, and earning wages and becoming more independent.

HISTORICAL AND INSTITUTIONAL BACKGROUND TO MIGRATION IN CHINA

Large-scale rural-to-urban migration has been a central component of social and economic change across the modern world, and it is easy to discern similarities between the Chinese case and that of other countries. However, it is important to note that certain aspects of the historical, socioeconomic, and political context of rural-to-urban migration in contemporary

China, which have a major bearing on the way it is understood and experienced, are unique. In particular, any analysis of contemporary migration in China requires a thorough understanding of the household registration, or *hukou*, system and the historical setting from which it arose.

The grand narratives of western modernism, including Marxism, were premised upon a fundamental divide between traditional rural society and modern urban society, and an understanding that development and modernization necessarily entail a process of rural-to-urban migration, urbanization, and the marginalization of rural life.[20] As Raymond Williams discusses in his book *The Country and the City*, the origins of the rural/urban divide can be traced far back in European history, to classical Greek culture.[21] However, Myron Cohen has argued that a rural/urban divide and the notion that urban life was superior to rural life were not features of traditional China, but emerged only in the late nineteenth and early twentieth centuries.[22] During this period, imperialism and industrialization brought about a functional and physical distinction between cities and the surrounding countryside.[23] This rural/urban distinction "on the ground," as it were, was accompanied by new discourses in which the countryside and its "peasants" were marked as essentially different from and inferior to urbanites.[24]

As Tamara Jacka has argued elsewhere, this new judgment was essentially the result of a process of "internal orientalism" on the part of a Chinese intelligentsia striving for modernity.[25] In the nineteenth century, as a result of defeat at the hands of colonial powers, the question, What is wrong with China? became of paramount concern, and a central plank in Chinese intellectuals' efforts to answer this question became the notion that the Chinese people, and the peasantry above all, were backward and in need of improvement and modernization.[26] These views mirrored western colonialist views of the Chinese people as a whole, which were likewise a mapping of a rural/urban divide onto an "other" nation, which like "the rural" was alternately abhorred and idealized.[27]

Thus, Chinese intellectuals adopted the western image of China as backward, but then deflected this inferiority onto an internal "other": rural "peasants." During the first half of the twentieth century, peasants and women became popular subjects for literature in which they were often portrayed as prime examples of the backwardness and oppression of traditional society, serving as a metaphor for the nation's ills. When woman and peasant were blended into one, the case for national reform became doubly effective.[28]

Subsequently, when the Communist Party under Mao Zedong came to power, it inherited an enormous amount of cultural baggage about "peasants," about the relationship between the educated elite and ordinary people, and about the relationship between the countryside and the cities, and then added its own interpretations. Mao rejected the orthodox Marxist view that peasants were too backward to constitute a revolutionary class, arguing in contrast that the poor peasants were the most revolutionary class of all. In addition, an important part of Maoist rhetoric was a commitment to the abolition of the "three great differences" (*san da chabie*)—the inequalities between the city and the countryside, mental and manual labor, and workers and peasants.

However, in the 1950s the Communist Party instituted two different forms of categorization and regulation that objectified and cemented into place a divide between rural and urban inhabitants. First, during the land reform campaigns of 1949–1952, all adults were assigned a class status (*jieji chengfen*), and children inherited the status of their father. Those living permanently in a village were assigned a class status according to how much land their family had owned during the previous three years. Those designated "landlord" were likely to have a large part of their land confiscated and redistributed to those designated "poor" or "middle" peasant. But this process was complicated by the existence of a great many people who were not permanent residents of a specific village, such as absentee landlords, itinerants, landless laborers, and those who worked part of the year as farmers and part of the year as workers in urban factories. In order to determine whose land was to be redistributed and to whom, all such people had to be assigned a specific place of residency. In towns and cities, in contrast, the designation of class status was based primarily on occupation before the revolution. The result of these two different processes was that people were defined as either permanent urban residents or permanent rural residents of a specific village, and the former were further categorized according to occupation while the latter were categorized according to land ownership.[29]

This rural/urban division was further reified in the late 1950s with the introduction of the household registration (*hukou*) policy, under which people were classified according to place of residence and as belonging to either agricultural or nonagricultural households. Household registration was inherited from the mother, and it was extremely difficult to transfer one's registration from agricultural to nonagricultural, from a village to an urban center, or even from a small town to a larger city.[30] In combination with other aspects of Maoist political and economic management, household registration effectively prevented rural-to-urban migration and reproduced rural/urban inequalities. In particular, when faced with the dilemma of how to develop and modernize a largely agrarian economy

scarce in capital, the Maoist government in the 1950s resorted to the So-
viet strategy of siphoning resources out of agriculture in order to finance
the heavy industrial sector. At the same time, it guaranteed subsidized food
and housing, lifetime employment, and welfare benefits to urban residents,
but not to those in the countryside.[31] This combination of central planning and household registration limited rural-to-urban migration, for it
became impossible to buy grain or to find housing in towns and cities
without local, nonagricultural household registration.

The institutional structure of the *hukou* system also reinforced gender
inequality as it combined with cultural constructions of gender and labor.
Permanent urban residency through *hukou* transfer was usually extended
only to those personnel who fulfilled the state's human capital needs. More
often, men were called upon in their roles as political administrators (i.e.,
cadres), skilled technicians, industrial workers within state-owned enterprises, military personnel, and postsecondary students or scholars.[32]
Transfer to urban *hukou* was less often awarded for the purpose of family
reunion, which largely curtailed the main path for rural women to achieve
social mobility: hypergamous marriage.[33] Thus, a greater proportion of
women are found among "unofficial" migrants than among "official" migrants in the cities.[34]

During the Cultural Revolution, Mao tried to redress the divide between urban and rural residents and that between intellectuals and ordinary people by sending urban intellectuals and students to the countryside
to learn from the peasants. In both the short and the long term, he failed
in that aim, for what most urbanites "learned" was how different and
"backward" the peasants were in comparison with themselves. With the
end of the Cultural Revolution and the demise of Maoism came the realization that China as a nation was still "backward" on the world stage, and
the question of What is wrong with China? reemerged. Answers to that
question were inspired by capitalism as well as by intellectual discourses
dominant in China in the first half of the twentieth century. Once more,
the inferior quality of the peasantry became a central preoccupation for
the intellectual and official elite. Consequently, as Sun illustrates in chapter 3, rural inhabitants and rural migrants have been portrayed overwhelmingly as inferior "others" in the media of the reform period. At
times they are depicted as criminal, barbaric, or, especially in the case of
women, immoral; at other times, they are portrayed as naïve and helpless.
These representations of peasants and rural migrants serve as a contrast
against which the civilization and modernity of the urban population (and
of the nation) is constructed.

In the late 1970s and early 1980s, economic reform began with efforts to improve the productivity of the countryside. The communal system was dismantled and replaced by various forms of a "production responsibility system," under which most decisions about work and the allocation of tasks were once again taken within the household. In addition, efforts were made to encourage diversification and specialization in the rural economy. Initially, these reforms were successful in stimulating higher levels of productivity in agricultural production, which in turn provided the capital and released the labor required for the expansion of rural industries and the development of private businesses. Income inequalities among different rural areas increased, but were offset by an overall rapid improvement in rural incomes and living standards and a narrowing of the rural/urban income gap. But from the late 1980s onward, real incomes in rural areas stagnated, while both intrarural and rural/urban income inequalities grew. By the mid-1990s, the rural/urban income gap was responsible for an overall level of inequality in China that was among the highest of all Asian developing countries.[35] Shortage of arable land, lack of local employment opportunities, falling prices for agricultural products, and rising taxes, not to mention unscrupulous and corrupt local leaders, pushed peasants out of their villages. A desire to see the world, now made more visible through television and increased flows of people across areas, and to improve one's material life relative to others, in addition to, in some cases, the need to escape oppression or familial conflict, further propelled rural peasants toward towns and cities.

Meanwhile, the growth of the urban economy resulted in a huge need for unskilled and cost-effective labor, especially in private and collective enterprises and the construction and service sectors. The majority of the new employment opportunities that have been created are temporary, offering no job security and very few welfare benefits; of low status; physically exhausting; and carried out in poor working conditions. Not surprisingly, these jobs have been largely rejected by urbanites, and consequently, demand has grown rapidly for rural migrant workers who accept the poor conditions and who are cheaper to hire.

With the development of a market economy, the state was no longer able to limit the allocation of goods and services exclusively to those with local, urban registration, and this enabled rural migrants to live away from their place of official registration. To adjust to these new circumstances, since the 1980s the state has undertaken several reforms of the household registration system, making it easier for certain migrants to reside long-term in urban areas. In addition, it has added supplementary regulations to the registration system so as to make it a more effective tool for tracking and policing migrants and restricting the settlement of rural migrants in certain urban areas.

In 1984, the State Council acknowledged a growing movement of rural people into small towns by allowing them to obtain a type of urban *hukou* in market towns, called "self-supplied food grain" *hukou* (*zili kouliang chengzhen hukou*). In order to qualify for this type of registration, applicants had to show that they were employed in a local enterprise or ran their own business, and that they could provide their own grain and accommodation in town. This type of *hukou* was only allowed in small market towns, and those who received it waived their right to village land. Between 1984 and 1988, some 4 million people took up *zili kouliang chengzhen hukou*.[36] However, it did not hold much appeal for new migrants and was abandoned in the early 1990s.[37]

By 1985, the Ministry of Public Security had implemented various nationwide measures aimed at regulating migration. In order to achieve a legal status, migrants are required to apply for a temporary residence permit (*zanzhu zheng*) at their destination, for a fee.[38] At the same time, the ministry instituted a system of personal identity cards (*shenfen zheng*), which all citizens were to carry on their person.[39] These two innovations made it acceptable and legal for rural residents to migrate to cities, but made migration more costly.[40] In addition, the central government requires that migrant women of childbearing age carry a "marriage and fertility permit" (*hunyu zheng*) issued by a body responsible for family planning in the place of temporary residence. The Ministry of Labor stipulates that migrants have an employment registration card (*waichu renyuan liudong jiuye dengji ka*) issued by the labor recruitment service in the county of the migrant's household registration, which is the basis for receiving an employment permit (*jiuye zheng*) at their destination. Some urban regulatory organs also require that migrants have a certificate of good health before they can register for other permits. On top of the cost of permits and certificates, migrants are frequently charged a range of fees and taxes, both spurious and legal, by various administrative bodies and by unscrupulous employers and landlords.[41] Migrants lacking proper documentation, stable residence, or secure employment may be considered criminals, and subjected to fines, deportation, or even arrest.[42]

In August 1998, the State Council approved a proposal allowing children to inherit *hukou* from either of their parents. In the past, as mentioned above, if a child's mother held rural registration, the child also would be assigned rural registration. This has meant that the children of migrant couples, and those of migrant women married to urban men, have been greatly disadvantaged in the city in terms of access to education, housing, and employment. As Tan and Short suggest in chapter 5, this reform will likely result in greater numbers of rural women marrying urban men and settling in the city. However, some local governments, especially of larger cities, have been slow to implement it.[43]

Of longer-term significance has been an increasing diversification and commodification of urban *hukou* since the late 1980s. The central government has opposed the outright sale of urban *hukou*, although numerous local governments have indulged in such lucrative practices.[44] In the mid-1990s, the central government authorized localities to issue provisional urban *hukou*s. The so-called blue stamp *hukou* (*lanyin hukou*), distinguished by a blue stamp rather than a red one as in the formal urban *hukou* book, became available in a number of towns, Special Economic Zones, and cities, including Shanghai, Shenzhen, and Guangzhou.[45] Its benefits have been locally determined, but can include such entitlements as access to public education and eligibility for a business license. The blue stamp *hukou* does not come with welfare or political participation rights, and thus differs from a bona fide urban *hukou*.[46] Eligibility is formally limited to professional or skilled workers, investors, those who purchase property, and others who make a "significant contribution to the urban economy," and their close relatives.[47] Most important, the blue stamp *hukou* costs anywhere from several thousand *yuan* to many times that much.[48] Given these stiff requirements, this registration has been secured only by a minority of relatively privileged migrants, most of whom already hold nonagricultural (i.e., urban) *hukou*.[49]

Recently, the central government has moved further toward relaxing issuance of urban *hukou*, or the privileges associated with it, in certain contexts and to migrants who meet particular criteria. As part of the effort to develop small towns and cities, in 2001 the State Council declared that all urban areas having a population of less than 100,000 should grant a local urban registration to those with a stable job and a fixed residence in the city.[50] In addition, as part of a movement to attract "talented personnel" (*rencai*) from other areas, several large cities have extended the privileges of urban *hukou* in the form of a "residence permit" (*juzhu zheng*) to qualified individuals.[51] Educated professionals, commercial home buyers, entrepreneurs who have made a substantial investment in the city, and employees of foreign enterprises, including overseas Chinese and foreign nationals, are some of the talented personnel who are now being exempted from the permits required of most migrants.[52]

Despite all the new reforms and regulations, in the early twenty-first century the household registration system and the division it maintains between those who have local, urban nonagricultural registration and those who do not remain influential. It has become easier for migrants to obtain local registration in small towns and for an elite group of migrants, few of whom are rural women, to secure a form of urban registration in medium-size and even some large cities. However, the majority of rural-to-urban migrants remain unable to transfer their *hukou.* Lack of urban registration makes it extremely difficult for them to become integrated into the urban community and limits their opportunities for social mobility. Without local urban registration, even those "rural" people who have lived in a city for many years face numerous obstacles: they are prevented from entering certain occupations and trades; they are denied work-related entitlements to housing, medical care, pensions, and social security; they are often forbidden to buy or build property and are thus relegated to "shantytowns" that have sprung up on the margins of large cities; they and their offspring are excluded from, or charged exorbitantly to attend, local institutions of higher education and elite local schools; and they are excluded from community- and work-based political, social, and recreational activities.[53] In short, they are treated as outsiders to the urban community.

Severely restrictive and discriminatory as they are, the household registration system and its affiliated policies and practices have not prevented large-scale and increasing rural-to-urban migration. In the following section, we take a brief look at patterns of migration among rural women and the ways these differ from those of rural migrant men.

GENDERED PATTERNS OF MIGRATION IN POST–MAO CHINA

Women have long been neglected in studies of migration, and the impact of gender on migration patterns and experiences has not received sufficient attention. Moreover, numerous misconceptions about female migration have prevailed in the field of migration studies, reflecting gender bias. For example, female migration has been treated as a deviation from the "standard" pattern of male migration and women's migration patterns have been attributed to traditional social roles and status, without consideration of political and economic factors.[54] Internationally, most studies of female migration have assumed that women are less inclined to migrate than men, are less likely to engage in longer-distance migrations, and migrate mainly as tied or associational migrants, following their families or husbands.[55] Likewise, in China there is a "widespread assumption that the decision to migrate requires more consideration for a woman than for a man; that it involves more physical insecurity and hardship."[56] The picture of female migration in contemporary China is far from complete and presents plenty of paradoxes. Yet it is clear from the available information, a summary of which we present in this section, that rural women, as well as men, are on the move in China today as never before.

Sex Ratios and the Direction, Distance, and Duration of Migration

Generally, sex ratios appear to vary according to the type of migration (*hukou* or non*hukou*), the direction of migration, the age or education level of migrants considered, and local and regional conditions. The consensus among various surveys undertaken during the 1990s is that nationally women comprise between <u>one third</u> to <u>one half</u> of the migrant population.[57] The 1990 census data found that approximately 9.1 million Chinese women and 12.9 million men between the ages of 15 and 59 migrated during the period 1985–1990.[58] According to this census data, male non*hukou* migrants comprised 1.9 percent and female non*hukou* migrants comprised 1.7 percent of the total population over the age of 5.[59] Interestingly, these proportions are reversed in data from the 1995 national one percent sample census, which defined the non*hukou* migrant population using a criterion of just six months' stay away from the registered place of residence, rather than one year, leading one analyst to suggest that "women's participation in non*hukou* migration . . . is not necessarily lower than men's."[60]

The proportion of women among the floating population has been found to vary a great deal, with conditions in certain regions seemingly favoring women's migration. A survey of 2,085 households in Anhui and Sichuan conducted in 1995 by the Ministry of Agriculture found that among migrants aged 18 and younger, women comprised the majority of the vast rural migrant labor force for these densely populated provinces (65 percent in Sichuan and 55 percent in Anhui).[61] Guangdong province's Pearl River Delta region, just over the border from Hong Kong and consisting of several cities (Dongguan, Foshan, Shunde, etc.), open economic areas, and the Shenzhen Special Economic Zone, is one of the most popular destinations for migrants from all over China, who are attracted by the employment opportunities created by the massive infusion of foreign capital.[62] An overwhelming majority of migrants to the Pearl River Delta are female; as elsewhere in Asia, young single women are the preferred labor for the transnational apparel, textile, toy, and electronics industries located there.[63] In the Shenzhen Special Economic Zone in 1996, 68 percent of migrants were women, according to officials.[64]

Surveys also give differing pictures of the relationship between the direction and distance of migration and sex ratios. According to the 1990 census,

migration since the early 1980s has generally followed a pattern of movement from the western and central inland regions to the coast, and within
the eastern region.[65] In addition, most migration occurs within provinces
and slightly more women than men move within provinces rather than between them (69.4 percent of women compared with 65.9 percent of men).[66]
These figures would seem to support the conventional wisdom that women
migrate shorter distances than do men.[67] Yet C. Cindy Fan argues that women in fact traveled longer distances than did men when they migrated
across provinces.[68] Moreover, rates of interprovincial migration rose among
both male and female migrants throughout the 1990s.[69]

Migration has been shown to occur mainly between rural and urban areas.[70] The 1990 census indicated that men outnumbered women by 2.3 to
1 in non*hukou* rural-to-urban migration.[71] Outside the Pearl River Delta,
larger cities attract fewer women than men, as the Ministry of Construction's survey of the floating population in eleven large cities conducted between 1989 and 1990 confirmed.[72] Yet the 1990 census data for Hubei
province, which includes a number of smaller cities, found that among unofficial migrants, women were more likely to be in cities than were men.[73]
This suggests that in smaller urban areas, the percentage of women in the
migrant population is greater than in large cities.

Most rural labor mobility is short-term or circulatory. This is partly because migrants often seek to maintain their ties to village and land, and because farm work requires additional laborers during the busy agricultural
seasons. In addition, the majority of migrants are employed in seasonal occupations, particularly construction.[74] Moreover, as indicated above, non-
hukou migrants face many barriers in settling in urban areas for long periods. Survey data indicate, however, that migrants' sojourns may be
increasing in length.[75] In particular, the observation that more couples are
migrating together to urban areas indicates a greater potential for family
settlement.[76] Among some women migrants, the tendency to stay away
from the village for long periods appears greater than for men.[77] This view
is supported by several single-province studies that suggest that rural women who migrate to the city are generally more satisfied with their situation at their destination than are men, and have a greater desire to stay
there long term and become official urban residents.[78] However, female
migrants to the Pearl River Delta appear to convey just the opposite. In
letters, songs, and poetry, young female factory workers in the Delta express a keen sense of homesickness and longing for return.[79] In surveys,
too, young migrant women express much less desire to stay than do their

male counterparts.[80] In fact, a 1997 survey of returning migrants across nine provinces found the mean duration of labor migration for women to be just 3.2 years, compared with 5.4 years for men.[81]

Age and Marital Status

Age and marital status are important determinants of women's migration in China as elsewhere,[82] although researchers are not all in agreement on the exact relationship between these variables, and there is some evidence that the picture is changing over time. To date, most surveys have indicated that the migrant population is on average younger than the rural non-migrant population, and that within the migrant population, women tend to be younger and less often married than men.[83] For example, the 1994 survey of labor migrants from 75 villages across 11 provinces conducted by the Ministry of Agriculture found that 83 percent of women were aged 30 or under, compared with just 55 percent of male migrants.[84] The 1995 Ministry of Agriculture household survey data for Sichuan and Anhui indicate that among migrants in the age group of 18 and below, women comprised 65.8 percent of the labor force in Sichuan and 55.6 percent in Anhui.[85] In general, among non*hukou* migrants, women are concentrated in the 15- to 19-year-old age group, whereas men are concentrated in the 20- to 24-year-old cohort. This is validated by both the 1990 census data for Zhejiang province[86] and a survey conducted in Foshan and Shenzhen in the Pearl River Delta.[87]

The predominance of younger women among migrants in part explains the fact that fewer migrant women than men are married. According to the 1995 data, only 31.7 percent of female migrants in Sichuan and 35.7 percent in Anhui were married, compared with 56.3 percent and 51.1 percent of male migrants in Sichuan and Anhui, respectively.[88] Likewise, in Foshan and Shenzhen in 1993, the percentage of unmarried women (about 60 percent) was higher than of unmarried men (about 55 percent).[89] Data such as the 1997 survey of the migrant population in Beijing, which found that 85 percent of female migrants were aged 15 to 49, with numbers peaking at age 19 and decreasing in successive years, suggest that many migrant women return to their villages to get married in their early twenties.[90] In China, the cultural convention is for men to marry a woman slightly younger, and the legal age for marriage for women is lower than for men (20 and 22 respectively). Thus at older ages, there are likely to be more single men than women found in the migrant population.

Education

The migrant labor force tends to be more highly educated than the rural labor force as a whole, and is becoming increasingly so. A study of migrant workers in the Pearl River Delta conducted during 1993–1994 found that 17 percent of migrants aged between 15 and 30 had only primary school education (*xiaoxue*), yet over 66 percent had junior secondary school education (*chuzhong*), and 15 percent had senior secondary school education (*gaozhong*).[91] In contrast, 1990 census data showed that among the total rural population aged between 15 and 30, 8 percent were illiterate, 43 percent had primary school education, only 48 percent had junior secondary school education, and 9 percent had senior secondary education or above.[92] According to Scott Rozelle and co-authors, the percentage of migrants holding at least a junior secondary school (*chuzhong*) education in 1988 was 61 percent; by 1995 the percentage had risen to 64.[93]

Among rural migrants, however, women are on average slightly less educated than men. According to the 1997 survey of non*hukou* migrants in Beijing, for example, 20 percent of women over the age of 6, compared with 15 percent of men, had only primary school education. Fifty-two percent of women, compared with 63 percent of men, had junior secondary school education; and about 13 percent of both men and women had senior secondary school education or higher.[94] This survey also showed that in the 14- to 16-year age range, female migrants outnumbered male migrants. As these are the ages when children should complete the last three of nine years of what is officially designated as compulsory education nationwide, these findings suggest that more young girls than boys are dropping out of school.[95] Thus, the lower levels of education among women migrants may be a factor of both their relative youth, compared with their male counterparts, and gender differences in educational attainment across rural China.

Migration Channels and Social Networks

Contrary to stereotype, the majority of the floating population do not blindly migrate, but respond systematically to information channeled to the villages mainly through social networks comprised of kin and co-villagers.[96] Most labor migrants follow relatives or co-villagers in migration. For example, 72 percent and 94 percent of migrants to Foshan and Shenzhen in 1993, respectively, had acquaintances at their place of destination.[97] The Ministry of Agriculture's 1995 survey of migrant households in Anhui and Sichuan likewise found that 51 percent of rural laborers migrated with fellow villagers, 15 percent with local relatives, 9 percent with family members, and only a small minority (3.1 percent) through direct recruitment by employers or through local government introductions (about 7 percent).[98] By relying on kin and co-villagers rather than institutions, migrants spread risk and lower the cost of migration.[99] Kin and co-villagers can be relied upon not only to supply information about job opportunities prior to migration but also to assist in finding work and accommodation.[100] And there are some data that suggest that personal connections are particularly important for women undertaking migration.[101]

Occupational and Wage Segmentation

For reasons we have explained previously in this introduction, rural migrants to large cities like Beijing and Zhuhai have a much lower occupational status, work longer hours for less pay, and reach double the rates of poverty than do permanent residents.[102] Migrant occupations are also segmented by gender, resulting in generally lower occupational attainment and earnings for women migrants than for men. Using 1990 census data, Quanhe Yang and Fei Guo determined that while migrants in general were mainly engaged either in industry or in the service sector, women migrants were overwhelmingly concentrated in the service and retail sectors, most as housemaids and restaurant workers.[103] Another analysis of the 1990 census data found that even after migration, women were much more likely than men to engage in agriculture, slightly more likely to be in clerical and sales jobs or services, and less likely to be either professionals, cadres, or industrial workers.[104] The latter is certainly true of the Pearl River Delta region, where few women are found in white-collar or technical positions, although they are by far the majority (90 percent) of workers on the production line.[105] When compared to nonmigrant rural women, however, migrant women have a much higher occupational attainment.[106]

The segmentation of occupations along the lines of gender and *hukou* explains why women migrants generally earn less than male migrants.[107] However, the extent of gender segmentation in the work force and of gender inequality in earnings among migrants varies considerably from one region to the next. On the basis of survey data, Xin Meng argues that in the mid-1990s, industries clustered around Dongguan city in the Pearl River Delta displayed relatively little wage inequality according to gender, as about 70 percent of migrants of both sexes were equally distributed in industrial jobs.[108] However, these results do not agree with the findings of the researchers affiliated with the Chinese Academy of Social Science, who found that in foreign-invested enterprises of the Pearl River Delta, women were disproportionately concentrated in low-skill, low-wage production assembly work, receiving average monthly wages in the 1990s of 300–500 *yuan*. Taking into account that workdays averaged twelve hours and that these wages included overtime pay, the researchers concluded that real wages were only about 200 *yuan* per month—barely enough for these workers to live on.[109] On the other hand, Xin Meng found that for Jinan city in Shandong province, gender was a key determinant of income among migrants. In Jinan, more than 50 percent of male migrants worked in construction while 40 percent of female migrants worked in domestic service, and the wage differential between these categories was large.[110] Differences in earnings between female and male migrants may prove less consequential in the long run than unequal access to technical training and skill development. Recent surveys demonstrate that "social and economic returns from urban labor-force experience are much greater for improved skills and abilities than those for accumulated income."[111]

WOMEN AND RURAL-TO-URBAN MIGRATION: ISSUES AND TRENDS

As the above survey data show, and as chapters in this volume further support, women not only migrate but often do so in patterns that run counter to common assumptions. The specific sociocultural and political-economic contexts of sending and receiving areas as well as individual factors result in both diversity and commonalities among women migrants and women's migration experiences. In this final section, we take stock of the discoveries reported above in light of ongoing debates about women and migration in China to which this volume contributes.

Associational Migrants and Marriage Migration

As stated previously, women have been generally assumed to be secondary migrants, who migrate to follow husbands and accompany family in an extension of their primary role as wife and mother, and unrelated to household economics. Thus, until recently, migration studies in China that did consider women focused mainly on their migration for marriage and its effects on host communities and on fertility rates. Much of this research has been biased toward the plight of male bachelors or blames migration, and rural migrants, for a breakdown in family values and a rise in human trafficking, as discussed in Sun's chapter. In contrast, the chapters in this book by Beynon and Tan and Short focus on women's agency in marriage. These chapters draw upon and contribute to recent scholarship that suggests that migrant women's decisions and experiences in the areas of marriage, social and economic mobility, and migration are integrally related.[112]

Women migrants have also been singled out by Chinese official researchers concerned about high fertility rates. This literature alleges that migrant women comprise an "over-quota guerrilla birth army" (*chaosheng youji dui*) that uses migration as a means to evade family planning.[113] This worry feeds on urban prejudices about rural migrants being associated with rising crime rates and social disorder. Recently, however, some studies have suggested that concern about high fertility rates among migrants may be exaggerated, and indeed that migration may even have a negative impact on fertility, for several reasons.[114] Chapter 7 of this volume confirms the hypothesis that migration depresses fertility and draws attention to women's agency in decision making about fertility, and to the experience of migration in changing women's attitudes toward, and knowledge about, contraception and reproductive health.

To date, statistical surveys have revealed that the majority of women who migrate are young and unmarried. This is in part because sociocultural factors, including gender ideologies, and institutional and economic factors have most often militated against the migration of married women. It is commonly assumed in rural China that upon marriage, women will assume the primary responsibility for child care and field work, and that husbands and sons will migrate before wives or mothers. A reversal of such gender roles, such as for a wife to go out to work for wages while her husband remains on the farm, can result in the loss of face for the husband,[115] though such a situation is by no means unheard of.[116] In addition, the lower earning power of women compared with men is also a factor in family decisions for the household head to migrate in lieu of, or prior to, his wife or mother.[117] However, there is some evidence that the probability that married women will migrate increases with the birth of a male child. Rural households' desire for a male heir is well documented historically and in the present. The birth of a son may provide his mother with bargaining power in the household, in particular the ability to demand child care from her in-laws, thus facilitating her own migration.[118]

Couples and families sometimes migrate together, but they do so in the face of numerous obstacles and usually only after certain conditions are met. The desire for families to hold onto their land, regulations regarding rights to land, and the cyclical, year-round nature of farm work all factor into the usual decision for at least one family member to remain in the village tending the land all year round.[119] In addition, migrants' lack of access to decent housing, schools, and health care in urban areas are further disincentives for family migration. In particular, migrant children without local, urban *hukou* face difficulties gaining entry into schools in urban areas, and few can afford to pay the higher fees (in the form of tuition fees or "donations") that they are charged in cities like Beijing.[120] Migrants from certain areas have overcome some of these problems by operating their own schools, charging much lower fees than urban schools. However, most such schools suffer from a lack of government support in terms of funding and legal recognition, so their ability to provide decent education is limited.[121]

Nonetheless, as chapters 4, 5, 6, and 7 demonstrate in varying ways, the common expectation for migrant women to return to the village after marriage, and for married women not to migrate, may not apply in some areas and may be less widespread in recent years.

Docile and Dutiful or Rebellious and Autonomous?

In addition to the factors limiting the migration of married women, there are also factors favoring the migration of young, unmarried women. An unmarried daughter's labor at home is often considered less integral to the operation of the farm household than that of other members, so families will not suffer economically by sending out a daughter.[122] Perhaps more important, the demand for young rural women in certain occupations and sectors exerts selective pressure on this segment of the rural population. Young women are highly marketable, whether in industry, service and sales, or clerical work. In certain of the export-processing industries clustered in South China, for example, young rural women are favored by managers who believe that they are inherently docile and therefore easier to manage, and are dextrous and nimble and thus well-suited to performing delicate manufacturing tasks.[123] These stereotypes of femininity have accompanied the export of capitalism around the globe. However, new research suggests that these stereotypes are challenged in some cases by alternative gender constructions, such as the "matronly workers" of the Hong Kong electronics factory studied by Ching Kwan Lee. As Lee argued, local labor market conditions in Hong Kong make the employment of married women not only feasible but even desirable.[124]

Lee and several other scholars have recently explored such gender ideologies in the context of the global factories of South China, through ethnographic investigation of the lives of rural women workers.[125] In her study of an electronics factory in Shenzhen, Lee elucidates the relationship between production politics and the construction of migrant women workers' identities. Lee shows that the factory regime is one of "localistic despotism," in which young migrant women workers are subjected to overt punishment-oriented control. The construction of their identities as "maiden workers" from particular regions of China is central to the exercise of this control. Yet Lee argues that women workers are not simply passive recipients of identities constructed through patriarchal and capitalist ideologies and in the interests of management. Rather, these identities provide a repertoire of available representations and images that women themselves recognize as meaningful. They interpret these images in their own ways and use them against management to their own advantage, thereby reproducing them. In another ethnographic study of an electronics factory in Shenzhen, Pun Ngai[126] likewise examines the construction of women workers' identities. With fascinating detail, she explores the everyday ways in which women workers as well as management deploy and manipulate difference and hierarchy, such as rural and urban, northerner and southerner, and male and female, between each other for power and gain.

These exciting new ethnographies build upon a previous generation of scholarship on the roles and identities of rural Chinese women in industrializing East Asia.[127] These early ethnographies located the meanings and outcomes of young women's migration in a recalcitrant rural patriarchy and lack of viable alternatives open to female workers. In Taiwan during the early 1970s, a daughter's incorporation into the workforce was viewed as a filial duty or repayment for the expense of raising someone who would eventually, in the patrilineal marriage tradition, become another family's daughter-in-law.[128] Typically, factory daughters dutifully remitted their earnings to parents, who in turn invested more in sons, reproducing gender inequality at the level of the family.[129] Although factory work often delayed marriages and widened women's choices, most daughters dutifully accepted marriages arranged by their parents.[130] In post–Mao China too, rural migrant women marry later than their nonmigrant peers, though there is some debate as to whether this leads to "marriage resistance"—marrying without parental approval or against parents' wishes.[131] In this volume, Beynon's chapter poignantly conveys the anxiety felt by rural migrant women facing marriage decisions, and analyzes the various factors that make their choices so difficult.

Chapters in this volume build upon and engage with the insights of previous scholarship into the ways in which rural migrant women workers are constrained and empowered by their competing and complementary roles as filial daughters, virtuous wives and good mothers, and independent wage earners and consumers, and emphasize the complexity of rural migrant wo-

Map 1

men's identities. The chapters situate experience and the negotiation of identities within the context of institutional structures, discourses, and practices of gender, kinship and family, capitalism, modernity and consumption, *hukou* and rural/urban difference, and above all, women's own agency.

Moreover, this volume complements the material on single female factory workers in South China by presenting studies of the lives of both unmarried and married migrant women working in a range of urban occupations, including domestic service, sex work, waitressing, factory work, and trade. In addition, the volume examines the situation of women who have remained in the village while other members of their household have migrated to the city, as well as women who have returned to the countryside after a period of time in an urban setting. These studies also range over a wide area, from Beijing (chapters 1 and 10), Liaoning (chapter 2), Heilongjiang (chapter 10), Jiangsu (chapter 5), and Guangdong (chapter 10) in the East to Anhui (chapters 3, 6, and 7) and Jiangxi (chapter 8) in central China, and Sichuan (chapters 4, 6, 7, and 10) in western China (see map 1[132]).

NOTES

1. The term "floating population" suggests that migrants move blindly or unsystematically. In fact most rely on social networks, as we discuss later in this introduction. The etymological roots of this term connote social transgression, as the term itself emerged from a long history of viewing mobile people with suspicion (Dutton 1998:62).

2. Despite a plethora of surveys and analyses since the late 1980s, estimates of the floating population vary tremendously and are imprecise, for several reasons. Mainly, the English term "migrant" has multiple referents in Chinese, where permanent "migrants" are distinguished from "floaters." Also, there are differences of opinion about what type and distance of movement and length of sojourn constitute migration. Finally, official classification of spaces as "rural" and "urban" have also changed (Chan 1994). These complexities only compound the already difficult task of census takers attempting to count a mobile population. The 1990 population census, which was the first to include discrete questions about migration, deemed a migrant as anyone away from their registered residence for more than one year, thus undercounting many short-term migrants (Fan 1999:961; Chan 1999:55n2). The available data from the 2000 census, however, improve upon the previous census by counting as migrants those who have lived six or more months away from their registered place, by asking questions about migrations of less than six months, and considering movements within counties and cities and not just across such administrative lines (Lavely 2001:3, 7). For additional discussions of such measurement pitfalls, consult Chan 1999; Mallee 1996; Scharping 1997; Solinger 1999:15–23.

3. The total rural surplus labor force is estimated to reach 220 million. See HRIC 2002:22; Lavely 2001; Solinger 1999:18. The 1990 national census calculated the entire floating population at only about 35 million (Fan 1999:961). However, a report commissioned in 1994 by the United Nations Food and Agricultural Organization (UNFAO) calculated that 120 million people with rural *hukou* were working away from their villages by the mid-1990s (Croll and Huang 1997:128n1). A more conservative but widely accepted estimate that drew from provincial survey data put the total floating population at about 80 million in the mid-1990s, including 50–60 million rural labor migrants and their families (Mallee 2000:35; Rozelle et al. 1999:374; Solinger 1999:18; West 2000:3–4).

4. Temporary migrants throughout the PRC's history have been predominantly peasants (Goldstein and Goldstein 1991:22). Studies from both Beijing and Shanghai in the mid-1990s reported that nearly 80 percent and 90 percent of the floating population in each city, respectively, were peasants prior to migration, comprising from a fifth to a third of the total urban population (Wang and Zuo 1997:276).

5. In this volume, we do not consider migrants who move between towns or cities, although they also belong to the floating population. This population is better educated than rural-to-urban migrants, and fares better in the urban labor force, but they too face hardship in the urban economy, holding less secure jobs and inferior housing compared with their local *hukou* counterparts (see "The survey of occupational mobility and migration," 2000). However, recent changes in residence registration laws indicate a rosier future for urban-to-urban migrants. See our discussion of *hukou* reforms below.

6. The literature on migration in China is too extensive to list here. However, we note that a concern with controlling the migration flow has been particularly evident in certain Chinese publications, as it reflects the concern of officials. See Li and Hu (1991) and Wang and Hu (1996), for example.

7. Some exceptions in the English literature include large- and small-scale questionnaire-based sample surveys. These may discuss migrants' motivations for migration, aspects of their lives in the cities, their personal evaluation of their work and living conditions, relations with residents and authorities, and changes in personal values and social status (e.g., Lan 1997; Scharping and Sun 1997; Zhou 1997). Questionnaire-based surveys on migrants' personal evaluations and values have limitations, however. They can give an indication of broadly held values, but a qualitative approach, based on more extensive interviews, is necessary for a thorough understanding of individuals' values and perceptions. Solinger's (1999) important book includes qualitative research on the experiences of rural migrants in urban areas, with a particular focus on their employment and their relationship to the state. This work provides a rather broad-brush view of the situation of migrants in various different cities across China. More recently, Li Zhang (2001a) has written a fascinating ethnography of Zhejiangcun, a community of rural migrants, mostly from Wenzhou, living in Beijing. Zhang is particularly concerned with the relationship between power and the production of social space. By examining the politics of the making, unmaking, and remaking of Zhejiangcun, she explores how space, power, and identity continually intersect to reconfigure the state-society relationship in a period of increased spatial mobility and marketization.

8. The small field of research on the lives of female migrants in China is discussed below and in note 125.

9. Bilsborrow and the UN Secretariat 1993:2; Buijs 1993:1; Chant and Radcliffe 1992:1; Pedraza 1991:303–4.

10. Buijs 1993; Kutsche 1994; Rodenburg 1993.

11. For example, see the story "I Am a Cloud" in chapter 10. In regard to the much-debated issue of whether rural women use migration as a means to evade draconian policies of family planning, please refer to the excellent discussion by Roberts (2000).

12. Lee and Kleinman 2000:224, 234. We caution that the causes of high suicide rates among young rural Chinese women are very poorly understood, and that the suggestion of a relationship between outmigration and (lower) rates of suicide made by Lee and Kleinman is highly speculative.

13. We use this term to convey "a sense of having the capacity, perceived or real, to direct their life choices and rise above their cohorts" (Smart 1999:431, discussing the effect of migration on rural women migrating to South China).

14. Among internal migrants internationally, "autonomy has been found to be fostered by legal migration, long duration in their destinations, urban destinations, work outside of the home and migration independent of the family" (Roberts 2000:6, citing Hugo). However, we caution that experiences of separation from home and exposure to new ideas may not translate directly to autonomy. For example, both Greenhalgh (1985) and Kung (1994), as well as Salaff (1995), in their respective studies of rural women workers in industrializing Taiwan and Hong Kong, found that while migration exposed young women to new ideas, it failed to liberate them from patriarchal control, as they dutifully remitted their wages to parents, who in turn continued to invest in the education of sons.

15. Knight, Song, and Jia 1999, cited in Roberts 2000:6.

16. Hondagneu-Sotelo 1994.

17. Ma 2001:242. The drawbacks to women's migration are also noted by Davin 1999:126–30.

18. As Davin (1999:130) observes, "women migrants have many adjustments to make when they return [to the village]," including potential loss of autonomy. Yet the family conflicts that may result, she notes, have a positive function of bringing about "a shift in family structures and gender roles which still constitute such a barrier to improving women's status in rural China."

19. Scott 1992.

20. Stockman 2000:46.

21. Williams 1973.

22. Cohen 1993:156.

23. Stockman 2000:48–49.

24. Cohen 1993:154–57.

25. Jacka 2000a.

26. Fitzgerald 1996:108.

27. See, for example, Smith 1894.

28. Feuerwerker 1998:245. Not all of the writers of this period portrayed rural women as symbols of the nation's backwardness, however. As Duara discusses (2001:359–85), some portrayed rural women as representing an essentialized, idealized traditional culture, and contrasted them favorably with modern, unfilial, or immoral women. Common to both representations was a denial of "coevalness," to use Johannes Fabian's term. In other words, whether portrayed positively or negatively, intellectuals positioned rural women as occupying and symbolizing the past, as objects that they, as the nation's educated elite, would work upon in order to build a modern future.

29. Kipnis 1995:116–17.

30. See Chan and Li 1999 for a description of the requirements for conversion from agricultural to nonagricultural *hukou*.

31. Chan and Li 1999:821.

32. Goldstein and Goldstein 1991:12–13, 28–29.

33. Rural women comprise the majority of marriage migrants, and marriage has long been a primary strategy for Chinese women to achieve social mobility (Fan and Huang 1998:229–31). Despite the guarantees of the 1950 Marriage Law, transfer of *hukou* to permanent resident status in larger urban areas has been difficult for rural spouses to attain (Fan and Huang 1998:232–33), although reforms in

the early 1980s did make it easier for spouses of cadres and intellectuals to become permanent urban citizens (Chan 1996:136).

34. Goldstein, Liang, and Goldstein 2000:218–19.

35. Khan and Riskin 1998:246.

36. Chan and Li 1999:835–36. A study conducted near Shanghai suggests that the majority of these were women who were already living in towns and whose spouses already had urban *hukou* (Solinger 1999:48–50). Thus, the new type of *hukou* helped to alleviate the problems of some people who had already settled, or whose family members had settled, in a market town.

37. Chan and Li 1999:836.

38. Ibid., 832–33.

39. Ibid., 833–34.

40. Wong and Huen 1998:976.

41. The high costs of permits and illegal fees levied against migrants have been hotly debated among policy makers, and the State Council in 2001 announced a plan for the gradual elimination of all fees, including for temporary residence permits. It remains to be seen whether such promises will be fulfilled in practice. See HRIC 2002:51–52.

42. See Dutton 1998:113–29. Detention under the "Custody and Repatriation" scheme more than tripled between 1989 and 2000, with 3.2 million instances of detention in the year 2000, according to Human Rights in China (2002:2). Official sources indicate that the great majority of those detained are rural migrants (HRIC 2002:2).

43. The editors found that as of 2002, this reform had yet to be systematically implemented in Beijing.

44. HRIC 2002:47.

45. Wong and Huen 1998.

46. Ibid., 979–80, 984–85.

47. Wong and Huen 1998:978; HRIC 2002:48.

48. Chan and Li 1999:839–40 and Wong and Huen 1998:991. Generally, the higher the administrative status of a city, the higher the price of the blue-stamp *hukou*. In 1994, prices ranged from a few thousand *yuan* for a town below the county level, to more than 10,000 *yuan* for a prefectural-level city, to between 20,000 and 40,000 *yuan* in Guangzhou, depending upon in which district of the city one chose to register (Chan and Li 1999:836–39). In Shanghai, a blue-stamp *hukou* is issued to firms for every million *yuan* of capital investment (Wong and Huen 1998:984).

49. Shanghai was one of the first cities to set up a formal blue-stamp *hukou* system, with rules on the management of the system taking effect in early 1994. However, between 1994 and 2000 the total number of blue-stamp *hukou* booklets issued in the city was well under 50,000 (HRIC 2002:49).

50. The American Embassy in China 2002.

51. In Shanghai, the talent scheme replaced the blue-stamp *hukou* system in 2001 (HRIC 2002:49; "Guanyu Shanghai shi juzhu zheng" 2002), and similar talent schemes are underway in Shenzhen and Beijing (HRIC 2002:48–50).

52. HRIC 2002:48–50. In short, numerous *hukou*-related changes are in progress in large cities, and all seem targeted toward creating hierarchy among

new migrants. We refer to the report by Human Rights in China (2002:48–50), as well as various news reports, including The American Embassy in China 2002; "Beijing cuts red tape for staff of foreign enterprises" 2002; "Household registration system plays vital role, says minister" 2002.

53. On employment discrimination, see Li and Li 1999:23–25. Regarding discrimination in education, see Ku 1999. In 2003, the State Council issued directives aimed at dismantling such employment and education barriers, indicating a sea change in CCP policy. When and how such improvements will be implemented locally awaits future research.

54. Rodenburg 1993:273.

55. Chant 1992:197–98.

56. Song 1999:76.

57. For example, a survey of the floating population in 11 large cities conducted between 1989 and 1990 by the Ministry of Construction found that women comprised 39 percent of the floating population, among which about half had migrated for work purposes (Song 1999:71–72). Likewise, a 1994 survey of 75 villages in 11 provinces conducted by the Ministry of Agriculture estimated that female migrants comprised about 33 percent of the 70 million labor migrants moving out of villages and rural townships (Lu 1999:2; Tan 1998a:118).

58. Huang 2001:264.

59. Fan 2000:426.

60. Fan 2000:427.

61. Du 2000:77.

62. Fan 2000:431, figure 1. According to Smart (1999:424), the Pearl River Delta "takes the lion's share" of foreign direct investment that enters China.

63. Scharping and Sun 1997:39; Tan 2000:292–97.

64. Tan 2000:296. Likewise, women comprised 78 percent of the migrant labor force in Dongguan's export-processing firms in 1989 (G. S. Lin, cited in Gransow 2000:6), and they outnumbered male migrants in Shenzhen and Foshan by a ratio of about 5:4 in 1993 (Scharping and Sun 1997:37).

65. Fan 1996:32.

66. Fan 2000:428.

67. Ibid.

68. Ibid. Similarly, Yang (2000:203) observes of the 1990 census data for Zhejiang that had movement across smaller spatial units, such as townships rather than counties, been measured, women's rates of migration would likely have appeared higher.

69. The research on 75 villages in 11 provinces by the Ministry of Agriculture found that interprovincial moves accounted for just 19.9 percent of migration in 1988, but rose to 36.2 percent by 1994 (Mallee 1996:120). Research conducted by the Ministry of Agriculture in Sichuan and Anhui provinces in 1995 found that the majority of labor migrants of both sexes from these provinces engaged in interprovincial migration, mainly to Guangdong (from both provinces) and to Jiangsu (particularly from Anhui), as well as to Beijing (Du 2000:77).

70. Mallee 1996:120.

71. Wang Feng 2000:236.

72. Cited in Song 1999:72; cf. Li and Hu 1991.

73. Goldstein, Liang, and Goldstein 2000:218.

74. Mallee 1996:121.

75. The Ministry of Agriculture's 1994 survey of 75 villages in 11 provinces na-. tionwide found that 16 percent of migrants left their village for less than three months; 24.6 percent stayed away for between three and six months, and 56.4 percent remained away for more than six months (Mallee 1996:121).

76. Roberts 2002.

77. Wang and Zuo 1997:20, reporting on their findings from a survey of migrants in Shanghai. They suggest the reason for this discrepancy is the fact that more male migrants are already married when they migrate and have families to return to, whereas most migrant women are unmarried and may have less motivation or fewer obligations to return to the countryside. See also Fan, this volume.

78. The evidence is from studies of Hubei province (Goldstein, Liang, and Goldstein 2000:227) and Hebei province (Song 1999:85).

79. Chan 2002; Tan 2000:305.

80. Woon 2000:157. Woon surmises that female migrants' negative outlook results from the employment opportunity structure of the Delta, which clearly favors male migrants.

81. Ma 2001:249.

82. Riley and Gardner 1993.

83. Not only is the migrant labor force younger than the rural labor force generally, but it is getting younger, and this may be attributable to an increase in women entering the labor flow (Rozelle et al. 1999:378).

84. Lu 1999:4.

85. Du 2000:77.

86. Yang 2000:205.

87. In both cities, roughly 75 percent of women migrants surveyed in 1993 were aged between fifteen and nineteen (Scharping 1999:80–81).

88. Du 2000:77.

89. Scharping 1999:80–81.

90. Zheng 1999:290; Beijingshi Wailai Renkou Pucha Bangongshi 1998:14.

91. Tan 1998a:71, table 1.

92. Ibid.

93. Rozelle et al. 1999:378.

94. Zheng 1999:290; Beijingshi Wailai Renkou Pucha Bangongshi 1998:170–71.

95. Zheng 1999:290.

96. Du 2000:83. See also Ma and Xiang 1998; Roberts 1997; Zhang 2001a.

97. Scharping 1999:88. Similarly, the 1995 census of the floating population in Shanghai shows that nearly half of all labor migrants to Shanghai found jobs through relatives and kin (Wang and Zuo 1997:9).

98. Du 2000:100, table 9.

99. Zhao Shukai 2000.

100. Scharping 1999:89.

101. Scharping 1999:88; Song 1999:74.

102. Details of a comparison between rural migrants and permanent residents in Beijing, Wuxi, and Zhuhai are found in "The survey of occupational mobility and migration" 2000.

103. Yang and Guo 1996:780. Similarly, the 1997 survey of Beijing's non*hukou* migrant population found that the majority of women migrants (69.2 percent) were concentrated in food and beverage retail and services (Zheng 1999:290).

104. Huang 2001:264.

105. Tan 1998b:119; Tan 2000:297.

106. Huang 2001:264.

107. Feng 1997:59–60.

108. Xin Meng 2000:256–58.

109. Peasant Worker Migration Project Group 1996:57; Tan 1998b:123–24.

110. Xin Meng 2000:256–58.

111. Ma 2001:247.

112. Davin 1999; Fan and Huang 1998.

113. Zhou 1996:189–94.

114. Davin 1999:130; Roberts 2000. First, unmarried migrants tend to marry later, in order to maximize their time away from the village earning money, and so have a shortened period of fertility. For married couples, migration generally requires periods of separation, which should further limit fertility. Third, for migrants residing away from the village, the opportunity costs for children are high, from the costs of education and housing to the lack of kinship networks and community supports, so migrants may be motivated to decrease risk by decreasing fertility. Moreover, migrants are specifically targeted by family planners, and may be made to comply more strictly with policy than rural nonmigrants (Hoy 1999:149). Migrants may also gradually come to emulate the smaller urban family as it becomes synonymous with a "modern" lifestyle.

115. Yang 2000:205.

116. See C. Cindy Fan's chapter. Tamara Jacka has interviewed married women in Hangzhou who left their husbands and children in the village to work in the city because there were better-paid employment opportunities for migrant women than for men.

117. Davin 1999:123.

118. Hoy 1999:144, 149.

119. Song 1999:78; Bossen 1994. Not all families maintain their farms themselves, however. Some families migrating to urban areas lease land to other villagers, and others leave their land untended (Tamara Jacka, interviews conducted in Beijing 2001).

120. Ku 1999. See also *n*53.

121. Eckholm 1999.

122. Lee 1998:74–75.

123. Lee 1998:135; and see Elson and Pearson 1984.

124. Lee 1998.

125. In addition to the studies of rural migrant women in contemporary China discussed here are several more that have been published recently in English, including Chan (2002), Feng (1997), Tan (2000), Tang (1998), Woon (2000), Xu (2000), Zhang, H. (1999a,b), and Zhang, L. (2000a).

126. Pun 1999.

127. These include Greenhalgh 1985; Kung 1994 (1978); Salaff 1995 (1981).

128. Greenhalgh 1985; Kung 1994:xxv–xxvi.

129. Ibid.

130. Kung 1994:127–42; Salaff 1981:266–70. Similarly, in the Shanghai factories of the colonial powers early in the twentieth century, unmarried rural daughters toiled well into their twenties, but eventually dutifully married the partners their parents arranged for them, according to historian Honig (1986:183).

131. Lee (1998:77–80) found that migration and factory life provide such an opportunity, while Smart (1999:433) found it did not.

132. Rendered by cartographer Chase Langford, UCLA department of geography.

>> *Part 1*

NEGOTIATING IDENTITIES

Arianne M. Gaetano

1. Filial Daughters, Modern Women: Migrant Domestic Workers in Post-Mao Beijing

>> In the broadest sense, the goal of China's reform platform is to achieve a modernity (*xiandaihua*) that involves "linking tracks with the rest of the world" (*yu shijie jiegui*) and otherwise overcoming a sense of having fallen behind the more economically advanced West.[1] This discourse of modernity constructs a chronotope[2] of rural/urban difference, whereby residing in the countryside and being a peasant imply being left behind temporally in the drive toward progress, and lacking the moral "quality" (*suzhi*) required of citizens to advance socialist modernity.[3] Rural women figure into this schema as paradigmatically traditional (*chuantong*) or backward (*luohou*).[4] As Harriet Evans notes, as China negotiates modernity coupled with global capitalism, the "modern woman" is constructed through images of "subordination and exclusion, most notably of the rural, uneducated, and poor."[5] According to this dominant schema, rural-to-urban migration is then a key means for rural women to cast off the peasant mantle and be "baptized in civilization."[6] But a focus on young rural women's actual lived experiences of migration disrupts this seamless narrative of modernity by exposing inequalities of gender and class that contour their everyday lives and confound their efforts to become modern. This chapter recognizes that while powerful cultural discourses and social practices of post–Mao modernity configure young rural women's motivations and expectations for, and experiences of, migration and work, the

women are agents who actively participate in, give meaning to, and shape the course of modernity.

In particular, during this period of rapid social and economic transition, young rural women who traverse the boundaries of the rural and the urban must contend with the contradictions posed by their position as temporary "outsiders" to both the city and the village, and the complexities of gender and class that structure their mobility. A desire for modernity, associated with urban living, in part propels young women out of the countryside. Distanced from village and kin, earning wages, acquiring skills, and navigating the urban landscape, migrant women forge new, modern identities. Yet their marginalized status in the urban milieu, due to structural barriers of the household registration (*hukou*) system and regulatory policies and practices that limit their full participation in the urban economy and polity, as well as more subtle forms of social discrimination directed at them by urban society, thwarts their ambitions for upward mobility as well as personal freedom.[8] Moreover, rural gender prescriptions provide few alternatives for young women but to ultimately marry and bear children, while *hukou*-based discriminatory policies and urban prejudices ensure that most young migrant women will return to the countryside to settle down. As a result, unmarried migrant women must be bound to dominant standards of social respectability or risk alienating their local communities and jeopardizing their own futures, even as their very mobility transgresses such standards and invites slander. These interconnected constructions of gender and class are captured in derogatory monikers like "working sisters" (*dagongmei*)[9] and "little nursemaids" (*xiao baomu*), which in popular parlance identify this population as both low-status workers and single and female youth. Such discourses configure young rural women as a "naturally" flexible labor force of temporary workers and secondary wage earners, reinforcing their primary identity as (future) wives and mothers. For young rural women, then, post–Mao modernity generates both desires and opportunities, through migration and off-farm work, to become modern, but limits the scope and duration of their pursuits.

Young migrant women's agency lies in their ability to fulfill their modern aspirations as rural women, by negotiating identities as both modern women and filial daughters across the social spaces of the "rural" and "urban." Agency, as explained by Stuart Hall, is located in the process of a subject's willful identification with forms of power that construct identities and create the "knowing" subject.[10] Identities, moreover, are but "points of temporary attachment to the subject positions which discursive practices construct for us."[11] As agents, then, rural migrant women are enmeshed in webs of power that determine the parameters of possible identities, but within which they may creatively fashion new identities that even reconfigure relations of power. Yet if identities are shifting and fluid, so too power is never just accommodated or resisted. As Lila Abu-Lughod observes, "if the systems of power are multiple, then resisting at one level may catch people up at other levels."[12] Conceiving of agency as productive of, as well as conditioned by, power in the particular historical and cultural setting of post–Mao China dispels the notion of either a universal (global) modernity or a monolithic (local) rural patriarchy, and in turn challenges the view of women as passive victims of these forms of power. Through attention to agency, fluid identity, and circulatory forms of power, I attempt to move beyond the polarizing "filial or rebellious daughters" debate that Yuan-fong Woon and others argue characterizes much previous scholarship on the changing identities of rural Chinese women in the process of incorporation into global capitalism.[13] Rather than pose the perennial question of whether such a process is liberating or oppressive, which has been shown to beg the question of "for whom,"[14] I illuminate rural Chinese women's own capacity to imagine and craft, through their gendered and classed locations in post–Mao modernity, meaningful identities that may have the potential to shift relations of power.

This chapter first provides background to the ethnographic research and next situates young rural women's desires and expectations for migration in the context of post–Mao modernity and rural women's life course. Finally, the chapter chronicles young rural women's everyday negotiations of identity through their decisions to migrate, their journeys to the city, and their job choices and in their urban lives, highlighting their struggles for survival, dignity, and value.

OUTSIDERS WITHIN: RURAL WOMEN WORKING IN URBAN DOMESTIC SERVICE

This chapter draws upon a larger project for which I conducted participant observation among young (single) rural migrant women working in Beijing's service sector for fifteen months between 1999 and 2000, and for two months in 2002.[15] Among my informants were twenty women with recent experience as live-in domestic workers. All had entered domestic service between the ages of sixteen and twenty, upon first migrating to Beijing from diverse rural origins. At the time of our first meeting, eight were currently employed as domestic workers; by 2002, only one remained in domestic service.[16] My particular interest in domestic workers was motivated by the extensive attention to them in the media and popular imagination, which identify the migrant maid (*baomu*) as an object of (urban) curiosity. The novelty of an outsider living and working inside an urban household is probably responsible for such excessive attention. In addition, the ubiquity of the domestic worker in public discourse reflects her unique place as the forerunner of the *dagongmei* phenomenon in Beijing. Since the beginning of the migrant labor tide (*mingongchao*), domestic service has been one of the main points of entry into the urban labor market for rural women migrating to Beijing, and thus was the logical starting point for my long-term investigation of rural-to-urban migration, work, and identity.[17]

In this chapter, my focus on domestic workers is particularly suited to the exploration of modernity and identity. While migrant domestic workers are marked as outsiders by their inferior class status accorded by their rural *hukou* and their low-wage, stigmatized occupation, they are also nominally incorporated into urban households, sometimes forming intimate relationships with employers. Thus, I argue, domestic service is a key site for examining the contradictions of *dagongmei* identity. This chapter draws upon my research mainly with these domestic workers, except where indicated, and presents their own narratives of migration and descriptions of their everyday lives, culled from my fieldwork notes and interview tapes.

MIGRATION DECISIONS AS EXPRESSIONS OF AGENCY

> I was 15, going on 16, when I announced: "I'm also going to Beijing." My father disagreed; I decided for myself. My sister-in-law didn't agree either, saying I was too young. But I had little to do at home. . . . Later I said to my father again: "I want to go out to work, and I won't come back for five years." I had made up my mind. I said, "I'll be back when I'm 22"—I was then 17. I said, "In five years I'll come back only once." They still didn't trust me. . . . Then my mother supported me a bit, and saw that I had nothing to do at home, that I didn't have any interest in farming. She urged [my father], "Let her go out to work." (Xie Aimin)

Following the implementation of reforms in early 1980s China, increasing numbers of bold young rural women have been compelled to venture forth from the village, headed for distant cities like Beijing. Like Xie Aimin,[18] most are initially opposed in their decision by one or both parents. Understandably, parents are concerned for their children's safety, their worries fueled by tales of unscrupulous employers and the dangers of city life as recounted by returning migrants.

> The elders in my village returning from work in Beijing said the city had lots of tricksters and bad people, people who wouldn't give you your salary or would cheat you. . . . Because of what returning migrants said, my parents worried, and didn't want me to come to Beijing. (Ma Ning)

Concerns for the safety of young women in particular may be compounded by the threat of sexual harassment and abuse, and of traffickers selling women into marriage or prostitution.[19]

> At home there are a lot of women who have been sold, especially from Sichuan and Anhui. I know some. They are adults, thirtysomething, who are unmarried [men] and can't get a wife through other means, so they buy one. There are lots and lots. They sell people like they sell commodities. (Ma Ning)

Yet despite the hardships that the journey and city life promise to present, certain young women are quite insistent in their efforts to win parental support and in their determination to leave the village. The magazine *Rural Women Knowing All* (*Nongjianü Baishitong*) provides some examples of the more extreme tactics deployed by determined young women. Gao Zhihua[20] writes that she "secretly left my parents a note, and hurriedly boarded a train headed far away," while Dai Chengjiao[21] refused to eat or get out of her bed until she won her parents' permission to leave home. Those young women who persist find comfort and strength in the knowledge that they have made an autonomous decision, and passionately resolve to accept the consequences.

> My mother and I are very close, like sisters even, so the first month that I was in Beijing, I missed home so much that I often cried, and I wondered why I had ever wanted to make myself suffer so! Later, though, I thought, "This was the path I myself chose," and there's nothing wrong with that! (Liu Fanmei)

Young women's efforts to overcome parental opposition, as well as their own fears and feelings of homesickness, suggest that the decision to migrate is ultimately an expression of their agency. Young migrant women I know clearly conceive of themselves as active initiators of migration. In their eyes, it is clearly not just a response to micro circumstances of poverty or macro results of uneven development.[22] Nor do they view migration as solely an outgrowth of Confucian filial piety,[23] or the result of a household strategy to better allocate scarce resources.[24] In the following sections, I explore the complex set of desires—escaping boredom and postponing marriage, seeking to acquire new skills or improve education so as to avoid a life of farming, seeing the world and satisfying curiosity about urban life—that factor into a young rural woman's decision to migrate.[25] These motivations must be understood in the context of a discourse of post–Mao modernity that privileges the urban, and in cultural constructions of gender and women's life course.

PLACING DESIRE: RURAL/URBAN DIFFERENCE AND "MODERNITY"

> Before, I didn't know anything about Beijing. I learned about Beijing from my elder brother's wife. She went to Beijing and said how everything there was so great. (Xie Aimin)

In heading to the city, often boarding trains or overnight buses for the first time, most young rural women carry only pocket money and dreamlike images of city life absorbed through television or gleaned from other migrants. Although potentially disorienting or dangerous, the city is also an object of fascination. Unlike most villages, Beijing offers the excitement of high-rises, superhighways, and multilevel shopping malls. Going to any large city, especially the nation's capital, is a chance "to see the world" (*kan shimian*) and glimpse life outside the village. Young women from the countryside willingly brave the potential dangers posed by migration because "going out to work" (*chulai dagong*) offers the chance to participate in China's quest for modernity, while remaining on the farm does not.

As China strives to catch up to the postindustrialized world through economic growth, the reform platform focuses on the "Four Modernizations" (industry, agriculture, science and technology, and national defense),[26] along with social and cultural development. China's version of modernization ideology, "socialism with Chinese characteristics," imposes a "developmental map of moral geography"[27] on its vast civilization. In particular, rural hinterlands appear economically sluggish in contrast to the dynamic urban and coastal areas, where favorable government policies and infusion of foreign investment have jump-started industrialization and spurred economic growth, resulting in rising per capita incomes and the emergence of an inchoate middle class. Rural agricultural regions, and rural peasants by extension, are paradoxically blamed as the causes of China's underdevelopment and seen as the objects to be developed; they are the necessary "other" against which progress and civilization (*wenming*)[28] are defined and measured. In this schema, being from a "poor and backward" (*pinkun luohou*) region takes on a social and moral taint that stains those least able to successfully accumulate capital and those geographically most remote from the urban centers of modern life.[29] Rural women are positioned as particularly distant from urban centers of modernity in part due to their increasing responsibility for rural household production (as well as reproduction), including farm work.[30] In addition, the media are rife with reports of how market reforms allegedly have revived "feudal" (*fengjian*) practices in the countryside, such as trafficking in women or denial of basic education to girls in poorer areas, reinforcing an association of rural womanhood with backwardness.[31]

The city, on the other hand, promises to expose rural migrants to new forms of knowledge and "raise their quality" (*tigao suzhi*). As many scholars of post–Mao China have noted, "quality" is determined by its relevance to state socialist modernity.[32] In the post–Mao era, technical training and intellectual scholarship have become increasingly valued over the manual labor and political dedication that were the hallmarks of Maoist learning.[33] Formal education and training, symbolized by the ubiquitous diploma (*wenping*), along with familiarity with media, computers, and the Internet, are important forms of cultural capital. Since modern technology favors the developed infrastructure and high concentration of centers for higher education found in the urban areas, the countryside and its residents appear technologically primitive in contrast. Migrant women likewise express their desire for formal education and value the prestige of mental labor, rejecting farming as useless knowledge.

> Rural folk for the most part, apart from farming, have never learned anything. [In Beijing] everyone reads books and the newspapers. But at home, we don't have these habits, nor the material conditions. (Zhang Xiaqing)

So long as wealth and status, accumulated through cultural capital of education and off-farm work, are considered predominantly urban prerogatives, migration to the cities is a key means for rural women to appropriate this modern identity.

Young rural women's desires and expectations of migration are thus forged in the context of a moral geography of development that denigrates peasants while privileging the city as the site of modernity. By leaving "backward" villages for a taste of the modern urban environment, young rural women themselves reinforce constructions of rural/urban difference and hierarchy, even though the opportunity offers them as individuals the chance to craft new identities.

GENDER AND RURAL WOMEN'S LIFE COURSE

The lure of urban modernity is also especially attractive to young rural women because of their gender and kinship position in the Chinese farm family. Following the completion of formal schooling[34] and prior to settling down, young rural women are liminally poised between carefree youth and responsible adulthood, which is traditionally conferred upon marriage. In all but the poorest of farm households, young women's labor is not crucial to the maintenance of the household economy, particularly when compared with potential wage remittances from off-farm work. Although young women generally help parents and other siblings with farm work, many complain of having "nothing to do in my village" (*mei shi gan; hen wuliao; lao xianzhe*).[35] At this unique moment in their life course, migration at the least promises diversion, even a chance to "find excitement" (*zhao renao*), before settling down.

For nearly all rural women, opting out of marriage altogether is not just impractical but also unthinkable. Marriage nevertheless looms large on the horizon because it signifies a certain loss of freedom and end of idealism. As it generally requires a daughter's spatial separation from the natal household, it symbolizes both an end and a new beginning. In anticipating marriage, young women imagine limitless possibilities for their future, only to be largely disappointed by reality.[36] Facing an uncertain future after marriage, they eagerly seize upon migration as the last chance for autonomy and independence.

Moreover, venturing to the city might also be a means of tempting fate or changing one's destiny (*mingyun*). Many young women hope to make a better match than what would be available to them in the context of their local community—namely, a fellow peasant. They set their sights on marrying someone with an urban *hukou*, or at least a skilled worker or entrepreneur, and most certainly someone with similar migration and work experience.[37] Whether enjoying a period of relative autonomy or pursuing an ideal mate, most young women postpone their return from the city for as long as they can.[38] In addition, by applying their earnings toward their dowry, they can improve the material quality of their prospects. Thus, to a limited extent, migration increases young women's chances to exercise control over their futures.[39]

Rural gender and kinship roles and identities foster young women's ability and desire to migrate, yet also reinforce their status as flexible workers. As they are mere secondary wage earners for their natal households, their low remuneration and lack of benefits appear justified, while their dismissal upon marriage without severance pay or pensions is attributed to the natural progression of a women's life course. In turn, these prescriptions compound young rural women's outsider status and class position in the urban environment.

RESPECTABLE MAIDENS, FILIAL DAUGHTERS

In post–Mao China, the migration of young rural women especially disturbs village parents and elders because it challenges their traditional authority in decisions about marriage and control over daughters' sexuality.[40] These two concerns are closely related: despite increasingly liberal attitudes toward premarital sex and cohabitation in urban China, rural women's marriage prospects continue to be linked to youth and virtuous character, among other factors.[41] The centrality of marriage in rural women's life course means that parents and daughters alike wish to maintain the young woman's good reputation. Young migrant women therefore must balance their aspirations for modernity with attention to their future marriage prospects.

The threat posed by migration to a young woman's reputation is historically conditioned. Although cultural discourse on moral propriety in China has varied over time, in the late imperial and Republican eras, women who sought work outside the village were considered lacking in feminine virtue. According to elite standards of behavior, women were to be confined to the "inner" sphere of physical environment and social life, interacting only with close kin. Often poverty or family tragedy, such as widowhood, was the catalyst for moving out of the village, and so women's migration was also associated with economic deprivation and the lower classes.[42]

In the Reform era, this gendered construction of virtue is further imbricated in a moral discourse on wealth.[43] Official support for increased consumer spending is tempered by popular outrage against corruption and official condemnation of excessive consumption outside the perimeters of law and order.[44] Such ambivalence toward wealth is mapped onto a discourse of women's sexual virtue, not least because some of the highest-paid jobs for female migrants in the city involve the commercialization of female sexuality, as in the entertainment sector.[45] In this sense, the bodies and characters of young migrant women become scapegoats for the challenges to social mores wrought by liberalizing consumption habits—particularly those of "deep-pocketed" (*dakuan*) middle-class men—challenges that threaten the stability of the nuclear household and the official construction of "woman" as a "virtuous wife and good mother."[46]

Thus in the early 1980s, rural elites were scandalized by the first exodus of unmarried daughters from the village, and lamented it would make the village "look bad."[47] Yet as more women from any one village or county participate in migration, criticism about the corruptive influence of wealth tends to abate, and local officials even facilitate young women's migration when they realize the value of their remittances.[48] Nevertheless, for her own sake as well as on behalf of her entire family, a young rural woman considering migration will weigh the consequences of being associated with such negative stereotypes of gender and mobility, and modernity and consumption.

> When I went out to work, my family didn't really support me. They worried that a girl who went out would ruin her reputation, so I told them that I wasn't "chasing money," I was just going out to work in a safe place. (Li Shanshan)

JOURNEYING TO BEIJING AND LOCATING WORK

Local social networks expedite young rural women's searches for work and journeys to the city. Someone familiar—a relative, co-villager, friend, or former classmate, usually someone older who is already established in Beijing—is trusted to provide accurate information about job opportunities, arrange for short-term lodging in the city or introductions to prospective employers, and ideally be accountable for a new migrant's personal safety and moral integrity.

> I had no way to go out, not knowing anyone. But then my mother sent some gifts to that old lady, who then took me out to work. . . . Her daughter was my primary school classmate. . . . In her employer's household there was a dormitory, like those ones they used to have at People's University specially for domestic workers. I lived with her there, for more than a month . . . later she found me a place . . . helping a couple care for an infant. (Xie Aimin)

In keeping with local practices of social networking (*guanxi*), the exchange of a gift establishes a reciprocal relationship between the two families.

Here, the local woman is made accountable to Xie Aimin's mother for the young woman's safe arrival and care in Beijing.

Commonly, a daughter's migration for work realizes the family's social obligations and widens their social network. Daughters gladly accept such jobs in their capacity as filial daughters.[49] Tian Weiwei became the domestic worker for the household of a revolutionary cadre retired from the Ministry of Finance, who had known her father, likewise a retired cadre but of much lower stature. Although neither Tian nor her father could easily refuse a request from a friend and superior, Tian interpreted the opportunity as an expression of her father's support of her: "My dad wanted me to go out and get life experience (*duanlian*)." For the sake of the social relationship between her father and her employer, though, Tian accepted absurdly low wages for her work with that family:

> I earned 50 or 60 [*yuan*] per month. It was low. Back then domestic workers were earning about 300 [*yuan*] a month, in 1993. Over three years my salary was raised to 100 [*yuan*]. . . . Usually, whatever humiliation I suffered, I didn't speak out.

Young women who accept the help of peers are obliged to extend the same helping hand to others later on. Rural communities depend greatly on migrants with urban connections or those already in the city for information about job opportunities and for job introductions. In a visit home to North China, hotel worker Zhou Lili was accosted by her fellow villagers demanding introductions to jobs, while her Beijing husband was approached by go-betweens inquiring about availability of prospective husbands from among his friends. She reacted to such pressure with some annoyance:

> You just can't help everybody, and not everyone has the capacity to do well in Beijing. Nor can I do much [to help them], as I make so little money myself and my husband is unemployed. But in their eyes we are better off, so if I don't help, they'll say I'm selfish.

Social networks based on kinship and native place facilitate young women's search for work in a secure manner, but also exact certain sacrifices and entail the burden of ongoing reciprocity. Nevertheless, relying on such networks provides the chance for daughters to actualize their own ambitions to go to the city with the approval and support of their local communities.

Fewer women pursue job opportunities independent of informal social networks, by relying on print advertisements or attending county labor

recruitment fairs. No matter how jobs are located, most young women accommodate concerns about moral propriety as well as personal safety in their journey to Beijing by traveling with an escort, such as a co-villager, male kin, or a county Women's Federation official.

> [In my village] some of the heads of households whose thinking was rather feudal said it was bad for girls to go out to work, that it was better for men to go out. But for me, my older brother was in Beijing, and he went out with me. My mom was worried at first, and I was a little worried about coming so far, but having relatives here helped. (Li Shanshan)

Even those who dare travel alone cautiously prepare for every emergency, carrying enough money to rent a hotel room or for return fare.

> Going out to be a domestic worker, I also worried that I would be cheated (*shoupian*); then what would I do? So that day that I went out I took some money, including enough for the return fare and three days' living expenses. This money came from my parents, because I'd only done house chores and worked on the family plot. If something happened, I would only stay in Beijing one day, visit Tiananmen Square, and then go home. (Liu Fanmei)

Liu Fanmei's description of her preparations for the journey out of the village, like the testimonies above, suggests that rural residents actively participate in moral discourse on wealth. Yet while urban residents hold a controlling image of the migrant as criminal or prostitute, rural peasants view cities as the domicile of cheats and greedy employers, and themselves as innocent victims. Nevertheless, the association of female mobility, money, and the corruption of innocence encumbers young women in their pursuit of modernity. In response, they utilize kinship networks and cultural notions of reciprocity to ensure their transition to "migrant worker" does not compromise either their personal safety or their status as dutiful daughters.

"SAFETY FIRST (ANQUAN DIYI)":[50] *CHOOSING DOMESTIC SERVICE*

Young rural women's choices in the urban job market are limited by notions of gender-appropriate labor[51] and by discriminatory policies that, alongside the *hukou* system, restrict migrants' access to coveted state-sector jobs and certain occupations.[52] Often they are further disadvantaged by their lower education level relative to their urban counterparts.[53] Although domestic service pays relatively low wages compared to other jobs available to migrant women,[54] it appeals to many newly arrived female migrants in Beijing as a matter of convenience. Live-in domestic service requires relatively little initial capital outlay yet resolves the immediate crisis of finding shelter.[55] Additionally, because domestic work is regarded by workers and employers alike not as skilled labor, but rather as an extension of women's social roles as mothers and wives, it is wide open to new arrivals with no prior work experience or with low education levels.[56]

In addition, many young women say they chose domestic service because it was "safe" (*anquan*), implying that it is not harmful to either one's person or one's reputation. As scholars of gender in China have shown, it is not so much the content of "work" as the spatial location of work and social relations of the worksite that imparts value.[57] Doing housework (*jia-wu*) and caring for the elderly, sick, or newborn is considered gender-appropriate work for women because of its location within the domestic sphere of the home, where it is performed for members of a family. Domestic work also is said to be "calm" (*tashi*) compared with other jobs that are available to young rural women new to Beijing: working as a waitress or hostess in a restaurant or bar, working in a beauty salon as a hairdresser's assistant or as a masseuse, or becoming a dance-hall escort. Wang Li-fang explains:

> When you first come out, getting a job in a home [as a domestic worker] is okay. You can't find any good job, and you have no place [to sleep], unless you go to a little restaurant, but that's so unsafe (*luan*)[58] . . . getting a job with a household is a bit safer.

Restaurants and clubs are undesirable in part because they are mixed-sex venues, where sexuality is marketed and consumed along with food and drink, and where one's virtuous reputation might be compromised.[59]

Women also consider the capacity of accommodations to accord safety and propriety in choosing jobs. Domestic workers' lodgings vary widely. Most reside with members of their employer's household in apartment buildings or in one-story brick houses similar to their homes in the village, often sharing a bedroom with their elderly or youthful charges. A few are lucky enough to be housed in "domestic worker quarters" offered by large work units, such as university campuses or the apartment buildings of a prestigious work unit. Such arrangements might include a private room or the chance to share a room with peers. No matter the degree of comfort, live-in domestic workers' accommodations may be preferable to those provided by employers to other workers. Restaurants are notorious for poor living conditions; waitresses often sleep on restaurant floors or tables and are forced to catnap during slow afternoon hours to ensure the equivalent of a full night's sleep. A dormitory I frequented, which housed the migrant workers of a professional cleaning company, consisted of dank and dark, mosquito-infested rooms in the basement of a high-rise. The two sisters who made the dorm their home for half a year expressed displeasure less at the physical conditions of the room than at the casual (*luan*) behavior they felt such quarters bred. They were especially disdainful of one female roommate, who spent nights with her boyfriend in the men's dorm room. Moreover, they were fully aware that errant young women might be forced to return home, either at the request of parents or at the discretion of bosses. At their previous job in a factory, a young woman had become pregnant and was summarily dismissed.[60] Domestic service thus offers a degree of physical protection and moral respectability that potentially more lucrative jobs lack, and is justified on these grounds.

STIGMATIZED AND "ENSLAVED"

> Zhang Xiaqing was the first migrant woman worker I met in Beijing, and over the course of three years we shared many experiences, including a trip to her hometown. When I met her, she had been in Beijing for only a month. Although she mentioned that she had come to Beijing once previously, when I pressed her about that time she deflected my questions and kept her silence. Just before I left Beijing she confided to me what I had long suspected: that in her first trip out to work in Beijing, she had been a domestic worker. Her father had objected to that job, which he felt was demeaning, low-class work that did not reflect well on either his daughter's reputation or the family's face (*mianzi*).[61] Though she shared her secret with me, Zhang entreated me not to tell her friends, neither co-villagers nor fellow migrants. Only through her hushed voice and body language could I know the chagrin and disgust she felt for domestic service and her experience of it. (field notes)

All the young migrant women I know acknowledge that domestic service carries a social stigma. This stigma appears to result from its historical association with poverty and gender transgression, like female migration generally, but is compounded by its association with servility. Performing intimate tasks not for one's immediate kin but for strangers, despite compensation, seems to be virtual servitude. In emphasizing to me the demeaning quality of domestic work, Xie Aimin gave the example of her first job, which involved "cleaning dirty diapers" daily.

Still others point to the lack of respect and human dignity accorded domestic workers as exacerbating the social stigma of domestic service. A rather extreme example was told to me by a part-time (live-out) domestic worker, whose employer refused to allow her to clean the toilet with anything other than her bare hand. Fortunately the worker was able to quit immediately, since it was only a part-time job. In addition, domestic workers may be perceived as offering sexual services, much as escorts (*sanpei*), as this quote suggests.

> We are looked down upon by Beijingers, especially those of us in the service industry, for in their eyes, all young women who enter the service industry then easily become "bad" women.[62]

Not only employers and urbanites but even fellow migrants might show disrespect for domestic workers. Tian Weiwei's general sense of strangeness and inferiority in the city was compounded by her interactions with migrant vendors at the produce market:

> I never regretted [coming out]; it's just that, doing domestic service, you feel like, when you've just started, like when you are going to market, everyone has a bad attitude toward you. . . . They hear by your accent that you have just come out. . . . [The vendors] know you are a domestic worker.

The stigma of domestic work threatens to ruin a young woman's reputation at home as well, damaging her pride and her family's face, and perhaps even her marriage prospects. In order to save face in front of other villagers and sometimes even family members, many women hide the truth of the work they do in Beijing: "Back home, if you say you are a domestic worker, it's like you are inferior (*diren yideng*)" (Tian Weiwei).

The location of domestic work in the home, while providing a patina of safety and respectability, paradoxically can make domestic workers particularly vulnerable to exploitation. The overlap of work and living space and the physical proximity of a domestic worker to her employer blur the boundaries between work time and rest time, and public and private space.[63] Not only because of living arrangements but also because of the demands of caregiving for infants or for the sick or incapacitated elderly, who demand round-the-clock attention, domestic workers may be called upon at all hours of the day and night. Characteristically, they frequently complain of being overworked and exhausted, and of "having no time to oneself" (*meiyou ziji de shijian*). At most, domestic workers rest one day a week, but most have no days off unless they return for a visit to their village: "They didn't offer [time off], and anyway, I had nowhere to go" (Tian Weiwei).

> Working in someone's house, you are restricted (*shou yueshu*). If they say you can't go out, you can't go out. If you go out, you still have to worry, afraid that they'll get angry when you return. (Li Shanshan)

Moreover, the tasks are all-encompassing and never-ending. Most domestic workers take care of housecleaning, laundering, marketing, food preparation, cooking, and dishwashing for the entire household each day, on top of ministering to the special needs of children and elderly and attending to visitors or guests. In addition, most employers require more than just the basic requirements of household operation, sometimes making demands simply to display their power over the domestic worker's very person, not just her labor.[64] Among the domestic workers I met, running errands, escorting children to and from school, and even helping out in the family businesses were routine demands made by employers. For example, Tian Weiwei had to care for a three-generation family of five. The household head demanded an extra meal each night:

> When I first started, the workload was very heavy. The [male] household head, at 10 P.M., would need to eat a midnight snack, so I prepared four meals [a day]. That elderly man had taken part in the revolution, and was used to eating a late-night snack.

The old man's status as a former revolutionary, a "national treasure," increased his authority over the younger woman, who would seem disrespectful if she refused to accommodate his wishes. Thus, protocols of age, generation, and gender may cumulatively exert a strong demand on a domestic worker's labor time.

Often domestic workers do not control where or for whom they work. Some are dispatched by their employers to care for a sick or terminally ill household member confined to a hospital, and must sleep in the hospital dormitory or even in the sick room with their charge and take orders from their employer, their patient, and the nurses alike.[65] Others are hired as domestic workers only to be employed as full-time workers in their employer's private business. For example, Ma Ning worked during the day for the family's dry-cleaning business, but also did laundry and cooking for the family as needed. Others are "lent out" part-time as a favor to their employer's friends, or are casually traded back and forth between related households.

Not only do domestic workers rarely control the content of their work, they also seldom control how they do it. As they learn their tasks, they are frequently supervised by their employer or a household member, and in turn have to police their own actions:

> Working in someone else's home is not like being in your own home. You have to remember that. You have to get used to their home. You must have a sense of propriety (*fencun*) when you do things in other peoples' homes. (Ma Ning)

Employers' control of workers' spare time, lack of privacy, and lack of freedom to manage the process of work leave these young women feeling psychologically "stressed and depressed" (*yayi*). For many, domestic work feels akin to indentured servitude or slavery: "I felt that I had been sold into someone's home" (Liu Fanmei).

The invisibility of paid domestic work to public scrutiny and its common acceptance as women's work or "chores" (*jiawu*) rather than skilled labor compromises migrant domestic workers' legal status. In fact, domestic workers are legally considered to be members of their employer's household, rather than independent workers. In domestic service, employee-employer relations are treated as interpersonal relations, covered only by the Civil Code, which is less comprehensive than the Labor Law.[66] Most rural women doubt that "the law" can protect them.

> There is no legal protection for *dagongmei*. [Only] if your relative is an official can you get legal help; otherwise, forget it. It [the law] is not for the people. (Gao Yamei)

Although domestic service in Beijing is somewhat regulated by guidelines promulgated by the municipal Labor Bureau, to be enforced by the domestic service introduction companies affiliated with the Women's Federation, these are suggestions without teeth, and workers are largely skeptical that companies could enforce the regulations.

> If little things happen, small things, and you find the Women's Federation directly, they might not care. Like my friend, she had some sort of disagreement with her employer, and so she returned to the company. The company said, "You and your employer can talk it out and resolve this yourselves. You don't

need to bother us." They didn't care. They said, "Resolve it yourself," and only come to them if you can't resolve it yourself. But we only went to them because we couldn't resolve it ourselves! . . . Those people there [in the company office], their talk is empty (*kong*) and they are irritable (*jizao*). . . . They don't have a very good attitude. (Ma Ning)

Though no comprehensive statistics exist to indicate what percentage of domestic workers experience mental or physical abuse, surveys of rural migrant women generally suggest rates could be as high as 65 percent, with verbal abuse predominant.[67] Women's Federation officials likewise acknowledge that sexual abuse of domestic workers by employers is not uncommon.[68] At a 1999 conference on migrant women workers' rights, one migrant woman testified publicly about the sexual harassment she experienced in her employer's household at the hands of her elderly male charge.[69] Cases of sexual and physical abuse of domestic workers have caught media attention. Yet often such reportage sensationalizes violence and perpetuates stereotypes of rural women; rarely does it offer critique of the systemic or institutional causes of such problems.[70] Moreover, mundane forms of exploitation are rarely addressed, perhaps because domestic work is not seen in the same light as other occupations.

In deliberating between cultural constructions of gender-appropriate work and the formidable barriers to migrant women in most urban employment sectors, many young women choose to enter domestic service. But such work is a mixed bag: the low status and remuneration position domestic workers far from the ideal of a modern lifestyle, and unique features further constrain their physical and social mobility. Bereft of political advocacy such as workers' unions that might help upgrade their labor status or expand their job opportunities, domestic workers nonetheless make the most of this job. In the next section, I delineate some individual strategies that they deploy to improve their work environment and their social status, including manipulating personalistic ties forged with employers.

"LIKE A MEMBER OF THE FAMILY"

The location of domestic work in the employer's household, its legal status, and its popular image all contribute to a notion that the domestic worker should be like "a member of the family."[71] Social relations between the domestic worker and her employer emulate kinship relations of the extended family, even adopting such forms of address. Hence, female em-

ployers are addressed as "granny," "auntie," or "elder sister," and male employers as "grandfather," "uncle," or "elder brother." Domestic workers
are referred to by their last names preceded by the diminutive "little"
(*xiao*), or as "little sister" (*amei*) or "little girl" (*xiao guniang*).

This kinship template accords both workers and their employers appropriate, ideal behaviors, and construes this class relationship as governed
by affective ties (*ganqing*). For their part, employers often perform "emotional work" for their domestic worker, caring about her health and well-
being, bestowing her with hand-me-down clothes, and sending her home
at holidays with gifts and good wishes for her family.[72] Affective ties com-
pel employers to take an interest in their domestic worker's intellectual
and moral development as well as her future. For example, they might provide reading materials to encourage their employee to improve her literacy, and might tutor her or even provide some tuition for a formal course
of study. When her services are no longer necessary, employers may help
their employee find a new position, and perhaps even introduce her to her
future husband.

Parents entrust employers with the supervision of their daughters'
moral character, such as closely monitoring and reporting on her social life
and activities. Employers might use this to their own advantage. For example, in restricting an employee's opportunities to meet with migrant
friends, a solicitous employer also ensures that her employee does not gain
knowledge of other available jobs or comparative wage rates that could be
used to exact concessions from her employer.

In return for employers' care and patronage, employees are obliged to
be respectful, loyal, and obedient, like dutiful daughters. Good domestic
workers place the needs of their employer in advance of their own interests. For example, I was to go to a park with Ma Ning and her friend on
their day off (Sunday), but only Ma Ning showed up to our appointment.
Her friend was invited at the last minute to accompany "her family," her
employer household, on an outing. Ultimately, affective ties maintain the
asymmetry between an employer and her domestic worker.[73] Even as fic-
tive kin, employers are still in a position of authority as elders who can,
consciously or not, manipulate emotional bonds to extract more labor
power from their employee. Although employers and workers can, and occasionally do, become companions, ultimately the needs of employers always come first. In fact, few domestic workers feel their actual situation
approaches the ideal of "like a member of the family." Even after four years
of loyal service and ongoing connection to her employers, Tian Weiwei
remarked, "Still, they aren't my own family."

Yet for a variety of emotional and practical reasons, most domestic workers strive to cultivate strong affective ties with their employer households. At the very least, the care of a kind employer helps young women combat homesickness. Wang Rong described how in her first few weeks at work she missed home so much that she was clumsy and absentminded in her work. Instead of scolding her for this behavior, her employer solicitously asked what was the matter and was sympathetic. Others felt a close relationship with an employer evidenced mutual respect and accorded the job dignity. Gao Yamei told of how, new to a job, she instinctively retreated to her own room when she learned her employers were expecting a visit by relatives. She was very pleased, though, when one of the guests, a CEO of a company no less, sought her out to say hello, asked her where she was from, and carried on a conversation about her home province. For her, "affection" (*ganqing*) meant treating employees as equals, despite the differences of social status. For still others, feeling necessary and useful— to one's elderly charge or to one's nation—was ample reward for a thankless job. Nurse's assistant Li Jianfeng expressed these sentiments in a letter of thanks to the Migrant Women's Club for their support:

> I've been in Beijing only three months. I first thought that domestic work was low-class work (*xiadeng de gongzuo*) and that I was inferior to others (*bi bieren di yi deng*). But after joining the Migrant Women's Club, I feel this job is noble (*guangrong*) and that I am making a contribution to the nation. Through my work, I make the last days of elderly people more pleasant and allow their children to rest easy.[74]

Young women also feel that they gain important experience of interpersonal relations in building a harmonious relationship with employers. In Liu Fanmei's words, "Doing domestic service, entering a household, it's like entering a minisociety: you must deal with human relations (*dei chuli guanxi*)." Ma Ning, who had located her first employer through a domestic service introduction company affiliated with the Women's Federation, spoke of the negotiating skills needed to be a successful interview candidate.

> At first, it was me who negotiated with the employer. Those people there [the company personnel], they don't go out and find an employer to talk to you. It's you who seeks out the employers. You must rely on yourself. Like, if the employer looks down on you, you must convince them [they can] rely on your

ability. They asked me if I could do certain chores. Then we signed the contract. I was really nervous. It's your first time seeing each other. Employers are really nervous too. You try to figure out what they are like, whether they seem okay.

Despite the social stigma of domestic service as drudgery, domestic workers take pride in their ability to do their job well by following their employers' rules and codes of discipline.[75] Li Shanshan boasted of her housework skills and ability to please her employer. Her superior performance distinguished her from the previous household help, whom she stereotyped as exhibiting more "rural" habits: being clumsy, undisciplined, and simple.

> The old lady wasn't happy before I came. Before I arrived, for a year she was not very happy and drove out another domestic worker. Our relationship, though, was very good. She said the first one went out too much and didn't know how to do the chores. Rural people who come out, they are different from urban people. Me, from when I was small I did housework, and I was attentive to hygiene. And I could do things carefully. In my hometown I helped my parents cook and wash clothes, so I could do all of those chores.

The exceptional quality of the employer-employee relationship that is modeled on kinship provides benefits to various parties. Parents feel at ease entrusting their daughters to an urban family. Daughters in turn can balance their life away from home with gendered expectations for behavior and character. Migrant women also present themselves to employers as exemplary and loyal workers in order to cultivate a harmonious relationship, one that might provide them with material as well as emotional advantages over the long term. In fact, numerous workers kept up with the employers they had cared for over long periods of time. Tian Weiwei still visits the elderly lady of the household where she worked for four years. "She and I are affectionate (*you ganqing*). Like right now, if I didn't have a job, she would help me."

Young migrant women make the most of domestic service, stressing their acquisition of modern skills like hygiene, time management, and interpersonal relations, or finding fulfillment in the feminine work of caring or in their status as disciplined professionals. Nonetheless, most domestic workers eventually become dissatisfied with the low status, low wages, and lack of freedom associated with domestic work and seek new employers or jobs, or at least pursue extra-work activities in their spare time.

PATHS TO UPWARD MOBILITY

Within the constraining structures of domestic work and the unique personalistic employer-employee relationship, young rural domestic workers do find ways to thwart employers' rules. Li Shanshan describes how she managed to find time to meet with friends (*laoxiang*).

> Sometimes when I had nothing to do, I would go out and chat with them. They were from my county. We all knew each other. Some of them ran stalls making snacks, some were resellers [of used goods]. I often went there to chat with them. I didn't have actual days off, but if there was something I wanted to do, I could say, "I've got something to do" (*wo you shi*) or "I'm going to mail a letter," and then I would have about two hours. Whenever I had nothing to do, I would leave. (Li Shanshan)

The contradictions of the intimate relationship between an employer and her employee often erupt in emotionally charged conflicts. At the center of such struggles is the issue of power and control. Wang Rong generally got on very well with the three-generation family she worked for. But she was really upset by the incident that resulted when her male cousin came for a visit and stayed the night in her room, a basement apartment that had a separate entrance from her employers' main apartment. The gatekeeper saw him arrive at night and leave the next morning, and reported this information to her employers. They immediately jumped to the wrong conclusion and scolded her harshly without stopping to hear her explanation. In anger and retaliation, Wang Rong did not speak with the family and boycotted work for the rest of that day. "I was so wronged (*yuanwang*), so humiliated (*weiqu*). They knew me for so long and yet they still mistrusted me?" But she was upset only by the lack of mutual trust, not by the principle that her employers should take an interest in her personal life and sexual relations. In fact, she is one of several domestic workers I know who accepted or actively requested an employer's help in meeting Beijing bachelors.

Liu Fanmei found herself more directly questioning the basis of her employer's care and protection as she struggled to assert her own desire for autonomy against concern for her safety and reputation:

> Now I'm in domestic work, and there are a lot of restrictions, like it's not convenient to make phone calls. At first I didn't really understand. Moreover, at the house I work in now, [my employer] doesn't want me to make friends; it's best if I don't socialize much.

> However, she lets me receive calls from my parents and encourages me to call them. She says I'm a young girl and I still don't understand the ways of the world. What if I encountered some bad guys, what then? She has a point, but I don't wholly agree, because one can grow up and mature, and can learn how to discern people's characters. Hence the Chinese saying, "with time you can see people's true nature" (*rijiu jian renxin*).

In retrospect, many migrant workers view their early job choices, especially domestic service with its low wages and restrictive work conditions, critically. Some even question those discursive practices that previously imbued their work with value.

> When I came out I was naïve (*danchun*). I didn't think much about how to make a lot of money. For example, going to work in a restaurant washing dishes and so on, that work can net more pay, but it's too unsafe (*luan*). . . . So even when the salary was high I wasn't willing. I just stayed in their [her employer's] house. I felt that I could be safe in their house. . . . [However,] each year I became more and more mature, and then I decided to do business for myself; I didn't want to work for others. (Li Shanshan)

Li Shanshan equated her naïveté with concern for safety and moral propriety rather than concern for her financial benefit or social mobility. Time spent in the urban environment, however, tends to change a young rural woman's mindset about earning money and significantly loosens her conservative attitude toward risk and social conventions.

Two experienced domestic workers here reflect a common opinion that time and experience transforms migrants from dupes to savvy opportunists:

> Yes, yes, those girls who have just come from the countryside are quintessential rural peasants (*didi daodao de nongmin*). (Ye Yanling)
> Yes, they are very naïve (*danchun*). (He Qinyin)
> They arrive in this big city and they don't understand anything. (Ye Yanling)
> Right. But when you come out, you don't stop reflecting. For example, at first you accept a low salary because at home you did household work and you didn't even get one penny. But after you get to Beijing and you live in this environment, and you gradually meet other people, you begin to compare yourself with others in this occupation (*tonghang*), and you realize that they are making more money. So [a girl's] point of

comparison shifts. At first she compared herself to people at home, then gradually she will compare herself with other people, including her superiors, and find areas where she is dissatisfied. (He Qinyin)

Young rural women agree that their experience in domestic work teaches them much about modern urban society. Yet by labeling newcomers naïve, experienced migrants imply that improving a situation is a matter of individual responsibility and is a natural progression. Experienced migrants thus reproduce the dominant discourses of rural/urban difference and class that blame rural migrants' low quality and essential characteristics for their own exploitation and deflect criticism of state policy or employer practices that structurally impede migrants' upward progress.

In the context of very restricted choices for upward economic mobility, migrant workers can best hope to increase their wages through lateral mobility.[76] Domestic workers therefore strategize to switch employers in search of higher wages. Sharing information about wages and work conditions with other migrant domestic workers, friends, or co-villagers is such an effective tactic for learning of new job opportunities that employers strive to minimize such contacts, praising domestic workers who keep to themselves and spreading malicious rumors about the tendency of certain workers to gossip or sneak about with friends. As employers keep close watch over them, domestic workers develop ways to contact friends who could help them locate new employers. Xie Aimin describes how she made a contact who, eventually, found her new work:

> [My employer] wouldn't let me go out. I really missed my friends (*laoxiang*) and I wanted to go see them, but she said, "No way. You've been here how long and already you want to go out?" I'd been there just about one month, when one day while I was helping her fetch fresh milk I spotted someone who appeared to be from the countryside. I asked if she was from Anhui, and she said she was! When I found that friend (*laoxiang*) and chatted with her, I felt so much calmer (*tashi*).

Migrant women also set their sights on moving out of domestic service into more prestigious occupations. Although doing sales (*pao yewu*) for small businesses or working as a cashier or typist are just as poorly remunerated as manual labor, young women in such positions celebrate their upward mobility. At the pinnacle of the job hierarchy is clerical work, as this quote by Yu Jing indicates:

> Since being in Beijing, I have gradually learned the importance of having a diploma, so I studied for a degree, and now I have found a job as a secretary, which may not mean much to others, but to me it is a big step forward from waitressing.[77]

Some domestic workers are rewarded for their loyal service to employers with help finding a new job. Li Shanshan, for example, had cared for an elderly lady and her temperamental husband for four years. In gratitude, their middle-aged daughter helped her find a cigarette-and-liquor stall to manage after her services to the family were no longer required. Li Shanshan reflected on the freedom she enjoyed in her new job, compared with domestic work:

> It's more free. You do things yourself. It's definitely better. . . . If I want to go out and play, I go out and play. Now if I'm tired, I can sleep. There's no one who manages me. It's more free.

Since most domestic workers realize they have few options other than lowly service work, they shift their attention to improving their skills through extra-work activities. Beijing affords numerous opportunities to embark on a formal course of study for a degree or earn a certificate in a particular technical skill. As Gao Yamei remarked, "Beijing offers educational opportunities that I can't find at home." Like most young women, Gao Yamei did not have a specific course of study in mind when she arrived in Beijing. But she quickly decided to learn Chinese medicine, inspired by a television report about a young Chinese medical doctor who established clinics in poor areas, thinking she could do the same in her hometown. Although she had not earned a secondary school diploma, she could become certified in a particular skill or trade, such as traditional Chinese medicine, hairdressing, cosmetology, tailoring, or tourism. Those with at least a secondary school diploma can set their sights higher, on the national high school equivalency exams, which could lead to a course of study resulting in a college degree (*dazhuan*).[78]

For young women pursuing self-study, domestic service is valued for providing relatively quiet accommodations, the leisure time in which to read or attend classes, and the petty cash to invest in study materials. In fact, domestic workers so oriented seek out employers they think will be more sympathetic to their cause. The unanimous preference is for an intellectual household, headed by a university professor or government researcher, whom they feel will be most amenable to demands for time off for study or who might provide ample reading materials in the form of a private library.[79]

The road to intellectual success is difficult, and only a few, like Ye Yan-ling, are able to achieve these objectives. Ye Yanling had been in Beijing working for the same family for seven years, caring for an elderly couple. A few years earlier, she determined to stop remitting her wages home to her mother, who had been keeping the earnings for her daughters' dowries, and instead to invest in classes and study materials. At first her employers were supportive of her attending night classes, and she earned a technical degree in accounting. Yet when she announced her intention to pursue a college degree program, her employers objected strongly.[80] She then offered to quit their service, but they were even more displeased. Ye Yanling said she understood their predicament: they felt she was irreplaceable, as only she could understand their habits and preferences. Eventually the two parties were able to strike a compromise. Ye Yanling's employers helped her find a new day job, doing odd jobs at their daughter's work unit, a government press. In exchange, Ye Yanling continued to board with them and provide help with the evening meal. Eventually she supervised her full-time replacement, a co-villager she had located for them through her social contacts.

Ye Yanling attributes her success to her patience, hard work, and dedication to her job and her employers, as well as her diplomatic skills:

> I think when you first start working in a household, you shouldn't think that you are going to be able to make demands like time off to study. You have to consider that you are being employed, and you have to get your work done and perform the tasks well. Then you wait some time and see that you [your employer and yourself] get along well, and then you can mention that you want to study, no problem. So when I introduce my co-villagers to jobs, I tell them just do your job well for a year or two, and wait until you have gotten used to the environment, and wait until you are more capable. . . . Anyway, after she [the co-villager] works for a year, her thinking will have changed though her environment has not! She'll go out on the street, look around, and she'll slowly start to reflect, "Hmm, shall I change my job? Should I study something?" It's certain her thought process will change. Myself, I appraised my situation and thought perhaps I could use the environment, my employer, or some other person. That's what I tell friends: "This isn't bad [work], you get along [with your employer], you can talk [with the employer] and have a place to live and to eat. You

> can wait until you understand the environment and you have the ability to figure out how to implement the next step, one at a time."

Ye Yanling's success at actualizing her aspirations for education rested upon her ability to delicately and patiently balance her obligations to family with her own goals and the demands of her employers over a long period of time.

Whatever the course of study chosen and the sacrifices it entails, most young women find great value in acquiring modern skills that they believe will be useful in their village or county. Many dream of setting up their own business, such as a tailoring practice or beauty salon. Pursuit of higher learning also imparts confidence and pride that negates the stigma of either domestic service or outsider status in the city. Ye Yanling had recently been stopped downtown by a patrolling Public Security Bureau officer. The officer most likely was suspicious of Ye Yanling's companion, her younger brother, because he was carrying a suitcase and looked the part of a recently arrived migrant (which in fact he was). As a longer-term migrant, Ye Yanling was required to have both a national identity card (*shenfen zheng*) and a temporary residence card (*zanzhu zheng*), as well as a work permit (*gongzuo zheng*). In fact, neither she nor her brother had the proper permits. Nevertheless, Yanling did manage to talk their way out of a fine (or worse, arrest) by claiming that she was a legal temporary migrant and that her brother was only visiting on holiday. After this brush with danger, though, she determined: "Next time, I will not say I am a migrant working (*dagong*) in Beijing. I will say I am a college student." College students in Beijing's prestigious universities often have nonlocal registration; by identifying with them, Ye Yanling revealed a confidence gleaned from her self-perceived rising social status.

Yet in their efforts to transform themselves from low-wage domestic workers to aspiring students, young rural women have to weigh the moral costs of withholding remittances from their families in order to invest in their own pursuits. That parents may judge harshly daughters who fritter away their money on clothes and disposable consumer items is evident from young women's emphasis on their own frugality and contempt for migrant peers who focus only on money. While families welcome their daughters' gifts brought home on visits, conspicuous displays of consumption back in the village might be linked to decline in virtue.[81] (See the discussion in the following section.) Moreover, the decision to withhold remittances or spend what might otherwise be put toward a dowry likely alarms parents already concerned with the delay in their daughter's marriage decision.

Education, however, is one consumer item available in the city of which parents generally approve. Ironically, parents who might have cut short their daughter's education in the past might now praise her new skills learned in Beijing. Ye Yanling felt personal triumph that her newly earned degree compensated for schooling that had been abruptly discontinued so that her younger brother could afford to attend school. Recollecting her father's orders years later, she sighed with regret: "Otherwise, I'd be in college now." But since undertaking study for the college degree on her own, she felt some satisfaction in hearing villagers praise her and use her successes as a model for village boys to emulate. Embarrassed, but with pride, she recounted:

> One of my father's veteran friends compared his son to me and scolded his son in my father's presence, saying, "Why can't you go out to work like Ye's daughter?"

Despite limited opportunities for upward economic and social mobility, domestic workers continually strive to better their lives in the city. Young rural women together share information that allows them to springboard to higher-paying or less-stigmatized jobs. Others set their sights on earning diplomas and certificates in their spare time in order to improve themselves and achieve future employment goals. Where possible, they manipulate their relationships with employers in order to further their goals. Migrant domestic workers find satisfaction away from the village to the extent that they can successfully acquire new forms of knowledge and modern skills, no matter how incrementally. Investment in better jobs and education may be due to desire for status in the eyes of rural or urban society, and a personal quest to raise one's quality. Whatever the reason, pursuit of such ambitions may be the most transformative effect of migration on rural women, as young rural women may directly expand the parameters of acceptable gender roles and identities.

CONSUMING BEIJING: ACQUIRING CULTURAL CAPITAL

Most migrant workers are limited by their finances, employment conditions, or education level from pursuing extra-work activities in a methodical manner. Nonetheless, nearly all agree that even the city itself can be a classroom that imparts new knowledge and teaches about modern life.

> Doing [domestic work] for one year, sometimes I was in a daze (*huanghu*), feeling that every day was the same, extremely dull. Look, there I was, a young woman, feeling I was wasting my talent (*qucai*). Afterward, though, I gave myself a goal: in one year I would tour Beijing and do things I wanted to do. Like, if I wanted to read I would just go to the Beijing Library. (Liu Fanmei)

Given the complex urban environment, managing to find one's way around the capital is educational and confidence-building. Two women from the Migrant Women's Club entertained me with humorous stories of their escapades getting lost on bikes and buses in Beijing's ancient alleyways (*hutong*). One shared with me her strategy for navigating the city: commit a few key routes to memory and never deviate from them!

On the few days off during the year, almost every migrant worker anticipates exploring Beijing's parks, temple fairs, or scenic and historic sites, often taking advantage of the discounted entry fees at holidays. Touring the city, young women can forget the stigma and oppressive conditions of domestic service, subvert the restrictions on their movement in public spaces of Beijing, and proclaim their equal right with Beijing citizens to enjoy public space. Liu Fanmei made the acquaintance of several Beijing elders, and from them learned how to participate in authentic Beijing culture.

> Beijing is also an immigrant (*yimin*) society, but among five people there will be two or three old Beijingers. They told me where the tastiest snacks were sold, and I wrote it down. One elderly Beijing man told me that Beijing people like to imbibe a particular drink a certain way, so I went to the Muslim temple and bought myself a bowl of it, swished it around in my mouth, and felt so happy.

Liu Fanmei is no stranger to public humiliation and discrimination due to her outsider origins. Once while she was browsing in a bookstore, a clerk cornered her and demanded proof of identification, as if implying that a migrant worker (apparently identifiable from her less-than-fashionable dress or from her accent) would not be buying books, only stealing them. Visiting historic and scenic sites, talking to Beijing elders, and learning about the capital's history legitimizes her right to a place in Beijing as a fellow citizen of the nation, and in part mitigates such moments of exclusion.

As the nation's capital, Beijing has a unique ability to catalyze migrants' emotions.

> People ask me, why did I come to Beijing? I say, because there
> is no Tiananmen Square in my hometown! It gave me a great
> impression in my youth. Beijing is China's cultural center, its
> political heart, so coming out is a way of experiencing that (*gan-
> shou*), gaining knowledge (*chang yixie zhishi*). Because if you
> don't come out, in the village you won't have such an apprecia-
> tion. (Liu Fanmei)

For most young migrants to Beijing, a trip to tour Tiananmen Square and
a photograph of the visit are mandatory. Mixing with Beijing families and
foreign sightseers, migrants too are transformed into worldly travelers. A
memento from Beijing shown to villagers at home might present an image
of a successful and exciting life, despite the reality of one's laboring existence. In fact, to return home without first visiting this most important
cultural symbol is tantamount to forfeiting face, a significant loss of opportunity to accrue cultural capital, as these sisters' letter home suggests:

> Although working here is a bit tiring, it's still better than being
> at home, because as long as you work, you'll be rewarded. . . .
> Since we've been here we've not even seen Tiananmen; if we
> went back now what would we have to say for ourselves?[82]

While migrants are outsiders in the city, the knowledge they gain
through firsthand experience of that environment seems sophisticated to
new migrants and villagers back home, to whom they appear to be insid-
ers to Beijing's secrets. For instance, upon returning home, Zhou Lili engaged in animated conversation with the village's most worldly members,
mainly her father's peers, discussing recent changes in Beijing. Yet her
conversation contrasted sharply with discussions I had overheard between
her and her spouse, a native Beijinger, whom she frequently relies on for
directions about how to get around Beijing. Such insider knowledge of the
capital is a form of cultural capital. Thus when a high official in Zhou Lili's
county town planned his first trip to Beijing, it was she who was called
upon to meet him at the bus station. She reported: "He couldn't have fig-
ured out his way out of the station. He's nearly illiterate!"

Another pleasurable pastime is visiting the many outdoor markets to
find bargains on clothes, cosmetics, and shoes. In addition to purchases of
clothes and shoes to send to their family members or to present as New
Year gifts upon their return home, young women also spend money on
their own adornment, in efforts to appear less "rustic" (*tu*). Young women
upgrade wardrobes with fashionable clothing and footwear, and purchase

moisturizers and whitening creams in the hope of having softer, whiter skin.[83] Many young migrant women cut or style their hair within months of arrival in Beijing, as long, straight hair is perceived as a marker of the village girl. Some avail themselves of technology, acquiring gadgets such as pagers, which not only are status objects but also facilitate communication with friends, undetected by strict employers.

The consuming pleasures of shopping and tourism are a significant means for young migrant women to partake of a modern, urban identity that is denied them in their role as service workers. Through clothes and gifts, photographs, and souvenirs that can be shared with fellow migrants and family and friends at home, migrants craft images of themselves as knowledgeable consumers and worldly travelers. Participating in shopping or tourism alongside urban residents, migrants likewise carve out their rightful place in the urban environment and identify themselves as consummate cosmopolitans.

But consumption must be balanced with filial obligations. Thus hotel worker Zhou Lili was pleased upon her return to her North China village to be called *tu* (rustic) by her peers, for this expressed the rekindling of their affection and approval of her. She complained:

> If I dress too poorly, they will gossip that my life in Beijing is hard. But if I dress too fashionably, they will be jealous and gossip about where my money comes from!

Due to such pressures, she passes several sleepless nights in advance of each trip home, planning carefully how much gift money she will bestow on each relative's household (through the young children). As with her appearance, it was necessary to maintain a balance between villagers' expectations based on their imagination of her wealth and her own means to indulge them.

> I can't afford to give much money, because I barely make a living myself. Yet if I don't give them enough, they will say bad things like I am stingy or I am a failure. But if I give too much, I will go broke, and they still won't be satisfied. It's really frustrating. That's why I don't want to go back home; that's why my sister and brother don't go home every year. If it weren't for my parents, I wouldn't give those relatives anything!

Zhou Lili, like other migrant women who reside long-term in Beijing, continues to make pilgrimages to the countryside and greet new arrivals from her county who come to Beijing, showing her respect and affection toward her parents, who indeed must interact with and rely on fellow villagers on a daily basis. Yet she cannot deny the pride and pleasure of being held in their esteem. Ultimately, such a feeling of respect—denied most rural migrant women in the city—is worth the (literal) price to be paid.

>>

In this chapter, I have argued that post–Mao modernity entails multilayered hierarchies of gender and class, largely articulated through discursive practices of rural/urban difference, which deeply affect the identities and experiences of young rural women. Their single status and peripheral position in the rural farm household contribute to their ability and desire to leave the village, while a quest for modernity leads them to the city. There, migrant women are channeled into low-wage, low-status jobs, and are subjected to new forms of authority and discipline. Yet they endure discriminatory labor practices and the social stigma of service work in their enthusiasm for the chance to experience the city and acquire cultural capital without sacrificing a sense of safety and social propriety.

Migration does not fundamentally challenge young rural women's exclusion from full participation in the urban economy or society, but rather reproduces their position in the national development hierarchy, as the cheap and flexible labor enabling urban consumption. Although migrant women frequently voice outrage at the discriminatory practices of urban employers and decry the unfairness of the *hukou* policy[84] or the policing tactics of the Public Security Bureau, their protests are individual.[85] Most adapt strategies of avoidance of institutional controls, preferring to rely on informal social networks to secure better jobs or to cultivate affective ties with benevolent employers rather than secure a labor contract.

Yet young women who leave rural villages for urban destinations are also agents with multiple motives who evidence a surprising tenacity in their daily struggles and express optimism about their experiences. Their perseverance is fostered by pride and satisfaction at gaining some independence, by improving social status and accumulating cultural capital in comparison to rural peers, and perhaps by their increased control over their futures. The value of migration for young rural women is not only symbolic, as Louise Beynon (chapter 4, this volume) argues, for it transforms a young woman's self-identity and relationships to urban and rural society, and even interrupts the flow of her individual life course.

Of course, this new identity as a modern, urban woman is always tenuously balanced against rural norms of gender and kinship, as well as against popular stereotypes about the corruptive influence of (urban) consumption on (rural) women's virtue. Rural women migrants are outsiders in the cities who live temporarily outside their rural communities. Yet by experiencing migration, work, and urban life, these women begin to form new relationships in urban areas while strengthening ties to the village, accruing *guanxi* with employers, migrant peers, and co-villagers alike, and thus are never wholly social outsiders. Whether as nontraditional (albeit increasingly typical) filial daughters or as budding modern women, young rural women migrants are carving out their space in China's socialist modernity project.

ACKNOWLEDGMENTS

Special thanks to Tamara Jacka, as well as Delia Davin, C. Cindy Fan, Marian Katz, and George C. S. Lin, for careful reading and helpful comments on previous drafts. This chapter draws from my dissertation research, which was made possible by grants from the following institutions: the National Resources Center (FLAS) administered through the East Asian Studies Center at the University of Southern California; the National Security Education Program (Graduate Enhancement Award); the Haynes Foundation (Dissertation Fellowship) administered by the University of Southern California Graduate School; the Peking University–University of Hawaii (Joint Fellowship); and the Urban China Research Network (UCRN). Drafts of this chapter were presented at the conference "Cities in China: The Next Generation of Urban Research," hosted by the UCRN, held at SUNY-Albany, June 14–15, 2002 and at the Association of Asian Studies annual meeting, New York, March 27–30, 2003.

NOTES

1. Zhen 2000:93. While "modernity" has generally been understood in development theory literature as the spread of particular institutional structures and ideologies of western capitalism, secular culture, and democracy to the rest of the world, anthropologists have recently made the case for "alternative," "other," or "local" *modernities*, which are historically and culturally specific, in the realization that specific "local" sites experience globalization in unique ways as well as produce their own versions of modernity. (I draw upon the following to explicate the concept of alternative modernity: Gaonkar 1999; Hirsch 2001; Miller 1994; Mills 1999:12–15; Ong 1999:29–54; Pred and Watts 1992; and Rofel 1999:1–37.) "Post–Mao modernity" thus implies a particular *time* and *site* in which discursive practices identified as modern are being produced and deployed.

2. Bakhtin (1981:250) discusses the chronotope as a literary device "materializing time in space," and I have followed Kipnis (1997:173) in applying the term to illuminate rural/urban difference in post–Mao China. The statist discourse on modernity, oriented toward the future (i.e., development and economic growth) and the urban (i.e., markets and consumption), overlaps with the socialist *hukou* system in organizing the populace into hierarchical categories of rural and urban.

3. See note 32. As articulated by the post–Mao Chinese state, modernity shares the "universal" (i.e., western) "prescriptive values" of progress and advancement (Mills 1999:13).

4. Rofel (1999) discusses how the figure of "woman" has been central to the construction of a socialist modernity (and see Barlow 1994a).

5. Evans 2000:238.

6. Meng 1995:257.

7. Following Ortner 1998, I too distinguish between the classic definition of class as an unequal relationship based on control of the means of production and the practical sense of class, *pace* Bourdieu, as understood through other social relations, including gender and rural/urban difference.

8. As explained in the introduction, rural household registration or *hukou* restricts migrants' access to urban subsidized housing, health care, and education. Since 1995, *hukou* is also the basis for restricting their employment in various occupations in Beijing (Beijingshi Laodongju 1995). Moreover, migrant workers are susceptible to the Public Security Bureau's surveillance tactics, such as random sweeps (*qingli*) of streets and stop-and-searches, aimed at rooting out vagrants (so-called "three withouts" [*sanwu*]: migrants without stable employment, residence, or identification). Dutton (1998:113–29) describes the consequences of detection for those without proper documentation.

9. On the class and gender significance of the label *dagongmei*, see Jacka 1998 and Pun 1999. Pun claims that this term originated in southern China's Pearl River Delta (a Special Economic Zone) following the implementation of economic reforms, and suggests that it is an identity imposed upon the rural female migrant labor force there by transnational capitalism to instill factory discipline. Yet the term has become increasingly ubiquitous, referring to any migrant woman worker, and also self-descriptive, as the names of organizations like the Migrant Women's Club (*Dagongmei zhi Jia*) imply.

10. Hall 1996:5.

11. Ibid.

12. Abu-Lughod 1990:53.

13. Woon 2000. Earlier ethnographies from Taiwan and Hong Kong, such as by Kung 1994 (1978) and Salaff 1995 (1981), emphasize the continued constraints of rural patriarchy on Chinese working women's autonomy, while more recent works from mainland China, such as Lee (1998), emphasize migrant women's agency, especially in migration and consumption decisions. Woon (149) concludes that migrant women might be both filial and rebellious (i.e., independent) at different moments of their migration trajectories. My position is rather that both qualities are expressions of women's agency (and empowerment), and ought not to be analytically opposed.

14. In her seminal essay, Ong (1988) criticized the women in development literature for using Third World women as a proving ground for western feminism, implicitly universalizing patriarchy and failing to account for agency.

15. See my acknowledgments.

16. I also interviewed sixteen employers of domestic workers.

17. The numbers of migrant women working in Beijing's domestic service industry have increased steadily since the early 1980s, although precise figures are difficult to come by. Liu Yida (1998:107) estimates there were about 50,000 rural domestic workers in Beijing in the mid-1980s; Tan et al. (1996) estimate that Beijing had more than 150,000 migrant women working in domestic service by the mid-1990s. The

official calculation by the Beijing Municipal Migrant Census Office (1998), of migrant domestic workers entered into the Public Security Bureau registry in 1997 in Beijing, is less than 30,000. Employment in domestic service is a factor of gender, historical migration and work patterns, and local labor market alternatives. In the early 1980s, women from Anhui province dominated domestic service in Beijing, in large part due to historical patterns of migration from that province. Since then, the composition of domestic workers in Beijing appears to reflect broader demographic patterns, comprised of greater proportions of women from Henan and Sichuan and, more recently, from such remote provinces as Gansu. In Beijing, domestic service serves as a springboard to other jobs for younger women, whereas for older migrant women, many of whom have little education or are even illiterate, domestic service may become a career. (On domestic service in China, see especially Croll 1986; Feng 1997; Gong 1998:57–61; Horizon et al. 1997:238–39; Jacka 1997:171–75; Liu Yida 1998:106–28; Meng 1995; Solinger 1999:223–25; Tang and Feng 1996.)

18. I use pseudonyms to protect informants' identities.

19. Trafficking in women is an officially acknowledged crime that has received widespread coverage in the domestic and foreign presses (e.g., Dorgan 2000 and Rosenthal 2001b).

20. Gao 1999.

21. Dai 1996.

22. For a critique of inattention to agency in migration studies rooted in modernization theory and neoclassical economics, see Abu-Lughod 1975.

23. Compare with Kung 1994 (1978).

24. For a summary and critique of the household strategies approach, see Wolf 1992 (chapter 1).

25. Similarly, Lee (1998) found that "due to poverty" was a knee-jerk response given as the reason for migration by young rural women working in a Shenzhen factory, yet additional questioning revealed a variety of motivations. My point is that within the context of rural/urban income differentials and discursive practices of rural/urban asymmetry, young rural women voice a variety of motives to migrate.

26. These were first articulated during Mao's rule, and were further promoted under Deng and throughout the post–Mao era as goals for the development of "socialism with Chinese characteristics" (Ong 1999:37).

27. Liu 2000:xi.

28. See Anagnost 1997, chapter 3, for a discussion of the politics of socialist "spiritual civilization" campaigns.

29. Liu 2000:xi. Interestingly, Kipnis (1995; 1997) argues that certain masculinist chronotopes of peasant "backwardness" have a subversive potential against state socialist modernity. He observes that elderly men seem particularly inclined to assert positive valuations of peasantness, or express a peasant subculture, that may critique urban and youth culture.

30. Jacka 1997 explores the feminization of farming.

31. See note 19 on trafficking and Rosenthal 1999 on education.

32. Anagnost 1995; 1997:75–97, and Sun, this volume. As a primary concern of the state, quality encompasses a moral outlook, physical health, and mental nimbleness. Thus, mastering rules of public etiquette and hygiene, obeying the law, and acquiring education or technical skills have all been touted by the Chinese

state as evidencing high quality. Nonetheless, "quality" is a term whose meaning is subject to contestation.

33. Potter 1983, cited in Schein 2000:241.

34. The state mandates nine years of compulsory education, through secondary school (*chuzhong*). Of nearly 800,000 female migrants registered with the Public Security Bureau in Beijing in 1997, 52.3 percent had secondary school education (Zheng 1999).

35. In very poor households having few laborers, young women's help in family farming is certainly critical to the economy, but those who can migrate are already somewhat peripheral to their household's economy. Hence their remittances tended to supplement the household budget, allowing for enhanced consumption power (see Lee 1998; and Fan, this volume).

36. This discussion draws upon Croll 1994:209–12. And see the testimonies collected in *Rural Women Knowing All* Project Committee, ed. 2000.

37. In a 1999 survey of mate choice among members of the Migrant Women's Club of Beijing, only a minority of respondents reported seeking a spouse in Beijing (6 percent). Nearly half (44 percent) said they "didn't know" and nearly as many said they would seek someone from their home county or its environs (43 percent) (cited in Tong 2001). However, my own research suggests that most women in fact would be interested in marrying someone from Beijing, but realize that there is little chance of making such a match and even less likelihood of finding an ideal Beijing spouse (e.g., one who is not too old, too poor, or too ugly), and so therefore they would be unlikely to state this intention or select this choice on a survey form.

38. See Beynon, this volume, for fuller discussion of how young women utilized migration as a strategy for manipulating their marriage choices.

39. Young migrant workers in Beijing are expected by their parents to choose their marriage partners from among networks of co-villagers or co-provincials. But increasingly young women are choosing partners outside these acceptable social networks, making decisions independently of parents, often over parental opposition.

40. This is also common elsewhere in Asia. See Wolf 1992. Mills 1999 also points to the importance of parental control of a daughter's labor power and earnings.

41. Although premarital sex among migrant youth is on the rise, most women migrants in large cities continue to view it as acceptable only when the couple intends to marry, according to the study by Zheng et al. (2001b:121). Their finding, that women's primary concern about engaging in premarital sex is not the sex act itself so much as their reputations in the eyes of villagers, corroborates my anecdotal evidence. The young women I know in Beijing are concerned to appear virtuous, and are therefore cautious about being caught acting too casually with members of the opposite sex. Such behavior could result in harmful gossip among peers or disciplinary action by parents or employers.

42. Mann 1997:30–44; Pruitt 1967. Rofel (1999:64–74) discusses the cultural schema of "inside/outside" in the context of pre–Liberation organization of gender and class difference, but does not find this spatial discourse applicable to contemporary gender relations. Both Jacka (1997) and Zhang (2000), however, find that this normative spatial dichotomy continues to organize gender, labor, and class in complex ways.

43. Liu (2000:12–14, 167–68) attributes the moral discourse on corruption and wealth, as well as Mao-era nostalgia of peasants in the northern Sha'anxi village he studied, to villagers' increasing sense of powerlessness and anxiety about being left behind in the quest for economic and cultural modernity. The moral discourse on consumption also reflects unease with increasing social stratification, a glaring reversal of Maoist ideals of equality and a hallmark of the Dengist legacy.

44. In addition to punishing corrupt officials or factory bosses, the state has periodically cracked down on "vices" such as prostitution, the production and marketing of phony goods, and so on.

45. See Tiantian Zheng, this volume.

46. Popular culture and media are rife with images and stories associating migration and mobility with greed, crime, and sexual licentiousness. See Sun, this volume; Zhang 2001b; and Zhao 2002. On the official construction of Chinese womanhood, see Barlow 1994a.

47. Gong 1998:60, citing an official from Wuwei county, Anhui province, which was the origin of many of Beijing's domestic workers in the 1980s.

48. Ibid.

49. That is to say, carrying through with the obligations of social relations (*guanxi*) and affective ties (*ganqing*) that migration entails is yet another expression of a young woman's filial devotion to her family. See Kipnis 1997 for a discussion of *guanxi* and *ganqing* in relation to daughters' filiality.

50. In Wang Rong's words: "I don't care anymore that domestic work is a low-status job. In my opinion, safety is most important."

51. Historically and into the post–Mao era, domestic workers in Beijing have been predominantly female and rural. Interestingly, some scholars argue that rural women in the city have an "advantage" in that domestic service jobs are explicitly reserved for them, but in fact migrant men have greater job choice and earn higher incomes (see introduction, this volume). Also, the stigma of service work as well as its exploitative features certainly offset some of its advantages.

52. In Beijing in 1995, for example, the Labor Bureau designated more than 200 jobs in a dozen industries off-limits to migrants (Beijingshi Laodongju 1995:139–49, 1999:57–67).

53. Female labor migrants have been found to be more highly educated than their nonmigrant peers but less highly educated than their urban counterparts (see introduction, this volume). Domestic workers I interviewed reinforced the larger trend, as over half had completed junior secondary school (*chuzhong*), but none had entered senior secondary school.

54. Wages for full-time domestic workers in Beijing in 1999–2000 ranged from 250–400 *yuan*/month, while migrants in petty retail or trade, or those with skills such as tailors, beauty technicians and typists, earned generally higher incomes of 600 or 700 *yuan*/month (see Feng 1997).

55. Official regulations in 1999 (Beijingshi Laodongju 1999:42–44) require that migrant domestic workers have a national identification card (*shenfen zheng*), a temporary registration card (*zanzhu zheng*), a certificate of clean health (*jiankang zheng*) issued at the county level, a marriage and fertility certificate (*hunyu zheng*), and a domestic service work permit (*jiawu zheng*). As most young women locate jobs through informal networks, whether they need to register with authorities is

largely at the discretion of their employers' neighborhood or residential committee. Usually domestic workers can bypass most requirements, avoiding the steep fees. However, by 2000 the strict enforcement of the temporary residence permit pressured a majority of migrants in Beijing to purchase at least this permit.

56. However, to promote the reemployment of urban women who have been laid off by state enterprises, the Women's Federation since the late 1990s has promoted (and renamed) "household service" (*jiazheng fuwu*) as a skilled occupation requiring training in home economics (*jiazheng xue*), making domestic work more professional and appealing.

57. See note 42.

58. I had originally translated this term as "chaotic," but have since translated it in numerous ways so as to reflect the contexts in which it is invoked. Thanks to C. Cindy Fan for sharing her understanding of what migrants attempt to express by invoking this term.

59. For example, on an application form required for an interview as a barmaid, Zhou Lili answered the question, "What are your job requirements/expectations?" with only the word "safety."

60. Urban women workers in various sectors of the economy likewise have encountered blatant disregard for the legal protection of their reproductive rights, as they have become increasingly vulnerable to the vicissitudes of the market and to layoffs (Wang Zheng 2000). But migrant workers in the informal sector have never received such entitlements (see Asia Monitor Research Centre et al. 1999).

61. On the concept of "face" see Hu 1944 and Yang 1945:167–72.

62. Xin 1999:30.

63. There is an extensive literature on the unique work conditions of domestic service, including Anderson 2000; Nakano Glenn 1986; Rollins 1985; and Romero 1992, to name but a few.

64. Anderson 2000.

65. Some hospitals retain a staff of such full-time nurse's assistants, but it is also customary for patients and their families to arrange for a full-time bedside caregiver.

66. This was confirmed by Zhou Wanling, a lawyer with the Federation of Trade Unions, at the 1999 Forum on Women Migrant Workers' Rights. See *Rural Women Knowing All*, ed. 1999:13–16.

67. Tang 1998.

68. According to Deng Xiaohui, a lawyer for the Women's Federation, in discussion at the Migrant Women's Club, May 11, 1999.

69. See *Rural Women Knowing All*, ed. 1999:99–101. According to scholar Li Qiang, personnel at the March 8 Domestic Service Introduction Company (affiliated with the Beijing Women's Federation) confirmed in an internal survey that both age and gender factor into domestic worker abuse at the hands of employers, and that rates of abuse are alarming (Research Center for Rural Economics 1999:4).

70. See Sun, this volume.

71. This is the image of the domestic worker as portrayed in the television series *Professor Tian's Household and Their 28 Maids* (*Tian Jiaoshou Jia de Ershiba ge Baomu*), which aired in late 1999 in Beijing.

72. The significance of "emotional labor" and gift-giving between employer

and employee in domestic service and other caregiving professions has been widely debated. Like Ozyegin (2001:150), I found that "power is constructed, maintained, and negotiated interactively by and between [the] domestic worker and [the] employer" through these exchanges.

73. Anderson 2000:122–25.

74. *Dagongmei zhi Jia Jianbao* 2000.

75. Constable (1997) demonstrates the pleasures of deference and submission to employers' ideals in her ethnography of Filipina domestic workers in Hong Kong. She interprets their personal body care and self-discipline as expressions of their agency and power.

76. Lee 2001.

77. *Dagongmei zhi Jia Jianbao* 2000.

78. There are two paths to attaining a *dazhuan* degree in Beijing. The first involves studying for a nationwide test (*chengren gaokao*) of five subjects, which is considered quite difficult. But ultimately that degree is less prestigious than a degree earned through fifteen courses of study at night school, whose prerequisite is the easier test (*gaodeng zixue gaokao*), yet whose duration is obviously longer and more arduous.

79. Unable to provide such perks, working-class employers, on the other hand, are less desirable. Usually these households only hire live-in help temporarily (i.e., to help a woman during the postpartum period), or hire part-time, live-out workers, because they have less physical space to accommodate a live-in domestic worker. Of the employers I surveyed, these types of households have a much harder time holding on to help, and therefore have many more complaints about the domestic service industry. Foreign employers, offering three times the wages of Chinese employers, are also highly desirable, but are relatively few.

80. Employer support for study toward a technical degree (*zhongzhuan*) but objection to pursuit of a college degree (*dazhuan*) is a common theme among the domestic workers I know who are part-time students. Employers likely realize that studying for a college degree will cut further into their domestic worker's time and budget, leading to increasing demands for time off and higher wages, and ultimately to a job change. Yet their objections also hint at a disdain for rural women's pursuit of upward mobility.

81. For example, this article in *Rural Women Knowing All* ("Meng gai xing le," 1996:34) insinuates that a returned migrant woman's money is unclean: "It was Ah Li, but it wasn't Ah Li of yesterday. She'd changed, completely changed. She wore rich clothes and gaudy makeup, every word out of her mouth was 'dirty.' I just couldn't believe it, my former friend had become like this in just two years."

82. Zhao 1996:27.

83. Schein (1994) discusses the connections among gender, global images of beauty and white skin, and rural backwardness in China. See also Evans 2000.

84. Most poignantly, Liu Fanmei referred to *hukou* as "an iron cage."

85. Chan 2002.

Tiantian Zheng

2. From Peasant Women to Bar Hostesses: Gender and Modernity in Post–Mao Dalian

> People will ridicule your poverty, but not your prostitution (*xiao pin bu xiao chang*).
> —common saying among bar hostesses

> Outside of this bar, whether in the city or in my rural hometown, no one knows where my money comes from. . . . With your wealth, everyone will respect you. They will think of you as a very capable person. It's no use being a pure and chaste rural woman. Nobody cares about that. As long as you show them your wealth, they will treat you differently.
> —twenty-year-old bar hostess from Heilongjiang

> Why doesn't society treat us as human beings? Why does society only allow men to go outside and flirt with women but not allow women to go outside? Who is better in this society? Those urban clients and women are no better than us. Who is better? Let's see who can earn more money and be more modern! Look at those urban laid-off workers, so pathetic and poor. We are much better than them. Remember, any means is justified as long as you can earn money.
> —twenty-two-year-old bar hostess from Jilin

>> This chapter offers a case study of rural migrant women working as bar hostesses in the port city of Dalian in Liaoning province. Called in Chinese *sanpei xiaojie* (misses accompanying [men] in three ways), referring to their escorting capabilities of drinking, dancing, and sexual services, these rural migrant women form a steadily growing contingent of illegal prostitutes or sex workers. This chapter examines the daily survival strategies of bar hostesses in Dalian and the ways in which these young women deploy their marginalization and oppression to defy and resignify their social status.

The argument developed in this chapter is based on a cumulative 14 months of fieldwork undertaken between 1999 and 2001. My research sample includes approximately 200 bar hostesses in 10 karaoke bars. In order to attain a full understanding of their life circumstances, I continually associated with hostesses both inside and outside of the bars. I sat with them in the bar lobbies waiting to be selected by customers, and I ate, shopped, and went to hair salons with them every day.

I gained access to the bars through a government official I knew, who was a close friend of the owners of three bars. He introduced me to the three owners as a researcher on the bars. For their part, the hostesses found it difficult to understand why anyone would want to study them. They generally felt that professional urban women would make a more suitable research subject. They thought their own lives were insignificant, undeserving of others' attention.

Fieldwork in the bars was not easy, safety being a major concern. I worked and lived with other hostesses in the poorest and most dangerous red-light district in the city. We had to maintain constant vigilance against police raids and attacks by thugs from competing bars (including other bar owners) and some regular clients. There were also substantial social barriers to overcome in the course of my fieldwork. At the beginning it was extremely difficult for me to socialize with the bar hostesses. My conservative attire and eyeglasses made me stand out as an outsider. Hostesses referred to me as "glasses" and "college student." They frequently derided me for my inability to participate in or make sense of their sex talk and dirty jokes.

As time went by, however, my interaction with the hostesses developed from a straightforward researcher-subject relationship into genuine friendship. The hostesses began confiding in me their hopes and fears about their professional and private lives, and as I became more familiar with their life conditions I grew increasingly concerned about the violence, abuse, and imprisonment they are subject to on a daily basis. Even while in the United States, I maintain frequent contact with many hostesses to stay updated on their changing life circumstances.

This chapter presents the dual cultural strategies that bar hostesses employ to reconstruct their identities, namely, commodity consumption and manipulation of the sexual image of rural woman as either "virgin" or "whore" to access economic, social, and cultural capital. According to Pierre Bourdieu,[1] relations of domination are ensconced in actors' strategies and taken-for-granted habits. In the post–Mao cultural system, consumption habits index a significant social difference. I argue that hostesses deliberately acquire and transform state-recognized and state-propagated consumption habits, thus attempting to negate their rural past and "country bumpkin" image and construct an urban and modern persona. Meanwhile, they adopt the sexual, virgin/whore image to attract more clients, to make more tips, to expand their social networks, to search for marriage partners, and to gain the opportunity to pursue further education in the city.

A scrutiny of hostesses' dual cultural strategies helps highlight the *interactive* rather than *oppositional* relationship between the state and bar hostesses. Previous research on migrant women tends to fall onto an optimistic-versus-bleak script: it either celebrates migrant women's resistance or deplores their victimization by setting the state and migrants in opposition. My chapter distinguishes itself from previous studies by exploring the interactive rather than antagonistic relationship between the state and hostesses. I argue that such a relationship is manifested in hostesses' embrace and emulation of state-propagated discourses on consumption and the stereotype of rural women as either virgins or whores. In performing and parodying these stigmatizing images and engaging in consumption practices, hostesses not only debunk their categorization as rural country bumpkins but also legitimize the state. Their self-representational strategy is a complex and contradictory process in which they are neither passive victims nor resistant heroines.

This chapter unfolds in four parts. First, I examine the appearance of new consumption spaces and practices in the post–Mao period. Second, I examine the production and reproduction of a rural/urban hierarchy through discourses on consumption and body culture. Third, I investigate how hostesses appropriate state-recognized and -approved consumption styles and use their sexualized cultural image to creatively reconstruct their own identities against the dominant constructions of their marginality. Finally, I conclude by pointing out that hostesses' contestation of their peripheral identities as rural women creates a parody of their constructed image and, at the same time, reinforces and reproduces hegemonic asymmetrical power relations and their marginality.

CONSUMPTION, MODERNITY, AND PROSTITUTION IN THE CITY OF DALIAN

Loud western music filled my ears as I stepped into the Romantic Dream, a karaoke bar in Dalian. As I made my way to the main lobby, my nose tickled from the pungent odor of cosmetics. Images from an American X-rated video flickered on a wide-screen television. More than a hundred *zuotai xiaojie* (literally, women who sit on the stage) stood poised in eager anticipation of the male customers. Hostesses were heavily made up and clothed in high-cut dresses, their heads topped with elaborate coiffures. Their eyes were riveted on the entering customers. *Mami* (Madam or "Mother"), dressed in sheer black tights, pointed at a dozen of the women

Figure 2.1 Nightlife in Dalian. *Tiantian Zheng*

with her long-antenna walkie-talkie and led them into the VIP rooms located on the second floor. There, a few would be chosen by customers as
escorts for the night.

As an escort, a hostess engages with her client in various activities, including drinking, singing, and dancing. Hostesses often permit customers
to grope their breasts in the expectation of more generous tips. At the end
of the night, clients may request that their hostesses accompany them to
their hotel rooms to provide further sexual services.

The ethnographic research comprising this study's database was conducted in Dalian, a seaport city situated at the southern tip of Manchuria
in North China. Following the promising test results of more liberal
economic policies in Shenzhen, Zhuhai, Shantou, and Xiamen, the State
Council granted Dalian Special Economic Zone (SEZ) status in 1984. By
the late 1990s, city government propaganda already boasted that Dalian
had developed into the "Hong Kong of the North," "International
Transportation Hinge," "Advanced Industrial Base," "Modern Environ-
mental City," and the "Center of Finance, Trade, and Tourism in Northeast Asia."[2]

The rapid growth of the city from a fishing village in the nineteenth
century to a metropolis with a population of five million today[3] has made

Dalian a magnet for labor migrants. By 1998 the most conservative estimate placed the number of the floating population in Dalian at around 300,000.[4] Institutional discrimination (i.e., the household registration policy) and social discrimination force the vast majority of these migrants to the lowest rung of the labor market. Migrants commonly work as construction workers, garbage collectors, restaurant waitresses, domestic maids, factory workers, and bar hostesses.

A substantial fraction of female migrants is employed in Dalian's booming sex industry. Karaoke bars can be found almost every few steps throughout the whole city. Jian Ping, a reporter for the *New Weekly* magazine,[5] calls the whole city "a gigantic sauna salon or KTV [karaoke] bar."[6] According to a city police chief, Dalian is currently home to 4,000 nightclubs, saunas, and KTV bars. This same police chief estimated that, as of 2001, 80 percent of the total population of migrant women worked as hostesses in the nightclub industry.[7]

China's sex industry emerged in the wake of economic reforms. During the Maoist era, consumption was strictly regulated and highly politicized. The Communist Party, in an effort to eradicate class distinctions and promote its egalitarian ideology, attempted to eliminate all forms of conspicuous consumption and individualistic or reactionary leisure activities.[8] The time, form, and content of leisure activities fell under the scrutiny and supervision of the state.[9] Leisure was conceptualized as a form of collective action. Unsanctioned activities were derided as capitalist behavior in political study classes,[10] and state propaganda advocated an ethos of "hard work and simple living."[11]

Deng Xiaoping, in order to boost China's sagging GDP and consolidate state power, initiated a program of economic liberalization in 1978. The shift from centralized planning to market mechanisms has led China's government to take a new attitude toward consumption and economic inequality, captured by the slogan: "Let one segment of the population get rich first and guide others along the way."[12] This drastic change in state policy marked the end of the old egalitarian ideals and has since led to pronounced social stratification. Post–Mao ideology encourages people to consume by linking consumption with the concept of modernity—a broad umbrella encompassing ideals of progress and a bountiful material life. Under the slogan of "make money and consume" (*nengzheng huihua*), materialism has become the hallmark of the new, modern citizen.[13]

Under the new policy, the central government and local regions have taken various measures to stimulate consumption.[14] In Dalian in 1998, the yearly per capita expenditure on consumption increased threefold over the expenditure in 1992.[15] Luxury commodities have become the hallmark of the new, "modern" Chinese way of life and of the new era of state policy making.

The reform state's more lenient stance toward consumption has opened the way for the reemergence of nightclubs and other leisure sites, which are especially prominent in the more prosperous SEZs. The Maoist state classified nightclubs, dance halls, and bars as emblems of a nonproletarian and decadent bourgeois lifestyle.[16] Such consumption outlets were condemned and eradicated from the Communist landscape. In order to avoid any residual negative connotations left over from the previous era, nightclubs in the current post–Mao period are referred to as karaoke bars, KTV plazas, or *liange ting* (literally, singing practice halls). Visitors to these bars are mainly middle-aged businessmen, male government officials, entrepreneurs, the *nouveaux riches*, policemen, and foreign investors. Clients can partake of the services offered by the hostesses and at the same time cement social ties or *guanxi* (literally, relationships) with their business partners or government officials. Hostesses, mainly rural migrant women, play an indispensable role in the rituals of these male-centered worlds of business and politics.[17]

THE PRODUCTION OF A RURAL/URBAN HIERARCHY THROUGH STATE DISCOURSES ON CONSUMPTION AND BODY CULTURE

The power of the post–Mao state, I argue, is legitimated not only through administrative regulations and policies but also through cultural discourses, including one relating to consumption and body culture. In this discourse, the state's hegemony is constructed and consolidated through the "privileged," "civilized," and "modern" urban population. A hierarchical power relationship between the self (city) and the other (countryside) is formulated by repudiating the other of rural migrant women. This discursive regime confines rural migrant women to stigmatized and marginalized identities, affecting their participation in employment, in education, and in social relations in profound ways.[18]

As I demonstrate in the following sections, stereotypes of rural women are constructed around a "country bumpkin" appearance and an uncivilized body and sexuality. According to Susan Bordo,[19] the body is a politically and culturally inscribed site shaped by specific historical junctures and regimes of control, exploitation, and power. In post–Mao China, the rural migrant female body is a site where the imperatives of state politics and layered configurations of gender, ethnicity, class, and sexuality become legible.

The "Country Bumpkin" (tuqi) Appearance

In the new market era, when women's pursuit of physical attractiveness and sexual pleasure has become officially acceptable,[20] advertisements and articles in the mass media relating to fashion and consumption abound in derogatory images of rural women. These often serve the purpose of elevating urban women. For example, articles on fashion techniques frequently use rural women as negative examples to avoid. As one author writes, "The fair lady is never a countryside bumpkin, but a refined city woman."[21] Following this same pattern, city women are bestowed with the modern address of "lover," while rural women are popularly referred to as "housewife" or "yellow-faced old woman."[22] City women are compared to "gourmet spices" and "champagne," and described as "the most beautiful scenery in the city."[23] Thus, urban women are associated with luxury goods and modern lifestyles, while rural women are linked with the domestic sphere and traditional feminine roles. They are ridiculed for their "peasant" attire, accent, and habits (e.g., their eating postures and hygiene habits).[24] Their bodies are adorned with unfashionable, outdated clothes and marked by dark skin, a working-class signifier associated with outdoor labor and excessive exposure to the sun (such as from agricultural toil)[25] that distinguishes them unfavorably from city women, who, armed with parasols and skin-whitening makeup, are able to achieve a "snow-white" beauty.[26]

The message to rural women is that, unless they transform themselves, they have no place in the modern world. They are instructed to emulate the consumption styles of urban women. A television advertisement for Ai Li Si (Alice) shampoo differentiates rural women from city women according to their hairstyle and hair quality. In the advertisement, three rural women have just arrived in the city. Their hair is tied into two long braids at the back of their heads. As they are marveling at the tall buildings, they catch a glimpse of a city woman entering a beauty parlor. Inside the salon, the city woman's hair is treated with the advertised shampoo. When she emerges, her shiny, straight hair sweeps freely along her shoulders. The three rural women are taken in by her beauty, and they too enter the salon to have their hair shampooed. When they emerge, their twin braids have been replaced by the city woman's hairstyle.

This advertisement follows a cultural script of personal metamorphosis similar to the story of Cinderella. The advertisement promises to transform the rural woman (Cinderella) into a modern urban woman (the princess) through the use of the advertised product. Cultural-symbolic meaning is attached to the distinct hairstyles as the markers of the urban and the rural woman: the tied braids of the latter signify tradition and immaturity, while the former's free-swinging loose hair indicates her maturity, independence, and sophistication. The product's English name, Alice, also emphasizes the urban woman's cosmopolitanism as a consumer of "western" products. The advertisement triggers peasant women's anxiety about being marginalized as "backward" and engenders a desire to imitate the modern, urban woman. The "modern hairstyles like those of urban women" become the symbol of, and the key to, attaining a modern, attractive, and sexually desirable persona.

The oppositional construction of rural and urban women's public images is also found in the state's discourse on modernity, which it links with the figure of the urban woman in several ways. First, urban women's consumption of luxury goods is taken as indirect proof of the success of economic reforms to deliver material prosperity. Second, urban women's connection to the city as the center of economic growth and commerce makes them an ideal symbol of China's modernization. Dalian city's propaganda appropriates the figure of the urban woman as its emblem. Since 1999, the city government has staged the "City Woman Fashion Contest" once every two years. The advertisement reads:

> Youthful and beautiful city women, this is your chance to beautify the city with your special fashion. . . . The city of Dalian needs you beautiful angels as its image spokeswomen. You will represent and display the city's beautiful fashion, culture, and landscape, and Oriental women's charm.[27]

The advertisement for this contest situates the metropolitan city in the fashion, body, and idea of city women. It is they who are the emblematic image of the city and the nation. They are the real "Oriental women," characterized by Oriental "restraint (*kezhi*), steadfastness (*jianren*), reserve (*hanxu*), and dignity (*ningzhong*)."[28] Rural women, on the other hand, have been completely left out of this picture of fashion, urbanity, and modernity.

The Passive Rural Body

According to the dominant discourse of the post–Mao era, only intellectuals and urbanites are privileged with the agency and the ability to assert their autonomy free from state control. Ruralites, in such discourse, are docile, passive, and dependent country bumpkins, still ignorant of how to voice their individual freedom through liberating consumption practices.

In the Maoist era, individual bodies were transformed into a public "docile body," subject to the demands of the state.[29] As Ann Anagnost notes,[30]

> Politicizing the body is not only a manipulative state project to ensure social control and ideological domination, but is essential to the party/state's own self-identity. It is through rituals of subjection and subject making that the party-state can produce docile bodies and transform these bodies into signifiers that figure in a master narrative of progress toward a socialist modernity. These rituals objectify subjects in a way that does not individuate them but causes them to be subsumed within a mass identity, the "people as one," for whom the party becomes the sole authorized voice.[31]

In the post–Mao era, people have started reacting against the collectivization of individual will. According to Xu Jian, "Along with the rejuvenated economy, the subjects of Maoist-politicized bodies began to desire a rejuvenated, depoliticized body."[32] Xu uses the case of the 1989 Tiananmen movement as an example of how "intellectuals, students and other sectors of the urban population" have stood up to claim individual and political autonomy and uniqueness. Xu observes that in contrast, ruralites were absent from the movement and argues that they lack the ability to assert themselves autonomously and politically. Many other Chinese intellectuals share the idea that only intellectuals and urban populations have the consciousness to envisage an individual autonomous body divorced from the state rule.[33]

The inability of peasants to exercise their new bodily freedoms is indicated not only by their political quiescence but also by their lack of cultural refinement as manifest in their tasteless consumption styles. The proliferation of commodities in the wake of market reforms has presented China's consumers with an unprecedented range of options. The element of choice has allowed consumption to be reconceived as an expression of individuals' inner being, and sayings such as "express yourself" (*zhanxian ziwo*) have become standard advertisement lingo. According to sociologist Li Shuang, however, peasants' lack of cultural taste prevents them from using commodities as expressive tools. As he writes, peasants "do not know how to consume even if they have money."[34] Without a cultural and aesthetic understanding of consumption styles, ruralites lack the ability for individual expression and the articulation of autonomy through the liberating practice of consumption. Their passive bodies need to be remedied, with the help of the urbanites. As Li declares, ruralites "need the guidance of the city people to be able to consume."[35] Chinese sociologist Zhou Xiaohong also characterizes ruralites derogatively as "weak, dependent, timid, passive, cold, conservative."[36]

The Sexuality of the Virgin/Whore

In state and popular discourse, rural women are stigmatized with the contradictory images of sexual purity and promiscuity. They are described as entrenched in "traditional" gender roles and sexual relations, obeying the customs of "feudal patriarchy," namely, strict premarital chastity and subservience and loyalty to their husbands. Expressions like "follow one's husband to the end" (*cong yi er zhong*)[37] and "marry a chicken, follow a chicken; marry a dog, follow a dog" (*jia ji sui ji, jia gou sui gou*)[38] capture these qualities. These attributes of passivity and subservience, coupled with their "naturalness and purity," make rural women the fantasized erotic objects for city men.

This script coexists paradoxically with the sexually available and promiscuous image of rural women. Some Chinese intellectuals have written that the countryside has a higher rate of premarital and extramarital sex and more frequent rates of sexual intercourse than the city.[39] According to these authors, peasant women's premature sexual development and strong sex drive account for their early average age of marriage and high rate of premarital sex and pregnancy. Tong Xia, for example, writes: "Many [rural women] have precocious sex biology but late-maturing sexual psychology. They experience strong sexual desires and weak sexual control. That is why peasant women will offer their virginity to their male partners in the most unbearable and unsustainable sexual hunger."[40] Other scholars claim that a rural woman's latent sexual desire and lack of "culturedness"[41] (*wen-hua diyun*) make her "sexually available" to men and willingly trapped into becoming a "fallen woman."[42]

As discussed in greater detail by Wanning Sun, this volume, the media frequently reinforce an image of rural women as either virgins or whores. The following news report from the *People's Daily* is an example:

> Several migrant women came from a Sichuan village to Chengdu looking for jobs. A club boss hired them as waitresses. In the club, the boss tried to force them into prostitution. One of the migrant women, Shengli Tang, jumped off the sixteenth floor and was paralyzed afterward. Hairou Liu, the Chairman of the Women's Federation (*Fulian*) eulogized her heroic act, as it em-

bodied the Chinese woman's spirit of self-respect, self-love, self-reliance, and self-strength. . . . The boss, who had his license confiscated, was sentenced to one year of labor education.[43]

The headline of this report, ANTIPORNOGRAPHY CAMPAIGN HAS TO PERSIST—CHUAN [SICHUAN] SISTER APPEALS IN TEARS, subsumes a migrant woman's horrendous abuse under the state's antipornography campaign. The term of address used to refer to the heroine, "Chuan Little Sister," conveys the lowness of her place of origin and her lack of power as a young unmarried woman. Without an identifiable individual name, the heroine is marked as an anonymous village girl, denied individuality and subjectivity. As the report indicates, the reason this migrant woman's conduct is eulogized is that she proves herself to be different from her sexually unbridled companions. The media thus appropriate her experience as an example to warn all promiscuous migrant women to discipline their bodies. As the report implies, her "heroic act" of resisting prostitution and crime manifests "Chinese woman's" self-respect and civility. The implication here is that the hidden "other" in this narrative—the rural migrant woman who does become involved in prostitution—lacks self-respect and civility and does not deserve to be considered a "Chinese woman."[44]

According to Partha Chatterjee, the nation is situated on the body of the woman as "chaste, dutiful, daughterly or maternal."[45] Women's sexuality and body must be kept under strict control, because women, as the bearers of national virtue and tradition, metaphorically mark the boundary of a nation.[46] In China, rural and migrant women's undisciplined morality and sexuality are seen as a potential threat to national and political purity. Their "menacing" and "contaminating" sexuality and their desires to "occupy" and "transgress" the urban space constitute a major concern to the state, whose propaganda frequently calls for the return of migrant women to their rural hometowns[47] (see Sun, this volume). When this propaganda fails to work and many more migrant women choose to stay in the city, the state has to reintensify the boundary between the moral, demure, and modest urban woman and the sexually unbridled rural migrant "whore."

Rural migrant women's bodies are, then, the battleground for the formation of hegemonic cultural norms. The discourse of modernity manifests the state's endeavor, with the help of moral police, to maintain its control by constructing the figure of the civilized, demure, and moral city woman in contrast to the docile and backward, or sexually promiscuous, rural migrant woman. Rural migrant women, defined by their sexuality as either virgins or whores, have little room for expressing agency.

THE POLITICS OF BECOMING A BAR HOSTESS[48]

Judith Butler argues, however, that the "discourse regime" that institutions impose upon a marginalized group is never established once and for all.[49] Rather, it is always subject to contestation by the marginalized's own interpretation and reinterpretation of identity. How then do migrant bar hostesses in Dalian construct identities for themselves? In the following sections of the chapter I argue that they do so by appropriating dominant discourses of modernity, namely, by both parodying and exploiting the rural/urban dichotomy and by engaging in consumption.

Entry Into KTV Bars

Rural women have limited employment opportunities in the city. As migrants, they often lack the social connections essential for job searching in the already saturated urban labor market. Their ability to find work is further hindered by the household registration system that denies migrants equal status with urban residents.[50] Among the jobs available to rural women, most are in labor-intensive industries that offer only meager wages. Under these circumstances, hostessing is a highly attractive employment option. Specifically, its attractive features include the following.

First, hostessing holds out the allure of high incomes and minimal time investment. Hostesses typically entertain a customer for one to two hours and earn an average tip of 200 to 400 *yuan*—the equivalent of, and often more than, other rural migrants' monthly wage and almost half the average monthly wage of an urban worker. Some hostesses can even earn 3,000 to 4,000 *yuan* a night for performing a striptease or doing the "shaking head dance" (*yaotouwu*).[51] Second, working as a hostess provides rural women access to a wide network of influential male figures in the city's business and political sectors. Third, hostessing requires only a minimal upfront investment of economic capital. Newly arrived hostesses typically borrow money from other hostesses or friends to purchase the clothing and accessories worn while servicing clients. Due to the high profitability of the job, the borrower can typically settle her debt with the earnings from one or two sessions with clients. Thus, rural women who lack economic resources can nonetheless enter the workforce.

Conspicuous Consumption

The rapid economic gains realized through hostessing open up a myriad of previously inaccessible consumption options. In Dalian, hostesses are a

Table 2.1 Bar Hostesses' Consumption Patterns

Expenditures	Percent of Total
Remittances to relatives in the rural sending community	50
Clothing and cosmetics	30
Education	10
Room and board	10

conspicuous component of the streetscape, easily recognized from afar by their fancy clothes, expensive shoes and accoutrements, distinctive hairstyles, lightened skin, and manicured fingernails. As Bourdieu notes, aesthetic choices in matters like cosmetics, hairstyle, clothing, or home decoration are "opportunities to experience or assert one's position in social space, as a rank to be upheld or a distance to be kept."[52] For the hostesses the body is the site of contestation, where displaying fashion, cosmetics, and luxurious objects as well as traveling become symbolic markers of their entrepreneurship. It refutes and resignifies hegemonic urban representations of them as inferior ruralites. Table 2.1 gives a rough guide to hostesses' consumption patterns.[53]

As seen from this table, aside from remittances, clothing and cosmetics capture the largest proportion of hostesses' expenditure. Hostesses' paraphernalia typically include the latest models in mobile phones and pagers. The more successful frequent the city's most upscale discos and luxurious restaurants. At one birthday dinner held by a hostess in Dalian's finest all-seafood restaurant, the final bill was 1,000 *yuan*. Hostesses routinely frequent "modern" sites, such as supermarkets and American fast-food restaurants (e.g., McDonald's, Kentucky Fried Chicken, Popeye's, and Pizza Hut). They consume "modern technology" in Internet bars, discos, saunas, beauty salons, and other new recreational places; they take taxis wherever they go, regardless of distance, and never wait for a bus; and they travel to other cities, such as Beijing and Shanghai, with clients or hostess friends.

These forms of consumption conform to the traditional definition of conspicuous consumption: the consumer purchases commodities in excess of her actual needs; and the object of consumption itself does not fulfill any practical need, but rather, because of its extravagance and showiness, becomes a pure public symbol of the consumer's economic power.[54]

Hostesses use various forms of conspicuous consumption to erase their rural origins and lay claim to a new, urban identity. During my research, whenever I asked a woman where she was from, she always tried to deny or to conceal her rural past. Instead of giving the name of her hometown, she would evasively utter the name of a province and then change the topic to her relationship with some VIPs in the city, some recently purchased commodities, her new hairstyle, etc. Hostesses believe that, with the help of money, they can cover their rural background and assume an urban persona. As an eighteen-year-old girl from Liaoning said, "We work like dogs to earn money, in order to spend it like a deity." Money to them represents the only real and practical thing they can grasp and exchange for the symbolic capital of respect.

Body Commodification and Refashioning

Hostesses are highly conscious of the fashion difference between rural and urban areas and the popular conception that only urbanites possess the cultural taste and refinement to dress well.[55] In my conversations with hostesses, they commented that the homemade, green and red garments they used to wear in the countryside made teenagers look like middle-aged women. In order to correct this fashion deficiency, they purchase luxurious apparel, such as fancy high-heeled dress shoes, the most fashionable and revealing dresses, designer handbags, foreign cosmetics, colorful fingernail polish, bracelets, and all kinds of other body ornaments. These fashion items are changed, exchanged, and eventually abandoned for new ones at a rapid rate. In addition, hostesses buy various forms of body-altering products and surgical services. This category includes both permanent alterations (plastic surgery) and non- or semipermanent bodily modifications, including skin-whitening creams, fake double eyelids, and permanent waves. Hostesses use these techniques of body refashioning and ornamentation to achieve two separate but interrelated goals: to make themselves more attractive to male clients, thereby increasing their earning power; and to efface their rural background and construct a new urban persona.

Hostesses' body refashionings demonstrate a defiant and creative agency by which they seek not only to achieve social parity with urban women but also to better them as their fashion superiors. They often negatively comment on the wardrobe of urbanites, using terms, such as *tuqi* (literally, earthy), usually used by city dwellers to describe peasants. They also comment on their own fashion proudly: "My boyfriend always says that I do not look like a rural woman at all. In fact, when I walk on the street, police never recognize me as a migrant, nor do they come to me asking for my temporary residence card (TRC)."[56]

Hostesses' body practices, in total, constitute a highly distinctive style that makes them an obvious feature of the city's human landscape. Many of the common accoutrements of their wardrobes are rarely, if ever, used by other social groups. These include a variety of incredibly inconvenient shoe styles, stick-on tattoos, false eyelashes, and so on.

Bars serve as crucial sites for hostesses' socialization into urban and globalized body culture. Their interaction with more experienced hostesses and male clients introduce these rural women to new aesthetic standards. In the bars, hostesses are also exposed to a myriad of media products that help shape their aesthetic sensibilities. They are avid students of television advertisements and fashion magazines. While waiting for customers, hostesses pass the time by viewing Hong Kong and Taiwanese films and pornographic videos (both western and Asian in origin). These influences form the basis of their unique vision of the ideal body.

Hostesses' subjective view of their own bodies is grounded in the economics of their profession. Hostesses, unlike prostitutes, do not necessarily engage in sexual intercourse (i.e., coital or oral sex) with customers. Rather, sexual contact is often limited to fondling performed during the course of other services (e.g., singing and dancing). This mode of sexual service leads to a highly differentiated system of pricing. Hostesses attach a "price tag" to different body parts and levy cash from customers according to the parts that they have touched. From lowest to highest value, these parts include the legs, breasts, and vagina.

The highest value is accorded the vagina—or, more precisely, the breaking of the hymen. This ranges in price from 1,000 to 10,000 *yuan*, with the woman sometimes anticipating marriage with that customer. To clients, the "red" blood from breaking a hostess's hymen and taking her virginity signifies wealth and good luck, and they therefore offer a lot of money for it.

Those hostesses who have "contributed" their virginity to the men they love free of charge are ridiculed in the bars. In fact, the "old" hostesses all urge the new hostesses to sell their hymen rather than "contributing" it to the man they love. A nineteen-year-old woman from Taiyuan offered her own experiences to instruct a new hostess who was reluctant to sell her virginity:

> I used to be so foolish. When I first worked in the bar, a client offered me 10,000 *yuan* for my virginity. I refused. Later on, a client from Taiwan manipulated my emotions and took away my virginity for free. Now I regret it so much! Virginity has a price. Who do you keep it for? I always asked myself: How long do you need to work to earn the equivalent of 10,000 *yuan*? Purity is

meaningless. No men are good in this society. They cheat you of your virginity and then abandon you. So do not save your purity for anybody. Earn money for yourself and enjoy it. That's the most important thing—to have money in your own pocket!

Hostesses' body commodification has profound psychic consequences that extend far beyond the sphere of work into their personal and imaginative lives. Hostesses view their own and other hostesses' bodies as an assemblage of fragmented parts. In my fieldwork I encountered many different behaviors manifesting this view. Hostesses would jokingly ask each other to cut off their breasts and legs to be weighed, so that they could compare them. They also developed a unique drinking game in which different parts of the body represent Hong Kong movie stars. In the game the buttocks are defined as Feifei (literally, "fatty"—a Hong Kong movie star famous for her full figure), the head as Zhou Runfa (a Hong Kong movie star who appears in an advertisement for a popular brand of shampoo), the breasts as Ye Limei (a Hong Kong movie star with large breasts), and the eyes as Lin Yilian (a famous Hong Kong singer with attractive eyes). One player says the name of one of these Hong Kong stars and the other player has to correctly point to the part of her body associated with that celebrity.

The following analysis separately discusses hostesses' body practices according to body part. I have intentionally chosen this mode of exposition in order to give the reader a better sense of hostesses' subjective view of their body as a collection of segmented parts to be manipulated.

Body Weight

While escorting customers, hostesses consume large quantities of alcoholic beverages, especially bottled beer. Over time this results in protrusive pot or beer bellies. To counteract this effect, hostesses use various diet formulas to achieve and maintain a slender figure. Many of these diet products are extremely harmful to their health. One of the most popular, a diet pill called Gudao, induces extreme nausea, frequent diarrhea, and a disgust for food. Despite the discomfort and obvious physical harm caused by these drugs, a majority of hostesses use them on a regular basis.

Breasts

Hostesses' change in attitude toward breast size reflects the gap between rural and urban body culture. According to them, in the countryside large breasts are interpreted as a sign of female licentiousness. It is typical for rural women to bind their breasts with a cloth band to restrict growth. This practice, however, is rapidly abandoned after migration to the city. There are at least two reasons for this transition. First, in the city hostesses' access to television and print media exposes them to a myriad of advertisements and messages that overtly and covertly promote large breasts as beautiful. Second, male customers' preference for large-breasted hostesses creates a powerful economic incentive for the women to increase their breast size. Full-breasted hostesses possess a clear advantage over small-breasted hostesses in the competition to attract clients. Customers often compare the breast sizes of different escorts, and during sessions they continuously fondle hostesses' breasts. As a result, those with large breasts are said to "have it made" and are the subject of other hostesses' envy.

These two factors lead to hostesses' intense preoccupation with breasts and breast size. They regularly swap tips on the most effective breast enlargement techniques, including breast-enhancing undergarments, creams, electric devices, herbal pills, and soaps. In addition to using these over-the-counter products, some undergo breast augmentation surgery. However, the high cost of the operation—Dalian's most upscale plastic surgery clinic, a Chinese–Japanese joint venture, charges 10,600 *yuan*—is prohibitive for most hostesses.

Skin

Skin tone is one of the physical indicators commonly used to distinguish rural migrants from urbanites, dark skin indexing a rural background, light skin indexing an urban background. Hostesses almost universally believe that their skin is too dark and make great efforts to lighten their complexions, commonly employing two means to create whiter skin.[57] First, they use whitening cosmetics and creams. One popular brand of "herbal" facial cream called Luhui burns off the outer layer of facial skin to allow a new layer of whiter skin to grow. Second, they often decorate their bodies with bright-colored body ornaments, such as red rings and multicolored bracelets, to create color contrast between the ornaments and the skin, so that the latter appears to have a lighter tone.

Hair

As illustrated in the advertisement example in the previous section, hairstyle functions as a diacritical marker distinguishing rural and urban women. Hostesses expend large amounts of time and money on hair products and styling. They change their hairstyle and color almost on a daily basis, and are very adventurous in their choices. They have their hair dyed in different colors or in stripes and made into a variety of fashionable styles. In part this is due to the demands of the profession. Hostesses need to constantly change their appearance in order to prevent returning customers from becoming bored. At the same time, hairstyle is a way of dissociating themselves from their rural backgrounds. According to the hostesses, dirty or unfashionable hair reveals a country background. They often critically comment on each other's hair, saying, "That looks so boorish (*tuqi*), like a peasant!"

In conclusion, hostesses defy the patriarchal morality of the state's laws against prostitution and its patriarchal proscriptions against premarital sex, and market their bodies for their own independent, autonomous, and instrumental use. Their body practices, I argue, should be evaluated as an integral part of their struggle for social respect in the city, through which they increase earnings and enjoy a better material quality of life. As illustrated, state-recognized symbols of consumption and modernity become resources with which to envision their own futures.[58] They deploy these dominant cultural symbols on their own terms to resist their marginality and construct an urban persona at the pinnacle of modern civilization. Such a hyperbolic performative agency, as I argue in the next section, parodies hegemonic representations of ruralites and ultimately calls into question those normative discourses.

Playing with Sexualized Images

The work of the bar hostess is to serve her male clients. In return, the clients compensate her with a certain amount of money. Within this seemingly simple exchange relationship, however, hostesses are in constant negotiation with male customers, attempting to extract from their clients additional benefits that go beyond the basic, flat-rate fee for their services. These benefits include perquisites such as tips and gifts, and, most important, access to the customers' social networks (i.e., social capital). One of my informants, a twenty-year-old rural woman from Hunan, explained to me that the key to being a successful hostess is one's ability to establish a stable relationship with the customer and then exploit him. To reach this goal, as she and many other hostesses emphasized, the hostess needs to play on the male customer's expectations and stereotypes of how a hostess should act. These women's repertoire includes three characters—the unruly whore, the demure virgin, and Cinderella—acted out according to their clients' social profiles. In general, hostesses classify clients as either old (above age thirty-five) or young (twenty to thirty-five), and as either local or outside clients. According to the hostesses, clients from the outside are the easiest to manipulate and cheat, and officials are the most generous with tips. Old clients are described as preferring sexually lewd and coquettish hostesses. Young clients, on the other hand, favor more pure and innocent-looking hostesses.

The Unruly Whore

Here is a scene in a KTV room that I witnessed during my fieldwork:

> About twenty beautiful women, sent in by *Mami* (Madam), lined up before several male clients in a KTV room. Ranging from seventeen to twenty-one years old, the women were in fancy sexy dresses, waiting to be chosen by the male customers for the night. The customers, casually sitting on the sofa, inspected the women from left to right, with critical expressions on their faces. The women, eager to be chosen, flirted with the men. Their legs were crossed, while one hand touched their hair and their eyes winked at the clients. Their provocative poses were designed to gain the clients' attention. In the middle of this examination process, *Mami* pulled a woman to the front and said, "What about this one? She's got big eyes!" A customer pointed at the woman and said, "Big eyes mean big vagina!", which was followed by fits of laughter from the other customers. At these words the woman quietly retreated into the group. This embarrassing remark did not stop *Mami*. "We also have one with tight buttocks. She will surely serve you well!" She called out, "Come over here, tight buttocks! Come to the front, tight buttocks!" At these words I saw a pretty woman in a tight Chinese traditional dress move to the front. A male customer raised one finger at her, motioning her to come over. At this gesture the woman almost jumped over to the side of the man, immediately hanging onto his arm. Shortly afterward, another customer pointed at a plump woman in the group and shouted at her, "Hey, are those breasts fake or real?" There was no response from the woman. She just stood there, gently shaking her full figure. The man, apparently unsatisfied, turned to all the women and cried out, "Whose breasts are the largest? Who wants her breasts to be fondled? Come and sit beside me!" Thereupon a woman, with the encouragement of *Mami*, sat beside him.

In this scene the hostesses performed hypersexual characters by using provocative poses and salacious winking in response to clients' licentious remarks. Such a hypersexual image invokes rural women's cultural portrait as sexually promiscuous and available. As shown, one hostess, despite the customer's insulting comments about her breasts, continued her erotic performance in order to gain his favor. The woman with "tight buttocks" demonstrated her willingness to be sexually dominated by jumping into the embrace of the customer.

To lure clients, hostesses present a lustful and sexually unrestrained image by winking, wearing revealing clothes, assuming seductive postures, pressing their whole body against their clients' bodies, and moving in sexually suggestive ways. Hostesses discuss these techniques as a form of body language through which they can communicate their intention to customers. For example, one said the following about her winking techniques: "Slightly closing your left eye seduces a man's soul. Slightly closing your right eye conveys your devoted affections to him. Slightly closing your two eyes communicates your agreement to have sex with him." Hostesses continually practice these body maneuvers in front of mirrors backstage. They are, so to speak, the tools of the trade.

In the karaoke room hostesses flirt with clients, using sexually provocative gestures and bodily contact. They purr, laugh, scream, or moan when clients prey on their bodies, and they sing songs to seduce clients and convey their "devotion." For instance, a hostess sang a song titled, "Why Do You Love Other Women Behind My Back?" As she was singing the song, she stuck her hands into her client's crotch, leaned her whole body over him, and coquettishly asked him, "My husband (*laogong*), why do you make love to other women behind my back?"

Outside KTV bars, hostesses send tantalizing phone messages to their clients, such as, "Making love is fun. A woman with large breasts is like a tiger or a wolf. A woman with flat breasts has unfathomably superior techniques. Let's make love." Hostesses commonly boast to each other about the "whorelike sexuality" (*sao*) their clients love most.

By allowing their bodies to be sexually fragmented and erotically staged for marketing, hostesses refute the state's attempt to regulate rural women's promiscuous and transgressive sexuality and to control it for purely reproductive purposes. By flaunting their hypersexualized bodies, hostesses intend to employ the hegemonic portrayal of rural women as the exotic and erotic other for their individual profit. How well they accomplish this determines how much profit they can extract from male clients.

The Demure Virgin

When young clients come in, hostesses immediately call out to each other, "Young fellows! They love virgins!" They run into the fitting room to exchange their sexy dresses for more conservative attire, letting their long hair down on both sides in the front and wiping off some facial makeup.

By this change of attire and appearance, they are transformed into "virtuous maidens" (*shunü*). In the karaoke room, they walk in short steps, seldom drink or talk, and sit somewhat far from the clients, knees tight together, their eyes innocently cast down, like "pure" and "shy" rural women fresh from the countryside who have just started working here out of desperation and poverty. Backstage, the hostesses often practice the "virgin" look through dress, hairstyle, makeup, and manner of talking and walking. All the while, they say, "I am a virgin. Good evening, big brother [a client]." A 19-year-old hostess, Sheng, is truly good at this. Clients always offer her a large tip of 300–500 *yuan*. She often says, "These stupid clients think I am pure and innocent (*chunzhen*). They say, 'Look how pure this rural woman is!' Fuck, I am just faking purity (*zhuang chun*)."

This virgin look requires not only more conservative attire, hairstyle, makeup, walking and talking styles, and so on but also demure manners. Hostesses must learn not to be too "bold and desperate" in front of clients. They comment that the more they retreat, the more the client is attracted to them. Knowing how and when to retreat, they project their virtue and purity. Also, a cultivated manner has to be displayed while socializing with clients. Once I had dinner with hostess Hui in her room. Being really hungry, I ate a lot. Feeling quite relaxed, I was shaking my legs a bit under the table. Appalled by my improper manners, Hui said:

> You cannot act like this. You have to look like a virtuous lady (*shunü*). Look, whenever I am with my clients, I always sit very straight, very quiet, never shake my legs, eat only a tiny little bit, and preoccupy myself with serving him the food he cannot reach. Even when extremely tired and starving, I am glad I project a virtuous lady (*shunü*) image, neither crude nor rough, with good education. Clients really like that.

As described in Hui's comments, clients love hostesses who are not only pure and virtuous but also servile and subservient. The key to being successful, as I learned, is to master the submissive skills to satisfy the clients' patriarchal demands. As the scene in the last section shows, male customers see the hostesses as sexual objects ready to be called upon and dismissed. They interrogate the hostesses about the "genuineness" of their breasts, compare the size of their eyes with that of their vaginas, demand to fondle their breasts, and so on. They dehumanize, degrade, and shame hostesses by calling them ugly, questioning their "three measurements," yelling at them, undressing and poking them, and beating them up. They call their hostesses merchandise: "My merchandise is right behind me."

These humiliating practices and physical abuse help clients assert their dominance over the hostesses and counter the power of the object of their desire—the women's promiscuous sexuality. As Roy Ellen states, "The more power attributed to objects, the more they are likely to be able to control the manipulator."[59] Fearful of being overpowered by their fetishized objects, male customers attempt to assert their subjectivity by repudiating and shaming hostesses with denigrating remarks. Such an "othering" process, however, could not be accomplished without the hostesses' assistance. Hostesses are there to ensure that the client's masculine ego is built up, secured, satisfied, and reinforced. Therefore, they need to be docile and obedient. A twenty-two-year-old hostess from Anshan narrated:

> When I first came here, fresh from the countryside, I did not know anything. I did not know how to make up, how to dress, how to behave. But I made up my mind to prove myself better than the urbanites. I went through several jobs before coming to the bar. Since working in the bar I have tried to learn from everybody, how they work, how they make up, and how they behave. If the other hostesses earned ten work points, I would earn fifteen. I knew I could do that. Gradually I learned how to dress up. I learned that customers are God. They are the most important channels through which I can reach my goal and gain my work points. Therefore, I always put them at the top of my list. Whenever a customer chooses me as a companion, I always serve him wholeheartedly. If I notice that he likes beer, I will always fill up his glass. If he likes to smoke, I will always light up his cigarette. I always give him a toast and drink up a full glass of beer first. Without demanding that he drink the same way, I convey to him my desire to please him. I always help him peel the melon seeds with my teeth until I have a handful and then serve them to him. It does not take very long, only about ten to fifteen minutes. But he always respects my efforts to serve him and often comes back to me, which earns me great respect from the other women and *Mami* for my ability to attract guests.

This Anshan hostess's experience illustrates how hostesses in general, in order to win the client's favor and procure a higher tip, have to compete with each other by performing the image of a subservient rural woman. As this hostess states, the motto of her service is: "Customers are God. I am here to serve them."

On stage, hostesses whiningly call clients "husband" (*laogong*). Those I interviewed had even written a humorous lyric to describe their work:

Entering the karaoke room, we smile our brightest smile.	*jin men xiao xi xi*
Sitting by the clients, we seem like man and wife.	*zuo xia xiang fu qi*
But as soon as the tip lands in our hands—	*xiao fei yi dao shou*
"Get the fuck out of here, you motherfucker!"	*qu ni ma le ge bi*

This poem not only expresses hostesses' antipathy toward their clients but also represents their desire to counterbalance their clients' power by extracting profits from them. In fact, hostesses confided to me that the only thing that they love about their clients is their money.

"You grow up in this place," one observed. "If you do not tolerate these small things, you will encounter a big mess (*xiao bu ren ze daluan*). Hold your nose and do whatever he says. Always be compliant. Never act against his will. Then he will definitely give you a 200-*yuan* tip. Otherwise, you will suffer the worst consequences."

Hostesses perform so skillfully that many clients believe that they actually are submissive, virtuous ladies. In fact, a KTV bar owner once commented that a hostess is the best wife candidate because she is both beautiful and gentle. He said:

> Look at how well a hostess serves a myriad of customers. She definitely will be a very good wife. First, coming from the rural area, she will value the opportunity to marry an urban man of means. With gratitude and devotion, she will serve him heart and soul. My friend married a hostess and always bragged about how servile, gentle, open-minded, and virtuous a wife she was. Look at our own urban wives—domineering and ferocious, incomparable. Second, a hostess with working experience has an advanced knowledge about sex and fashion. She appears sexy, coquettish, alluring, and fashionable. She also grasps kinky sex techniques. These will cater to the husband's sexual needs. Moreover, she understands men's inherent physical desires. So she will be very open-minded with her husband's extramarital affairs.

This male bar owner believes that a hostess's rural background makes her a good candidate for a wife because she is not only easily controllable but also tolerant of her husband's sexual promiscuity. According to him, "Men do not like capable professional women because they feel challenged. Professional women are too difficult to control."

While clients desire hostesses as the erotic and submissive other in order to solidify their male ego, hostesses aim for economic gain and social advancement. Hostess Guang obeys all of her client-boyfriend's orders, including how to dress, make up, and do her hair. She said, "I have to. He gives me a lot of money, buys me clothes and a mobile phone, pays my rent and telephone bills, and tutors me in English every weekend." After they first met at the KTV bar, he took her to dinner and on trips. She loved sightseeing in a number of tourist cities. These perquisites were all predicated upon her obedience.

Playing Cinderella to Prince Charming

Hostesses also play upon the stereotype of a poor, vulnerable rural woman in order to entice clients into playing a "savior" role. Hostesses often recount to customers their horrendous experiences of being raped or sexually abused. One said, "I told my client that I, as a rural woman, came to be a hostess because my previous city boyfriend raped and abandoned me. My client was so touched by my story that he was literally in tears!" The other hostesses all laughed. I asked her if this was true, because I often heard clients say that this was the main reason hostesses "fell" into their profession. In response, she laughed loudly and looked at me as if I came from Mars, saying, "Who ever tells clients the truth? You are a fool if you believe it! Of course I made it up!"

Hostesses create such stories to evoke customers' sympathy and desire to save the "fallen" woman. Often clients are so moved by the tragic existence of such pretty and vulnerable rural women that they offer them larger tips, finance their education, and establish enduring sexual, and sometimes emotional, bonds. As one hostess recollected, by playing the role of an abused and vulnerable rural woman, she had established several fairly long relationships with such "caring" and "sympathetic" men. However, as she regretfully added, since some of them were traveling businessmen from other parts of the country, she eventually lost these economic benefits once they left town.

Economic Benefits and Access to Clients' Social Networks

Hostesses consider their job as both a sacrifice and a stepping-stone to reaching their goals. Almost every hostess enjoys various degrees of social, cultural, and economic advantage from her relationship with clients, as I describe in detail below.

First, clients often act as hostesses' teachers, instructing them in English and computer skills and even offering them computers to practice on. Hostesses also use their earnings to attend classes and learn occupational skills.

Second, clients often take care of hostesses' rent and phone bills as well as buy them clothes, jewelry, the latest model mobile phones (3,000 *yuan*), and driver licenses (3,000 *yuan*). Some hostesses have multiple male lovers at the same time, without being discovered. Hostesses May and Wang are good examples. Hostess May had six client lovers. On her birthday she managed to participate in six birthday parties, one for each of them. Similarly, Hostess Wang was kept by three clients, from whom she had gleaned a great deal of economic profit. For each commodity she bought, she asked the money back from each of her three clients. For instance, all three clients offered to take care of her rent. She rented the house using one client's money and deposited the other two clients' money in the bank. If one man bought her a necklace, she immediately would ask the other two men for the money to buy a necklace. After getting thousands of *yuan* from those two, she would put it in her account. Then she would wear the one necklace before the other two men, telling them that this was the necklace she bought with their money.

Third, clients often drive hostesses around the city or take them along on sightseeing trips. Hostesses showed me photographs they had taken with client lovers while traveling in Shanghai, Beijing, Shenyang, and other major cities.

Fourth, clients frequently introduce hostesses to new job opportunities, which can include work in other industries (e.g., beauty parlors) as well as in more upscale bars where the bar owners and Madams are the clients' friends.

Fifth, officials sometimes issue their hostess lovers free temporary resident cards or urban household registration cards (*hukou*). Hostess Yu's client arranged for her temporary resident card to be stamped for a whole year free of charge. Likewise, Hostess Han's client issued her an urban household registration card for free. In fact, she is now holding two registration cards, one rural and one urban. She deems herself "a very successful woman."

Sixth, a great number of hostesses are either married to or kept by wealthy clients as legitimate wives or second wives. In this way they become not only "legitimate urbanites with urban residency cards" but also entrepreneurial owners of businesses, such as sauna bars, gift shops, karaoke bars, and restaurants. Among the 200 hostesses I have studied, a total of six are married to their clients. To give an example, Hostess Han is married to the treasury director of a prestigious hotel in Dalian. Before marriage, Han earned enough money to buy a house for her family in her rural hometown in Heilongjiang and another one in Dalian. In fact, nine people in her family were supported by her income alone: her parents and seven other brothers and sisters. Han gave her brother 25,000 *yuan* as a marriage present and similar amounts to her sisters upon the births of their children. She has been married for a year now and runs a hair salon bought by her husband in Shenzhen.

Besides these women, almost every other hostess has been kept as a second wife or lover at one time or another, and some more than once. For example, Hostess Yu's sister used to work in a low-class bar. One of her clients introduced her to an upscale bar in the city, where she gained employment. After a couple of years she was kept by a client as his second wife. He opened a sauna bar for her in the provincial city of Shenyang. She is now the owner of this sauna bar. She often came to Dalian to visit her sister Yu in the low-class bar. Every hostess gasped at her glamour. Every possession of hers sparkled with wealth and status. Each accoutrement that adorned her body—her bag, necklace, dress, cell phone, shoes, wristwatch, etc.—was worth thousands of *yuan*; her watch alone, 10,000 *yuan*. Everyone expressed envy and admiration. She, however, just smiled and advised them all to transfer to upscale bars as she had. Her visit caused such a stir in the bar that, immediately after she departed, her sister Yu and ten other hostesses left their current employment in search of greener pastures.

The above examples illustrate the ways in which hostesses glean a great deal of economic, social, and cultural capital from their clients by manipulating the image of the rural woman as either a virgin or a whore. As Mayfair Yang[60] points out, in postsocialist China *guanxi* (social networks) arose as a way of defusing and subverting the restrictions of a powerful modern state. As I have demonstrated, the shrewd *guanxi* manipulation in hostesses' negotiations with clients enables upward mobility in an illegal profession. Each hostess has triumphant tales of the different advantages they have extracted from their male customers. Oftentimes, they share these experiences with one another and compare their gains. For them, these profits are the basis for judging the depth of their clients' feelings toward them.

CONCLUSION: REPRODUCING HEGEMONY

In defiance of state laws against prostitution and patriarchal control over women's bodies and sexuality, hostesses market their bodies for their own independent, autonomous, and instrumental uses. Their work entails not just the sale of sex but also the sale of a performance as unruly whore, docile virgin, or victimized peasant woman. Their manipulation of rural women's images not only enables hostesses to become active commodity consumers and debunk their image as country bumpkins but also gives them access to their clients' social networks in order to reap cultural capital, social advancement, and economic security.

As illustrated by the many examples cited, hostesses deploy the dominant cultural symbol of consumption to project an exaggerated image of an urban woman antithetical to their popular representation as naïve peasants incapable of being full-fledged urbanites. Their conspicuous consumption allows them to contest these stereotypes and lay claim to urban membership and legitimate citizenship. Consumption, however, requires money, so in order to realize their agency, hostesses must reproduce the stereotypes of rural women for their male clientele. Their performances help redistribute male clients' socioeconomic resources into their own hands and enable them to negotiate a space for themselves in the city.

The state discursive regime of consumption and body culture constitutes the available cultural repertoire that hostesses appropriate for their social advancement. Their dual cultural strategies are created through, rather than outside of, the simultaneously constraining and enabling state structure. Their very agency paradoxically binds and limits them by reinscribing and reproducing the hegemonic state discourse that legitimizes and naturalizes their docile virgin/promiscuous whore image. Thus, their agency becomes what is held against them and reinforces their marginality and low status.

ACKNOWLEDGMENTS

I am very grateful for supportive funding provided by YCIAS and the East Asian Council at Yale, and the helpful, detailed suggestions and critiques offered by the editors, Arianne Gaetano and Tamara Jacka.

NOTES

1. Bourdieu 1984.
2. Gu 2000 and Zhang Haibing 2001.
3. This is the official figure of the city population (in the central four districts).

4. Zhang Haibing 2001:142. Municipal officials interviewed estimated a floating population in Dalian of one million people, from all over China.

5. Jian 2001.

6. Jian 2001; Khan and Riskin 1998:44.

7. Interview conducted in 2001.

8. See Wang 1995. He argues that only very few leisure activities were organized by work units so as to prevent any bourgeois "counterrevolutionary decadence."

9. Wang 1995:156.

10. Ibid.

11. Gan 1958; Yan 1997.

12. Khan and Riskin 1998.

13. Yan 1997.

14. Li 1998.

15. See the chart in Zhang Haibing 2001:400.

16. Farrer 1999.

17. Karaoke bars, although legal, have always been one of the government's main "culture purging" targets. They are claimed to work against the state's cultural logic in three aspects: 1) socialist business should prioritize the needs of people and serve the people. It should be different from the commercial system, where the pure objective is to pursue and procure sudden huge profit. Many bar bosses operate their business by cheating customers and providing erotic services; 2) "erotic companies" (*seqing peishi*) are illegal and immoral and are counter to socialist "spiritual civilization." Such "ugly phenomena" associated with capitalism should be wiped out to maintain the healthy and inspiring socialist cultural environment and "civilized consumption"; 3) juxtaposed against socialist recreations enjoyed by the masses, karaoke bars are more individually based, where individuals pursue and express their "repulsive and hideous" desires to show off their performing talents and satisfy their sexual demands. In view of the above three reasons, karaoke bars regularly undergo a purging process to become part of "spiritual civilization." Frequent police raids are part of this process.

18. See also Moore 1994.

19. Bordo 1993.

20. Brownell 1995:235.

21. Luo 2001.

22. Chu 2001.

23. Ibid.

24. He and Shi 2000:12–16.

25. Brownell 1995:235; Cheng 1999; Li 1999.

26. Brownell 1995; Schein 1999.

27. *Zhongguo Di Er Jie Dushi Nühai Fushi Fengcai Dasai Dalian Sai Qu* 2001.

28. Barlow 1997:530.

29. Anagnost 1994.

30. Ibid.

31. Ibid. 139.

32. Xu 1999:986.

33. Wang Xuetai 1999; Zhou Xiaohong 1998.

34. Li 1998:334.

35. Ibid.
36. Zhou Xiaohong 1998:193.
37. Song 2000:94, 228.
38. Tong 1995:94.
39. Tong 1995; Wang and Guo 1993:31–35; Liu 1995:199–200.
40. Tong 1995:103–4.
41. "Culturedness" here means "modesty" and "refinement."
42. Lin 1999; Shen 1999; Wen and Ma 1991:224.
43. Bai 1998:1.
44. See also Gladney 1994.
45. Chatterjee cited in Parker et al. 1992:6.
46. See Clarke 1999; Cook 1996; Finnane 1996.
47. See Liu Li 1998; Zhou 2001.
48. This title is a reference to the title of Pun's 1999 article.
49. Butler 1993.
50. See introduction, this volume.
51. The latter is a strip show performed under the influence of the drug Ecstasy. After dosing, the performer cannot stop shaking her head and dancing until the drug wears off.
52. Bourdieu 1984:57.
53. Information in this chart is drawn from interviews with more than a hundred hostesses and participant observations in hostesses' everyday life.
54. Bourdieu 1984; Ellen 1988.
55. Cheng 1999; Li 1999.
56. In reality, police did stop them on the street demanding a display of their TRCs. However, they were extremely reluctant to admit the fact that their hyperbolic "modern" appearance gave their identity away.
57. See Brownell 1995.
58. Baudrillard 1997 (1981). He argues that consumption is more important for its symbolic meaning than for its instrumental use. See also Liechty 1995. Lietchy argues that individuals use consumption to construct their imaginative identities, to draw social boundaries and improve group solidarity.
59. Ellen 1988:229.
60. Yang 1994.

3. Indoctrination, Fetishization, and Compassion: Media Constructions of the Migrant Woman

THE STORY OF AN ANHUI WORKING SISTER / AN INTRODUCTION

>> Hong Zhaodi[1] is a twenty-year-old woman from a village in Suxian county, Anhui province. She, her parents, and two brothers live off the land. Poverty forced her to drop out of school at the age of thirteen. In early 1998 she heard from one of her friends that an acquaintance named Liu Feng ran a factory in Guangzhou and was looking for someone to do the bookkeeping. Seeing this as a way to get herself and her family out of poverty, Hong left home and traveled south. After arriving in Guangzhou, Hong was taken to see her prospective boss. Little did she know that she was heading for hell. She was hired, but on June 12, 1998, Liu told Hong that she was to work as a prostitute. She refused. Liu then kicked her in the groin many times, stripped her naked, and photographed her. Two days later, Hong started to hemorrhage and was taken to the county hospital. She appealed to the hospital staff for help, asking them for permission to notify the police. Her appeals were ignored. Out of despair, Hong attempted to end her life. She threw herself out of a second-floor window and ended up with first-degree spinal damage.[2]

Hong's desperate suicide attempt finally caught the attention of local police, who took Hong to the city hospital. On June 22, 1998, *Guangzhou Evening News* (*Yangcheng Wanbao*), a metropolitan commercial paper in

Guangzhou, ran a story about Hong entitled WORKING SISTER PUSHED TO HELL—KILLS HERSELF TO AVOID PROSTITUTION[3] that gave detailed coverage of the incident. The provincial authorities subsequently took note and issued an order to prosecute the perpetrators and penalize the apathetic hospital staff. The story also moved the readers of *Guangzhou Evening News*, who donated 60,000 *yuan* to help with Hong's medical expenses. Liu, the perpetrator of the violent crime, was sentenced to ten years' imprisonment and required to pay compensation of 120,000 *yuan*. Various levels of the All-China Women's Federation (*Quanguo Funü Lianhehui* or *Fulian*)[4] also reacted to the news story and public outcry. Money was raised in support of Hong's brave action and she was praised as a *lienü* (a woman who would rather die than have her virtue compromised).

The day after the story appeared in the *Guangzhou Evening News*, Gao Fumin, the president of the Anhui Women's Federation, was interviewed by the paper. Gao praised Hong's bravery, thanked the paper for exposing the crime, and extended her appreciation for the support from various women's federations and other organizations in Guangzhou province. On the same night, the vice president of the Anhui Women's Federation reported the incident to the provincial authorities, who, in turn, issued instructions to the various departments concerned to handle the matter with sympathy and care.[5]

At the end of June 1998 representatives from the Anhui Women's Federation, together with a reporter from the *Hefei Evening News* (*Hefei Wanbao*), a provincial commercial paper, journeyed to Guangdong to see Hong. They told her that she exemplified dignity (*zi zun*) and self-respect (*zi zhong*) and had brought pride and honor to the women of Anhui. In July *Anhui Women's Movement* (*Anhui Fuyun*), an official monthly journal of the Anhui Women's Federation, ran an article calling on Anhui women to learn from Hong's brave action and also urging them to learn a lesson from the violent incident. The article advised rural women not to leave their hometown and to seek work locally instead. It also cautioned those intending to migrate to be careful and wary of possible deceptions and criminal activities.[6]

The story of Hong Zhaodi is worth recounting at length here because it raises some important issues concerning representations of the young, rural migrant woman, or working sister (*dagongmei*), in Chinese media. Regardless of differences in ideological orientations, audience segmentation, and institutional contexts, both "official" and "commercial" media[7] have paid constant and consistent attention to the phenomenon of the working sister in the reform era. In this chapter I shall argue that these various representations construct the working sister at the intersection of indoctrination, fetishization, and compassion, all of which subject her to a "controlling gaze"[8] and none of which adequately expresses her agency and subjectivity. I shall demonstrate that the representational strategies of indoctrination, fetishization, and compassion point to the complex interplay and complicity among the socialist state, the market, and the emerging middle class. More specifically, I will show that both the official and the commercial press construct stories of crime and the abuse of migrant women's human rights in sometimes lurid and gory detail, not only to shock and titillate but also to assist in the construction of party-state hegemony. Dramas about working sisters routinely feature the stock characters of the victim, the villain, the kindhearted, the police, and the paternal figure of the party-state. Such dramas usually end with all the characters getting "what they deserve," but, more importantly, it is almost always the state, as embodied in the police and the Women's Federation, that is given the symbolic power to rename these women as "good" or "virtuous." I shall also argue that, as the example of Hong Zhaodi makes clear, stories of the working sister may sometimes be a voyeuristic peep into the private lives of an "other" community. However, at the same time, they highlight the importance of equality and basic human rights and, in this way, may be seen as contributing to the formation of "cultural citizenship."[9]

My comparison of representations of migrant women in official and commercial media throws open the fundamental question of the relationship between the power of the state and that of the market. Are the images of migrant women in these representations competing or complementary, and how do they reflect and reproduce the contradictions of the post–Mao socialist state in the throes of commercialization and globalization? The analysis also raises the question of the prospects for democratization. While official media may be losing ground in the ideological battle to define "good" or "bad" citizens, may the commercial media create new possibilities for cultural citizenship, not through indoctrination but through democratic participation, albeit limited? Within the parameters described above, and in the hope of shedding some light on these questions, I will turn to the figure of the working sister from Anhui[10] and examine first the official position—via some publications of the Women's Federation—on issues relating to rural female migration: "staying home," "leaving home," and "working away from home" (*dagong*). I refer to this position as "indoctrination." I will then consider the burgeoning voyeuristic and fetishistic representations of the working sister in the commercial media. Finally, I will discuss representations of the working sister in what

I refer to as "compassionate journalism," which has emerged as an important reporting practice in some segments of the commercial media as well as among some of the official media, and address the questions of whether or not such journalism contributes to cultural citizenship and whether or not it offers a space for migrant agency or voice that is denied in other forms of journalism.

THE WOMEN'S FEDERATION, INDOCTRINATION, AND THE "IDEAL WOMAN"

The Women's Federation is what is termed a "mass organization," with the official dual role of furthering the interests of women and promoting party policy among them. In practice, the federation comes under the direct leadership of the party and, at all levels, receives its funding from the government. It should therefore be considered part of the state apparatus. Its publications are part of the official media and are largely mouthpieces for party rhetoric, even though, like other official media, it has had to react to competition from the commercial press and has become more diversified, both in appearance and in content.[11]

As may be clear from its somewhat tardy and weak response to Hong Zhaodi's case and the moralizing tone that it took in reporting her story, the role of the Women's Federation is increasingly ambiguous and awkward as it contends with the rapid economic and social changes of the reform era. It tries to provide support to women, but it does not work effectively and is certainly not feminist in intent or practice. This is because the Women's Federation is largely devoted to mobilizing women around state expectations of the "ideal woman," or what Tani Barlow refers to as the "imbricated national Chinese woman subject."[12] Such discourses, according to Barlow, assume that the interests of individual women and the interests of the state are one and the same. Women are encouraged by the Women's Federation to be four things: independent (*zili*), strong (*ziqiang*), confident (*zixin*), and proud (*zizun*). They are also expected to acquire four qualities: to be motivated (*you lixiang*), to be educated (*you wenhua*), to have a strong determination (*you zhiqi*), and to have goals (*you baofu*).[13] Women's Federation publications routinely exalt exemplary individuals who qualify for the title of *si you* (four qualities). Since stories of model women appear in a rhetoric that places family, community, and nation above individuals, they should be understood in exactly this context. In other words, although these concepts, in a different context, may sound strikingly similar to what some western feminist discourses would privilege, they are nevertheless intended to shape and mold women into citizens who can be recruited into the political, social, economic, and sexual roles carved out for women by the Chinese state. It is precisely for these reasons that Judd argues that the "desirable" qualities listed by women's federations are imposed on women externally and from the top, and serve as much as to sort women into hierarchical order in the state's nation-building project as to strengthen their competitiveness in the market economy.[14] Claiming to promote the interests of women, but obviously part of the project of nation building at a time when economic reforms have exacerbated the disparities and inequalities between the sexes, classes, and regions, the Women's Federation is having an increasingly hard time explaining its function and justifying its existence. Many of its publications, as certainly is the case with Anhui Women's Federation publications, are therefore fraught with tensions and contradictions: they preach the ideals of independence and gender equality to women but are not critical of structural inequalities between the sexes.

Its response to female migration is one of the most telling examples of the Women's Federation's ambivalent position. The movement of women from the countryside to the city, and between provinces, is considered to be beneficial to the national economy, since it enables gaps in the labor market to be filled. A mobile, readily available, and flexible workforce is an important component of a successful market economy. Therefore, the Women's Federation helps to connect village women and their prospective employers in the city to create employment opportunities in domestic service and other types of work. It also publicizes stories of rural-to-urban migrant women who return to their villages with entrepreneurial skills and capital. Zhao Yuemin is one such success story publicized by the Women's Federation. She was born and brought up in Wuwei, Anhui, the hometown of the famous Wuwei *baomu* (maids). Zhao's mother and grandmother had been domestic maids in Beijing. In 1985 Zhao followed in their footsteps and went to Beijing as a maid. However, she refused to see domestic service as her fate. While working as a maid, she started studying modern techniques for raising chickens. She subsequently left her job as a *baomu* and started her own chicken farm outside Beijing. Finally she returned to her hometown and became a shareholder and manager in the village-run farm, generating an annual income of 200,000 *yuan*.[15]

Zhao's story of entrepreneurial success, however, is not typical of most women migrants. Women's experiences of leaving home and venturing into the unknown cities are often treated with ambivalence and suspicion by the Women's Federation and its media. The visibility of certain mobile people—particularly prostitutes and criminals—in the already crowded cities is often seen as a source of anxiety, fear, and moral panic. Mobile women seem to compromise the implementation of location-bound family planning policies and to threaten to erode traditional feminine values and destabilize the institution of the family, since the traditional view holds that a woman's place is in the home and tends to equate women with domestic duties and men with public affairs.

This contradictory view of female migration is symptomatic of the conundrum facing the cadres of the Women's Federation in the new socio-economic reality. While "thought work"[16] in the socialist era aimed at the mobilization and socialization of women, this ideological task today is much more challenging, due to the fact that more women than ever are on the move. On the one hand, rural women like Zhao are seen as successfully indoctrinated; they exercise the four qualities of "independence," "strength," "dignity," and "self-respect" in the domestic realm of the home or the village, returning to the village after a brief period of time in the city. Those rural women who "go out" and do not return to the village, or become "fallen" by turning to vice or crime, are not seen as "good" or ideal. Certainly, the qualities expected of women are impossible goals for many who, with limited resources and options, are forced to take up work that is "indecent" or criminal, and therefore morally unacceptable to the Women's Federation.

The official narrative of the ideal woman is overtly anti-individualistic and, at the same time, implicitly patriarchal. Hong Zhaodi is a "good woman" in the official view and was given both financial and moral support because she refused to work as a prostitute and preferred to die to maintain her virginity rather than to surrender. She is therefore decorated as a *lienü*, a Confucianist concept that describes a woman who defends her virtue by taking her own life. Although a *lienü* is a strong-spirited woman defying masculine oppression, her virtue lies as much in her determination to defend her virginity and reputation as in her feistiness and strong will. In other words, where a woman's virginity is not the issue, a woman who allows herself to be exploited and oppressed in other ways is a "virtuous wife and good mother" (*xianqi liangmu*), and hence an exemplary citizen. She is an "ideal woman" because she works to reinforce the stability of the state and of the family. A virtuous migrant woman, by this logic, is therefore one who allows herself to be exploited for the sake of national development.

While Anhui Women's Federation publications tirelessly promote "ideal women" like Zhao and Hong, who are docile and "disciplined,"[17] they consistently shun the presence of "bad" women and their "unruly" bodies. For instance, the topic of prostitution seldom appears in Women's Federation publications, and when it does, it always has a condemnatory undertone. The following commentary from *Anhui Women's Movement* adopts such a moralistic position:

> In recent years, as many of 70 percent of divorce cases have women as the guilty party. The "third-party" phenomenon and extramarital affairs are also caused mostly by women. It is no longer unusual for a woman to assume the role of a "personal assistant," mistress, and concubine. . . . These women do not hesitate to sell their body for money; some women seek lovers outside marriage. In the shameless business of prostitution, some women appear both as victims and perpetrators, polluting the morals of the community and poisoning the soul of people.[18]

The complicity between the discourse in some Women's Federation publications and the patriarchal position on the issue of prostitution is most clearly evidenced in the official interpretation of the relationship among migration, prostitution, and erosion of the family, according to which prostitution is a result of women succumbing to the seduction of a materialistic and hedonistic lifestyle brought about by westernization and made possible and easy by the growing number of mobile women. In other words, official representations of migrant women reflect the Women's Federation's discourse that rewards *lienü* and those who value virginity (*zhenchao*) and chastity (*shoujie*), denies the possibility of political agency to women who become prostitutes, and fails to recognize the oppression experienced by the vast number of women forced into prostitution by violence or poverty in contemporary China. In praising Hong, who preferred death to loss of virtue and forced prostitution, the Women's Federation's discourse of the *lienü* rescued her from the status of a "fallen" woman and through renaming restored her "virtue" and moral "purity." This is how the power of the state is seen to work most effectively, as Anagnost argues succinctly:[19]

> The bestowal of status honors, through the issuing of ritual markers and public processions, demonstrates the power of the state to define discursive positions in political culture through its classificatory strategies, its power to name, to sort persons into the hierarchically arranged categories of a moral order.

Through Hong's story the Women's Federation conveyed two clear patriarchal messages to rural women: "don't leave your village home" and "your life is not worth living if you are a 'fallen' woman." By linking prostitution and

sexual servitude to morality and by disassociating it from economic and political realities, the state, through the Women's Federation and its press, appears to adopt a fundamentally sexist position akin to Confucianism. The
Women's Federation must portray migrant women ambivalently—as both
positive and negative. Portraying them as "fallen," as the above commentary
from *Anhui Women's Movement* does, justifies paying little attention to their
individuality and to the social causes of their condition, thus allowing the
state to sidestep the contradictions that economic reform poses for rural women. Should the government admit that economic reform is exploitative of
rural women, it would lose legitimacy and support for its reforms.[20]

FETISH, VOYEURISM, AND THE "OTHER" WOMAN: THE WORKING SISTER IN THE COMMERCIAL MEDIA

Officially the Women's Federation, in line with the state's approach more
generally, does not encourage rural women to stay in the city long-term
and, therefore, rarely promotes rural women who have "made it" but who
live permanently in the city. Furthermore, in response to cases of gross exploitation or abuse of migrant women, the federation tends to offer little,
if any, support and makes little effort to challenge the institutional and ideological underpinnings of such abuse. As we have seen in the example of
Hong Zhaodi, it is often only when incidents or events involving individual women victims reach the commercial media, arousing public sympathy
and pressure, that the Women's Federation and other authorities are forced
to take action to protect women and punish the perpetrators. On the other hand, judging from the content of the commercial media, one can also
surmise that, as in the West, sex, violence, and crime sell well in contemporary China. Commercial Chinese media rely on images and stories of
women to sell. For both these reasons, while the Women's Federation's
press can afford to ignore stories of "fallen" working sisters, in commercial
publications, including *Xin An Evening News*,[21] such stories abound.

In other words, while official journalism represents migrant women only
through model images and deals with issues such as prostitution and sexuality by avoidance and censure, commercial media represent working sisters
as alternately the objects of fetishization and voyeurism and the objects of
moral outrage and compassion—in both cases, as voiceless and passive. The
working sister of popular urban myths falls into several tropes. She is sometimes a country girl who becomes a *baomu* (maid), a *xiaojie* (an euphemistic
term for prostitute), or the victim of abduction and human trafficking. Or
she might be a *xiagang nügong*[22] (laid-off urban woman worker), who leaves

home to seek employment in a distant city. I argue that, whether a *baomu*, a prostitute, or an abducted woman, the rural migrant woman is portrayed as a social vagrant, occupying the liminal space between the "civilized" and the "uncivilized," the urban and the rural, the public and the private, or what Stallybrass and White refer to as the "cultural categories of high and low."[23] For this reason, stories of working sisters generate sales because they suggest the possibility of transgressions—moral, cultural, and ideological—that are not tolerated by the state or represented explicitly even in the commercial media. Very often "transgressive acts," when told as media stories, can only be hinted at or implied. Yet it is precisely the hidden or forbidden nature of such transgressions and their representations that promises both voyeuristic and fetishistic pleasures.[24]

The voyeuristic gaze of urban readers is clearly present in most popular representations of migrant women. The construction of the *baomu*, for instance, exemplifies the nature of this gaze. Urban, well-to-do residents—both male and female—often find themselves caught in a situation where they cannot trust their *baomu* yet have to put her in charge of duties in the house involving a great degree of intimacy, responsibility, and confidentiality. Like the maid in Victorian England, whom Anne McClintock describes as "a threshold figure,"[25] the *baomu* transgresses the boundaries of the public and the private, the paid and the unpaid, and those of the family. For this reason, she is the object of intense social scrutiny, anxiety, and fascination. Consequently, mass-appeal papers often tell stories about maids' escapades, ranging from stealing money from employers, being negligent of babies in their care, or seducing the man in the household (sometimes the husband and other times the son) to being sacked after proving to have unclean habits or being diagnosed with a contagious disease.[26]

The voyeuristic gaze of urban readership as well as a controlling gaze of the state—embodied in the enforcement of law and order—are both clearly present in the trope of the abducted woman. Her experiences of being lured, drugged, kidnapped, and sold by traffickers far from her hometown, then rescued or saved by police, provide rich fodder for recreational reading in the commercial media and inspire the "action story." The popularity of this journalistic genre involving police, the perpetrators of crimes, and the victim lies in its dramatic effect. The use of catchphrases such as "night raid" (*yexi*), "narrow escape" (*tuoxian*), "operation" (*xingdong*), "bizarre crime" (*qi'an*), and "crime scene" (*xianchang*) heighten the suspense and drama. These stories also appeal to readers' voyeurism by including detailed information on the abduction, rape, and assault of rural women or lurid scenes of prostitution.

Xin An Evening News runs regular columns entitled ANHUI POLICE (*Anhui jinfang*) and EVENTS AND HAPPENINGS (*shishi zongheng*), which supply a regular diet of dramatic stories of this type. The following *saohuang* (crackdown on prostitution) "raid story" is typical:

> Headed by Chief Inspector Kong Xiaoliang, a special team from Hefei's Public Security Bureau heads for a dance hall on Suixi Road for an unexpected inspection. Our reporter is allowed to come along. Upon arriving they are greeted by a cacophony of music coming from those private rooms with closed doors. The boss standing in the foyer spots the "uniform," gives his employees a wink and a nod, and then walks up to us with an ingratiating smile. Our team is not to be distracted by him. Inspector Yu heads straight for one of the rooms and forces the door open with a violent push, revealing a good-looking *xiaojie* in a mini-skirt and a skimpy top, struggling to sit up from the arms of a middle-aged man.[27]

The most horrifying tales relaying the worst forms of female mobility, stories such as these probably appeal because they present a familiar and clear narrative structure, the innocent victims versus the evil perpetrators, and definite closure, since usually they end with the "rescue" (*jiejiu*) of the helpless woman and her "escape from danger" (*tuoxian*) with the help of the police. They may also have the mythological function of providing acceptable explanations for frightening or baffling events, such as abduction, or undesirable phenomena, such as prostitution, and reassuring responses, such as evidence that justice is done and the law enforced. These stories are usually presented to the urban readership as "bizarre" and "horrific" tales involving criminals deprived of human decency, to be read and savored at a safe distance and with an unambiguous sense of moral superiority. More important, they appeal to an urban middle-class sensibility. This, I argue, is characterized first of all by an intense curiosity about the lower classes[28] and secondly by a paradoxical relationship to the notion of privacy. On the one hand, a secret self that needs privacy is regarded as a signifier of middle-class status, but on the other hand, middle-class readers are often very interested in learning about other people's private secrets.[29] Finally, the urban middle-class sensibility is marked by a desire for basic social justice, the protection of individual rights, and the certainty and effectiveness of the law.[30]

The multiplicity of gazes directed at the migrant woman in the commercial media in contemporary China is exemplified by exposé journalism, written by reporters working undercover (*anfang*) and almost always claiming to be eyewitness (*jishi*) accounts. The selling point of these tales is that they expose a shady world of which ordinary people are unaware or that they have not experienced. Although the rationale for *anfang* and *jishi* reportage is supposedly to expose what is wrong in society, its real appeal lies in its capacity to blend moral surveillance and control with titillating sex, crime, and intrigue, the object of the gaze being, in both cases, the migrant woman.

For eight consecutive days in July 2000, *Xin An Evening News* published a group of undercover investigative and eyewitness accounts of the sex industry in Anhui. The editor noted:

> Currently, the provincial police have mounted a campaign to crack down on the rampant practices of prostitution, gambling, and drug trafficking. In order to collaborate with this initiative, this paper sends our own staff reporter to investigate undercover a number of recreational business premises. What follows is a series of true accounts of these investigations.[31]

A closer reading of these stories reveals that this form of investigation satisfies a desire to know an "other" world, including the interior of a brothel, the appearance of the women working inside, and the brothel clients. Written by an anonymous "staff reporter," the series publishes, sometimes in great detail, the undercover reporter's detailed descriptions of brothels found in several counties and towns of Anhui, and his conversations with brothel owners, prostitutes, and clients. Such reports, while arousing and satisfying the reader's curiosity about the other world, are nevertheless inscribed with a sense of secrecy and intrigue: the "brothel" and "prostitute" are seldom overtly labeled as such, and sexual services are usually described in coded language:

> A "cultural and recreational center" appeared on Xiangyang Road, Wuhu City on July 1. Though it's only been half a month since its business started, it has already gained quite a reputation. According to local taxi drivers in Wuhu, the center is definitely the "fun" (*hao wan*) place to go. Exactly how is this a "fun" place? On July 18, we sent one of our journalists there to check it out. The center is a five-story building, offering, as listed on the notice board in the foyer, a range of services including sauna, massage, foot bath, and karaoke. The floor manager walks up to our journalist the moment he walks in. "Welcome.

We have all sorts of service provided by our *xiaojie*," the manager says. "Do you have *that* kind of *xiaojie*?" our journalist asks. The manager replies, "The *xiaojie* I refer to is exactly *the* kind of *xiaojie* you ask about. This is your first time, so I don't want to be too explicit." The manager walks the journalist up to the fourth floor and introduces him to a *xiaojie*. She charges an x number of *yuan*, and is willing to perform all duties short of "*daowei* [climax or orgasm]."[32]

The *xiaojie* in these "cultural and recreational centers" and "entertainment clubs" are portrayed as shadowy figures, some of whom promise to deliver "all-channel services" (*quan pindao*, implying the entire range of sexual services). Exposed, but somewhat indirectly, they are constructed as symbols of danger or taboo and as objects of the voyeuristic and fetishistic gaze.

Police/action stories and exposé/investigative stories, as discussed here, constitute staple reading in entertainment-oriented dailies such as the *Xin An Evening News*. In the former the controlling gaze comes from those representing law and order, whereas in the latter it comes from reporters and the media institutions they represent. The popularity of both genres derives from these stories' capacity to provide, first, a clear-cut delineation of what is right and wrong, moral and immoral; second, voyeuristic or fetishistic pleasures through reference to a dark, forbidden, and hence intriguing world; and third, assurances of law and order being upheld. For this reason, stories from both genres are significant in articulating and reinforcing a middle-class sensibility.

The juxtaposition of these stories with the moralistic discourse on prostitution and the stories of "ideal women" found in the Anhui Women's Federation publications points to the complex and paradoxical nature of the relationship between the state and the market: while they are sometimes competing and oppositional, often what we see is more of an ideological alignment and coalition, with both subjecting the migrant women to a controlling gaze. It is also conceivable that such a complex and paradoxical relationship nevertheless contains a democratizing potential: while the moralistic indoctrination of "good" or "bad" citizens promulgated in official publications may be seen to be virtually bankrupt, popular narratives in the genre of police stories and investigative stories, both of which are framed within a law-and-order discourse, seem to demonstrate a new possibility for the formation of civic consciousness, characterized by a concern with law and order as well as a respect for human and individual rights.

SYMPATHY AND CARE: THE POLITICS OF COMPASSION

While the commercial media actively participate in exploiting the image of suffering women as objects of fear and desire, they also provide one of the few contact zones between individual victims of abuse and the public. This contact zone—though highly problematic—is nevertheless one of the few places where victims can air their stories to the public and the authorities. For example, Hong Zhaodi's luck turned not so much with the assistance or support from the state authorities like the Women's Federation but as a result of the initial exposure of her misfortune by the commercial media and the reader sympathy it generated. Despite their fetishized images of sexuality and crime, some stories in the commercial media, including Hong Zhaodi's, appeal to readers' concern for social injustice and compassion for human suffering. As the gap between the rich and the poor widens, the lives and misfortunes of the socially marginal become objects of intense curiosity and staple fodder for urban folklore. Hong's change of fate was thanks to compassionate journalism, or what one might term "perennial stories."[33] These are tales of the misfortunes of the poor, the vulnerable, and the powerless that struggle to negotiate an underlying tension between discourse on the commonality of humanity and fellow citizenry and an innate "us-versus-them" narrative structure.[34] Perennial stories articulate the concerns with social justice and individual rights that, as I argued above, are characteristic of the urban middle-class sensibility. Increasingly, journalistic professionalism is defined, in both commercial and state media, not only as the courage to expose evils and uphold justice and morality but also as the capacity to sympathize with and care for the weak, the poor, and the downtrodden.[35] Some media are particularly known for sympathetic attention to the suffering, misery, and hardships of certain social groups. Examples are commercial media such as the *Southern Weekend* (*Nanfang Zhoumo*) and *Southern Metropolitan Daily* (*Nanfang Ribao*) in Guangdong, and state media outlets such as the TV show *Focal Point* (*Jiaodian Fangtan*) in Beijing, the highest rated current affairs show on Central China Television (CCTV).[36]

While some perennial stories invite readers to take direct action, as in the case of Hong Zhaodi, others encourage less concrete forms of sympathy. One example of the latter is the regular stories run by *Southern Weekend*, drawing urban readers' attention to the injustices, inequalities, and poor working conditions suffered by rural migrants. According to one report, tens of thousands of migrant workers from inland and northern provinces working in places like Shenzhen live in extremely basic conditions with no privacy and little comfort. Moreover, due to the long hours of factory work, stringent management regulations, and low pay, married migrant couples cannot even live together. The editor's note says:

> We must pay attention to this marginalized and exploited community. They exist at the bottom of our society and their basic rights as private citizens are being taken away from them. Yet nobody can deny that these people have already sacrificed too much for the development of our society. They deserve more sympathy and care.[37]

We may do well to juxtapose the exposé of the brothels from *Xin An Evening News* with this story of a migrant community. Both bring the private lives of individuals to the public's attention, thus rendering the invisible visible. However, these stories operate according to different social semiotics of the migrant body. The former uncovers the prostitute's body yet still withholds it from full view, adhering to the principle of fetish and disavowal, thus appealing to the voyeuristic desires of middle-class (and other) readers. The latter also directs the public gaze onto the migrant body, but only to evacuate eros and desire from it in order to articulate another aspect of the middle-class sensibility—the concern for justice and individual rights.

Although the article advocates for migrants' human rights, it does not point to the fundamental social and economic inequalities that have given rise to the violation of those rights. In this type of narrative, migrant workers frequent the discursive field of urban middle-class audiences, but mostly as objects to be represented. Stories such as these, with their detached language of reason, law, and human rights, may not elicit emotional identification or immediate action such as donations, but may do just as much as Hong's story to humanize migrants and change perceptions of them, or even effect a change of policy toward them. Perennial stories are thus another example of how the commercial media may do more to develop a consciousness of cultural citizenship among urban middle-class readers by encouraging compassion and care than do the official media with indoctrination into state-prescribed understandings of citizen rights and responsibilities.

I speculate that the appeal of these compassionate stories derives from their capacity to generate a range of emotional responses, which in turn can be translated into various types of reading pleasure. For instance, stories of gross injustice such as Hong's elicit moral outrage. Such outrage can be closely linked to a "feel-good" factor, for stories such as these with a "good vs. bad" structure can have the function of validating and confirming one's moral beliefs and values. In addition, the communication of this sense of outrage through the regular consumption of media gives readers the pleasure of being connected to a community of other like-minded, though anonymous, readers. Furthermore, these stories of compassion deliver a reassuring sense of familiarity and continuity: a feeling that in spite of the injustice and ugliness in the world, at the end of the day, justice is done, life is blessed with human kindness, and society returns to a "normal" state.

Another kind of reading pleasure may come from the "do-good" capacity of the reader, which in turn can produce a "feel-good" effect. No longer given the likes of Lei Feng, the model soldier and icon of socialist heroism during the Mao era, as a standard to follow, audiences of compassionate stories are not likely to be burdened with the high socialist rhetoric of altruism. Rather, they may simply desire to live with a good conscience or gain empowerment through generosity and morally uplifting deeds. The hundreds of readers of the *Guangzhou Evening News* who donated money to Hong Zhaodi upon reading of her misfortune were probably not expecting public recognition for their generosity, but it may have made them feel good nevertheless. In other words, although their action may have made a difference to the victim, it may also have benefited them morally and emotionally.

Readers of this and other perennial stories may also gain pleasure from the affirmation of a class- or geography-based difference between the self and the other. Although the "other"—those rural migrants who live at the periphery of "our" existence as the most economically disfranchised, culturally inarticulate, and socially marginalized group in Chinese society— deserve "our" sympathy or help, they are nonetheless not "us." To put it another way, urban middle-class readers may sympathize with those they help, but their feelings and donations do not necessarily erase their sense of a class-based difference. In fact, as I have shown, such a juxtaposition of sympathy and class consciousness is essential to the formation of a middle-class sensibility.

It is clear by now that compassionate journalism may take a number of forms, ranging from issue-related social critiques (e.g., the migrant couples' bedroom) to emotionally stirring narratives of the misfortunes of the weak in the hands of the strong (e.g., the story of Hong Zhaodi). As a narrative form, it is testimony to a growing civic consciousness of the urban middle class. It appeals to the public's sense of justice (*zhengyi*) and moral conscience (*liangzhi*). At various times and under different circumstances, compassionate journalism has the effect of raising awareness, inviting sympathy, or generating social action. It has attracted a growing urban readership and generates profits, not in spite of but precisely because of its attention to the socially disadvantaged. This is the paradox of compassionate journalism: its emergence is a response to increasing social stratification and inequality in the era of globalization and urbanization, yet the effect of stories from this genre is to reproduce the very social inequalities that they purport to address and evoke outrage about.

CONSTRUCTING THE WORKING SISTER: A BRIEF SUMMARY

My analysis of some Women's Federation publications points to the increasing ineffectiveness of the state in addressing problems of injustice and inequality arising from female mobility, and its inability to step beyond orthodox party discourse on social issues such as gender and sexuality. At the same time, the analysis highlights an unyielding desire of the socialist state to maintain ideological supremacy and a strong capacity to make its presence and power felt in a market culture.

Unlike official media, commercial journalism eschews indoctrination. However, much like some Women's Federation publications, the commercial media treat migrant women as either victims of crimes in need of rescue or figures of transgression in need of control. In both state and popular narratives, migrant women are the objects of a controlling gaze, although in the former the gaze is controlled by the state, whereas in the latter it comes from a fetishistic and voyeuristic urban readership.

It thus appears that the politics of representation of migrant women is indeed complex. Any argument for giving an institutionally sanctioned voice to the working sister has to contend with both state and market forces as well as growing social stratification along the lines of geography, class, and gender. In spite of the apparent tension and contradiction between the state and the market, the ideological positions and discursive strategies of representing migrant women in the two domains appear to be convergent rather than divergent. The strategies of indoctrination and fetishization both contribute to a hegemonic representation of the working sister. Consequently, she has emerged as a highly popular trope in urban narratives, but as a speaking subject she remains faint-voiced and largely unheard. Therefore, the prospect of constructing an array of female subjectivities *of* and *by* the working sister looks remote.

The politics of representing the working sister in contemporary China is further complicated by the emergence of compassionate journalism across state and commercial media. On the one hand, like the state's discourses on female mobility, the humanistic discourse of compassionate journalism renders invisible the structural inequalities causing social stratification. This allows the urban middle class, including both media practitioners and their audiences, to sympathize with the disenfranchised without threatening the foundations that underpin the middle class's relative comfort and superiority. Consequently, migrant women—cast in the light of difference, however sympathetically—suffer a reproduction of their deprivation that is both social and discursive.

On the other hand, like many stories in the "action" and exposé genres in the commercial media, stories of compassion are usually told within the framework of law, order, and human rights, and therefore constitute a significant discursive space where a civic consciousness and a concept of citizenship that is an alternative to the state may gradually emerge. Thus such stories generate some hope for the prospect of a more profound social change in the direction of empowering the working sister.

ACKNOWLEDGMENTS

Many thanks to both editors for their tremendous support in the rewriting process. Their suggestions and comments were instrumental in sharpening the theoretical and conceptual focus of my chapter.

NOTES

1. *Zhaodi* means "beckoning a younger brother" in Chinese.

2. Information about the incident used in this chapter comes from the article "Hong Zhaodi shijian fasheng yihou (After the Hong Zhaodi incident)," published in *Anhui Women's Movement* (*Anhui Fuyun*), an official publication of the Anhui Women's Federation (Anhui Province Women's Federation's Legal Consultation Office 1998:20–21). This publication is publicly circulated but targeted toward women cadres.

3. The story in the *Guangzhou Evening News* is entitled "Dagongmei bei ren tuijin huokeng, Hong Zhaodi ningsi bukeng maiyin (Working sister pushed to hell—kills herself to avoid prostitution)," June 22, 1998, quoted in the article from *Anhui Women's Movement*, cited above.

4. The All-China Women's Federation is a mass organization under the leadership of the Chinese Communist Party, comprising a hierarchy of organizations reaching from the national level down to the village. For a discussion of the relationship between the Women's Federation and the Chinese Communist Party, and of the structure, power, and status of the Women's Federation in the reform era, see Judd 1994:213 and Judd 2002.

5. See Anhui Province Women's Federation's Legal Consultation Office 1998:20–21.

6. Ibid.

7. Economic reforms and subsequent processes of globalization and commercialization in the media have resulted in an uneasy coexistence between the "party line" and the "bottom line." On the one hand, media outlets under the auspices of the Communist Party and mass organizations such as the Women's Federation continue to "toe the party line"; on the other hand, there is a burgeoning media sector, largely funded by nonstate sources, which is profit-seeking and entertainment-oriented and has broad popular appeal. See Zhao Bin 1999:291–306; Yuezhi Zhao 1998, 2000:3–24. Also found in the commercialized sector are "metropolitan" papers and evening dailies, such as the *Southern Weekend* in Shenzhen and Guangzhou and *Xin An Evening News* in Anhui, which are considered to have the function of articulating sensibilities of the emerging middle-class and urban readership. In addition, this bifurcated media structure is unstable and subject to ideological convergence and splintering. For instance, although Central China Television's (CCTV) *Focal Point (Jiaodian Fangtan)* is a television program under the direct auspices of the Chinese Communist Party (CCP), it nevertheless relies on advertising income and therefore has the imperative of ensuring ratings. Its high-quality investigative journalism appeals to a broad cross-section of the Chinese audience, including urban and rural, rich and poor. By the same token, the metropolitan presses, which are often referred to as "mass-appeal papers," also operate along a spectrum ranging from tabloid sensationalism to socially responsible serious journalism.

8. The concept of "the gaze," which has been widely used in critical media studies, originates in film theory. In a seminal article called "Visual pleasure and narrative cinema," Mulvey (1975:6–18) observes that classic Hollywood films present men as active, controlling subjects and treat women as passive objects of desire for men in both the story and the audience, and do not allow women to be desiring sexual subjects in their own right. Such films, she argues, subject women to the controlling male gaze, presenting woman as image or spectacle and man as bearer of the look. I am appropriating the concept to include a way of "looking" sanctioned by both gender- and class-based inequality and the political and institutional power of the state.

9. "Cultural citizenship" refers to the "broadening of the traditional idea of the rights and responsibilities of states and citizens" (Rowe 1999:87–88). The importance of the media in the formation of cultural citizenship lies in their ability to contribute to the "creation of informed, critically reflective persons capable of taking an active part both in their own lives and in those of the collectivities of various kinds." Also see Hartley 1999.

10. Anhui is a largely rural and underdeveloped province in central eastern China. Many rural Anhui residents have migrated to the city, including the well-known figure of the "Anhui maid." See Sun 2002:153–78 for a detailed discussion of economic and social change in Anhui.

11. For instance, while the Women's Federation of Anhui runs a boring, didactic, and monochrome publication called *Anhui Women's Movement*, the women's federations in some other provinces have taken on a much more colorful, entertainment-oriented format, and appeal to a wider female readership.

12. Barlow 1994b:345.

13. See Gao 2000:15–16.

14. Judd 2002.

15. See Yang and Guan 1999:24.

16. "Thought work" (*sixiang gongzuo*) is an official Chinese term referring to work for the purposes of ideological indoctrination.

17. Anagnost 1997:95.

18. Wang Xia 1999:19.

19. Anagnost 1997:100.

20. I am indebted to both editors for helping me to clarify this connection.

21. Like thousands of other tabloids in China, *Xin An Evening News* is funded purely by circulation and advertising. Unlike *Anhui Daily (Anhui Ribao)*, the mouthpiece of the provincial CCP, or the *Anhui Women's Movement*, which are noncommercial publications funded by the state, *Xin An Evening News* strives to keep its circulation high through retail and subscription sales.

22. A social group that is rapidly becoming the urban underclass, it is also one of the most visible casualties of economic reforms. Although the misfortune of being laid off (*xiagang*) falls on both male and female workers, women bear the brunt.

23. See Stallybrass and White 1986:4. This is not the place to discuss the politics of transgression in detail, but suffice it to say that I have found their framework of theorizing transgression, whereby they conceive the high-low opposition in "four symbolic domains," psychic forms, the human body, the geographic space, and the social order, useful. According to Stallybrass and White, there is an undeniable ambivalence in European bourgeois representations of the "lower strata" (of the body, literature, society, place) in which the "low" are both reviled and desired. The "top" discriminate against the "low" for reasons of status and prestige, but at the same time find themselves dependent upon the low; in other words, the "low-Other" are excluded and opposed at the social level but desired or eroticized at the level of fantasy.

24. Mulvey (1975) distinguishes between two distinctively male modes of looking by the film spectator: voyeuristic and fetishistic. Voyeuristic looking is marked by a distance between spectator and spectacle, which allows the spectator a degree of power over what is seen. Fetishistic looking, in contrast, abolishes the distance between the seer and the seen, thus involving direct acknowledgment of the object viewed. As Ellis (cited in Neale 1997:332), explaining Mulvey, puts it succinctly: "The voyeuristic look is curious, inquiring, demanding to know. The fetishistic gaze is captivated by what it sees, does not wish to inquire further . . . and has much to do with display and the spectacular." Voyeurism and fetishism, though representing different ways of looking, are nevertheless imbricated in each other. Hall (1997:268) points out that fetishism operates at a level "where what is shown or seen, in representation, can only be understood in relation to what cannot be seen, what cannot be shown." This desire to both expose and hide is a paradox crucial to the strategy of fetishization, which, as Hall (Ibid.) observes, "is a strategy of having-it-both-ways: for both representing and not representing the tabooed, dangerous or forbidden object of pleasure and desire," and as such [it] inevitably "licenses" voyeurism.

25. McClintock (1995:77) examines the relationship between power and desire in the imperial metropolis of Victorian England through a case study detailing well-known Victorian barrister Arthur Munby's lifelong obsession and erotic fascination with his maid, and maids in general.

26. The experiences of *baomu* and their relationships with employers also provide staple fodder for feature films and television dramas. See, for example, the

films *The Girl from Yellow Mountain* (1984) (*Huangshan Lai de Guniang*) and the television dramas *Professor Tian's Household and Their 28 Maids* (1999) *(Tian Jiaoshou Jia de Ershiba ge Baomu).*

27. "Muji shengcheng 'saohuang' (Eyewitness to Heifei's crackdown on prostitution)," *Xin An Evening News*, July 30, 2000, 15.

28. Writing about the emergence of the penny press in the United States toward the end of the nineteenth century, Hughes (1968) considers the ways newspapers cater to the taste of the middle class and the wealthy in the city in the process of urbanization and immigration. She observes that one of the traits of the middle class is its increasing curiosity about the poor and immigrants.

29. For a full statement of this point, see Teng 2000. Teng argues that the paradoxical relationship to the notion of privacy is clearly evidenced in the popularity in the late 1990s of "*yinsi* (hidden self) literature," which describes and narrates the secret world of the private self.

30. This is obviously not the place to discuss and debate in detail what constitutes the middle class in contemporary China. However, I agree with Robison and Goodman's observation that the question of what constitutes the middle class in Asia is complex. I also find their description of the middle-class outlook to be very useful: it is marked by "high levels of consumption and a greater emphasis on leisure; a greater concern for education as a central mechanism for securing positions and wealth; a desire for predictability and certainty of laws; and access to information and analysis" (Robison and Goodman 1996:11).

31. Editor's note, alongside Liu Weizhang and Yang Sheng's news story "Shuishang leyuan le zai hechu? (Where is the fun bit in the fun park?)," *Xin An Evening News*, July 17, 2000, 1.

32. "Women zheli ershi si xiaoshi yingye (Here, we are open 24 hours a day)," *Xin An Evening News*, July 22, 2000, 1.

33. I am borrowing this term from Hughes (1968), who uses it to describe stories with "human interest," such as those of lost children, hurt animals, and change of fortune, which frequently and regularly circulate in the American penny press. According to Hughes, they are age-old stories that will remain popular due to their enduring humanitarian interest.

34. This common journalistic narrative structure is extensively discussed in Hartley 1992.

35. This emphasis on justice, equity, and conscience is evidenced in, for instance, the titles of the anthologies of the best news stories written by reporters from *China Youth Daily*. The trilogy *Bengbao Jingri Chuji* (The Target of Today's Paper) is thematically organized respectively around the themes of *liangzhi* (conscience), *gongping* (equity), and *zhengyi* (justice) (Lu and Luo 2000).

36. There is a popular saying in China about quality journalism: "In the north we have *Focal Point*, and in the south we have *Southern Weekend (Bei you Jiaodian Fangtan, nan you Nanfang Zhoumo).*" It is estimated that as many as 0.3 billion people watch *Focal Point* every evening. This is a state television program that is, however, funded mainly by advertising revenues. It is, therefore, an example of the "bifurcation" of official-commercial media. For a good discussion of *Focal Point* and the impact of investigative journalism, see Li Xiaoping 2002:17–34.

37. Sun Baili 2000:16.

Part 2

SEEKING A FUTURE

Louise Beynon

4. Dilemmas of the Heart: Rural Working Women and Their Hopes for the Future

> A cultural approach to migration does not ask what migration does, how it comes about, or how it is structured, but is concerned with how migratory experiences are tied into the web of ongoing discourses of belonging, separation and achievement.[1]

>> The growing incidence of female rural migration in China has been reflected in the increasing number of surveys and papers documenting the migration paths and characteristics of female migrants. Drawing on this material, this chapter seeks to take a more cultural approach to migration, as defined by Frank Pieke above. Rather than detailing the ways in which young rural women come to the city and their daily working lives, I seek to link their experiences of migration to their changing attitudes to life and the choices they have to make in crafting a future for themselves. In particular, I try to assess how the experience of leaving home and working in the city influences young rural women's attitudes toward marriage and their choices and opportunities for finding a good husband and securing a future home, either in the city or back in the countryside.

The chapter draws on extensive interviews with young, unmarried rural women working in Chengdu as nannies or daily domestic helpers, as shop assistants or sweatshop workers, or in restaurants and teahouses. These young women lead particularly unsettled lives compared with other migrants in the city. Having migrated within their own province, they often return home to visit or help out in the busy farming season, frequently changing jobs and living quarters and taking little or no part in any organizations. These women are "urban guerrillas," living neither in collective dormitories linked to enterprises nor in migrant villages found in some Chinese cities, but in between these spaces.[2] For some of these rural working women the main focus in the city was a small government-run household services labor market in the center of Chengdu—Huang Wa Jie labor market—where they gathered every day on benches in a crowded courtyard, waiting to be hired. In weekly visits over the course of two years, between 1996 and 1998, I conducted informal interviews with more than a hundred working sisters, ranging from casual conversations during a single meeting to more in-depth discussions developed over several months' contact. These interviews often evolved into small group discussions and arguments between migrant women as they took up issues of urban prejudice, work conditions, life at home, and the vexing question of marriage and the future.[3]

During my research at the labor market I realized that, despite the different ages and situations of these women working in Chengdu and whatever plans and ideals they confided to each other, the issues of marriage and of their future were never far away. This chapter, therefore, argues that there is a complex interconnection among migration for work, marriage, and securing a future for unmarried female migrants in China. Taking a cultural approach, I outline the motivations for migration of this group of females, and the contradictory and often unconscious impulses of avoiding early marriage and childbirth while seeking to secure a better marriage through such movement. Next, I look at the lives of this group of rural working women in Chengdu and show that there is a sharp contrast between the barriers to achieving actual economic independence and social standing and the women's perceptions of independence and liberation and pragmatic acceptance of their temporary and difficult working conditions. The precarious and temporary nature of their lives in the city and the urban prejudice they face reinforce rural working women's sense of living in between the city and countryside and plays a major role in their deliberations over their future.

Central to these deliberations is a confrontation with a serious dilemma: the longer migrant women stay working in the city, the more difficult (and undesirable) it is for them to return to the countryside to marry, but the alternatives of marrying an urban resident or remaining unmarried are either remote or untenable. Although momentarily evaded, the question of the future and marriage has to be faced, for it is only through marriage that young rural women secure their future "place." The notion of place for these women is multilayered; it signifies not only a geographical sense of a physical location but also a psychological sense of belonging, of feeling comfortable in or being part of a community. Contemplating marriage, working sisters also have to decide where to live in the future, and what kind of life they want and can realistically achieve. The pertinent question for rural working women in Chengdu is, therefore, not "What does tomorrow hold?" but, rather, "Where is tomorrow?"

A CULTURAL APPROACH TO THE MIGRATION OF WOMEN TO CHENGDU

Migration for this group of rural working women in Chengdu is characterized by a complex mix of push and pull factors, including the economic poverty of their home villages, their desire to lessen the burden on their family by leaving, and a sense that they are unproductive and without value as unmarried daughters. Thus, on one hand, their migration can be conceptualized as a displacement rather than a positive movement.[4] However, there are also strong pull factors, attested to by these women in phrases such as "to test myself" (*duanlian ziji*), "to open my eyes" (*kaikuo yanjie*), and "to change myself" (*gaibian ziji*). Young rural women leaving for the city seek a sense of independence and value while recognizing the drudgery and narrowness of their present and future rural lives. Most important, they use migration for work to evade early marriages and deflect pressure from parents to control their marriage choices, and at the same time view such migration as an opportunity to make a better marriage. Thus, on the other hand, their migration can be conceptualized as a positive desire to escape, to gain autonomy, and to try to change their fate.

The complex motivations encouraging an increasing number of rural women to leave home necessitate a reexamination of how we should conceptualize female migration. Theoretical literature on migration tends to subsume female migration under a household strategies model, in which it is assumed that families or households decide who should migrate to benefit the household economy.[5] But this model ignores individual motivation and the complex process of conflict and compromise among household members.[6] Some writers have emphasized that household welfare is the underlying influence on patterns and selectivity of migration in China,[7] but recent research in China and other Asian countries shows that never-married women often migrate against their households' wishes.[8] My own research among rural working women in Chengdu supports the notion that individual motives are greater for women than for men in contemporary Chinese rural migration.[9]

The portrayal of female migration as part of a household strategy, downplaying the individual motivations of women leaving home, is complemented by another male-biased model that views women as passive objects in marriage migration. Actually, women often make rational and autonomous choices in marriage migration as a means to achieve economic, social, and geographical mobility.[10] Their use of migration for work as a strategy to gain a sense of independence and as a means to improve their chances of finding a better place through marriage suggests that migration should be conceptualized as a "motive path," not just through geographical space but also through life space.[11] A focus on migration as a constantly shifting biographical event rather than an economic household strategy draws out the ways in which women are using migration to craft a future. I argue, therefore, that it is impossible to disentangle marriage migration and migration for work in the lives of rural working women.

The patrilocal system of marriage predominating in rural China, in which daughters leave their natal families upon marriage, has meant that rural families consider their daughters to be "another family's member" (*renjia de*). Indeed, expressions labeling daughters as "goods one loses money on" (*peiqian de huo*) and "water thrown out of the door" (*po chuqu de shui*) when they marry illustrate the precarious and temporary place rural daughters occupy in their natal homes. But a different reading of patrilocal marriage suggests that, historically, marriage has also been a means for Chinese women to achieve social mobility. Certainly, in pre-reform China, marriage was rural women's only opportunity for upward mobility. In the commune era, under Mao Zedong, a system of spatial hypergamy existed, in which women were able to marry up and out of poverty-stricken areas, in contrast to the general immobility of rural society, although such movement was never classified as migration.[12] Evidence suggests that this spatial hypergamy is continuing and increasing in the postreform era; the high rates of interprovincial migration of Sichuan women to both rural and urban areas point to the significance of marriage migration.[13]

With the rise in rural migration of both men and women, migration for work is expanding the opportunities for women to marry away. One survey showed that of more than 17,000 women marrying into north Jiangsu, 9,627 came after meeting men who were working outside of that region, 4,591 found husbands after visiting female relatives who had already married into the area, 2,554 were sold into marriage, and 884 found spouses through advertisements.[14] Thus, although the postreform era has witnessed the trafficking of rural women, many more women are actively marrying farther away as they meet partners while both are migrating for work. It is important, therefore, to recognize the positive side to the norm of patrilocal marriage.

For rural daughters, marrying out can be a painful and difficult separation of their present and future lives, but it also provides a chance to escape poverty, family conflicts, and even rural life altogether. One rural woman in Chengdu said:

> I come from a very poor mountain village. If I hadn't had the chance to come to Chengdu to work I would have had to marry there and would never have been able to leave. It's better being a daughter than a son, because if I find someone here in Chengdu, I won't have to go back. If you are a son, then you have to return home, however poor it is. A son is tied to the soil, but I can get free.

From the perspective of this rural woman, patrilocal marriage can be an opportunity for a daughter to change her fate and begin life anew, while in contrast, rural men are bound by filial duty to return to their native place and cannot stay away permanently.[15]

In my research with rural working women in Chengdu a paradoxical attitude to marriage emerged. Most of the unmarried women had migrated for work as a conscious or unconscious means to evade early marriage and motherhood. Several young women interviewed said that they had left home because their parents had arranged a marriage for them and the only way to resist was to leave. Others said that avoiding marriage was not a conscious motivation for leaving, but that having gone, and especially after returning home for a visit, they realized how differently their lives were turning out from those of friends left behind. One woman remarked:

> All my friends who didn't go out to work are married now with a child. I have nothing to say to them anymore; they just talk all the time about their mothers-in-law and their children. It's so boring! I suppose if I hadn't come to Chengdu my life would be like theirs; that's why I am so glad I decided to leave. I hadn't thought about leaving to escape marriage, but now that I look back on it, that's what it was.

The increasing pressure on rural young people to marry early (and therefore have children early) has been documented in the Chinese press.[16] Letters written to the journal *Rural Women Knowing All* (*Nongjianü Baishitong*) also describe the continuing pressure of parents on their children and the difficulties in resisting such pressures; these letters illustrate rural daughters' ambivalent attitude to marriage and their desire to postpone it for as long as possible. This relates to their perception that a rural marriage entails a constriction of their future and a narrowing of their aspirations to the domestic sphere. One woman, for example, justified her

refusal to marry early by writing: "As soon as I marry I will lose my freedom and become a little housewife."[17] Another argued that marrying early, when she was in the golden age of youth, would be wrong, as she does
not know what she wants or how to achieve her ambitions.[18]

On the other hand, the rural working women in Chengdu recognized
that marriage continues to be the deciding factor in a rural woman's life,
and the question of future marriage was never far from their minds.[19]
They responded to my suggestion that they could remain unmarried with
amused tolerance at my foolishness; if they didn't marry, they explained,
they would not have a house or a viable economic future. As unmarried rural daughters, their place after migrating for work is not their natal home,
because they are expected to marry out.[20] One woman responded to my
question of where she felt her home was by saying:

> Chengdu is not my home, even though I have worked here now
> for five years. But I can't really call my parents' home mine ei-
> ther, because I will marry out eventually. I can only call it my
> temporary home.

So marriage is more than finding a partner; it is securing a future place.
This may not seem new in areas where women have traditionally always
married out of their own villages and thus gone to new places. However, I
would argue that migrant women now face a unique dilemma, because migrating for work has not only opened up the possibilities in marriage
choice to include long-distance or urban marriage but also raised their expectations for a future partner and increased their desire for a different
lifestyle by giving them a taste of independence and freedom and by exposing them to different lifestyles and attitudes. This suggests a further
meaning to the term "place"; in addition to a geographical location and a
sense of belonging in a particular space, rural women are trying to gain a
better and happier future, both economically and emotionally.

In this quest for a better future place, marriage is the key. To what extent, therefore, can rural migrant women actively seek a good marriage
while working in the city? To what extent can they exercise agency and
control in their decisions on a future partner and a future place? These
questions necessitate a closer look at rural women's lives in the city.

THE IMPACT OF WORKING AND LIVING IN THE CITY

As many surveys have shown, the jobs available to rural women and the
conditions under which they work are often harsh and difficult.[21] Howev-

er, as I have suggested above, many young women do not migrate in the expectation of gaining a real economic and social value through a good job. Rather, the decision is related more to the symbolic value of the work.[22] That is to say, for this group of rural women in Chengdu the actual wages and conditions of their migrant jobs are less important than the benefits of leaving home and gaining status as a wage earner, however small that wage might be. This sense of status is accentuated by their perception of their lack of economic and social value as unmarried rural daughters at home. As one young woman said:

> When I left school I just helped around the house and did some agricultural work, but I felt I was a burden on my family and life was very boring. I thought I was useless and no good to my family, and lots of other girls in the village had gone away already to work, so I felt even more lonely and useless. That's why I decided to come to Chengdu to look for work.

In reality, it appeared to me that the contributions of the unmarried rural daughters that I interviewed were considerable, but undervalued by both daughters and other family members. When I asked them to describe these "helping out" tasks, it emerged that these young women actually took on major responsibilities in both the agricultural and domestic spheres. This supports Tamara Jacka's argument that the major role expectations of rural women—to maintain a harmonious home, look after and be respectful to parents-in-law, sacrifice their own interests to other family members and raise children—all relate to married women.[23] The value that women accrue in the eyes of others is from their work as rural wives and mothers.[24]

Going out to work challenges their own perception and that of their families that they have little value as unmarried daughters, in part because working for a wage makes their contribution as economically productive workers visible and gives them a sense of value through work, and in part because they establish their worth as individuals separate from their families. Working away from home transforms the time spent waiting between leaving school and getting married—a liminal period of "helping out"—and gives them a sense of value as an independent person, however temporary. One young woman argued forcefully:

> I love working in Chengdu. I have my labor power and I exchange it with my employers for money. I don't feel inferior to anyone, not even urban people who look down on us rural migrants.

However, the majority of rural working women in Chengdu are unable or unwilling to break out of the traditional gendered division of labor that places them in unskilled service jobs with low wages and no welfare benefits, jobs that mitigate against their chances of creating an independent, secure economic and social position. One woman expressed a pragmatic acceptance of her situation by saying:

> It's impossible for me to get a good job with my background. I've got no skills and I left school at fourteen. But there's no point in my going back to school or learning new skills, it's just not worth it. I'm happy to get by as I am.

Few migrant women are able to save much money or to go to night school to improve their skills. This points to the difficulties in achieving actual autonomy and economic independence.

However, what could be more important is their *perception* of autonomy and independence. The opportunity to see the world, gain new experiences, and feel a degree of independence was emphasized by many rural women during interviews, rather than the actual wages and conditions of migrant work. Indeed, they admitted that a significant attraction of migrating to Chengdu was the chance to develop a new and freer life. One means of gaining a sense of autonomy and independence is through making a "space of their own" in the city. For example, an increasing number of rural working women at Huang Wa Jie labor market and elsewhere have chosen to rent a room in Chengdu rather than live at their place of work.[25] Being able to rent their own room rather than working as a live-in nanny or living in a factory dormitory has enabled these rural women to craft their own home in the city and to make friends and aquaintances outside work and family ties. Appreciation for this freedom was echoed in a letter to *Rural Women Knowing All*; the woman wrote that she had little money, lived in a tiny room, and worked long and hard hours, but that "in my heart I feel I have some space that is mine."[26]

Even if actual living conditions in the city are difficult, the chance to have a space of one's own can make it worthwhile. The young women working in a park teahouse in Chengdu very rarely left the confines of the park and knew very little about the city. However, one said:

> I feel that the world is so much bigger here in Chengdu, there is so much more space! Everything was so small and stifling in the village. I know I hardly go out of the park and don't know Chengdu at all, but my space is still bigger.

In contrast to the traditional fear of being a stranger in a strange place (*rensheng dibushu*), some women recognized the positive aspects of being a migrant, distanced from one's native place and a stranger in the city. One woman said, for example:

> I love being a stranger in Chengdu, as it gives me the freedom to do what I want, make the friends I want. Nobody can judge me, because they don't know my background or my history. Chengdu isn't my place, but I feel I can belong here.

It is significant that none of the rural working women I interviewed belonged to any native place association in Chengdu,[27] and that many actively sought to live with fellow migrants who were not fellow villagers (*laoxiang*). An ambiguous attitude to networks based on village and kinship ties was noticeable among them. While many had come to Chengdu through such networks, they did not automatically count fellow villagers as either friends or trustworthy acquaintances. One woman explained the desire to evade old ties by saying:

> Just because a person is a fellow villager doesn't mean they can be a friend. In fact, I prefer friends who come from outside my village. Otherwise it can get too complicated. They might tell tales about me to the village or gossip too much. I like making friends through my own choice.

This common attitude among the rural working women in Chengdu is in stark contrast to existing literature on the importance of native-place ties. Much attention has been focused on "migrant villages," especially "Zhejiang village" in Beijing.[28] However, it could be argued that not enough attention has been paid to the negative or constricting effects of living in such a community, especially for unmarried rural women who are migrating in part to escape the restrictions of rural life.

What was also apparent in conversations with rural women at Huang Wa Jie labor market was the fact that they compared their working conditions not to other, better jobs in the city, but to their rural life. They felt that however hard work was in the city, it was infinitely preferable to the rural drudgery they had left behind. This was vividly expressed by one of the few married rural women at the labor market; she said that after years doing rural work and bringing up her child, she felt she had been liberated (*jiefang*) by leaving her husband and coming to Chengdu to do casual work and could not imagine returning to the countryside. Accruing a sense of economic and social status through outside work, therefore, is complemented by a sense of space and liberation, even if actual living conditions in the city are difficult.

I have argued that for rural working women in Chengdu the advantages of gaining a sense of value, independence, autonomy, and space outweigh the actual economic and social conditions of their life in the city. However, the type of work they do and their pragmatic recognition of its temporary nature limit their integration into city life and even turn them away from considering long-term residency. Dorothy Solinger has detailed the many ways in which rural migrants are excluded from urban economic and social life and the barriers to their integration,[29] though research suggests that migrant women have more opportunities to integrate than migrant men.[30] This is especially true of those who find work as nannies, shop assistants, and restaurant workers, since such work involves considerable physical and social interaction with urban residents. At Huang Wa Jie labor market, for example, it was hard to tell that some of the women were from the countryside; they dressed in the latest Chengdu fashions and had learned to speak standard Chinese.

But, despite the greater opportunities to integrate, most of the women interviewed did not make much effort to know urban people or copy their ways. One woman who had worked in Chengdu for six years looked as if she had just arrived from the countryside. She argued:

> Chengdu is a good place to work and have a good time, but it's not a place I can stay in forever. I feel too insecure and hate always being an outsider (*waidiren*). Because of the household registration (*hukou*) system, city people will always think of me as a rural girl, so what's the point in adapting?

Thus, in addition to the barriers of work and economic standing and the temporary nature of their sojourn in the city, the continuing experience of urban prejudice is a major factor preventing rural women from being able, or willing, to become citified. The constant reminder of being an outsider reinforces their perception that the city cannot become "their place." As one woman writing to *Rural Women Knowing All* explained, the experience of working in the city made her realize it was not her place, and returning home brought relief and happiness because at least it was her own place.[31]

When issues of discrimination and urban prejudice were raised in my conversations with women at Huang Wa Jie labor market, the response was universal anger and bitterness at the prejudices and actions of city people toward them. The women frequently expressed sentiments that city people "looked down on us" (*qiaobuqi women*), and were sly (*jiaohua*), arrogant (*jiao'ao*), and selfish (*zisi*). The women blamed their unequal treatment and inferior social status on the *hukou* system that excluded them from the city social networks and cast them as long-term sojourners. Urban prejudice also encouraged most of the women to seek friends among fellow rural workers rather than urbanites; many had spent years in Chengdu and had no urban friends or desire to make any. Likewise, the women who rented rooms preferred to live in courtyards with other rural migrants, where they said they felt more at home. Thus, it could be argued that living in the city reinforces rural working women's sense of identity as rural people. One woman's letter to *Rural Women Knowing All* described how working in a small city had brought her face to face with the gaps between city and country people and made her realize that rural people have their own path and destiny and cannot become city people.[32]

The experience of living in the city but being excluded from it by low economic and social status and the prejudice of urban residents created a particular sense of in-betweenness for all the rural migrant women interviewed. This was especially true for those who went home several times a year to see family and friends and help out in the busy season. The frequent movement across rural and urban boundaries caused them to reflect on questions of place, belonging, and identity. Many women said that coming to the city threw into relief the economically backward state of their homes and the drudgery of women's lives in the countryside. Still, most maintained an attachment to a rural way of life and were nostalgic for the simple and friendly relationships of the village in contrast to the rude and discriminatory attitudes of urban residents toward them.

The frequent movement between two places also accentuated their sense of lack of belonging and feelings of cultural marginalization.[33] One woman said:

> When I go home I don't tell my parents about my Chengdu life, as they wouldn't understand. I just slip back into being their daughter, even though I feel I've changed. I like going back home, but after a few days I start to miss Chengdu. When I get back to Chengdu I start to miss home!

The women who had spent several years working in Chengdu were all ambivalent about returning home, whether for a visit or permanently. They worried that they would not be able to adjust to being a rural worker and wife after so long in the city.[34]

The sense of in-betweenness, of being culturally rootless and marginalized, is of special significance for rural working women. Unlike migrant men, who have a certain and fixed home to return to, these women have an accentuated sense of insecurity about their future because their natal home can only be temporary. Their experiences of living in the city, outlined above, have a critical impact on their decisions about a future husband and a future place. Their dilemma in relation to this issue will be detailed in the next section.

DECISIONS ABOUT THE FUTURE: CHOOSING PARTNERS AND PLACES

The above outline of rural working women's lives in Chengdu highlights the constraints on rural migrants in crafting a permanent place in the city: their low-paid and low-status employment prevents them from achieving real economic independence and a social standing among urban residents, while the continuing influence of the household registration system and deep-seated urban prejudice against rural incomers reinforce the notion of a cultural divide between rural and urban society and prevent migrants from becoming fully integrated city residents. The experiences and feelings of migrant women in Chengdu living between urban and rural spaces suggests that the constraints are particularly acute for them, and even more so because they are caught in the contradiction between the need to marry and their changing expectations. Most women, ultimately, feel they have to choose; they cannot move between their rural home and urban work indefinitely. Yet in making marriage choices they are faced with difficult decisions relating not just to their prospective partner but also to their future place.

Expectations of marriage increase with migration, as women are influenced by urban mate-selection values, see more clearly the burdens of rural life for married women, and become more critical of prospective rural husbands. Living in the city, gaining a sense of independence and value, and absorbing new ideas on love and marriage, many of the women at the labor market were unwilling to settle for a traditional rural husband. One woman said:

> The last few times I have been home my parents have tried to introduce me to some local men. But I don't like any of them. It's hard to explain, but I feel my life would be so dry (*kuzao*) if I married them and became a rural wife. If only I could be like the "single aristocracy" (*danshen guizu*) that I see in Chengdu. Then I wouldn't have to marry at all.

For many migrant women it is hard to settle for a rural husband, to whom they disparagingly refer as "dirt-head, dirt-brain" (*tutou tunaode*).[35] Migrant women have to go back home to marry rural men and fit into a traditional marriage relationship, even though going out to work and seeing the world has given them self-confidence, a sense of self-worth, and different attitudes toward work and marriage. Thus, there is a contrast between the abilities of migrant women and migrant men to adapt back to rural life; men do not experience such a sharp conflict in returning to customary patterns of obedience, because the traditional marriage relationship favors the rural husband as head of the household.[36]

Marrying an urban man would appear preferable, but there are practical and cultural barriers. At Huang Wa Jie labor market there was great skepticism about the benefits of finding an urban husband as a means of staying in Chengdu. Two women there had married men with urban residence, but they were looked on with pity rather than envy. In both cases the husbands maltreated their wives, which the women at the labor market attributed to the different social statuses of the partners. They argued that no good urban male would want to marry a rural woman; only the bad and desperate men would consider it, and use their higher social status to exert power in the relationship. Although household registration regulations have relaxed and new guidelines allow for children to take on either parent's registration[37] (previously a major barrier to intermarriage between rural women and urban men), there is still considerable prejudice against such intermarriages.

As outlined in the previous section, rural women working in Chengdu expressed deeply ambivalent attitudes about living long-term in the city, where they will always be considered strangers and outsiders. Similarly, one woman argued in *Rural Women Knowing All* that most migrant women cannot find their own path in the city and will always be strangers and "rural girls" (*yatou*) in the eyes of urban residents; she concluded that rural women ought to go home in the end.[38] In fact, several letters to *Rural Women Knowing All* illustrate this dilemma of choosing a future place. One woman wrote that, for ordinary migrant women, working in the city can only be a temporary solution to their existence. Finally, most have to leave behind the freedom of migrant life and return to the confines of rural life, and the few who decide to stay on in the cities face an insecure future. Another woman wrote that she was resisting pressure to return home to find a husband, but that it would be hard for her to establish a place for herself in the city if she stayed.[39]

The dilemma facing the rural women in Chengdu lies in having to choose between a rural life that many have come to hate and fear and a city life where they will always be considered strangers and outsiders. Most of the younger women interviewed at the labor market resolutely evaded this question, arguing that they didn't have to think about marriage yet, or that they could only live one day at a time (*zou yitian, suan yitian*). Some women had started relationships with male rural migrants, though these were often very insecure. For example, one woman had been her urban employer's mistress for five years but claimed she didn't want to marry yet because she was too young to have children. The lack of suitable solutions to this dilemma was expressed by one older migrant woman:

> I am now twenty-seven years old. I don't like going home anymore, as all my family talk about is how to marry me off. I have my land still at home, but no real home, as my brother is married and has children. But I don't want to marry a rural man, I don't want to be a rural wife. So I come back to Chengdu and carry on working. I have tried finding a husband here, but it isn't easy and, to be honest, I don't really want to get married. But I worry about the future, how I will live when I am older.

The accounts of rural working women suggest that not only are they having to choose between an urban future and a rural future but also that they are pressured to choose before a certain time. At the labor market there was considerable gossip about two women who were twenty-eight and still unmarried. Other women said that they had left it too late and would never be able to marry now. Worries about becoming rural "old maids" (*daling guniang*) were expressed by many rural women working in Chengdu, and the fear of being left on the shelf was a major impetus to grapple with the problem of marriage. One woman warned against staying away from home too long and wishing to marry late. She said that she had worked outside for ten years, refusing all introductions to partners, but when she returned to her village she found that all the good men had already married; her expectations of a partner were high after living in the city, but she could not find anyone suitable.[40] Two recent Chinese studies have pointed to the disruptive effects of migration on rural women's cycle of marriage and childbirth, arguing that a failure to marry by the age of twenty-five and have children is reinforcing a sense of rootlessness and an inability to adapt back to rural life among increasing numbers of migrant women.[41]

These women's fear of not finding a suitable partner if they postpone marriage beyond a certain age is paralleled by a recognition that their working life in the city is contingent on their youth. Apart from self-employment in the small-scale retail sector, most employers prefer to hire young migrant women, and many job advertisements explicity exclude wo-men over thirty.[42] The women at the labor market felt that their only cap-ital was their youth; most said they had to take advantage of their few years to make some money and see and experience the world. One woman ex-pressed this sense of temporariness by comparing her lot with that of the growing number of middle-aged urban women also seeking daily domes-tic work after being laid off from their factories. Pointing to these urban women, she said:

> I really feel sorry for these women; it must be hard for an urban person to look for this kind of work. They don't have any eco-nomic security, and no one wants them if they are too old. But you know, the only real difference between us is age; I am young still, but what will happen to me when I get to their age? It will be difficult for me to find a job, and then what could I do?

For many of the migrant women interviewed in Chengdu, marriage was necessary to secure a better future, however ambivalent they might feel about it. Those who had been in Chengdu for several years complained that their lives never changed: they did the same menial work and had not realized any of their ambitions. They had migrated to the city to escape being a "frog in a well" in the countryside, but after a few years in the city they felt trapped once again. One woman who had worked as a nanny for over six years in Chengdu said that her dream was to open a small restau-rant, but she needed a husband to help raise the capital and run the busi-ness. She was unable to save enough money or find reliable enough part-ners to set up a restaurant herself. Marriage, therefore, is an important step to achieving economic and social mobility, because it allows for the pooling of resources and the sharing of burdens. This attitude mirrors that of Taiwanese rural factory women who saw marriage as the only way to se-cure a better standard of living by pooling resources with a husband. After several years working in the factory with no opportunities to advance, they felt the same narrowness of life they had left home to escape.[43]

I would argue, therefore, that most rural working women in Chengdu are "playing with time" by working in the city. The very temporary nature of their life in the city explains their difficulties in formulating coherent plans for the future and imagining marriage. However, at some point, these women do have to choose, as time runs out for them. The differing attitudes of two women in Chengdu illustrate this well. One woman was twenty, had finished secondary school, and was confident of succeeding in Chengdu. She enjoyed being a rural migrant in the city, being an outsider and free to make friends and find work as she pleased. She had no plans to get married for some time, if at all. Listening to my description of this woman, another rural migrant, who was nearly thirty, almost illiterate, and widowed with two children left behind in her husband's village in Shanxi had this to say:

> If I were twenty I would think like her, I wouldn't want to settle down. I would try to make something of myself. But it's different for me; I can only be a nanny, and there's no future in that. I need a home (*jia*). I'm nearly thirty. I can't go back home because my family consider me to be married out; but I can't go back to Shanxi. I have to create some new roots, make a place for myself. I need a husband to make a home. Otherwise, what will I do when I am old? Who will look after me, where can I live?

The accounts and feelings of migrant women in Chengdu outlined here point to the impact of migration on their attitudes toward and expectations of marriage. Not only do they gain a sense of independence and value by working in the city, they also absorb new ideas on love and ideal relationships and critically examine rural life for women. But their rising expectations are hampered by the difficulty and undesirability of finding an urban spouse or staying long-term in the city. While many women express a desire to remain single, in practice marriage is a necessary step to gaining economic security and creating a sense of home. The pressure of time forces them to confront the issue and make some sort of choice.

Returning to the labor market a year after my fieldwork, I caught up with some of the women I had interviewed and heard their stories. A few had married a fellow migrant and remained in Chengdu, working together as small-scale traders or continuing their domestic work. Others had given in to parental pressure and had gone home to be introduced to a partner. The woman from Shanxi had married a divorced urban resident and said she was relieved to have a secure home of her own. But another woman said she was trapped in her marriage to an urban man who had become a petty criminal; he had forced her to have a child, and she felt unable to leave. Migrating for work, therefore, has opened up opportunities for some rural women to actively shape their future and make their own marriage choices, whether marrying fellow migrants and staying in the city or finding migrant men from wealthier villages and securing a more comfortable rural life.

But other rural women cannot be such active agents. Many eventually have to return home to be married and have fewer opportunities to migrate after marriage and childbirth. Others marry urban residents to secure a place and are uncertain of happiness. Many of the single women interviewed accepted that their ideals could only be dreams, while few married women expressed real satisfaction with their situation. On one level, these follow-up stories confirm that marriage is, indeed, a weighty issue for migrant women that determines their entire future. But on a deeper level they suggest that rural women's dreams and expectations of a better "place" in the future are, in fact, rarely achieved and that migration, while widening choices and raising expectations, also increases the possibility of disappointment.

>>

Life in the city for this particular group of rural women in Chengdu is fluid, rootless, and insecure; jobs, homes, and friendships are brief and unstable, and frequent movement between the city and home accentuates a sense of impermanence and in-betweenness. Their low-paid and low-status work and harsh working conditions make it difficult for all but a few to achieve real economic independence and social status. Yet, although they acknowledge the myriad problems and discriminations they face, many women emphasize the positive sides to being rootless and an outsider in the city: their perception of economic autonomy and their liberation from rural drudgery. These contradictory feelings, I have argued, relate to their motivation for migration: rather than seeking economic gain, most desired to escape the narrowness of rural life, the hardships of rural women's work, and the threat of early marriage and childbirth.

However, conflicting feelings arose from the necessity to face the prospect of marriage and secure a future place. What was significant in interviews with these rural working women was the real ambivalence they felt; they recognized the necessity to marry eventually, but the contrast between their hopes and reality, and their understanding of the impact of marriage on their future lives, made it difficult for them to grapple with these choices. As one Chinese researcher has noted,

> Marriage is a turning point in the lives of rural women in terms of mobility and non-mobility, of factory employment and self-employment, and the "career" of migrant women often ends with the start of married life.[44]

Younger women temporarily evaded this conflict by claiming they needed to improve themselves first or make some money and see the world. All the women saw their lives as "living one day at a time" (*zou yitian suan yitian*). This inability to actively plan and craft a future for themselves points

 idealistic

to the temporary nature of their life as migrants and their situation as outsiders in the city. Thus, their subjective experiences of working in Chengdu have had a profound impact on their ideals for the future and the actual decisions they have to make.

Ultimately, the rural working women in Chengdu were caught in several paradoxes: they had left home to gain economic independence, but most
could not create a secure life in the city; they wanted to postpone marriage
for as long as possible because they saw it as a constraint on their freedom,
but they knew that it was a dangerous strategy, as marriage was necessary
to secure a future; their attitudes to rural life, rural relationships, and their
own sense of identity had undergone a significant change in the city, but
new expectations were almost impossible to realize. The very inarticulate-
ness of most women in talking about the future and their ideas on marriage
points to their underlying awareness of these paradoxes and difficulties.

Caught between traditional rural ideas of marriage and the role of women and their new sense of identity, and between hopes for a future partner and the reality of their economic and social status, this group of migrant women face an uncertain future. While they are unmarried they
experience an acute sense of in-betweenness, as neither urban residents
who can stay in the city nor rural women happy to return to the village.
The pressure of time and the need to secure an economic future and a
sense of a stable home means that marriage choices eventually have to be
made, but they are rarely made freely or according to ideals.

NOTES

1. Pieke 1999:16.

2. Feng 1997:64.

3. My experience of conducting fieldwork at the labor market mirrored the inherent instability of these migrant women's lives; discussions and burgeoning
friendships were cut short as women were hired and disappeared forever. However, some migrant women, especially those working as daily domestic cleaners, used
the labor market as almost their only fixed place to meet informally and chat with
fellow migrant workers, and it was possible to develop closer relations with these
women.

4. It is significant that wealthy areas have low levels of outmigration, especially
among women. See Croll and Huang 1997:128–46.

5. Chant 1992:197–98; Hugo 1993:60.

6. For example, one study on female migrants in Java argued that "we find not
strategies, but motley and assorted decisions and behaviours to which others responded by desisting, withdrawing or accommodating" (Wolf 1992:5).

7. Rowland 1994:131.

8. Phongpaichet 1993:184; Riley and Gardner 1993:203.

9. Pieke 1999:7. See also Gaetano, this volume.

10. Hugo 1993:56. See also Tan and Short, this volume.

11. Pryor 1975:14.

12. Lavely 1991:310.

13. Davin and Messkoub 1994:18. Sichuan women from poor rural areas have developed marriage networks into the richer eastern provinces. One study showed that over 42 percent of women marrying into Jiaxing city, Zhejiang, came from Sichuan. See Wang Jinling 1994:61. See also Tan and Short, this volume.

14. Zhang Hesheng 1995:91. Although most women surveyed expressed satisfaction with their long-distance marriages, which illustrates the active agency of women in using marriage migration to escape poverty, evidence suggests some are less lucky and vulnerable to control and abuse by their new family. See, for example, You 1992:114.

15. This comment, echoed by several other migrant women, is an extremely interesting new perspective on patrilocal marriage; existing literature emphasizes the better opportunities for men, both before and after marriage, to move away and work in business or industry.

16. Jiang 1996:26–27; Li and Zhang 1994:60–61.

17. Miao 1996:36.

18. Zhang 1996:15. For another example illustrating the pressure to get married that young rural women feel, see the story by Zhou Rencong, this volume.

19. This dilemma was vividly expressed in a rural working woman's letter to *Rural Women Knowing All*. See Song 1996:9–11.

20. Several women interviewed said their decision to leave home was made after their brother had married and brought a wife into the house, creating tension and disputes between the sisters-in-law.

21. See, for example, Andors 1988; Pun 1999.

22. Evidence from Taiwan similarly suggests that the greatest impact of migration on rural women was the fact of leaving home, not the income or type of work they found in factories or in the cities. See Kung 1981:186; 1983:88.

23. Jacka 1997:72.

24. See Judd 1994:246. She argues that unmarried daughters do have considerable value to their families and village, but that they do not enjoy the (deferred) benefits of working for the household economy or village industry because they marry out.

25. This perception of autonomy, particularly among rural working girls who lived away from their work, was also noted by Davin 1999:128.

26. Sun 1996:29.

27. Although Chengdu does not have the structured native place associations found in Guangdong, for example, male migrants did say there were some more informal associations in Chengdu.

28. Ma and Xiang 1998; Xiang 1999.

29. Solinger 1995:129; Solinger 1999.

30. See Yuan and Wong Xin 1999. Their study describes male construction workers as living in an environment cut off from the city, in which it is impossible for them to become city people.

31. Mei 1996.

32. "Xiao chengshi liugei wode . . . " (Small city life has given me . . .), 1996.

33. See also Feng 1997:62.

34. Similarly, a survey of rural migrants in Hangzhou characterized them as "two-dwelling people" (*liang qiren*) or "borderliners" (*bian jieren*), yearning for city life but maintaining a sentimental attachment to home that leaves them vacillating between the two, resulting in a sense of cultural rootlessness, as they find it hard to assimilate back into their rural homes but feel excluded from city life (Ma 1995).

35. Tan 1996.

36. Chinese studies of the marriage difficulties of rural working women include Chen 1997; "Dagongmei: bianyuanren de hunlian gushi (Working sisters: Love and marriage stories of borderliners)," *Zhongguo Funü (China Women's News)*, June 1997.

37. See introduction, this volume.

38. Xiao 1996.

39. Wei 1996; Xu 1996.

40. An 1996. This sense of missing the right time to marry a good man is shared by urban women; several urban friends in their twenties who read this letter exclaimed that their situation was exactly the same.

41. Feng 1997; Tan 1996.

42. This age barrier is also increasingly true for domestic work, especially as rural women are now competing directly with middle-aged urban women for this type of work. Many urban employers prefer younger and more inexperienced rural nannies, because they are more "innocent" (*chunpu*) and easier to manage and control.

43. Kung 1983:164.

44. Huang 1999:98.

Lin Tan and Susan E. Short

5. Living as Double Outsiders: Migrant Women's Experiences of Marriage in a County-Level City

>> A significant increase in migration, and especially rural-to-urban migration, has accompanied China's economic reforms. Although initially scholars described women as "associational" migrants (who migrated because their spouse migrated or lived elsewhere), more recently, significant independent migration among women has been widely acknowledged.[1] As a consequence, attention is now devoted to women who move from rural to urban areas to take advantage of jobs or other opportunities to earn money.[2] Though the shift in focus is warranted given that most women report that they migrate for economic reasons, we contend that researchers must be careful not to focus solely on migrant women's working and living conditions in urban places. Marriage and family remain important dimensions of their lives.[3]

The 1990 Population Census revealed that nearly one third of female permanent migrants, i.e., those who changed their *hukou* (household registration) upon migration, reported moving for marriage.[4] In addition, many temporary female migrants, who move initially for economic reasons, marry and settle away from their home villages. In this way, they too become permanent migrants.[5] Women who move for economic reasons sometimes marry someone from the urban town or city where they work, a suburb just outside, or perhaps another village.[6] Usually, they will reside in their new husband's village or hometown. Irrespective of the destination, the experience of migration has implications for marriage. Women marry differently because of their migration experience. In this chapter we ask: How are these marriages through migration different from other marriages? Moreover, how do migrant women, particularly rural-born women, fare when they marry into another setting?

In China, a migrant and a wife share something in common. Both, albeit in very different ways, are outsiders in a new community. From the perspective of local people, migrants are outsiders who bring with them different ways of speaking, seeing, and living. In the context of family life, women are similarly seen as literal and symbolic outsiders. This is because marriage is traditionally patrilineally and patrilocally organized. Upon marriage, women typically leave their natal family to join the family of their husband, moving into that community. To the marriage union they bring their own surname, a daily reminder to those around them that they come from outside the family and the community. Sometimes, when women migrate *and* marry some distance away from their home village, often moving into a more prosperous community and family, these two statuses converge; such women negotiate day-to-day life as "double outsiders." One married migrant woman, originally from northern Jiangsu, explained her experience this way:

> Yes, local people really look down on us because we come from a poor area. I suffered terribly from the negative attitudes of my husband's relatives. It is not such a problem that other people look down on outsiders from poor places, since I do not have to see them often. But it is a different feeling to find that the whole family looks down on me and my mother's family. I have to endure this attitude all the time. And I have to meet the relatives often. I really feel I'm a sad outsider to this family when the whole family gets together at Chinese New Year. Then I always cry and miss my distant mother. But according to custom I have to stay in my mother-in-law's home during Chinese New Year.

Our chapter considers the marriage experiences of these "double outsiders." Drawing on fieldwork completed in 1998, we examine migrant women's marriage experiences in the Special Economic and Tax Waiver Zone (hereafter referred to as SEZ) of Zhangjiagang in Jiangsu province. We observe that rural women who marry in their migration destination experience marriage differently from local women in the same community for multidimensional reasons. First, their marriages are different because of whom, how, and why they marry. Second, they experience married life differently because as migrants, they are outsiders in the local community, often physically distant from networks of family and friends and perceived differently within their new families because of their outsider status. Within this context, however, migrant women who marry deploy active strategies to negotiate their "double outsider" position. Before we begin our analysis, we first describe marriage migration in contemporary China more generally, then introduce our fieldwork site.

TRENDS AND CHARACTERISTICS OF MARRIAGE MIGRATION

Rural women in China have almost always migrated at the time of marriage. Until recently, most of them married within a radius of 20 *li* (10 kilometers/6.2 miles) of, and usually in the same township as, their native village, or in a nearby township within the same county.[7] However, since economic reform women have increasingly migrated farther to marry, often into different counties or even into different provinces.[8] Figures from the 1990 Population Census reveal that approximately four million women migrated significant distances for marriage between 1985 and 1990.[9] The exact numbers depend on the data source and the definition of a move. Because many marriage migrants are not officially registered in marriage or household registration records, it is unclear how they would respond on a census form, and therefore some researchers suggest that even four million is a conservative estimate.[10] In general, research suggests an increasing trend toward long-distance marriage migration.

Women's motivation for marriage is multifaceted and depends on personal and family factors. Some women have a strong personal desire to escape poverty and achieve a more comfortable lifestyle through marriage; they view it as a means to staying in a better place. Their personal desires have a strong influence on marriage choice, but family context remains relevant. These women will likely promise to send money back to their families when they can. Other women do not necessarily desire to marry far away, but respond to family need. Family circumstances may shape their marriage options. Poor families may strongly encourage a daughter to accept a particular marriage that brings money into the family. This type of marriage, organized around family exchange, mirrors an older custom not much practiced today called "exchange marriage" (*huan qin*), where families exchanged daughters for their sons to marry. Today, families are more likely to "exchange" a daughter for the money that a good bride-price will bring and that can be used, for example, for an older brother's marriage or a younger brother's education.

Women who migrate and marry over long distances fall into three basic groups. The first group leave home specifically for the purpose of finding a husband. Their goal is usually "to find a better husband" (*zhao ge hao zhangfu*), often someone from an area more prosperous than their natal village.[11] The second group is sometimes called working sisters (*dagongmei*). They are usually young and single temporary migrants who initiate their rural-to-urban migration for the purpose of looking for a job, learning a work skill, or, more vaguely, "to expand their horizons and get a glimpse of urban life" (*jian shimian, kankan chengliren de shenghuo*). These young women often have a secondary interest in marriage, or "changing their lives forever," should they meet a suitable partner.[12] Many working sisters do settle down in their new localities, which are often richer villages, city suburbs, or small county-level cities.

The third group of women who marry far from their natal villages are those who have been tricked, abducted, or otherwise forced into marriage by human traffickers (see Sun, this volume). Some of these women may have been sold into marriage by their impoverished families. Trafficked brides usually marry poor men from the poorest of rural areas, or older or otherwise handicapped bachelors desperate for wives.[13] Such marriages are illegal and relatively rare, but occur nonetheless. Our discussion in this chapter concerns only the first two groups of marriage migrants, women who told us they moved initially for marriage or work.[14] These women married local men in our study site, and are both temporary and permanent migrants.

RESEARCH METHODOLOGY AND FIELDWORK SITE

The fieldwork that serves as the basis for this chapter was completed in April and May 1998 in Zhangjiagang, a county-level city with an SEZ in Jiangsu province. As part of this fieldwork, 120 formal interviews were completed with married women and men between the ages of 20 and 30 in four of the different townships comprising Zhangjiagang—Houcheng, Gangqu, Zhongxing, and Nansha—with 30 interviewees in each township. The interviews were designed to allow comparison. Sixty were completed with women, half of whom were locally born and half of whom were migrants. Of the latter, 17 had household registration in Zhangjiagang and 13 did not. All had marriage registration, or legal marriage, locally in Zhangjiagang.[15]

Likewise, 60 interviews were completed with men, half of whom had married a local woman and half of whom had married a recent migrant. To gain insight into the marriage experiences of migrant women, we detail migrant women's depictions of their own marriages and implicitly (and sometimes explicitly) contrast these with descriptions of their marriages by others. We also describe how those we interviewed represented marriages that involved migrant women differently from those that involved local women.

In addition to these individual interviews, twelve focus group meetings, three in each of the townships, were coordinated. Each group differed in the characteristics of the participants. One group included eight to ten migrant wives. Another included local men who had married migrant women. The final group included local officials who worked in departments that consider issues related to migrant women, such as the Civil Affairs Department, which registers marriages; the Family Planning Office; the Women's Federation Office; and the Public Security Bureau, which registers migration. We use these interviews to gain insight into local and official perceptions of migrant women's marriages and to strengthen our understandings and interpretations of individual experiences. They also provide insights into normative ideas regarding migrant women and the social implications of migration.

Zhangjiagang is a popular migrant destination and a relatively rich county-level city, where the net per capita income reached 5,409 *yuan* in 1996. This figure compares to a national average net per capita income of 1,926 *yuan* and a provincial measure of 3,029 *yuan* for the same year.[16] Zhangjiagang includes 26 towns and townships that are diverse in nature and that have characteristics of both rural and urban areas. Located between Shanghai and Suzhou, two modern and industrialized cities, Zhangjiagang had a population of about 820,000 in 1996. Although it is called a "city," more than half of its residents hold rural household registration records.

Zhangjiagang's status as a county-level city is significant. In this special category, the city government does not operate most of the work units, including factories. Work units tend to be organized at township levels of government or by village management committees. Other places of employment include private or joint venture enterprises. One consequence is that most people do not need urban household registration to legally work in nonagricultural jobs. Zhangjiagang, then, serves as an interesting site for this analysis; county-level cities, although popular migrant destinations, have received relatively little attention in studies of migration in China.

Social life in Zhangjiagang has a rural flavor to it. Local people are usually very familiar with their neighbors. Neighborhood women and men gossip with one another, and know and care about one another's families. Marriage customs also reflect practices that are more common in rural areas than in cities. Marriage is universal, and it is still important that the bride and groom be "matched" in terms of socioeconomic status (*men dang hu dui*). Although some young people date before marriage, formal introduction through a matchmaker, or go-between, is still widely practiced. Generally, the groom's family takes financial responsibility for the marriage, paying to build a house, paying the bride-price, and covering other expenses. After marriage, the couple is expected to stay in close contact with the groom's parents and support them in old age. A new bride is expected to face the big challenge of getting along with her in-laws, especially her mother-in-law.

Despite its rural character, Zhangjiagang has been changing rapidly in recent years, and residents suggest that the influx of migrants has grown considerably. Local people told us that since the 1990s many young women have been arriving to look for a "new world," with the intertwined hope of finding work and a desirable marriage. The marriage registration data provided by the civil administration offices of the townships where we did fieldwork confirm what we were told. For example, in 1996, nearly one third of all marriages in Zhongxing township involved a woman who had recently migrated.

In the following three sections we turn to our analysis. We begin with a description of the most common kinds of marriages among migrant women in Zhangjiagang. Next, we discuss migrant women's marriage experiences, highlighting the difficulties they describe. Finally, we outline the strategies they use in support of their marital and personal fulfillment.

MARRYING INTO ZHANGJIAGANG

Marriage migrants in China tend to originate in the poorer areas of the southwest and travel to the rural villages, towns, or county-level cities of the rich areas on the eastern coast. Jiangsu, with its rapid socioeconomic development, is one of the richer coastal provinces receiving marriage migrants. One study showed that 71 percent of the female marriage migrants in Jiangsu came from one of four provinces: Sichuan (29 percent), Guizhou (16 percent), Anhui (13 percent), and Yunnan (13 percent).[17] Our interviews similarly revealed that most of the migrant brides in Zhangjiagang came from these less economically developed provinces, and also from northern Jiangsu, which is far less developed than the south of the province.[18]

All the migrant brides came from agricultural backgrounds, although more than half had worked in township or private factories in Zhangjiagang before marriage. In Zhangjiagang, marriage migrants have not, for the most part, been able to switch their rural residence registration for urban registration through marriage. Even those who moved from a rural village to a rural Zhangjiagang township were not always able to change their household registration record. Wealthy rural townships, such as those where we conducted interviews, try to limit their population so that the official local economic statistics appear favorable. The central government evaluates local governments' success in maintaining a healthy economy through collecting a series of per capita economic measures, which are affected by population accounting. Wealthy communities also want to preserve limited resources, such as land, for local residents.

In addition to their rural roots, marriage migrants in Zhangjiagang are characterized by relative youth. The men and women we interviewed emphasized the youth of migrant brides. They reported that migrant women marry at younger ages than local women and are more likely to be in marriages with larger age differences between spouses. The average ages of those we interviewed are consistent with the patterns local people perceived. Among the 30 local men who married migrant women, the average age difference between husband and wife was 4.3 years. Among the 30 local men who married local women, the age difference was 1.1 years. A closer look at these patterns suggests that the larger age difference between spouses in migrant marriages is due, on the one hand, to older men marrying migrant women and, on the other hand, to migrant women marrying earlier than their local counterparts. We hesitate to draw any firm conclusion from calculations based on our limited sample, but we think it notable that the marriage patterns observed by local and migrant women and their husbands are consistent with the simple tabulations our data allowed. At the very least, youth is a salient characteristic of migrant brides in the eyes of the married people we interviewed in Zhangjiagang.

The interviewees described a host of reasons they thought helped to explain why migrant women marry younger than local women. Key among them is the marriage custom in a woman's home village. Those who come from places where women marry young expect, and are expected by their families, to marry at younger ages. Also, working sisters are eager to marry because they seek stability and legitimacy in their new place of residence. Their hope is that marriage will help to anchor them in the locality and diminish their outsider status. In addition, through the permanency marriage suggests, they symbolically achieve the better life they sought when they migrated. Marriage thus adds certainty and a measure of success to their quest. Practically, it may provide women, through permanent residency, more—and more secure—work opportunities. Local employers may also view married migrant women as more trustworthy than "temporary" working sisters, unconnected to local families. As one migrant woman who had two years' experience as a working sister before marriage explained:

> I came here as a working sister in this garment factory four years ago, when I was eighteen years old. [According to custom in my hometown in Guizhou], women at this age need to think about looking for a future husband. But I never thought about going back to my home village to get married. I didn't want to spend my lifetime in that poor village just like my parents. In truth, I wanted to change my status here from an outsider to a resident. I like not only working here but also living in a good place like Zhangjiagang. Marrying a local man was the best way to reach my aim. So I married my husband two years ago, after being introduced to him by a colleague in our factory. Now I can think of my future as a woman of Zhangjiagang. It is very different from being a working sister. As a working sister, I felt I had no clear future; it was just a matter of living from one day to the next, and I could have been laid off at any time. . . . Yes, almost all of my working sister friends have the same feeling as me. We left our home village looking for a better life. But the life of a working sister is uncertain. We should get married to a local man if we really want [to stay here and have a] stable life.

To better understand migrant women's marriages, we need to have a sense of the men they marry. Our interviews made it clear that one reason migrant women's marriages are unlike those of local women is that they marry different kinds of men. The migrant women who participated in our research tended to marry men who were poorer, both economically and educationally, than other men in the area, or men who were in poor health. In many instances, migrant women married men who had difficulty finding local women to be their wives. Often, neither these men nor their families perceived a migrant woman to be the ideal marriage partner. These findings are consistent with those reported by C. Cindy Fan, this volume, based on her analysis of interviews with rural women migrants from Sichuan and Anhui provinces.[19]

The system of patrilineal, patrilocal marriages makes the characteristics of husbands' families relevant, especially when a woman marries at a distance from her natal family. Migrant women in Zhangjiagang tended to marry into four kinds of families: relatively poor families; families with only one or no in-laws; families with a son who had a physical or mental disability; or richer families who made money doing business outside of town. We describe each of these situations in greater detail below.

In Zhangjiagang, as elsewhere, men from poor families have always had more difficulty than others in finding a wife. In the past, these men usually found brides in the poorer villages of northern Jiangsu. Since economic reforms and the associated relaxation of migration restrictions, women have been migrating to Zhangjiagang in greater numbers from northern Jiangsu and other impoverished areas. Poor families with unmarried sons, and especially sons over 25 years old, tend to be the "receiving" families of these women. Among those we interviewed, average annual family income was consistent with this story. Family income was markedly lower for couples that included a migrant woman (6,600 *yuan*) than for couples where both spouses were local (11,700 *yuan*).

These differences in wealth were also reflected in bride-prices. Among the men we interviewed, those with a migrant wife reported that they paid on average 14,742 *yuan*, while men who married a local woman spent on average 28,154 *yuan*. While the women we interviewed reported lower bride-prices than the men,[20] they too indicated that bride-prices for local women were at least double those for migrant women.[21] We caution, however, that bride-price is not always about the wealth of a family. Richer families who have sons with undesirable characteristics may be unable to attract local women even if they can pay the high bride-price. Moreover, the price may be paid in different ways when a marriage occurs to a migrant woman whose natal family lives far away. There may be fewer smaller gifts or just one large lump-sum payment rather than many separate payments.

Although in Zhangjiagang migrant women on average marry poorer men than local women, for most migrant women these marriages nonetheless provide what they consider to be comfortable living circumstances. Jiangsu is a wealthy province and Zhangjiagang, while still a rural county-level city, is a relatively rich community. Thus, even though migrant women marry poor men in Zhangjiagang, they can expect a much higher standard of living than they might have had in their home villages.

Migrant women are also more likely than local women to marry into families with absent or deceased in-laws. Such families, especially when there is no mother-in-law, tend to be less desirable to potential brides. In families with no mother-in-law, young brides are expected to take on more household responsibilities, for they will not have help with domestic work or taking care of a baby. This pattern was striking among our interviewees. Among the 30 men who had married migrant women, 18 had lost one or both parents by the time they were looking for a wife. Even when his parents are alive, a man can have difficulty finding a local wife if one or both parents are ill. Potential new brides know they will immediately carry responsibility for the care of sick in-laws. Families with sick in-laws may also have economic difficulties due to the lost labor of the sick people and the medical expenses associated with treatment.

Families with a son who is physically or mentally disabled are also more likely to embrace a migrant woman as a daughter-in-law. Because of the strong discrimination men with disabilities face in China,[22] they tend to have difficulty finding a local marriage partner. The women in our study who married men with disabilities in Zhangjiagang were not themselves disabled. Among the 30 female migrants, two married men with mental disabilities. Both women were healthy and literate, but came from very poor families in rural northern Jiangsu. One woman told us that she chose this marriage because it provided money that could be used for the bride-price her older brother would need to pay to marry. The other woman told us that she married her husband because his family promised to give her family 10,000 *yuan*, a very large sum of money for a family in a poor village. It was to be used for day-to-day survival and for the school fees of her two younger brothers. Neither of these women was inclined to talk about herself much, however. When we asked about their lives after marriage in Zhangjiagang, they emphasized only that they were satisfied with being well treated by their in-laws. It is difficult to know how to understand their comments. It may be that the comfortable life they enjoy in Zhangjiagang makes the other difficulties they encounter worthwhile. Or it may be that they discuss their satisfaction relative to their expectations for happiness. Although these women may have grown to love their husbands, they indicated that they married to satisfy the needs of their natal families, not to maximize their personal fulfillment. We might expect them to discuss their satisfaction in this context as well.

Finally, some migrant women marry into well-off Zhangjiagang families. This is the ideal for many but the good fortune of only a few. Among the 30 female migrants we interviewed, eight came to know their husband at work. Some met their spouse in the factories of Zhangjiagang and others met their Zhangjiagang husband while working together with him in a factory elsewhere, and moved to Zhangjiagang, their husband's home, upon marriage. Our discussions revealed that the "receiving" families tended to have migration experiences of their own and were more comfortable with migrants and "outsiders" in general. Many earned money through some business experience outside of town. It is unclear whether the women who were in these marriages had different background circumstances than other migrant women. Certainly, as a group they appeared to have more choice about the men they married. Their marriages reflected this difference and their relationships with their husbands seemed a more prominent feature of their family lives.

Many working sisters aspire to marry into successful Zhangjiagang families, but it is usually not an option because they come from poor families and are less educated than daughters from wealthier families in Zhangjiagang. In fact, for most working sisters, finding *any* suitable marriage partner is difficult. Their migration experiences often lead them to be more urban and independent, compromising their ability and desire to marry in their home village. Additionally, they quickly age out of their home marriage market, where younger ages at marriage prevail. Because working sisters become less attractive potential wives in their local villages, they may be more willing to consider men who are thought to be the least desirable marriage partners in Zhangjiagang. As families in rural villages see their daughters' local eligibility decline the longer they are away, they too express concern, creating additional pressures for working sisters to find a husband. There is little question that this is an important dimension to being a single working sister. One migrant woman with five years' experience as a working sister said:

> In the winter of 1990, just after the Spring Festival of that year, when I was only eighteen, I went to Suzhou SEZ with three other girls from my home village in Sichuan. We worked on the factory production line for three years. After that, I worked in a beauty salon for another two years. Time flew by, and in 1995 I realized that I had turned twenty-three years old in a flash. I still did not want to go back to my hometown to get married. According to the custom of my hometown, girls should be betrothed before twenty. My parents were really worrying about my getting married at that time, but they did not ask me to go back home. In other words, they just hoped I would get married no matter where I stayed. At that time, someone from my village who got married into Zhangjiagang several years ago introduced me to my husband. . . . Then I married into Zhangjiagang in late 1995. I finally settled down in Jiangsu. My parents were very glad to see that I had finally married. A friend who went to Suzhou with me is still single and working in Shanghai now. It is difficult for her to find a husband in Shanghai, even in

the suburbs, since she is a rural girl. Yet she never thinks of going back to our hometown. Now, according to the custom of our home village, she is too old to find a suitable husband. Her parents feel sad about their daughter's life; it is unusual for a woman to be single with no reason. Compared to her, I am lucky to have settled down in Zhangjiagang.

As we have detailed in this section, migrant women experience marriage differently than local women, not only because of the experience of migration but also because they marry different men and may come from rural, poor families. Migrant women in our study were more likely than local women to marry men from relatively poor families; men from families with one or no parents-in-law; men with a disability; or men from richer families doing business. Thus, we should expect their marriages to be different than those of local women. Likewise, migrant women's natal families differ from those of local women. These differences shape how migrant women experience married life in Zhangjiagang, the subject of the next section.

LINKING LIVES AND FITTING IN: BEING AN OUTSIDER IN MARRIAGE

In the previous section we discussed how marriage provides a sense of permanency that is welcome to working sisters living in Zhangjiagang. With it, however, come new demands and expectations. No longer short-term residents, married migrants in Zhangjiagang have a greater desire to fit in. They want to become part of their husband's family and part of their neighborhood. Simultaneous with marriage and their new desire to build these linkages is some loss of community with the other single working women with whom they used to live, work, and share day-to-day experiences. Now they must negotiate daily life with a husband, and often in-laws and neighbors as well. For many this transition is difficult at first, and isolation is a very common feeling during the first year of marriage. It is especially strong for migrant women. Although all but two said that they had had a "smooth" family life since marriage, almost every migrant woman we interviewed in Zhangjiagang told us of a personal experience of isolation. Often it was not limited to the first year of marriage.

Migrant women who marry into Zhangjiagang feel isolated for several reasons. First, they often have little connection with their natal family. Due to physical distance, migrant women do not have much opportunity to return home to seek advice on marriage and other matters. Many sent home letters and some sent money once or twice a year, usually before the Chinese New Year. However, seventeen of the thirty migrant women interviewed had never returned to their mother's house after marriage.[23] Beyond that, however, migrant women may feel cut off from their family because their ability to communicate with their parents is limited. Their parents probably do not have access to a telephone and may not be able to write letters easily. By contrast, local married women do retain significant ties with their natal family; they often ask for suggestions and help from their mother and other family members when they face problems with their husband or parents-in-law. Some even stay in their mother's home for a while to "adjust" their feelings as they make the transition into their new family. Unfortunately, migrant women generally do not have this support, nor can they easily turn to their new neighbors to seek help and win sympathy. For most, this means that the relationships they build within their husband's family are especially important, and they work hard at being a good wife and daughter-in-law. These contrasts between the situations of local married women and migrant women are illustrated in the following quotations.

Local woman

My parents are living in another town, Zhongxing, which is about 10 *li* (5 km/3.1 mi) from here. I usually go back home once a month. Sometimes I take my daughter and go to see my mother and stay there overnight. . . . I went to my mother's house when I had a row with my husband, but this has only happened two or three times since we got married four years ago. . . . Yes, there is a telephone in my mother's house, and I call my parents when I want to talk to them. I also often call my older sister who is living in Yangshe town. I ask for advice from my parents and my sister when I have difficulties.

Migrant woman

My home is very far away in rural Guizhou. I really missed home when I first came here, although I feel my mother-in-law is very nice to me. I often feel lonely and homesick. I did not understand the Zhangjiagang accent when I first came here, but now I can talk with a local accent. I have never gone back to see my parents since I got married to my husband three years ago. . . . Yes, I keep in touch with my parents with letters, not by telephone; that is not available in my mother's house. I write two to three letters to them each year, but I get only one to two letters back. They need to ask my brother to help to write letters, as they do not know how to write. Sometimes, people from my home village (*laoxiang*) come and convey oral messages from my parents. I try never to tell my parents about my problems in my letters. I always report good news, because I do not think they can help me in any way, and I would not want to make them worry about my life here. So I have to solve any problem by myself. Unlike local girls, we cannot do things just as we please. We have to build a good relationship with our in-laws.

Migrant women can also feel isolated because they are less well acquainted with their new husband than are local married women. Some migrant women, particularly those who are not working sisters, hardly know their husband at all before marriage, while some local women may have grown up with their husband. When migrant women marry a man with developmental disabilities, the feeling of isolation can be more pronounced. These women indicated that their relationships with their in-laws were very important emotionally and financially. The situation of one such migrant woman was described to us by the Women's Federation cadre living next door to her:

> She came to Zhangjiagang from a poor village in northern Jiangsu and got married into our town last year. Her husband is somehow mentally disabled. Fortunately, her parents-in-law have been treating her very well. This poor woman, her husband cannot speak clearly. I don't think she could continue to live in this family without good relations with her parents-in-law, who are very nice and care about her. Of course, she also tries hard to maintain good relations with her parents-in-law. She has to if she still wants to keep this marriage. It is a pity, the husband can't even talk to his wife clearly. She [the wife] does not often talk to our neighbors. People in this town often look down on migrant women, especially those who come from rural northern Jiangsu. People don't say anything, but you can tell from their attitudes. . . . Why? I don't know, maybe because they are poor and not well-educated. There's no clear reason.

As the Women's Federation cadre alludes to above, another reason migrant women feel isolation has to do with the way others, both within their new family and in their community, perceive them. Women, their spouses, and community leaders gave numerous examples in our interviews that suggested that migrant women were perceived as untrustworthy and self-interested. They thought migrant women were less committed to their marriage and family and were interested only in personal, short-term economic gain. There is little question that these perceptions shaped the day-to-day experiences of migrant women as wives, family members, and community members.

Tensions about the trustworthiness of migrant women often arose over issues involving money. Here, the nature of the marital arrangement itself was often relevant. Because migrant women came from poor families, the agreement usually included a lump-sum bride-price that went to the bride's family either before or after the wedding to help them overcome economic difficulties. This form of bride-price payment reinforces the "economic transaction" aspect of the exchange. Because of this arrangement, some migrant women were thought to be always plotting to get more money from their husband's family to support their poor natal family. One repercussion of this stated or unstated suspicion was that migrant women were much less likely than local women to have control over managing their household's resources, particularly cash. This was true regardless of whether the couple shared a house or other resources with their parents-in-law. There was some indication that migrant women were considered more trustworthy once they had given birth to a child. However, even this did not render some women trustworthy enough, according to our interview participants. Local women and men told us that some marriage migrants in Zhangjiagang ran off after gaining access to enough money. The following quotations illustrate the differing financial arrangements in households where the wife is a local and those where the wife is a migrant.

> *A local woman who has been married three years*
> Yes, I, just like other women, need to manage our family income and expenses for everyday living. We separate our income from my parents-in-law's. My husband does not care about buying everyday things. We discuss big decisions about our family life, including buying expensive things and financial support for our parents. I take the responsibility for everyday life. . . . Of course, I know that he trusts me, why not? In Zhangjiagang, most women manage their family's finances. The husbands give their salaries to their wives to manage.

> *A migrant woman who has been married two years*
> Yes, I take care of our family's everyday expenses, such as buying food in grocery stores. But my husband manages our

family income and our savings accounts. It is hard to say whether he trusts me or not. I am his wife and we have a son together. But I know my in-laws feel my husband should take care of our family resources.

A family planning official

It is hard for migrant women to be trusted. There are some problems, particularly in the first few years. In some cases, migrant women just used marriage to get money . . . so families with migrant brides feel nervous. They are afraid to give them money. Maybe they will run away someday. Some husbands in these families also worry that migrant wives will try to send some money to help their poor parents in their hometown without telling them. This kind of thing happens sometimes in Zhangjiagang.

A migrant woman's husband

I think my wife and I trust each other. Her parents are living far away in Sichuan. We send some money to support them before every Spring Festival. . . . Yes, I manage our family savings and income, but I discuss our family expenses with my wife. We make decisions together. My mother has some traditional ideas. . . . Yes, she always worries about my life. But she has felt much better since we had a son last year. She thinks my marriage and family life are now more stable. In fact, it is hard to see it this way. There have been many divorce cases in Zhangjiagang in recent years.

Feelings of isolation come from family experiences but also from experiences living in the community as an outsider. In every township and village where we conducted research, we found that people clearly remembered and easily pointed out migrant brides, suggesting that they continued to be considered outsiders. Of course, migrant women's dialects were a daily reminder of their status. A migrant woman from Sichuan who speaks very good Zhangjiagang dialect told us:

People in Zhangjiagang look down on people from outside of south Jiangsu, particularly people from the north of Jiangsu and other poor provinces. When I first came here three years ago, people never tried to understand what I said with a Sichuan accent. I could tell they looked down on me by their attitude even when they said nothing to my face. They only used the local dialect when they talked with me, regardless of whether or not I

> could understand. I was cheated many times in the free market because I couldn't speak like a local woman. My husband and mother-in-law thought I was stupid when I was cheated. Fortunately, I learned Zhangjiagang dialect very quickly. Two years later, I talked just like a local woman. I felt my husband's relatives and neighbors started to accept me once I could talk with them using the local dialect.

Because migrant women tend to have less dense family networks locally, friendships are all the more important. However, it is not always easy for these women to communicate and develop friendships with local people. Frequently, migrants, perceived as outsiders, are not asked to participate in neighborhood activities. For example, few migrant women had been invited to join in the preparation for a neighbor's wedding or the delivery of a new baby. To be included in these kinds of traditional activities in the neighborhood is often a symbol of respect and friendship. Many migrant brides found it difficult to gain acceptance at this level.

When we interviewed men married to migrant women, we found that few were sensitive to the isolation their wives felt. The men thought discrimination against outsiders was understandable, since local people typically look down on people from northern Jiangsu and other poor areas. In short, husbands were often not their wives' allies when it came to confronting the negative perceptions in their communities and families. Indeed, husbands shared and perpetuated some of these perceptions.

Local stereotypes about migrant women abounded. In focus group discussions, local women told us that migrant women experience discrimination because they are lazy, having grown up in poorer areas where the pace of life is slower. One local woman said that some migrants are swindlers who will leave for another place and another marriage once they get their bride-price money in Zhangjiagang. A family planning officer told us that some local people hate working sisters because they are young and eager to find boyfriends or husbands, tempting local men to cheat on or abandon their wives. This officer emphasized that there was some truth to this perception. She explained that the divorce rate in Zhangjiagang increased dramatically in the early 1990s, and that the increase coincided with the influx of migrants. Local women were most concerned about this issue. A family planning worker told us:

> One really bad thing the working sisters did was to destroy local people's marriages and family relations. More and more local men divorced their local wives and then remarried young and

beautiful working sisters. Of course, the problems are not only on the side of working sisters but also on the side of local men. But local people, particularly married women, just hate those migrant girls. After getting married to a divorced man, a migrant woman will still face negative attitudes from her local neighbors, and the family members and relatives of her husband.

In sum, migrant women's experiences of isolation in marriage and feelings of being an outsider are borne out by their own stories, by the accounts of their marriages that men provide, and by the discussions we had with others in the community. Their isolated, outsider status was further confirmed in local power structures. Our focus group discussions included twenty Women's Federation cadres in four townships. Despite the strong presence of migrant women in Zhangjiagang, all twenty cadres were local women. Even at the village level, no outsider worked as a Women's Federation cadre in these four townships.

SEEKING A PLACE: STRATEGIES OF INTEGRATION

Despite its symbolic permanence, marriage in Zhangjiagang does not transform working sisters or other migrant women into locals. Marriage to a local man, though the dream of many working sisters, does not always bring happiness. In fact, more often than not, it heightens feelings of isolation. Still, many of the migrant wives in Zhangjiagang expressed positive outlooks and told us of the ways they devised to find happiness in their married lives. Most had a two-part strategy—though the word "strategy" may suggest more planned, deliberate action than was directly conveyed by the women themselves. Nonetheless, the women told of behaviors that were intended either to win the respect, love, and trust of their husband's family or to build social networks within their community.

Although a good relationship with the husband's family is usually desirable to wives elsewhere, it seemed especially important to migrant women in Zhangjiagang. A striking feature of the interviews was that the women emphasized good relationships with their husband's family, and especially their mother-in-law, more than they did a good relationship with their husband. The isolation from their natal family and status as outsider in the village, as described earlier, played a role in this desire for a strong relationship with their mother-in-law. Most migrant women strove to avoid conflicts with their husband and his parents and tried to make their parents-in-law like them. Thus, a migrant woman from Guizhou said:

> When I was on my way to come to get married in Zhangjia-
> gang, my mother told me again and again about the saying
> "Marry a chicken, follow a chicken; marry a dog, follow a dog
> (*jia ji sui ji, jia gou sui gou*)." She also suggested to me that I nev-
> er argue with my mother-in-law, since I would have nobody to
> support me. As a migrant bride, I knew that I had to follow my
> husband and respect my mother-in-law when I first came to this
> family. My husband is the oldest son of my mother-in-law, and
> his father passed away two years ago. So my husband and I have
> been trying our best to work for this family and to make my
> mother-in-law happy. I have also tried very hard to get along
> with my two married sisters-in-law and two unmarried
> brothers-in-law.

Migrant brides know of two important things they can do to make their husband and in-laws happy. The first is to have a child, particularly a son, as soon as possible after getting married. Many migrant women have their first child within the first two years of their marriage, a little sooner than most of their local counterparts. Local family planning officials explained that migrant women are eager to have a son to gain a stable and smooth life in the family. In fact, they can be so eager that they violate the one-child policy, which is strictly enforced in Zhangjiagang. Two of the thirty migrant women tried to have a son after giving birth to a girl, despite family planning policy prohibitions against a second child, even for those whose first was a girl.[24] A woman who had been a family planning worker since 1989 said:

> The migrant women are the main target group of our family
> planning work. I have found that the migrant women are more
> likely to have earlier marriages and pregnancies than local wo-
> men, and compared with local women, they have a stronger de-
> sire for a son to please their parents-in-law and enhance their
> status in the family. Some local people feel that a daughter is
> better than a son when it comes to caring for parents in their
> old age. But most migrant women are still trying to have a son.
> Some have tried to violate our local population policy by get-
> ting pregnant a second time.

Another way women attempt to win the favor of their husband and his family is to make economic contributions to the family. It seemed that migrant women in Zhangjiagang were somewhat more likely to continue working after marriage and childbirth than local women. Although most mothers of young children in China work, among those who participated in our interviews, local women indicated that they spent more time at home caring for a child under the age of three than did migrant women.[25] Whether or not they were in paid employment, migrant women told of the great energy they put into domestic work and child care to show their husbands, parents-in-law, and neighbors that they are hardworking, virtuous wives and daughters-in-law. Attention to domestic work and child care is also one way that migrant wives try to dispel myths that they are lazy.

Migrant women's strategy in the community is somewhat different. Although certainly many of the women we interviewed tried through hard work and a positive attitude to win the respect and friendship of neighbors and other community members, more often than not they relied more on friendships with other migrant women in Zhangjiagang for support.[26] For some this worked well. A migrant woman who had worked for two years as a working sister said:

> I got married last October. I have some very good friends from my hometown still working in Zhongxing town. We try to see each other and talk for a while when we miss each other. When my friends from my hometown run into difficulties, they come to see me in my home. I have always tried my best to help them, particularly those women who have no family. There are more and more people coming from my hometown, and we keep in touch and help each other. When people go home and then come back here, I always get some news about my home. Occasionally, I ask my friends to take gifts to my parents, and my parents also ask them to bring something back for me.

Not all women had access to such well-developed networks. Instead, many built new networks, inviting other women from their home villages, and sometimes family members, to Zhangjiagang. They would persuade relatives and friends to come to Zhangjiagang to work or marry by telling them about the economic advantages of the place. Among the migrant wives we interviewed, eighteen told us that relatives or others from their villages had come to Zhangjiagang since they themselves had arrived. Twenty-six of the thirty migrant women had experience creating this type of linkage. One migrant woman even introduced her best friend from childhood in Guizhou to her new husband's brother. Her friend then became her sister-in-law in Zhangjiagang. The woman told us that she felt much happier after her sister-in-law moved into the family, because the two women were able to talk every day and they understood each other well. Building these networks has spillover effects too. Through introducing relatives and villagers to others in Zhangjiagang, migrant women expand their network of social relationships with local people. This is particularly true when they introduce men in Zhangjiagang to marriage partners. Successful introductions allow them to play the well-respected role of the go-between in marriage. A migrant woman who had come from a village far away in Yunnan three years ago said:

> I felt terribly lonely in the first few months, although my mother-in-law was very nice to me. My husband has two younger brothers. To pay bride-price for three sons was a heavy burden for my mother-in-law, particularly since my father-in-law died several years ago and left unpaid bills. After asking for the agreement of my mother-in-law and brothers-in-law, I wrote to my friends in my hometown to introduce my brothers-in-law and to give them some background information on Zhangjiagang. Finally, a friend in my home village decided to marry one of my brothers-in-law. I was even happier than them, as I got a friend into this family! My mother-in-law and husband were also very happy with this result.

When migrant women marry they often must navigate life as "double outsiders," outsiders in both their family and their community. Marrying far from home, they are usually less able than local women to rely on their natal family for support and advice after marriage. In addition, because they are usually from a poorer rural area, community members and family members, including their husband, may hold negative stereotypes about them. In particular, they are thought to be less trustworthy and less hardworking. Despite these obstacles, many of the migrant women we met in Zhangjiagang told of their happiness at marrying into the area, and of their amicable family life. Their "smoothing" strategies suggested they went to great lengths to create a fulfilling marriage and family life. Many worked hard to be a model daughter-in-law and wife, a woman who works hard, spends money wisely, and takes care of her family. By also recruiting other women from their home families and villages to come to Zhangjiagang, they expanded their social networks and reduced their feelings of isolation. Although migrant women described the difficulties they encountered as double outsiders, they were quick to emphasize that their lives were better than they might have been had they married in their home villages, and rarely expressed regret.

Although some officials and many locals in Zhangjiagang see marriage migrants as a social problem, there is little reason to think that rural women will stop marrying into Zhangjiagang anytime soon. In fact, we should expect these marriages to become even more common. Recruitment networks gain momentum as they grow, and married migrant women are actively strategizing to expand their networks. In addition, the reform of household registration rules has allowed children to take their father's household registration. Prior to this reform, at the end of the 1990s, children had to take the registration of their mother, which made starting a family with a rural woman less attractive to men with urban registration. Now that urban-registered men are assured that their children can also be assigned urban registration status, thus receiving better benefits such as education, more local men may be willing to marry a rural migrant woman.

Focusing on Zhangjiagang allows us to present a picture of migrant women's marriages in a typical county-level city. Despite the substantial migration to these smaller cities, research on migration has tended to focus on the larger cities of China and their associated SEZs. Migrant women who marry into Zhangjiagang experience marriage differently from migrant women who marry into cities such as Beijing and Shanghai. Working in and marrying into a county-level city allows women to both maintain and reshape some of their rural traditions in their new setting. At the same time, they are less likely to encounter or live among extensive communities of migrants from their home area (i.e., migrant enclaves), compared to women who migrate to larger cities. Thus, many women who migrate and marry into a county-level city have marriage and family experiences that differ not only from those of local women but also from those of their sisters migrating to big cities. Our analysis suggests that women who migrate and marry into a county-level city, despite being double outsiders, can and do successfully make themselves "a place" that, even if it is at times isolated, can also bring happiness.

ACKNOWLEDGMENTS

Our collaboration on this work was made possible through a Fulbright Award to Lin Tan. We are most grateful to Arianne Gaetano and Tamara Jacka, who carefully read this chapter and provided excellent substantive and editorial suggestions. We also thank Yu-Hua Chen, Aaron Katz, and Michael White for insightful discussion, and Juhua Yang for thoughtful written comments and assistance with reference material. Kelley Smith and Cendhi Arias of the Brown Population Studies and Training Center provided excellent assistance with manuscript preparation.

NOTES

1. Yang 2000.
2. Cai 1997.
3. Yang 1992; Yang et al. 1999.
4. Tan and Gilmartin 1998.
5. For a discussion of the distinction between "permanent," "official," "*hukou*" migrants and "temporary," "unofficial," "non*hukou*" migrants, see introduction, this volume.
6. Liu and Li 2000.
7. Gu 1991.
8. Tan and Gilmartin 1998; Tian 1991; Yang 1992.
9. Li Shuzhuo 1994:26–28; Tan and Gilmartin 1998.
10. Zhang 1994.
11. Li 1995; Tan and Gilmartin 2001.
12. Tian 1991; Wang 1992. See also Beynon, this volume.
13. Zhang Zhenhua 1990.
14. We acknowledge our simplification. The reasons women move are complex and hardly singular. Indeed, women can move for work *and* marriage, as well as for other reasons.
15. To be legal, a marriage must be registered with the Department of Civil Affairs. Usually this requires that either the husband or wife have local household registration. However, in some rural areas, "de facto" marriage, or marriage without legal marriage registration, is practiced. In Zhangjiagang de facto marriage is not common.
16. China Population Information and Research Center 1997.
17. Yang 1992.
18. The social networks that develop between migration origin and destination communities shape this distribution. For more on migrant networks, see Massey and España 1987. Historically people in Zhangjiagang have thought of northern Jiangsu as a poor place, and there is a long tradition of stigmatizing women from this area. In the past, when most marriages occurred between men and women living in the same county or township, women from northern Jiangsu would occasionally marry in the south to bring money to their families. The discrimination experienced by people from northern Jiangsu, or Subei people, is widespread, extending well beyond Zhangjiagang. See Honig 1992.
19. See also Fan and Huang 1998:227–51.
20. Bride-price includes cash and other transfers, such as furniture, household goods, and clothing. Men and women may count what is included differently. For example, men whose families purchase the furniture may be more likely to include the cost of these items in bride-price calculations. Women may be less likely to count furniture and more likely to count cash and clothes, because these are more

clearly items transferred to them or their families. Men likely have greater incentive to inflate bride-price.

21. The bride-price figures we use do not include building a house, which is becoming another necessary cost in Zhangjiagang.

22. See, for example, Rosenthal 2001a.

23. Although, as discussed by Judd 1989:525–44, the *niangjia*, or mother's family, is important for married women in China, migrant women from very poor, distant places are less able to visit and communicate regularly with their natal families.

24. In many rural areas since the beginning of the 1990s, couples whose first child was a girl have been allowed to have a second child. This is not the case in urban areas like Zhangjiagang, however. For more details on the one-child policy and local variation in the one-child policy see Greenhalgh 1986; Short and Zhai 1998; and Winckler 2002.

25. Data from an eight-province multipurpose survey in China reveal that working mothers are common and their work involvement is not especially responsive to the birth of a child. For more details on the relationship between work and child care see Short et al. 2002. For more details on changes in work in response to a birth see Entwisle and Chen 2002.

26. See also Fan, this volume, on migrant women's social networks.

>> *Part 3*

CHANGING VILLAGE LIFE

C. Cindy Fan

6. Out to the City and Back to the Village: The Experiences and Contributions of Rural Women Migrating from Sichuan and Anhui

>> A great deal of attention, scholarly and otherwise, has focused on the massive rural-to-urban migration in China since the beginning of economic reforms, but researchers have only recently begun to examine the role of gender in migration.[1] Most of their works highlight structural relations, such as the impact of political, sociocultural, and economic determinants on men's and women's positions in the labor market and on their roles in the village household. Relatively little attention has been given to the agency of migrants and the contributions they make. This is due in part to a lack of empirical field-based information, and also to researchers' general emphasis on broad trends rather than migrants' direct experiences. In this chapter, I use data from a survey of village households in Sichuan and Anhui to examine rural women migrants' experiences. The data consist of first-person and detailed accounts by migrants of their migration and job search processes and of their views about a variety of issues. The survey is a rare and valuable source of qualitative data that is uniquely suitable for studying migrants' experiences and contributions. I compare male and female migrants in broad terms, but I highlight the experiences of rural women.

Most Chinese rural women who migrate to work in urban areas maintain close ties with their home village. The vast majority are young and single, and they return to the countryside upon marriage. The experiences that they have gained during migrant work and the contributions they make to their village enable them to be potential sources and agents of social and economic change in China's countryside.

In this chapter, I emphasize four aspects of migrant women's experiences. First, I examine the economic motivations and contributions of women migrants and stress that rural women, when given the opportunity to pursue off-farm work, are as economically active as their male counterparts, and that their remittances[2] are important means for improving their families' well-being. Second, I illustrate the central role female migrants play in forging networks of rural-to-urban migrants. These networks are highly gendered. They facilitate the migration of inexperienced women migrants but also channel them into segregated jobs and homogenize their urban experiences. Third, I show that urban work experiences can empower women migrants and enable them to become potential agents of social change in rural areas. Fourth, I argue that the sociocultural constraints facing rural women remain powerful limitations on their economic contributions and their agency in fostering social change. Central to these constraints are expectations of marriage and the traditional gender roles within marriage.

THE SICHUAN AND ANHUI SURVEY

The Sichuan and Anhui Survey was conducted by the Research Center for the Rural Economy in the Ministry of Agriculture in 1995.[3] Sichuan in western China and Anhui in central China are two major origins of rural-to-urban migrants, especially those headed for destinations in eastern and southern China. Though Anhui is geographically closer to China's developed eastern seaboard, it shares with Sichuan relatively low levels of economic development and a large surplus of rural labor. The survey consisted of two parts. The first part involved three villages each from two counties in Sichuan and two counties in Anhui. In each village, 15 migrant households (where one or more household members had migrant work experience) and 10 nonmigrant households were randomly selected. A total of 300 households from the 12 anonymous villages were interviewed. The interviews were conducted during the Spring Festival (late January and early February 1995), a time of year when many migrants returned to the home village. The result is a valuable volume of transcribed material (the Interview Records),[4] consisting of first-person accounts of migration, labor market processes, and farming and evaluations of migrant life and other household and family issues. The second part of the survey consists of systematic data on 2,820 households in Sichuan and Anhui (the Household

Survey) and provides supplementary information about labor migrants from the two provinces.

In this chapter, I focus on the transcribed material from the first part of the Sichuan and Anhui Survey—the Interview Records. Specifically, I examine the records of interviewees[5] who migrated to urban areas or their outskirts to work and are therefore considered rural-to-urban labor migrants. Based on the migrants' narratives, I conduct two types of analysis. First, I reconstruct aggregate patterns of migration processes and consequences for the purpose of comparing male and female migrants. Second, I use women migrants' narratives to interpret their experiences, contributions, and constraints.

In the Interview Records, male migrants are more highly represented, older, and more likely to be married than their female counterparts. Of the 191 migrant interviewees[6] included, 160 or 83.8 percent are men and only 31 (16.2 percent) are women. The average age is 24.7 for female migrants and 31.7 for male migrants, and the age group 15–24 accounts for 75.9 percent of female migrants and only 25.0 percent of male migrants. The majority of male migrants (78.1 percent), but only a small proportion of female migrants (22.6 percent), is married. The high proportion of male migrants may in part be due to a smaller number of migrant women returning to the home village during the Spring Festival, but there is no compelling evidence that this is the case. Rather, the sex ratio is consistent with the conventional wisdom that more men than women participate in rural-to-urban migration. Women's lower representation in migration is also related to migrant women's age concentration, which reflects the sociocultural traditions that govern the life cycle of rural females.[7] In rural China, it is common for young women not to pursue education beyond junior secondary school. Many, in fact, quit after primary school; and a significant proportion is illiterate. They are too young to get married, and their labor may not be central to the family's farm work. During the several years between school and marriage, therefore, they constitute surplus labor. If they do pursue migrant work during these years, however, they are under pressure to return to get married when they reach their mid-twenties.[8] Marriage almost always signals a termination of migrant work.[9] As a result, the vast majority of female labor migrants is single. For men, on the contrary, marriage may not be a deterrent to migration but can actually facilitate continued migrant work. I shall elaborate these processes in greater detail in the "Constraints" section.

Table 6.1 describes the demographic characteristics, destinations, and migrant work of the 31 women migrants included in the Interview Records.

Table 6.1 Characteristics of Women Migrants

Number	Village	Age	Marital Status	Education	Destination	Migrant Work
1	Sichuan, Village 1	32	married	primary	Wujiang, Jiangsu	machinery factory worker
2	Sichuan, Village 1	23	single	NA	Huizhou, Guangdong	electronics factory worker
3	Sichuan, Village 2	18	single	junior secondary	Shenzhen, Guangdong	eyeglasses factory worker
4	Sichuan, Village 2	30	married	primary	Dongguan, Guangdong	accessory factory worker
5	Sichuan, Village 2	29	married	primary	Dongguan, Guangdong	toy factory worker
6	Sichuan, Village 3	26	single	primary	Guangzhou, Guangdong	metal factory worker
7	Sichuan, Village 3	41	married	junior secondary	Boluo, Guangdong	vegetable farm worker
8	Sichuan, Village 3	18	single	primary	Xiamen, Fujian	art products factory worker
9	Sichuan, Village 4	21	single	junior secondary	Guangzhou, Guangdong	electronics factory worker
10	Sichuan, Village 4	22	single	junior secondary	Zhongshan, Guangdong	shoe factory clerk
11	Sichuan, Village 6	19	single	junior secondary	Emeishan, Sichuan	hotel service worker
12	Anhui, Village 1	23	single	junior secondary	Tianjin	food processing factory worker
13	Anhui, Village 1	16	single	illiterate	Wuxi, Jiangsu	restaurant worker
14	Anhui, Village 1	21	single	junior secondary	Chongming, Shanghai	garments factory worker
15	Anhui, Village 1	20	single	primary	Luoyang, Henan	shoe factory worker
16	Anhui, Village 2	22	single	junior secondary	Beijing	nanny
17	Anhui, Village 2	23	single	junior secondary	Suzhou, Jiangsu	tour guide
18	Anhui, Village 2	47	married	illiterate	Beijing	nanny
19	Anhui, Village 2	46	married	illiterate	Beijing	nanny
20	Anhui, Village 3	22	single	primary	Changzhou, Jiangsu	shoe factory worker

Table 6.1 (continued)

Number	Village	Age	Marital Status	Education	Destination	Migrant Work
21	Anhui, Village 4	NA	single	NA	Changzhou, Jiangsu	garments factory worker
22	Anhui, Village 5	18	single	junior secondary	Shanghai	painter
23	Anhui, Village 5	20	single	illiterate	Changchun, Jilin	garments factory worker
24	Anhui, Village 5	20	single	junior secondary	Changshu, Jiangsu	seamstress
25	Anhui, Village 6	24	single	primary	Changzhou, Jiangsu	tailoring business owner
26	Anhui, Village 6	24	single	NA	Shanghai	grocery store salesperson
27	Anhui, Village 6	23	single	illiterate	Shanghai	restaurant worker
28	Anhui, Village 6	23	single	illiterate	Shanghai	nanny
29	Anhui, Village 6	NA	single	NA	Danyang, Jiangsu	fishery worker
30	Anhui, Village 6	22	single	primary	Wuxi, Jiangsu	garments factory worker
31	Anhui, Village 6	23	single	illiterate	Changzhou, Jiangsu	construction worker

NA = not available

Among them, only six were married. Their ages ranged from 29 to 47. The 25 single women range in age from 16 to 26. Regardless of age and marital status, the women migrants' educational attainment was low, with seven illiterate, nine primary, 11 junior secondary, and four unknown. This is a profile similar to that reported in macro-level studies.[10] In the next section, I shall examine the spatial patterns of migration for both men and women and highlight the economic motivations and contributions of women migrants.

ECONOMIC MOTIVATIONS AND CONTRIBUTIONS

The Sichuan and Anhui data record patterns of migration specific to gender. Contrary to conventional wisdom that women migrate shorter distances than men, women migrants in the Interview Records migrated long distances to work. Figures 6.1 and 6.2 document the destination

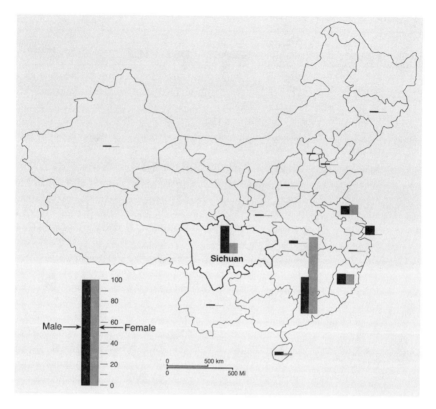

Figure 6.1 Destinations of Sichuan Migrants (percent)

provinces of male and female migrants. Clearly, except for the home province, eastern coastal provinces are more popular than inland provinces. Sichuan migrants favored Guangdong, Fujian, Shanghai, and Jiangsu. Anhui migrants were especially attracted to the adjacent provinces of Jiangsu, Shanghai, and Zhejiang. Male and female migration patterns differed in two ways. First, the home provinces were important destinations for men, accounting for respectively 25.3 percent and 24.7 percent of male migrants from Sichuan and Anhui. By contrast, only one Sichuan woman migrated to work within her home province, and none of the Anhui women migrants worked in their home province. This difference suggests that women migrants are at least as likely as, and perhaps more likely than, male migrants to pursue work in distant destinations. Second, female migrants are more concentrated in their migration desti-

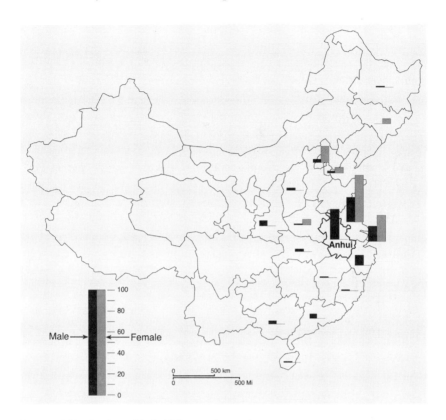

Figure 6.2 Destinations of Anhui Migrants (percent)

nations. Guangdong (72.7 percent) was especially popular among Sichuan women, and Jiangsu (45.0 percent) and Shanghai (25.0 percent) were favored by Anhui women. It is possible that a smaller sample of women compared with men resulted in the former's more concentrated distribution. But table 6.1 shows that women migrants' destinations were mostly large cities, such as Shanghai, Beijing, Changzhou, and Guangzhou, or special economic zones/regions, such as Dongguan and Xiamen, suggesting that they were attracted to places known for economic and employment opportunities. Though male migrants were also attracted to these places, their destinations were more dispersed. The concentration of women migrants' destinations highlights the role of gendered social networks, which are further examined in the next section, in channeling migration streams to specific destinations.

In their narratives, migrants mentioned three types of reason for migration. These are detailed in table 6.2. "Push" refers to the lack of resources, especially farmland, in the village and migrants' or migrant households' inability to make ends meet based on village resources; "pull" refers to the desire to increase income for improving family well-being; and "noneconomic reasons" refers to motives not directly related to income. These three types of reason are not mutually exclusive, but push reasons emphasize the village's lack of resources, pull reasons focus on economic betterment expected from migrant work, and noneconomic reasons highlight factors other than economic benefits. Interviewees often mentioned more than one reason, and therefore all responses are included in the percentage calculation. More women's responses (47.7 percent) than men's responses (34.2 percent) referred to push reasons, and more men's responses (50.9 percent) than women's responses (34.1 percent) fell under pull reasons. Similar proportions of men's and women's responses involved noneconomic reasons. These results suggest that economic motives were prominent among both male and female migrants, and that women's migration was more likely a result of economic difficulties and the lack of village resources. "Surplus labor," for example, indicates that some women's labor in farming is rendered unnecessary because there is little farmland to begin with. These women are, in essence, surplus agricultural labor. This Sichuan woman's comment (#6 in table 6.1)[11] is similar to many young women migrants' remarks: "In our family there is plenty of labor but very little land. I had nothing to do at home, and so I decided to find migrant work."

More than one quarter of migrants indicated that economic reasons like "job opportunities" and "better income" explained their selection of migration destination (table 6.2). However, the social network consisting of "fellow villagers, relatives or friends" was the leading reason for the majority of male and female migrants to select their migration destination. By contrast, "proximity to home village" was not an important factor for either group.

The average duration of migrant work was 9.3 months for male migrants and 10.7 months for female migrants. The difference suggests, first, that men are more likely than women to return to the home village during the busy farming season. Indeed, a higher proportion of men (33.6 percent) than women (12.9 percent) returned to help with farming during 1994. Second, it suggests that women are as economically active during their period of migrant work as men.

Women migrants, however, earn considerably less than their male counterparts. The average income of female migrants was 355 *yuan*, a mere 55.3

Table 6.2 Reason for Migration and Choosing Migration Destination

	Men	**Women**
Reason for Migration (Multiple)		
Push	34.2	47.7
insufficient farmland or food	17.9	18.2
education fees for family members	4.3	9.1
to pay off debts	6.0	2.3
surplus labor	6.0	18.2
Pull	50.9	34.1
increase income	41.9	31.8
build new house	6.0	0.0
marriage expenses	3.0	2.3
Noneconomic reasons	13.2	13.6
broaden horizon and learn skills	9.8	11.4
dislike farm work	3.4	2.3
Other	1.7	4.5
N	234	44
Reason for Choosing Migration Destination		
fellow villagers, relatives, or friends	58.4	60.7
better income	14.6	10.7
job opportunities	10.9	17.9
proximity to home village	3.6	3.6
other	12.4	7.1
N	137	28
Duration of Migration in 1994 (Mean Months)	9.3	10.7
N	154	31

percent of the average income of male migrants (table 6.3). This discrepancy is likely related to a persistent gender gap in educational attainment in rural China, to women migrants' young age, and to labor market segmentation in urban areas. In the Interview Records, 64.8 percent of male migrants, compared with only 40.7 percent of female migrants, had junior secondary education. Women migrants' young age is likely correlated with lack of seniority and experience, and hence, lower income. Moreover, the urban labor market is segmented in such a manner that women migrants are highly represented in gender-segregated and low-paying jobs.[12]

Despite the discrepancy in income, male migrants and female migrants alike saved an average of about 61 percent of their income (table 6.3), indicating that women spend less during their period of migrant work. The ability of female migrants to save at a rate similar to men's suggests that

Table 6.3 Income and Saving

	Men	Women
Monthly Income (mean *yuan*)	642	355
N	129	23
Monthly Saving (mean *yuan*)	378	255
% of income	61.4	61.3
N	100	16
Annual Saving or Remittance (mean *yuan*)	3,783	2,178
N	127	24
Use of Saving or Remittance (multiple, %)		
building or renovating house	31.9	21.2
agricultural input	19.2	15.2
living expenses	11.8	18.2
education fees for family members	11.4	12.1
to pay off debts	10.0	6.1
marriage expenses	2.2	9.1
future use	6.6	3.0
other	7.0	15.2
N	229	33

women are as economically driven as men to use their migrant income to support the village household. The average annual remittance of female migrants—taken or sent home, mostly during the Spring Festival—was 2,178 *yuan*, which was 57.6 percent of that of male migrants. That percentage is higher than the income percentage (55.3 percent), which is probably due to female migrants' longer duration of migrant work during the year.

Household and living expenses consume the bulk of the remittances from both male and female migrants. Some migrants have multiple uses for the remittances, and all these uses are included in the computation for table 6.3. "Building or renovating a house" was mentioned most often, followed by "agricultural input," "living expenses," "education fees for family members," and "to pay off debts." Their order of importance was similar between male and female migrants. Except for "building or renovating a house," the differences in percentage points between men and women were less than 10, again suggesting that male and female migrants have relatively similar priorities in the use of their savings. Expenses in the future, including "marriage expenses," "future use," and "other," accounted for relatively small proportions of the responses. A higher proportion of female responses (9.1 percent) than male responses (2.2 percent) for "marriage expenses" suggests that dowry, in addition to bride-price, is a common concern. "Future use" and "other" refer, for example, to savings for opening a business.

The above statistics suggest that, when given an opportunity to pursue migrant work, women do make important contributions to improving household well-being. The story of a forty-seven-year-old Anhui woman (#18) illustrates the economic contribution one migrant can make:

> The big flood in 1991 destroyed our harvest. There wasn't enough food for the family. My husband is not a tactful person and he would get into trouble if he worked in the city. Instead, I decided to look for migrant work. My departure would also save the family food. After the 1992 Spring Festival, I followed a fellow villager who had worked as a nanny in Beijing, and worked there until harvest that year. After helping my older son to build his house, we were again in debt. So in 1993 my daughter and I went to Beijing again. . . . I returned for the harvest in 1994, and after that my younger son also followed me to Beijing and worked as a kitchen hand in a restaurant. . . . My husband and my mother-in-law take care of the farming and housework. In addition to the money we sent home, at the end of the year we brought home 1,900 *yuan*. We paid back some debts, built three rooms, and bought a cow. . . . After the Spring Festival the three of us will go out again, because the family still needs money. We still have some debts; we should get prepared for my son to get married; my daughter will be marrying soon and we need to prepare for her dowry.

In this household, the wife was not only the main provider of funds for renovating the house, paying debts, and investing in agricultural input but also the pioneer migrant who paved the way for other family members to pursue migrant work. This type of "reversed" division of labor, in which the wife does migrant work and the husband stays in the home village, is rare but was shared by all six married women in the Interview Records. I shall elaborate the context and dynamics of such an arrangement in the "Constraints" section.

More common among female migrants are young, single women. Traditionally, rural women's labor in housework and farming is not remunerated, their lives revolve around the village, and they have few opportunities for social or economic mobility. Migrant work, on the other hand, is rewarded financially, increases rural women's exposure to new ideas and opportunities, and enables them to make a significant economic contribution to the family. This Anhui woman's (#15) determination to migrate, when she was only 15, helped her family tremendously:

> After my father passed away, we had accumulated a debt of 6,000 *yuan*. After finishing primary school I stayed home to work on the farm. But farm work barely feeds my family and does not produce income. In 1990, I secretly borrowed 40 *yuan* from a neighbor and planned to go to Luoyang to find work. My mother found out and tried to stop me. I finally left with tears in my eyes. I just wanted to make some money. . . . This year I brought home 800 *yuan*, which was all used to pay back our debt.

Migrant work is an important opportunity for wage earning that is not available to most rural women, as illustrated by this eighteen-year-old Sichuan woman (#3) who worked in an eyeglasses factory in Shenzhen:

> We have very little farmland, and so I wasn't of much use staying in the village. All the young people in our village were working outside [the village]. I too became restless and did not want to stay home. By working as a migrant I can at least support myself rather than depending on my parents. . . . How much did I bring home? I am embarrassed to say. I brought home very little money . . . let's say 300 *yuan*. Some of my friends cannot even support themselves and need their parents to send them money.

This woman was not under pressure to support the family, which was probably a reason for her small remittance. She seems to have been driven more by the desire to make productive use of her labor and to earn her own living. When young women cannot be economically productive and have no access to wage work in the village, migrant work becomes an important, perhaps the only, means for them to generate earnings for themselves.

While most rural migrants are employed in wage work, the more adventurous are able to find opportunities to be creative and enterprising. This twenty-four-year-old woman (#25) from Anhui only had primary-level education. But after seven years of work as a migrant, she managed to start a tailoring business in a large city:

> I started to do migrant work in 1988. In 1994 a *laoxiang*[13] introduced my sister and me to work in a clothing factory in

Changzhou. But the boss delayed paying us for eight months. In the end, my sister and I decided to leave the factory, rent a place, and start our own tailoring business. We wrote to our home village and recruited six young women to help us. Even though my sister and I did not make any money in the first eight months of last year, in the last four months we each made 3,000 *yuan*, and together we were able to bring home 4,000 *yuan*.

This young woman's experience suggests that migrant work is fraught with exploitative practices as well as opportunities. Her enterprising ability is perhaps an exception to the popular image of women migrant workers as docile, obedient, and tolerant. Nevertheless, sending home remittances from migrant work is something shared by and expected of almost all migrant women.

The evidence described here suggests that rural women migrants do travel long distances to destinations that promise economic opportunities, that they are as economically active as men during periods of migrant work, and that they actively send home remittances to improve the village household's well-being. In other words, migrant work has become an important means for rural women to make efficient use of their labor, to engage in wage work, and to perform as economic agents for the family.

MIGRANT NETWORKS

Research on China has highlighted social networks as an important source of information for migrants.[14] Evidence from the Interview Records shows that women migrants play an important role in forging gendered networks, facilitating the migration of other rural women, and directing other women to specific gender-segregated urban work.

In rural China, fellow villagers and relatives play a very important role in providing information about possible migration destinations and job opportunities. Table 6.4 shows that respectively 92.3 percent and 68.9 percent of female and male migrants in the Interview Records undertook their migration together with fellow villagers, family members, or relatives. The very small proportion—7.7 percent—of women who migrated on their own suggests that company was crucial to them, and that the journey away from home can be a factor in impeding migration. Many rural Chinese, especially women, have never traveled to places far from their home village and must rely on people they know who are familiar with the route. Furthermore, there is a widespread and valid perception that the journey

Table 6.4 Migration Company and Job Information

	Men	Women
Migration Company		
fellow villagers	26.7	57.7
family or relatives	42.2	34.6
no company	30.2	7.7
other	0.9	0.0
N	116	26
Information About Work		
fellow villagers	23.6	25.0
family or relatives	27.9	28.6
self	33.6	17.9
recruitment	3.6	10.7
other	9.3	0.0
N	140	28

to and from the destination is dangerous. Migrants are especially wary of robbers. Traveling with someone they trust is a risk-reducing strategy. To this thirty-two-year-old Sichuan woman (#1), the trip from her home village to Wujiang, Jiangsu, where she worked as a machinery factory worker was almost overwhelming:

> I left the village right after the Spring Festival of 1994. I went with my cousin and five other fellow villagers. We took the train to Zhengzhou, changed to Xuzhou, Nanjing, and then Suzhou. From Suzhou we took the bus to this town in Wujiang. That was my first time journeying a long way from home. We made so many connections that I felt dizzy. The entire trip I followed my cousin closely and didn't dare to move around lest I got lost. The trains and buses were very crowded and disorderly. We had some problems with the connections, but luckily we didn't come across any robbers during the trip.

This Anhui woman's (#21) encounter with robbers likely added to her concern over the migration journey:

> The journeys to work and back home are unsafe. My fellow villager and I [traveled from Changzhou to Nanjing and] took the bus to return from Nanjing to the village. At three in the morning, four robbers got onto the bus and searched our belongings. Fortunately, my bag was with the driver and wasn't taken away.

> But my fellow villager's valuables were robbed. Not only that, the robbers beat her up because she argued with them.

Not only do fellow villagers, family members, and relatives provide company during the migration journey, they are also the main source of job information for the majority of migrants (table 6.4). Rural migrants have weak affiliations with the state and little access to institutional support.[15] Other than the more experienced migrants, rural Chinese have few means to obtain and evaluate information about the urban labor market. Even if state or urban agencies are available, migrants may still prefer to use social networks as a more reliable source of information. The prominence of specific destinations, such as Shanghai and Changzhou among those from Village 6 in Anhui (table 6.1), for example, suggests that social networks give rise to migration streams from the home village to the destinations familiar to experienced migrants.

Social networks play an important role in directing migrants not only to specific destinations but also to specific types of jobs. After the Spring Festival, in particular, inexperienced migrants follow fellow villagers to find work. Often, these informal groups are determined by gender. For example, this twenty-two-year-old Anhui woman (#16) was first recruited by an employment agency to work as a nanny in Beijing. As a pioneer migrant, she became a magnet and guide to other potential female migrants in the village:

> In the past several years, I have brought more than twenty young women from my home village to Beijing to work as nannies. . . . After I returned to the village this time [during the Spring Festival], another ten or so women asked me to take them to Beijing.

Sometimes, employers use migrants as a conduit to recruit more migrant workers from the home village. This twenty-two-year-old Anhui woman (#20) who worked in a shoe factory in Changzhou played such a role:

> My boss asked me to introduce several fellow villagers to him. All the workers in that factory are women. Several young women from the neighboring village also want to join me.

Many migrants who have benefited from urban work are willing to be purveyors of information for fellow villagers. In fact, they have a sense of obligation to their neighbors, further reinforcing the role of networks in directing migrants to specific types of work. A forty-six-year-old Anhui

woman (#19) working as a nanny in Beijing remarked, "I have always wanted to connect fellow villagers to good jobs. When I fail I feel very bad."

Relatively few female migrants found their job on their own (17.9 percent), compared with their male counterparts (33.6 percent) (table 6.4).
This discrepancy suggests that women migrants are more reliant on information provided by others, via social networks or recruiters. Fellow villagers, family, or relatives were the main sources of information for 53.6
percent of female migrants and 51.5 percent of male migrants. Recruitment—referring to formal recruitment by employers and employment
agencies of labor in rural areas—accounted for the employment of 10.7
percent of female migrants but only 3.6 percent of male migrants, reflecting the efforts by some employers to target rural women workers. Social
networks play a role even in migrants' access to recruitment information.
This twenty-two-year-old Sichuan woman (#10), for example, learned
about a recruitment opportunity by a Taiwan-invested shoe factory
through her relative:

> One of my relatives is the manager of an employment agency.
> In 1992, through him I learned that a well-established factory
> in Guangdong was recruiting workers. So I applied and was
> selected.

Furthermore, social networks connect migrant women to employment
agencies at the destination. For example, all four nannies in the Interview
Records traveled to their destinations with other fellow villagers and con-
tacted specific employment agencies as a group. Their job search experiences, including details such as how much they were charged by the
agency and how long it took to find an employer, were very similar. This
Anhui woman's (#28) account was largely echoed by other nannies:

> In 1990, I followed four young women from the home village
> to go to Shanghai. Of the 50 *yuan* that my family gave me, only
> 20 *yuan* was left when I reached Shanghai. We paid one *yuan*
> per day to stay in a nanny employment agency. After three days
> I was matched with a family who needed a nanny for their child.
> The family and I each contributed one half of the 14-*yuan* fee
> charged by the employment agency.

Both the marginal institutional positions of migrants and the prominent
role of social networks have fostered the channeling of such workers into
specific types of jobs.[16] To rural migrants, the urban labor market consists
of segments specifically targeting their labor rather than a range of oppor-

Table 6.5 Top Three Occupations of Migrants

Rank	Men	% of All Nonagricultural Occupations	Women	% of All Nonagricultural Occupations
1	construction worker	35.6	manufacturing worker	51.6
2	manufacturing worker	20.6	nanny	12.9
3	construction contractor	7.5	service worker	12.9
Sum		63.8		77.4
N		160		31

tunities. Their value to this market is tied to their membership in a labor force that is reputedly hardworking, tolerant, cheap, and disposable.[17] Without local household registration (*hukou*), they are the "outsiders" who are brought in only to satisfy urban demand for workers for low-paying and less prestigious jobs.[18] Much of the existing research on migration in China has emphasized how urban labor practices and regulations limit migrants' job access, and little attention has been paid to the role of social networks in fostering labor market segmentation. Through such networks, new migrants replicate the work of earlier migrants. Furthermore, social networks are often gendered, and they reinforce the sorting process that matches employers with workers and deepens segmentation and gender segregation of work. This is a process that homogenizes rather than diversifies migrants' experiences. Thus, migrants in the Interview Records were highly concentrated in a few occupations, namely, construction worker, manufacturing worker, and construction contractor for men and manufacturing worker, nanny, and service worker for women (table 6.5). This type of gendered sorting is widely known among migrants. For example, a twenty-three-year-old Sichuan woman (#2) who worked in an electronics factory in Huizhou, Guangdong commented: "Most men [migrants] from our village work in construction in Jiangsu, and most women [migrants] work in Guangdong factories."

Most of the manufacturing jobs available to female migrants involve labor-intensive work in factories producing such goods as electronics and garments.[19] Domestic work is another popular occupation, especially for older women. Two of the four migrant women above forty years of age were nannies. Service work in hotels or restaurants was also quite popular. In addition, two women were hired as agricultural workers in the rural outskirts of urban areas (#7 and #29). Agriculture is the least preferred work and is usually picked up by migrants who have failed to find other work in urban areas. Many employers in urban areas target young, single migrant women, because they are perceived to be more dexterous, efficient, capable of handling delicate work, and easier to manage than men or older women.[20] The forty-one-year-old woman who worked as a vegetable farm worker (#7), for example, was deemed too old for preferable factory work:

> Vegetable farming is hard, poorly paid work. Most people prefer not to do such work. But I have no choice. I am too old for factory work. Factories won't hire me. The minute they see my identity card they turn me away.

Administrative positions are rarely open to rural migrants. Only one woman (#10) in the Interview Records had an administrative position, as a clerk in a Taiwan-invested shoe factory in Zhongshan. Most rural migrants have little job mobility, and in this regard her experience is rather exceptional:

> The factory provides training to new employees. After that, they assign employees to different types of work. Opportunity certainly plays an important role. I was initially assigned to manage the shop floor. After three months, the factory head noticed that I did very well and asked me to do some administrative work. . . . I am happy that I am a clerk rather than an ordinary worker.

The networks that facilitate migration and the search for a job remain strong in the destination. For example, the pioneer migrant from Anhui (#16) who brought more than twenty women to Beijing maintained close contact with most of her fellow villagers:

> Every Sunday I go out with 15 or 16 *laoxiang*, all of whom have worked as nannies in Beijing. We go to the park, go shopping, or go to the movies. It's a lot of fun. . . . Presently, some of my *laoxiang* continue to work as nannies, some are washing dishes in restaurants, and some have become food vendors. Three women married *getihu* [private entrepreneurs] or farmers from the Beijing suburbs. One woman died from a gas leakage while working in a restaurant. Her family received only 3,000 *yuan* in compensation. I have lost contact with three other women.

Among some women migrants a sense of sisterhood and mutual responsibility has developed, further reinforcing gendered networks. Such networks can also evolve into something resembling a collective front for negotiating options in the labor market. Rather than functioning as an individual job seeker, the migrant may become part of a group that works its way through the complex urban labor market as a single unit. After working in Shanghai as a nanny for four years, this Anhui woman (#28) contemplated changing jobs:

> Since 1990, I have gone to Shanghai every year to work as a nanny, and I've been with seven different families. Last year, after the Spring Festival, three other women from my home village and I decided we wanted to try out factory work. So we traveled to Nanjing together, and then took the train to Changzhou and entered a private enterprise. After nine days, we all felt that factory work was too exhausting, and so the four of us returned to Shanghai and continued working as nannies.

Furthermore, social networks bind migrant women together so that many are part of a native place-based community that serves social functions not provided by urban natives. This Anhui woman (#12) who worked in a food-processing factory in Tianjin said:

> Workers in that factory came from eight different provinces, including many *tongxiang* from Anhui. We take care of one another and do things together—like taking photographs and going to karaoke bars. Every week all the *tongxiang* have a party, and sometimes we invite friends from other provinces as well. In the four years I have been at the factory, no one has ever harassed me. Even though I could have made more money working in another factory, I do not want to give up my job. It's fine that I make less money than I could have. Fellow workers in that factory are mostly in their late teens and early twenties, and are friendly and full of life. As a result, factory life is a bit like campus life. We seldom interact with the Tianjin natives.

There is no question that networks—especially those involving *laoxiang* and fellow villagers—are crucial for migrant workers to endure the dreaded migration journey, to find work, and to enjoy social and community life. Moreover, gender influences the formation and composition of such networks, with the ironic effect of both homogenizing migrants' experiences and occupations and providing a basis for companionship and support.

SOCIAL CHANGE

To rural women in China, migrant work presents more than just an important opportunity for wage work. By removing themselves from rural areas, at least temporarily, migrant women not only earn money for themselves but also are exposed to new ideas, which may infuse village life with economic and social changes.

Exposure to new ideas leads some women to contemplate ways of investing long-term. Those who are enterprising may use their earnings to broaden their future options. This twenty-two-year-old Sichuan woman (#10) wanted to start a business in the future:

> Young people should try to go somewhere and increase their exposure. Life is more meaningful if you are making money rather than relying on your parents. . . . I send home 500–550 *yuan* every month. Over the past two years I have sent home a total of 7,200 *yuan*. . . . I still want to work for another two or three years, to save up some money in order to start a business in the future.

Similarly, this twenty-three-year-old Anhui woman (#12) planned to invest her savings:

> In 1994 I made about 3,500 *yuan*. I saved every cent and plan to use it to buy a store in town (20,000 *yuan*). My boyfriend is from this county. After we get married we can rent out the store. . . . Migrant work really helps increase our exposure.

To many rural women, migration may offer the only opportunity to engage in nonagricultural labor, and is therefore especially attractive to those who dislike farm work. This nineteen-year-old Sichuan woman (#11) was happy to work in a hotel in Emeishan:

> I want to have a new life. I don't want to live the rest of my life as a farmer, trapped in this poor village like my parents. . . . After many attempts to persuade my father to permit me to do migrant work, he finally agreed. He talked to a relative who found the connection for me to work in this hotel.

Women migrants who engage in wage work rather than staying in the village as surplus agricultural labor feel an increased sense of independence from the family. This twenty-one-year-old Sichuan woman (#9) commented:

> The past two years I was in Guangzhou I didn't save up much money. Still, I found the experience rewarding. I earned my own living. I was naïve when I was staying in the village. When I was away from home I had to be independent and make my own decisions.

Many migrant women commented on their changes in lifestyle and outlook as a result of migrant work experience. A twenty-three-year-old Anhui woman (#12) summarized these changes:

> Many changes have occurred to migrants. They turn huts into large houses, dress better, and are more open. Those who stay behind look less smart. As far as meeting and seeing people of the opposite sex, migrants are more open and nonmigrant women tend to remain feudalistic [*fengjian*]. Many migrants have learned some skills and figured out a way to make money, and they build houses and buy electrical appliances. They eat better now, and kill a pig during the Spring Festival. Villagers used to be simple-minded, but are now more cunning. . . . Older cadres in the village are too slow and conservative. They should retire and let younger people do their job.

Her remarks suggest that migrants have not only improved their material well-being but also incorporated new views and lifestyles into village life. Her critique of cadres is an example of migrants reflecting on and evaluating rural life in relation to their increased exposure. Furthermore, migrant women may perceive nonmigrants as unsophisticated. This twenty-three-year-old Anhui woman (#27), for example, felt distant from nonmigrants:

> When I return home to the village I usually hang out with other young women migrants. I have little to talk about with nonmigrant women. We have different lifestyles, and we don't see eye to eye. To us [migrants], nonmigrant women wear reds and greens[21] and look unrefined. To them, our permed hair makes us look strange and alien.

Migrants bring back elements of the urban lifestyle, especially from places where they work.[22] This woman who worked in Beijing (#16) commented:

> Beijing is wonderful. It is big, sophisticated, and it has so many things not found in the village. . . . Through migrant work we learn skills and knowledge and make money. . . . Our quality of life has improved as well. In particular, we dress much better now. Migrant work increases our exposure, so that we talk more politely and we become wiser. Villagers imitate migrants. They buy western-style furniture and decorate their homes following the styles in Beijing. . . . Villagers are now more concerned with sanitation. Their taste for food has also changed. I don't respect

those who prefer staying home doing nothing to migrant work. More than 90 percent of the young women in our village do not go to school. When they go to Beijing, they look especially dumb and are likely to get into trouble.

Critical evaluations such as the above may prompt migrants to make changes to the family and to the village. This twenty-two-year-old Sichuan woman's (#10) comment further reinforces the notion that returned migrants become agents of social change in the village:

After migrants have been to more developed areas, their attitudes change. They become dissatisfied with their situation and want to improve their family's well-being by working harder.

Among married women, the most significant changes brought about by migration relate to the division of labor within the household, whereby one spouse does migrant work and the other takes care of the farmland and housework. Such an arrangement is necessary if the married couple wishes to improve the well-being of its household via migrant work, without giving up farm work. Giving up contract land is not common, especially since most rural migrants do not have access to permanent residence in urban areas and so must eventually return to the village. The most widely adopted division of labor is one where the husband does migrant work and the wife stays in the village. Of the 126 married migrant households in the Interview Records, 69.1 percent were split households where the husband was the migrant worker and the wife stayed in the village, 26.2 percent were households where both the husband and the wife were migrant workers, and less than 5 percent (six) were split households where the wife migrated and the husband stayed in the village (see also migrant #18's narrative in the "Economic Motivations and Contributions" section). The last type of arrangement—the "reversed" division of labor—is the exception rather than the rule, but does suggest that migrant work opens up alternative forms of household division of labor that deviate from traditional norms of village life. Women engaging in this "reversed" division of labor are not only wage earners but also empowered by their economic contributions to the family. After seven years of migrant work, this Anhui woman (#19) decided to return to the home that she helped build:

My husband is a contented farmer. In 1987, my three daughters were still small. We were very poor then, and so I decided to find migrant work in Beijing. . . . Later I also brought my daughter along to Beijing to work in a factory. . . . I am returning to the village now, because I want to help my husband in farm work. During the past several years my daughter and I brought home 8,000 *yuan*, which we used to build four big rooms. I am very happy about that.

In short, the Interview Records indicate that women migrants have gained a sense of independence and exposure to new ideas as well as income, and are thus better equipped to plan their future, to critically evaluate rural life and traditions, and to engage in alternative gender divisions of labor. All of this suggests that women migrants are potential agents of social change in rural China.

CONSTRAINTS

Despite the many contributions women migrants make to their families, their fellow villagers, and their villages, they continue to be constrained by deep-rooted sociocultural traditions as well as an inferior institutional status. These constraints limit their opportunities to engage in nonvillage, nonagricultural, and wage work, and undermine their agency and ability to contribute to the village and to foster social change. In this section I focus on the constraints posed by the patrilocal marriage system and expectations of marital roles in the household.

First of all, the pressure for rural women to get married escalates once they have reached their early twenties. Parents are eager for their daughters to return to the village before they are past "marriageable age." A twenty-three-year-old Sichuan woman (#2) who worked in Huizhou described the pressure from her parents:

> My parents think that I have reached the age for getting married and are anxious that I find a husband. They don't want me to do migrant work anymore. But I still want to work some more and make some money. I like my work and I like Huizhou, but I won't find a husband there. I'll find someone in my native place to marry. It's more convenient and it's safer.

Women migrants in the Interview Records almost unanimously agreed that they should return to the countryside to find a husband. Though young rural women may desire to marry urbanites in order to "leave the farm for good" (*tiaochu nongmen*), their inferior backgrounds and lack of urban residence render them among the least desirable in the urban marriage market.[23] In addition, most rural women consider finding a husband in their native place less risky. Both considerations reflect the marginal and outsider status of migrants in urban areas. To most rural women, therefore, marriage denotes the termination of migrant work and the return to the village. A twenty-three-year-old Anhui woman (#28) who worked in Shanghai summarized succinctly women migrants' marriage considerations:

> I have never considered finding a husband in Shanghai. Among Shanghai natives, only men who are twice our age, widowed, or disabled would marry women with our background. Marrying migrant workers is risky, since it is hard to tell what kind of people they are. It is much safer to find a husband from one's native place.

Villagers' concern over undesirable urban influences may prompt fiancés and parents to pressure women migrants to discontinue urban work even before they get married. This twenty-four-year-old Anhui woman (#26) who worked in Shanghai suffered from such pressure:

> In our village, most women my age are already married. After they get married, most will not pursue migrant work anymore. . . . Three years ago my sister introduced me to a young man. We have been seeing each other since that time. It went really well at first, but he works as a cook in Changzhou and we don't see each other that often. As a result, we have had some misunderstandings lately. He wanted me to write to him, but I didn't go to secondary school and cannot write well. Plus, his family is not supportive of his seeing me, and he has become somewhat suspicious of me. In our village, there is a common view that migrant women are loose. So after you are engaged, your fiancé and his family discourage you from migrant work.

The notion that migrant women are immoral[24] is related to the age-old belief that women's proper place is within the domestic sphere. Confucian prescriptions relating to social positions popularize the notion that women's place is "inside" the family, whereas men are responsible for the "outside," including making a living to support the family. Though the state's intervention, under Mao, mitigated the constraints on women's labor force participation, sociocultural traditions are deeply ingrained in the social fabric of China and are reproduced in various ways as the state turns its attention to economic development. Tamara Jacka[25] has shown that the boundary between the inside/private and outside/public domains has shifted as women have become the primary labor force in agriculture.

Specifically, in rural China today, "inside" refers not only to the home but also to the more stable and sedentary village life, including agriculture. To those who hold strongly to traditional views about gendered boundaries, cities may be perceived to be disorderly, corrupt, and fraught with bad influences.[26] For women migrants, pressure from their prospective husbands and future in-laws, the deep-rooted tradition of getting married before the mid-twenties, the limited marriage market in urban areas, and the advantages of returning to the native place for marriage combine to keep opportunities for pursuing economic mobility through migrant work short and temporary. Therefore, urban work represents only an episode, primarily in the late teens and early twenties, of most rural women's lives.[27]

For rural men, in contrast, marriage does not necessarily disrupt migrant work but in fact facilitates labor migration. The patrilocal tradition ensures the transfer of a woman's labor to the husband's household upon marriage. A wife not only represents an augmentation of labor resources but also becomes the designated person to take care of farming, housework, and child rearing, making it possible for the husband to pursue migrant work. The high proportion of married men among migrants and the less concentrated age distribution of male migrants observed earlier further underscore that marriage is less disruptive of rural men's migrant work. As discussed earlier, a division of labor by gender, with the wife tending to the "inside" and the husband working "outside," is a popular strategy among rural families for augmenting household income while holding onto farmland. In China, as in the West, women are stereotyped as the nurturing family members and are expected to be the primary caregivers in the household.[28] Accordingly, married women in rural China have little choice but to stay in the village to care for children and elderly in-laws. This division of labor also ties women to agricultural work and reinforces the feminization of agriculture that has been well documented in recent research.[29] In this regard, to women migrants, marriage is disempowering because it requires leaving their wage work and thereby decreases their own economic mobility, forcing them to rely on their husbands' wages for improving the household's well-being.

The experiences of the six married women migrants who engaged in a "reversed" division of labor with their spouses further illustrate the endurance of sociocultural traditions about gender roles, even as they are the exception to the rule. A "reversed" division of labor denotes a deviation from traditional gender role arrangements, and in all six cases that strategy was the household's last resort rather than its preference. Economic hardship and the desire to build a house motivated these couples to pursue wages through migrant work. Most important, all six women considered their husbands' poor or potentially poor performance in migrant work a reason for a "reversed" division of labor. In other words, married women migrants are but replacements: men remain the preferred candidates for migrant work, and it is only under circumstances where their work has failed or is likely to fail that the wife has the opportunity to pursue off-farm employment. Although all six married women managed to improve their household's financial well-being through migrant work, the three younger migrants (#1, #4, and #5, ages ranging from twenty-nine to thirty-two) were under pressure from their husbands to return to the village. This thirty-two-year-old Sichuan woman (#1) described her dilemma:

> Many fellow villagers have started to build new houses. We decided to do the same. But after building a house four years ago we have been in serious debt. Migrant work is the only means to pay back the debt. During the past several years my husband had done migrant work in mining, construction, a brick factory, etc. He is unskilled and can only do manual work, work that is dirty, tiring, and dangerous. . . . He is impatient and has a bad temper, and he cannot tolerate the tough life of migrants. . . . The past several years the money he made from migrant work wasn't enough to pay for his food, cigarettes, and drinks. Even he himself admits that he is useless [*meiyong*]. For several years he didn't bring back a cent. In the village you could at least produce some income from farming and raising pigs. Fellow villagers all tease him. He feels embarrassed and doesn't want to go out anymore. . . . I suggested that he take care of the home so that I could try my luck outside. He said, "Don't you look down on me. Migrant work is harder than you think. Try it if you don't believe me." So I went out, and he stayed home to farm and watch the kids. . . . In one year I brought home 3,000 *yuan*. This money helped us to pay back our debt, purchase fertilizers and pesticides, pay the children's school fees, and buy a TV set for them. . . . I still want to return to work after the Spring Festival, but my husband doesn't want me to go. . . . He wants me to stay home and help him raise some pigs. . . . We have been fighting about this matter.

This is a vivid example of how the "reversed" division of labor is considered deviant and is hotly contested. Even though this woman was happy about her economic achievements, her comments on the husband's failure in migrant work show that she was heavily invested in constructions of gender and the institution of marriage, even as she simultaneously contested and felt constrained by them. Men who stay in the village while their wives do migrant work risk being perceived as "useless" and tend to put pressure on their wives to return.[30] Similarly, in cases #4 and #5 the wife's economic power was being pitted against her expected village and household roles. By contrast, the older women migrants (#7, #18, and #19, ages ranging from 41 to 47) and their husbands were more relaxed about arrangements. All three couples had grown children, so it is likely that the husband viewed the woman's caregiving labor as less necessary. The differences in household dynamics between the younger and older migrant couples further demonstrate that the woman's role as caregiver, especially when the children are young, is a predominant factor in the household division of labor.

In summary, evidence from the Interview Records suggests that the sociocultural constraints that rural women face considerably limit their opportunities for migrant work and off-farm work, in turn decreasing their economic contributions to the family and to the village. For both single and married women, marriage and their expected role within it take precedence over their autonomy, economic betterment, and other benefits of migrant work.

SUMMARY AND CONCLUSION

Based on the Interview Records of the Sichuan and Anhui Survey, in this chapter, I have argued that rural women migrants make important contributions to their households, forge lasting networks with other women migrants, and have the potential to foster social and cultural change in the countryside. Their agency, however, is tightly constrained by sociocultural traditions of marriage and gender roles within marriage.

Rural women migrants are mainly young and single and have low levels of education. Many are surplus labor in rural areas where farmland is limited, and migrant work puts their labor to productive use. They travel long distances to specific destinations, in part drawn to economic opportunities and in part guided by social networks formed by fellow villagers and relatives. Even though women migrants have lower incomes, they are as economically active as male migrants, and their remittances are an important means of alleviating village households' economic difficulties and improving their well-being.

Gendered social networks play important roles in rural-to-urban migration, providing information to new migrants, facilitating their migration and job search processes, and reducing the risks of migrant work. At the same time, however, they reinforce the segregation of urban work, by resident status and by gender, and homogenize migrant women's work experiences.

Migrant work is an important, and sometimes the only, means for rural women to engage in wage work, through which they gain independence and greater exposure to new ideas and opportunities to earn their own living. Women migrants are critical of rural life and strive to incorporate elements of the urban lifestyle into their own lives and those of fellow villagers. Migrant work even leads some to experiment with new gender divisions of labor in the household. Through wage earning and making economic contributions to the family, women are empowered and become potential agents of social change in rural China. However, women migrants' agency is constrained by sociocultural traditions. Blocked from the urban marriage market by their inferior socioeconomic and institutional status and driven by the preference for a husband in their native place, most young women return to the countryside to get married before they reach their mid-twenties. Once married, rural women are expected to stay in the village, while their husband's migrant work is permitted to continue. Even though a "reversed" division of labor exists, whereby a woman rather than her husband leaves the village for migrant work, it is considered deviant and is hotly contested. Marriage, in essence, usually terminates rural women's migrant work, cuts off their opportunities to engage in off-farm wage work, and undermines their agency.

Although this is a case study focusing on only twelve villages in two provinces and on a small sample of 31 rural women migrants, the qualitative data examined in this chapter provide depth, richness, and texture that can not only complement other case studies but also enhance our understanding and interpretation of large-scale studies and representative surveys. More than analyses that use only quantitative data, migrant women's own narratives foreground their agency in the household and in the village and also emphasize the structural constraints that limit their contributions.

ACKNOWLEDGMENTS

An earlier version of this chapter was presented at the Second International Symposium on WTO and Chinese Rural Development in the 21st Century, jointly sponsored by the Rural Development Institute of the Chinese Academy of Social Sciences (RDI-CASS), Maoming Municipal Government, and the China Society of Foreign Agricultural Economy (CSFAE), Maoming, Guangdong, June 25–29, 2001, and the 2001 International Forum on Rural Labor Mobility in China, jointly sponsored by the Department of Research on Rural Economy, Development

Research Center (DRC) of the State Council, the Research Center for Rural Economy (RCRE) of the Ministry of Agriculture, and the Department of Training and Employment of the Ministry of Labor and Social Security, Beijing, China, July 3–5, 2001. This research was supported by two research grants from the National Science Foundation (SBR-9618500; SES-0074261), a subcontract award from the Luce Foundation, and funding from the UCLA Academic Senate. I wish to thank Zhou Daming and Luo Zhaoyuan for helping me access the data used in this chapter, and Wenfei Wang for research assistance. I am grateful to Frederick Crook, Arianne Gaetano, Tamara Jacka, and Eduard B. Vermeer for comments on earlier versions of the chapter.

NOTES

1. For example, Cai 1997:7–21; Chiang 1999; Davin 1997, 1998; Fan 2000, 2003a, 2003b; Fan and Huang 1998; Huang 2001; Yang and Guo 1999; Wang Feng 2000.

2. In this chapter, I use the terms "savings" and "remittances" interchangeably, because in the data migrants do not distinguish between them. Both terms are used to refer to the portion of income that migrants send or bring back to the village, either for their own use or for the use of the household.

3. See Du 2000.

4. Nongyebu nongcun jingji yanjiu zhongxin (NNJYZ) 1995.

5. The material also includes selective accounts by the interviewees of their household members, but these are too sketchy for detailed examination and are not included in this chapter's analyses.

6. In the vast majority of migrant households, only one migrant was interviewed. Among households where more than one migrant was interviewed, only two had detailed accounts of all those interviewed. In both cases, two migrants were interviewed. In other words, the 191 migrants analyzed in this chapter represent a total of 189 households.

7. See Fan 2000, 2003a.

8. For example, Tan 1996.

9. Wang Feng 2000; Yang and Guo 1999.

10. For example, Fan 2000.

11. In this chapter, the interviewees are kept anonymous and are identified only with numbers listed in table 6.1. Hereafter, "#" refers to the number in that table.

12. Fan 2000, 2003a; Huang 2001; Yang and Guo 1996.

13. *Laoxiang* and *tongxiang* both refer to people from the same village, and are sometimes used more broadly to refer to people from the same county or province.

14. See, for example, Fan 2002; Lou et al., this volume; and Solinger 1999:176.

15. Solinger 1999:242.

16. Fan 2001.

17. Zhou Xiaohong 1998:3–23.

18. Fan 2002, 2003a.

19. See also table 6.1.

20. Chiang 1999; Lee 1995; and Tam 2000.

21. This expression is commonly used to describe rural people whose wearing of colorful clothes is interpreted as due to lack of sophistication and taste.

22. See also Lou et al., this volume.

23. Until recently, a child born in an urban area had to inherit the mother's household registration. This discouraged urban men from marrying rural women, since their children's survival and education in the city would be extremely difficult. Starting in 1998 and in selected parts of China, new regulations have been approved that allow children to inherit their father's household registration (see Chen 1999; Davin 1998). But it is unclear whether this regulation has been fully implemented across the whole of China, and whether it can offset the inertia in the urban marriage market that disadvantages rural women. See also Beynon, this volume; Chen 1999; Chiang 1999; Fan and Huang 1998; Fan and Li 2002; and Tan and Short, this volume.

24. See Pang Hui's story, this volume. When she returned home from migrant work, her husband thought of her money as dirty and refused to let her stay back home.

25. Jacka 1997:193.

26. For further discussion on this point see Gaetano, this volume.

27. See Fan 2003b; Lee 1995.

28. McDowell 1999:126; Yu and Chau 1997.

29. For example, Davin 1998; Jacka 1997:128–39; and Zhang 1999b.

30. See also Lou et al., this volume.

Binbin Lou, Zhenzhen Zheng,
Rachel Connelly, and Kenneth D. Roberts

7. The Migration Experiences of Young Women from Four Counties in Sichuan and Anhui

It is not easy to make money by peddling; there's more bitterness than sweetness. But there is sweetness if you bring money back.
—a married woman from Anhui

I changed greatly. I lacked self-confidence before. My marriage was not very successful. My parents-in-law did not accept me. Now I am confident. I can work independently, and I want to run my own company in the future, since I am very familiar with the market right now.
—a twenty-six-year-old secondary school graduate from Anhui, with one daughter

>> This chapter draws upon research conducted with rural women from Anhui and Sichuan who migrated to a town or city outside of their home county and then returned to rural life. It seeks to explore these women's understandings of and feelings about their past experiences of migration and life in the city, and the impact that migration had upon their present circumstances and their perceptions of the future.

Our analysis is based on fieldwork carried out during August and September 2000 in four counties of Anhui and Sichuan provinces, as part of a larger study of the effect of migration on women's reproductive health and on women's status in their rural families. Anhui and Sichuan are both high-migration provinces, ensuring an adequate proportion of returned migrants in the study. Both are poor, with similar levels of per capita income and economic structure, but they have very different migration histories. Thus our selection of these two provinces allows areas of both comparison and contrast. The investigation included a survey of individual women, focus group discussions, and household and individual interviews. Information used in this chapter mainly comes from the focus group discussions and individual interviews.

The chapter focuses on three separate aspects of the migration experience: leaving home, urban life, and returning home. Given the different migration histories of the two provinces—women from Anhui began to migrate during the 1980s but women from Sichuan did not migrate until the early 1990s—we anticipated and found substantial differences between provinces in the circumstances of leaving home and some differences in the effects of migration upon returning home, but we were surprised to discover few locational differences in migrants' views of urban life. Generally, women from both provinces migrate between the ages of eighteen and twenty-five, for economic reasons. However, in the 1980s Anhui women migrated very young, as early as age thirteen. The age of first migration has increased over time in Anhui and is now, for the most recent cohorts, more similar between the two provinces.[1] Still, women in Anhui tend to migrate at a slightly younger age, and thus more often before marriage, than their Sichuan counterparts. Perhaps because of their province's longer history of migration, Anhui parents seem less afraid of migration for single women. Anhui women migrate for shorter periods of time, returning home often between episodes. The majority work in small businesses while away from the village. Women from Sichuan, on the other hand, are more likely to migrate after marriage and to have a single migration experience. They work mainly in factories, stay away longer, and have relatively more stable jobs. The majority from both provinces migrates with someone else and to a destination where they know someone.

Despite substantial differences by location in the circumstances of migration, its timing in women's lives, the destinations, and the occupations engaged in while "out," our major finding is the similarity of the migration experience for all the women in our study. This is not to say that there are no differences, but that the similarity overwhelms what differences emerge, and that those differences that do emerge are not primarily location-based. Rather, to the extent that we can identify differences in migrants' views of their experience, age and marital status (which in rural China are so highly correlated that it is impossible to separate the two effects) are the relevant categories of distinction.

In talking to women in rural Anhui and Sichuan, we were struck by the level of ambivalence or even internal conflict they felt about their migration experience. Most of them both enjoyed it and missed their home. They were at the same time happy to come home yet looking forward to going out again. The bittersweet metaphor with which we began this chapter is indicative of these ambivalent feelings. The complexity of returned migrants' memories of the migrant experience comes from the very different opportunity sets available in urban and rural areas.

Based on our focus group findings, the pace of life is slower and the number of hours of hard labor are lower on average in rural than in urban areas. This slower life can be boring for some young women. Boredom and the lack of cash income push rural women to urban areas. The physical demands of factory, retail, or service employment (shifts are often twelve hours, six or seven days a week), the language and cultural barriers of urban life, and the psychological costs of separation from families, children, and/or spouses pull migrants back to the villages. These push and pull factors remained relevant for all the returned migrants we talked with, even those who had migrated many years ago, though aging seems to reduce the boredom factor and having already migrated reduces the need for cash income. Thus, migration out of Sichuan and Anhui declines with age as it does for almost all migrating peoples.

In addition to the commonality of bittersweet views of their migration experience, there was also a uniformity in the effects of migration on the women's lives upon return. Again we were a bit surprised by the lack of provincial differences in reported effects of migration. The majority of women felt changed by the experience in a way they viewed as positive. They talked about changes in the way they dressed, their standards of hygiene, and their expectations for their children. Many expressed dissatisfaction with rural life. Similar results emerged from our statistical analyses of the survey data, where no consistent significant differences across provinces were found.

There was a difference between married women of Anhui and Sichuan in their reports of the reaction of fellow villagers to returning women migrants. Migrants from Sichuan felt pressure to renounce their urban-learned customs, whereas the Anhui women did not. Again, we attribute this finding to the different migration histories of the two provinces. Perhaps criticism of urban ways will lessen in Sichuan over time as migration becomes a more common experience among villagers. In addition, in terms of the women's own reactions to having returned, significant differences emerged between younger and older women. We cannot tell whether these differences are cohort-specific and thus will remain over time, or whether they are age-specific and thus will dissipate as the women fall into their prescribed roles in the rural community as mothers and as caregivers for the elderly. In both the Anhui and Sichuan locations, young unmarried women tell different stories than married women. The latter are concerned about family and children, while the former are more focused on themselves and their career paths. Single women are more likely to dream about their future, while married women are more focused on the present. Both a period effect and cohort effect are at work; the age of first migration and year of first migration both represent different experience paths for these women. Part of the effect of the year of first migration is a selection factor. The older respondents, those aged thirty to forty, almost all from Anhui, migrated during a period when migration was more daring and rarely undertaken, whereas the younger women migrated along with the majority of their cohort, during a period when migration had become a common practice. The combination of two effects—women of all age cohorts migrating more in recent periods and younger cohorts migrating more than older in each period—means that migration is becoming much more prevalent among all women in Sichuan and Anhui provinces and has taken on a rite-of-passage quality that was absent in earlier years. Especially in Anhui, it is difficult to find women in their late teens who have not migrated.[2]

The rest of the chapter proceeds as follows: "The Study Locations" provides details on the counties included in the study. "Basic Characteristics" discusses some basic attributes of the survey respondents. Although most of the evidence we report in this chapter comes from the focus groups and individual interviews, the women who participated were similar to the survey respondents in every way. The next three sections follow the migrant experience from "Leaving Home" to urban life ("Life as a Migrant") and then returning home ("Back at Home").

THE STUDY LOCATIONS

The four counties from which we collected information share common features: the land is quite limited given the size of the population; household income depends heavily on agriculture, mainly on rice production; and about 90 percent of residents live in rural areas. There are few township enterprises in any of the four counties. These common characteristics ensured that (1) there were enough returned migrants to interview; (2) the influence of having migrated would be easily identified given the local situation; and (3) the economic status of households was about average or slightly below the national average, neither too poor nor very developed. Although they share these common characteristics, the four counties also show a variety of migration patterns.

Table 7.1 provides some basic information on the four counties. Of the two counties in Anhui, the economic situation of Huaining is better, for although both counties are major grain producers, the farmland in Zongyang

Table 7.1 Population and Economic Statistics of the Four Counties

County	Population (thousand)	Percentage Population Rural	Gross Agricultural Output (1990 prices, million *yuan*)	GDP/capita (*yuan*, 1999 prices)	Land Type
Huaining, Anhui	779.4	89.6	836	3,576	alluvial plain
Zongyang, Anhui	946.0	91.2	796	2,445	alluvial plain
Xingwen, Sichuan	423.0	89.4	302	1,974	mountainous
Changning, Sichuan	422.0	90.5	423	2,969	hilly

DATA SOURCES: Sichuan Statistical Bureau, *Sichuan Statistical Yearbook 2000* (China Statistics Press, 2000); Anhui Statistical Bureau, *Anhui Statistical Yearbook 2000* (China Statistics Press, 2000); State Statistical Bureau, *Social-Economic Statistics Summary by County (City) of China, 2000* (China Statistics Press, 2000)

is easily flooded. This has led to a long history of seasonal migration from that county. In general, residents of Anhui share a tradition of commerce; for the last several centuries the *Hui shang*, or merchants from Anhui, have been renowned for their travels all over China selling manufactured goods to rural dwellers. At the time of our study, a larger proportion of Anhui returned migrants worked in "commerce" (a term of the state statistical bureau), which can be an enterprise as large as a company or as small as one single individual.

Xingwen, in Sichuan, is the poorest of the four counties. Being mountainous, it lacks arable land and is officially designated a poor county (*pinkun xian*) by the national government. The local government, as part of its poverty alleviation program, has encouraged all families to send their youths to the cities to work. Changning has a better economy, is closer to the city of Yibin, and has a large bamboo forest that attracts tourists from southern China. The lack of economic opportunity in all four counties is the primary motivator of migration. Agriculture does not fully employ all the residents all of the year, and thus many are looking for work outside. Migration itself requires start-up money, so it is not necessarily the poorest of the poor who migrate. Instead, migrants "go out" with a variety of economic goals. While some are working for basic living expenses, many are trying to amass funds to build a new home.

As mentioned above, outmigration from both counties in Sichuan started later than from those in Anhui and has only become common since the mid-1990s. We attribute the later onset of migration both to Sichuan's geographic distance from the rapidly developing manufacturing centers of southern and coastal China and to the lack of easy access to transportation in this remote and mountainous region. The result was that, at the time of our research, hardly any Sichuan women over thirty years old had migration experience, while in Anhui grandmothers in their fifties could tell stories of their migration experience in the city in the early 1980s, when there were very few migrants. A cohort difference is observable in villagers' attitudes toward migration; for example, their comments on who can go out and when to go out (see "Leaving Home"). As we note in "Basic Characteristics," Sichuan women are more likely to be married before their first migration. With such substantial differences in the circumstances of migration, we were surprised at the similarity of returned migrants' reflections on their experiences (see "Life as a Migrant") and of their reports of the effect of migration on their current lives in the village ("Back at Home").

BASIC CHARACTERISTICS OF THE PARTICIPANTS

In each of the four counties, two townships were selected for fieldwork, and a stratified sampling design resulted in a survey sample of 3,186 women. One third of them had had migration experience. Table 7.2 presents basic information on those survey respondents who had migrated, showing the differences and similarities among the four counties. Note that since the survey was conducted in the village, it included only those who were in their rural home, not local women who were away from home at the time of the interview.

In each township we also organized six focus group discussions: 1) married female returnees; 2) single female returnees; 3) married women who had never migrated; 4) single women who had never migrated; 5) women whose husbands had migrated; and 6) husbands. The focus group participants were between sixteen and forty years of age. Since most women in rural China get married soon after reaching age twenty, single participants were almost all under age twenty-four, and most of them had graduated from secondary school (i.e., they had completed nine years of education). The ages of married groups varied from twenty to thirty-seven, and the majority of them had received primary or secondary school education. More Sichuan women than Anhui women had graduated from secondary school. Most participants who had migrated had done so in their teens or twenties.

Table 7.2 Information on the First Migration Episode

	Anhui/ Huaining	Anhui/ Zongyang	Sichuan/ Xingwen	Sichuan/ Changning	Total
respondents	401	285	211	256	1153
mean age at first migration episode	23.48	20.94	24.62	24.38	23.26
migrated before marriage (%)	37.9	58.6	25.1	17.6	36.2
migrated to another province (%)	88.3	74.3	78.2	75.7	80.2
destination was big city (provincial capital or Beijing or Shanghai) (%)	31.3	20.8	40.8	30.7	30.3
destination was mid-small city (%)	45.0	58.5	36.0	52.4	48.3
average period of stay (months)	8.67	12.5	14.53	13.69	11.79
employment status (column percentage)					
unemployed	3.0	11.9	5.2	4.3	5.3
self-employed	54.1	6.0	3.3	12.5	23.7
employee	42.4	81.4	90.5	80.0	69.2
manager	0.5	0.7	1.0	3.1	1.2
major job (column percentage)					
factory worker	22.9	46.7	64.5	48.6	42.1
restaurant worker	19.2	12.3	12.3	13.7	15.0
retailer	49.1	4.6	1.9	8.6	20.5
other	8.8	36.9	21.3	29.1	22.4

DATA SOURCE: Authors' survey

Almost all the married women focus group participants were active and participated fully in the discussion, whether they had ever migrated or not. But the two single women's groups were quite different: single returned migrants were much more open and willing to talk than single women who had never migrated. The former did not hesitate to express their feelings, discussing them with facilitators and with each other, and they spoke more like urban youths, without a heavy local accent.[3] The latter were much more shy, answered questions very briefly, and did not engage in discussion. From this evidence alone it seems that the migration experience had a strong cultural impact on single women, though one that to some extent was compensated for by age, as evidenced by the older married women who had never migrated.

Figure 7.1 Young single returned migrant women of Huaining county participating in a focus group discussion. Binbin Lou

LEAVING HOME

Timing of First Migration

Figure 7.2 shows the marital status of migrant women by age of first migration in the two provinces and graphically demonstrates three major findings of our research, which we discuss in turn.

First, most migrant women were married by the time of their first migration, unless they migrated very young, before the average age of marriage for women in the sample, 21.7. By the age of 22, three fourths of the women in both provinces were married by the time of their first migration.

Second, a much larger percentage of women in Anhui were single at their first migration than in Sichuan, where the majority of women first migrated only after marriage. The figure demonstrates that one reason for this is that they started migrating at a younger age in Anhui, some going out with their older brothers or sisters when they were only thirteen or fourteen years old. Throughout the early 1980s in Anhui the pattern was one of very young women migrating. As one older Anhui

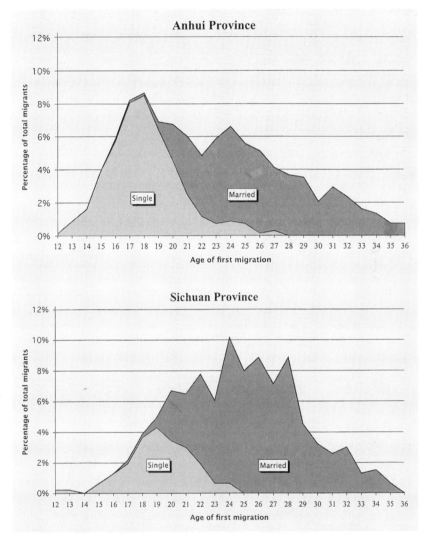

Figure 7.2 Marital Status by Age of First Migration in Each Province (migrant women)
Data source: Authors' survey

woman recounted: "I went out with my uncle to Jiangxi, Hubei, and Henan to sell cloth, when I was fourteen. . . . All the young people here have migrated; my two younger sisters did too." Clearly, strong social networks helped facilitate the migration of young girls from Anhui. The central location of the province and ready access to both water and train transportation helped as well. Recently the age of first migration in Anhui has risen, as young people stay in school longer and family income is higher.

Third, counter to commonly held views, these rural women do migrate in substantial numbers after marriage. The sense that marriage ends migration for them is simply not correct.[4] Although it may have been more accurate in the 1980s, we also met plenty of women who had migrated after marriage even then.

While most Anhui women migrants, including some Anhui girls who dropped out of secondary school to work in the city, were single at first migration, the situation in Sichuan was quite different.[5] Indeed, not long ago migration by unmarried women was discouraged in the Sichuan villages we visited. Villagers believed that "bad girls migrate out before marriage" and gossiped about them. A village leader in Sichuan told us that about seventy women in his village had migrated. Most were married women who migrated together with their husbands, which is considered very respectable. However, the village leader we spoke with also included in his count both unmarried women and married women who migrated without their spouse. There was much less social concern about married women migrating alone than about unmarried women. Furthermore, in the case of husbands and wives migrating together, it was more commonly held that the wife went along to keep her husband out of trouble than the reverse. The village leader told us, "It used to be unmarried men who migrated. But now unmarried women migrate also. People's opinions are changing, and nobody blames them [unmarried women migrants] anymore."[6] Similarly, an unmarried returned migrant from Sichuan summarized the change in attitude that seems to have taken place in Sichuan in the late 1990s regarding the migration of unmarried women: "When I first migrated out I was quite young. I didn't care what people said about me and just wanted to see the outside world. People in their forties talked a lot about me behind my back. Now the migration of unmarried girls has become normal." Thus, until recently social stigma dissuaded most young Sichuan women from migrating, but migration after marriage was considered "okay," whereas in Anhui the taboo about unmarried women migrating had broken down much earlier.

Motivation

The major category of difference in terms of motivation to migrate is not location of residence but marital status (recall that age is highly correlated with marital status, so that it is difficult to distinguish between these two factors). Among married women, economic reasons were usually at the top of the list. "To make money (*gao qian*)" was what most Anhui women said, while in Sichuan they said "look for money (*zhao qian*)." Either way, the implication was that they were unable to earn money at home. Although few families worry about food shortages, most lack extra cash. As a thirty-five-year-old woman from Anhui said, "We are losing our arable land. We now only have a small amount of land to work on, and we get hardly any income from it. We only grow enough vegetables for the family; we even need to buy grain. Everything requires money." It is important to recognize that rural incomes have grown over time, so that the need for money should not be greater in recent years, but several economic factors lead to the increased sense of "need." Consumer goods are available for purchase that were not available before. Locally produced building materials are being replaced with manufactured building material, so that where previously the family would gather stones for a wall or have a dirt floor, now they will purchase cement and tile. In addition, economic reform has resulted in an increase in the tax burden and a large increase in the cost of education, which is one of the major reasons rural families need cash.

In both provinces, widowed women are particularly hard hit economically. A woman in one of the Anhui villages told us that she migrated in 1984, among the earliest "movers." Her husband had died, leaving her with three children. If she had not migrated to earn money, it would have been very difficult for her to feed her family. Now she is a grandmother living in a comfortable, well-decorated two-story house, and all her children have successful careers.

Among the younger respondents there was less sense of urgency, as they did not support families. Nonetheless, younger people still felt the need to make more money for themselves. Some of what the younger unmarried migrants earn they retain to use for a dowry or to contribute to building a new home for themselves and their husbands. The rest is remitted to their parents. That money may be used to pay for the education of a younger sibling or for the bride-price for a younger brother's marriage.[7]

Both married and single migrants in both Anhui and Sichuan used their income for two major household expenditures: building a new house and paying for children's education. The largest household expense in contemporary rural China is the construction of the house, a primary symbol of wealth and status in the village. It is a matter of pride for young couples to have their own house instead of living with their parents. A Sichuan woman told us, "My husband has four siblings, and we did not have our own house after marriage. I had to live in my in-laws' house, and gave birth in their house. It was shameful. So I decided to migrate out to work." Now she has a new house for her own family. It is not uncommon to see half-finished new houses in these villages. The explanation is that the owners ran out of money, so they went out to make more and will come back to finish the work later.

After house construction, children's education was the priority for most of the women with whom we spoke. A returned woman with three children in Anhui told us, "There are mainly two things of importance for migrants: the first is a house and the second is children's education. Nowadays the tuition fee for one semester is 400 *yuan*. If you include other [school-related] expenses it comes to 800 *yuan* for half a year." School fees have increased all over China since the education reform act of 1986 that decentralized the responsibility for financing education. Villages are now required to both offer primary school to all children up through the sixth grade and pay for it out of local revenues. Secondary school is also compulsory and is provided at the township level.[8]

Most of the women we talked with felt it was important that their children get an education, so that they could get a better job and have a brighter future. For some that meant migrating to earn the money needed for fees. Some women who had temporarily come back to help with the rice harvest told us that they would go out again afterward to make more money to pay their children's school fees. An Anhui couple in their forties said that they had come back to see their second son off to university. Their oldest had already gone to college. Both parents had worked for eight years in a private factory in rural Zhejiang making umbrellas, putting almost all the money they earned toward their three boys' educational expenses. In other cases, however, aspirations for their children meant that women returned to oversee the education of their school-age offspring. It seems that grandparent care is acceptable for infants and preschoolers, but parental care, particularly a mother's, is preferred for school-age children. Perhaps this is due to the differential between parents and grandparents in terms of literacy; many grandparents cannot help children with their homework or are less effective at motivating them to do it.

Among women who migrated with their husbands, a few told us that their main motivation was to increase the savings rate out of his income, and others were motivated to "keep an eye" on him. A village leader in An-hui told us, "There used to be only men migrating out in this village, not women. Married women who now go out with their husbands do not in-tend to make money, but to save money. Their husbands would spend all the money if no one looked after them. Some of the wives are also con-cerned that their husbands may have affairs with other women if they are not there." Here, the gendered assumptions that women are less selfish or profligate than men supports married women's migration with or without their husbands. While historically the migration literature has modeled the wife in a "joint migration" as passively accompanying her husband, here it is suggested that the wife's role is active—she's looking out for the purse and for her own well-being.

For still other married women, migrating without one's husband can be an escape from abuse or a failed marriage. A twenty-nine-year-old Anhui woman said, "My friend went to Beijing one year after she had her child. Her husband treated her badly. He had girlfriends from a nightclub in town, and changed [lovers] frequently. My friend had to go out to work."

Among the unmarried women, the reason most often mentioned for migrating was to see the outside world or to look for a better future. A twenty-one-year-old secondary school graduate from Anhui said, "It is not because my family needs money. I want to go out all by myself, to see, to feel, and to experience." Another secondary school graduate from Anhui said, "There is no future staying home. I learned to be a tailor, but there is no clothing factory here. So I have to go."

Migrating was also the way for some to escape unwanted engagement. A thirty-five-year-old Anhui woman said, "My father died when I was young, and I live with my stepfather. They asked me to marry him [her husband], but I did not want to. I went out to work for a year and hoped that they would give up. But after I came back he frequently visited; then I had no choice but to marry him."

In sum, although the motivation for migrating out differs by individual, there are certain patterns. In the early 1980s more women migrated for economic survival, while in the late 1990s it seems that more women mi-grated to earn money to improve their own or their family's quality of life. Of those who migrated most recently, more young single women migrat-ed in the hope of having a brighter future, for personal development, and to escape from rural reality, while more married women migrated explic-itly to earn money. These differences in motivation between single and married women are more pronounced upon repeated migration, as we dis-cuss in "Back at Home."

Traveling Partners, Destinations, and Occupations

A strong commonality among almost all the women with whom we spoke was that they migrated with somebody they trusted: siblings, spouse, relatives, classmates, close friends, or neighbors. Several women in Sichuan who had never migrated gave as their reason the fact that they had no one they could trust with whom to go along, even though many other women in the village had migrated. As one twenty-one-year-old secondary school graduate from Sichuan said, "You will be lost out there, if there is nobody to introduce you. If you have a reference and a secondary school education, and you're a hard worker and are willing to work, you will definitely find a job."

An alternative to going *with* someone they know is going *to* someone they know. An unmarried young woman from Anhui who had come home to visit her parents said, "My aunt went to Beijing in 1990 and worked for a family as a nanny (*xiao baomu*). She met a boyfriend there and got married. I went to Beijing in 1999 and cooked for my aunt and her family. The life in Beijing is much better than here."

Forty-seven percent of the married women who migrated were in the company of their husbands during their first migration episode. Joint migration was particularly common when the couple did not yet have children, but it was also common when the husband and wife were in occupations, such as commerce, where they could work together. In a married returnee focus group discussion it was explained to us that the reason couples migrate together is that it is safer that way, and that husband and wife can help each other. Some of the other 53 percent of married women migrated alone, to a place where they had friends or family, but a substantial number migrated from the village with a sister, sister-in-law, or some fellow villagers. Also, as we discuss below, some of the Anhui women were traveling in groups.

There was certainly neither a single migration destination nor a single occupation that engaged all the women in our sample. Even from a single village there was variation in the destinations from the local large city to the provincial capital to Beijing, Shanghai, and the southern coastal region, and variation in occupations from factory work to service jobs such as waitressing to small businesses such as vegetable selling or tailoring. Still, there were patterns of migration destinations, and destinations were often linked with jobs. We found that women in the same village often migrated to similar places and to do similar jobs. This is similar to C. Cindy Fan's finding, this volume, of the homogenization of women's experiences.

We learned that each village had its own preferred destinations and occupations. For example, migrants from Huaining were mostly engaged in commerce. Those Huaining women who were not involved in commerce mostly went to Zhejiang and Jiangsu and worked in clothing factories. Migrants from Zongyang were also mostly in commerce, with very distant destinations. Men from one of the townships in Zongyang tended to do interior house decoration in Beijing, and therefore almost all their wives and children had been in Beijing at least once. Women in Xingwen, Sichuan, either went to Guangdong to work in footwear factories or went to Beijing to become waitresses. Women from Changning were most likely engaged in factory work in Guangdong or went to Chengdu, Sichuan's capital, to work as store clerks or waitresses.

Unique to Anhui was that groups of women would become traveling retailers. A group of four or five people would leave the village together, buy some products, and travel together. After a while, when they felt that they had made enough money, they went home together. These Anhui women had been in most of China's provinces, following those who made good money selling similar merchandise to the same destinations, no matter the distance. The following quote from a twenty-three-year-old married woman from Huaining, Anhui, illustrates this particular pattern of migration:

> The first time I left home was when I was seventeen. I was not interested in making money. I just wanted to go out like the others. My cousin took me along. We sold small merchandise. We went to large cities, small cities, and towns; anywhere, as long as we could sell. . . . I have been in northeastern provinces, Hunan, Guizhou, Sichuan . . . lots of places.

No one we interviewed from Sichuan engaged in this type of traveling entrepreneurship. Sichuan women were much more likely to be factory workers than were Anhui women, and more likely to migrate just once but for a longer period of time. This pattern is related to their position as factory workers, whose work schedule is very prescribed.

In sum, we found substantial differences between the provinces in the age and the marital status of first migrants, though the age of first migration has increased in Anhui over time to nearly match that in Sichuan. In addition, the women from the two provinces differed in their destinations, occupations in the urban area, and durations of migration. Gender interacts with migration in interesting ways: until recently it inhibited the migration of single women from Sichuan who feared being seen as "bad," while enabling the migration of wives with husbands as a way of "keeping an eye" on the latter. We have also seen that migration certainly does not end with marriage and that many married women migrate without their husbands. They travel with relatives or fellow villagers or join family or friends who have migrated before them. While every village exhibited a large variation in destinations and occupations, patterns did emerge. Women from Sichuan were more likely to be employed as factory workers, while Anhui women often engaged in commerce. A subset of Anhui's women migrants were really traveling salespeople or, perhaps more accurately, peddlers traveling from town to town selling their wares.

LIFE AS A MIGRANT

Contrary to what one might expect, the differences in the timing and duration of migration and the destination and occupation of the migrants summarized above do not have a substantial effect on women's views of their lives as migrant workers. Though the timing and duration of migration differed between Anhui and Sichuan, the motivation differed by marital status, and the destinations differed by village, there was an extraordinary commonality in the women's retrospective feelings about their lives as migrants. Almost every returned migrant with whom we talked expressed ambivalence about the migration experience; no matter whether they worked in a factory or sold goods on the street, they remembered the experience with both happiness and bitterness.

Finding a First Job

Finding a "good" job was the strongest desire of almost all the women who had migrated, and their success at work brought them confidence and pride. For them, a "good" job meant a relatively high salary and good working conditions. Many women made it through their migration experience by sheer hard work, especially in the early stage of securing a position and learning a new set of skills. Some reported obtaining certain positions by their cleverness and initiative. During focus group discussions and individual interviews, they displayed their pride and self-confidence as well as their pleasure in their success, as demonstrated in the following two quotes:

> My first job was weaving. I did not know how to do it. I just followed another woman who took me there. After four to five days of learning and practice I could do it, and then I got a job

in a weaving factory. (a thirty-four-year-old secondary school graduate from Anhui, married and with a son, who currently runs her own grocery store in the village)

I learned from a newspaper that a newly opened large supermarket needed clerks. I applied. After an interview and one month training I got the job. Other newly recruited clerks all had higher education and were older than me. The boss thought that I was good at communicating with the customers. (an unmarried woman from Sichuan, who is temporarily back home to help her sick mother run a family shop)

Not all succeeded right away. A young woman from Sichuan told us the story of how she failed the first time and succeeded later:

I learned CAD (computer-aided design) in 1998 in Hefei (the capital of Anhui), and my husband studied advertising design on his own. We went to Shanghai with some application materials. We did not know anybody and had no place to stay. Our money was stolen when we fell asleep on the train. I cried. A good person we met on the train gave us 100 *yuan*. We went out every day in Shanghai trying to find a job. Nobody would hire us, since we did not have a diploma or household registration.

Yet the couple was not discouraged and went to Hefei and tried again. This time they succeeded:

A printing factory was looking for a person for design. Although I did not have a diploma and only had secondary school education, I was capable, confident, and skilled at typing. I applied. I told them that I knew how to design. I prepared a very good resumé, and I displayed it with self-confidence. They asked me to do some work, and I passed at once!

Certainly, not every story has a happy ending. A woman in Anhui told us how she failed in her entrepreneurial efforts and had to go home, since she was out of money. Another woman said that she could not find a satisfactory job. In the end she was hired at a private sweatshop with very bad working and living conditions. "I missed home and my child, but I had no choice. I had to work to earn money to pay the travel costs to get back. I returned home after two months."

None of the women we talked with had been prostitutes (or at least none admitted to it), but most had a story to tell about women who had taken that path. The storytellers were highly critical. Women in a village in Sichuan told us that there were some fellow villagers who did "that job" (meaning prostitution) to earn easy money, and who traveled back home several times a year by airplane. One woman said, "They are lazy and do not like to work. Although we work very hard, our money is clean. Their money comes from a dirty place."

The issue was seldom that someone had trouble finding a job; more often, it was not easy to find a satisfactory job that was not only profitable and "clean" but also not too physically exhausting. A substantial proportion of work in the cities is physically demanding. Only a few migrants had made their way "up" to a more respectable or better-paid job. The barriers to landing such jobs are substantial. They include *hukou*-based discrimination, dialect-based discrimination, and lack of networks, knowledge, and skills. Those who succeeded tended to be younger and better educated. But all who were able to find a satisfactory job had more cash than they had before, which in turn made life more tolerable, even in poor living conditions.

Living Arrangements

Living arrangements in urban areas were closely related to what kinds of jobs women found and with whom they migrated. From our survey we learned about the living arrangements of migrant women on their first migration. For Anhui, the percentage who lived in a dormitory was 28.3 and for Sichuan it was 47.2. More women from Anhui lived in rented rooms (57.1 percent) than did women from Sichuan (38.0 percent). The major reason for the difference was the type of job the women were doing (see table 7.2). More Anhui women, especially those from Huaining, worked in retail and had to travel more frequently and find their own places to stay. More Sichuan women, on the other hand, worked in a factory that usually provided a dormitory for workers, commonly one room for as many as ten people. Some small, privately run enterprises allowed workers to live in the boss's house.

When couples migrate together they may live in a shed on a construction site or rent a room in order to live together. A twenty-four-year-old woman from Anhui reported, "My brother and sister-in-law, and sister and brother-in-law run a shop together in a Beijing suburb. They rent a house, and my brother's child is with them." Single women or married women without their husbands who did not live in dormitories often shared rented rooms with relatives, classmates, or friends. For example, the supermarket clerk from Sichuan mentioned earlier told us that she rented an apartment with her co-worker. Anhui women employed as traveling merchants usually stayed in small hotels with fellow villagers.

It is interesting to note that most of the returnees did not comment on living conditions, which did not seem to be so important to them. However, a few complained that the employers should provide better accommodations, as demonstrated in the following quotation from a twenty-year-old single woman from Sichuan:

> We lived in a dormitory of the factory. It was too restrictive. We worked until eleven or twelve o'clock at night, and had to walk a long distance back to the dorm. It was almost two or three o'-clock in the morning by the time we had finished bathing and washing our clothes. We had to get up at five o'clock in the morning. We asked to live in the same building as the factory, but the boss wouldn't allow it.

Happy and Unhappy Memories

For some of our interviewees the experience of migration was an old memory; for others it was still fresh. We found that women were more willing to talk about the happy events in their migrant life, although they all complained that the work was hard. In each focus group we asked women to tell us about the most memorable event in their migration experience. Generally, happy memories came from feelings of accomplishment, having spending money, making friends, and feeling human kindness.

Many told stories of personal triumphs, such as one young married woman from Sichuan: "When I worked in a clothing factory in Guang-dong, the pay was based on pieces completed. There was a big contract that needed to be done. We worked very hard for a month. I did the best job. I was awarded the first prize! It was a new blanket. I was so proud!" Others enjoyed the rewards of their labor, such as this thirty-four-year-old married woman from Anhui: "The happiest time was when I got my first pay. I could buy what I liked. It was also a happy time to me when I received letters from home. I cried while reading them—I was happy but homesick. It was also a pleasure whenever my sisters or brothers visited me."

Others were touched by the kindness shown to them, such as in this story told by a twenty-five-year-old married woman who once worked in a clothing factory in Hangzhou: "When I was sick and lay alone in the dormitory, I felt so helpless and alone. At that time a fellow villager visited me with fresh fruits and medicine. I was so moved!" A twenty-three-year-old married woman from Sichuan was shown compassion by an attentive boss:

> I worked in Guangdong in 1998. I was having a baby, but it was a difficult labor. My husband was so scared! He called an ambulance at midnight but nobody answered; then somebody found a car. The doctor said that if we wanted the baby to live, my life would be in danger. It was so lucky that we both survived. My boss's wife was with me for the whole night. I can't imagine what I would have done without her. When I was discharged from the hospital, the whole family was together again and safe!

There were also quite a few stories of joyful escapades with fellow workers, such as:

> There was a film showing, but the boss wouldn't let us go and we did not have enough money to buy the tickets. We sneaked in over the fence. We were caught and fined for not having tickets. But we didn't have any money anyway. They first took our watches. We stayed there and would not leave. Later they returned the things they'd taken, and then we left. We laughed all the way back. It was such fun! (a twenty-seven-year-old primary school graduate from Anhui, with one son)

However, life in the city was not always fun. Some stories were told with tears. For example, migrants often got stuck in difficult circumstances due to the high costs of travel. A 35-year-old married woman from Anhui said, "It cost more than 1,000 *yuan* to travel to Urumqi [the capital city of Xinjiang Uygur Autonomous Region]. We could not earn any money without working hard. When I knocked at doors, some people refused to buy politely, some shouted at me and threatened to call the police. When business was low, I missed home so much."

There were also many stories of being cheated by labor recruiters and exploited by bosses, as illustrated below:

> The outside world is very complicated. People are sly. One of my classmates told me that she was cheated by a couple that tricked her to go to Yunnan. She expected that she would work in a barbershop, but it was a nightclub. The boss asked her to change into fancy clothes and she refused . . . the boss kept her inside the house. She asked somebody to call her home, and her father res-

cued her. I was so shocked by that story. I will always remember it and must keep alert so as not to be cheated. (a nineteen-year-old single female vocational school graduate from Sichuan)

I worked in Changzhou in 1994. It was a factory that made screws. We were paid 7 *yuan* for 10,000 screws. The money was taken if we did not meet the quota. The boss used abusive language. Sometimes I was so angry I couldn't eat for three days. (a 27-year-old married woman from Anhui)

I worked in a small textile factory in Zhejiang. The boss was mean. His dinner was good; I only had water and rice. I worked 18 hours a day. I only had four or five hours' rest. The boss promised to pay me 500 *yuan* per month, but only paid me 300. I argued and cried for three days, and finally got my pay. Then I changed jobs. (a 29-year-old married woman from Anhui)

I was introduced to a footwear factory in Guangdong. There were lots of workers from my county. The boss was very mean and strict to workers. We got up very early, had only one hour break at noon, and worked overtime at night. They told us that there would be a bonus for overtime, but it turned out to be nothing. We staged a strike, since the overtime exceeded what was allowed under the Labor Law. Then the manager told us to go immediately [weeping]. There were about thirty of us who left without pay. The factory accountant was the wife of the head of the local police station. The boss called the bosses of other factories and told them not to hire us! (a twenty-seven-year-old unmarried woman from Sichuan)

Migrant women are particularly vulnerable to acts of violence. The following story was told to us by a married woman from Anhui: "Last year I checked into a small hotel at night. I was alone and couldn't sleep. I kept the light on. At 3 o'clock in the morning I heard a noise at the window. A man broke into my room. I shouted, but he did not go. The concierge dialed 110, and the police came and caught him."

In a focus group with husbands, one insisted that it is easier for women than men migrants to find a job, since they are more obedient. However, through women's own stories a different picture emerged. Not one of those we spoke with seemed to fit the stereotype of the docile female factory worker. These women fought to improve their situation actively, through arguing or even going on strike; others removed themselves from negative situations by quitting. They bravely faced the challenge of the outside world, dealt with difficulties, and solved problems, and most more or less succeeded.

BACK AT HOME

> The happiest time was getting ready to go home. I called home and packed my bag. The journey was exhausting, but I was happy, since I was going home! (a twenty-eight-year-old woman from Anhui, with a son at home)

Strong ties to family and the land cause rural migrants to return home often. In addition, legal constraints, particularly the household registration system (*hukou*), mean they seldom make the city their permanent home.[9] In one village the woman village leader told us that there were 72 households in the village, with about 300 people, one third of whom were working outside the county. Yet only a few families had locked up their houses and left their farms in the care of others and completely migrated out. They may or may not ever come back, but nobody ever said that they would live outside and never return. In another village a new house was being built for a couple working in a state-owned forestry center in western Sichuan. The wife told us that they built the house for their retirement. It was not so easy for them to leave the land, even though city life was very attractive.

Motivations for Going Home

When survey participants were asked the primary reason for returning home from the first migration episode, the most frequent reasons stated were: family need (33.8 percent), to visit a family member (22.7 percent), and unable to find a satisfactory job (17.5 percent). The other reasons stated were: marriage (7.7 percent), childbirth (4.2 percent), my husband's request (4.2 percent), to look for a job at home (1 percent), and other (8.9 percent). Table 7.3 shows the variation in the reasons for returning home by the timing of initial migration.

The rural women with whom we talked spent a lot of time thinking about the needs of their families. As the following quotations indicate, an ill or vulnerable parent could require the attention of an unmarried daughter.

> I came back because my mother needs me. She did not feel well. I am the oldest in the family; my three younger sisters all work outside. (a twenty-five-year-old single secondary school graduate from Sichuan)

Table 7.3 The Reason for Returning Home from the First Migration Episode by Status at Leaving Home (column percentage)

Reason for Returning Home	Before 1st Marriage	After Marriage, Before 1st Childbirth	After 1st Child Born	After the Last Child Born
marriage	19.7	—	—	—
childbirth	1.7	25.9	2.2	1.7
family need	19.0	24.1	46.9	41.3
visit family member	30.0	18.5	17.1	22.1
husband's request	.7	5.6	7.6	2.9
no satisfactory job	17.3	16.7	17.3	19.2
found job at home	1.4	.9	.7	1.2
other	10.1	8.4	8.3	11.6

DATA SOURCE: Authors' survey

> I came back because of my mother. My parents have a very bad relationship. But it is impossible for my mom to take any action [meaning divorce]; she is numb. She accepts fate. She does not like us going to the city to work. She cannot understand us. My elder sister could not stand it anymore and migrated out. She won't be back again. Now I run a small shop. I don't want to always be with my mother, but I can't get rid of her either. I don't want to leave her alone. (a seventeen-year-old single secondary school graduate from Sichuan)

One of the major findings from our survey was that two thirds of the migrant women were married. Many of them had children who were being taken care of by relatives at home. Some women reported having returned home to care for their children themselves. Married women returning home generally stayed there if there was nobody else to take care of the children, elderly, the farm, or the housework.

> I came back this year to start my own business in cloth making. In fact, I can earn more money working in a factory, but my family needs me. My husband works in the village in construction. I have to cook for him and take care of my child who is in primary school. (a thirty-four-year-old married woman from Anhui)

A thirty-four-year-old married Sichuan woman, who migrated in order to make money and build her own house, came back home after the house was built to care for her child, but also because to stay out might be viewed unfavorably by the community:

> My husband thought that if he stayed home and I worked out-
> side to make money, he would lose face. The fellow villagers
> would laugh at him. He said that's a man's responsibility. I came
> back, and now he is working in Guangdong. He makes more
> than 1,000 *yuan* a month and sends home 600–700 *yuan*. The
> major reason I agreed to come back was our child. The school
> fees are too high in the city; it is impossible to earn enough
> money to pay them. I stay home and take care of our child. I can
> also raise pigs. We let others take care of our farm.

Three fourths of the migrant women in our survey had husbands who
were themselves migrants. Who should stay and who should go were conscious decisions the couples made. During the interviews, they talked
about the careful balance between costs and benefits in making such decisions. The opportunity cost of migrating is higher for the wife, since the
husband is usually not experienced with the "inside" duties of housework,
child rearing, and so on. However, in many cases the benefits of the wife
migrating are evaluated to be higher than the costs. In a focus group discussion with husbands, a man told us that originally he and his wife had
both migrated (they had met while working in a factory). Later, his wife
worked in a footwear factory in Guangdong, while he stayed at home and
worked on the farm. His seventy-five-year-old father took care of housework and the child. This husband said that women not only could earn
money but also were more likely to save money, as they neither smoked
nor drank. His wife sent more money home than he ever did.

   In some cases migrants returned home after being unable to find a good
job. Often they lacked the education or skills necessary for a good job. A
thirty-five-year-old secondary school graduate from Anhui with one
daughter followed her husband to Shenzhen, but could not find a job:

> Thirty to 40 percent of the people in Shenzhen work in high-
> tech. If you have poor education, you can't find a job there. . . .
> I decided to come back home and bring up my daughter. I told
> her to study hard and do better than her father. Let her have a
> better education; that is the most important wealth. We can't do
> anything well without good education. We can't catch up with
> developed countries.

   Others found jobs too difficult or too dangerous and quit and came
home. A twenty-year-old unmarried primary school graduate from
Sichuan told us that she worked in a footwear factory in Guangdong.

Afraid that the job was harmful to her health, she quit: "I went to Guangdong with my friends. The footwear workshop had a kind of chemical that makes skin peel off. And the Guangdong food did not taste good. Although it was fun out there, we all came back."

Some young women returned home because of particularly bad experiences of labor exploitation. A twenty-year-old single secondary school graduate from Sichuan said:

> I felt discriminated against by rich people. I worked for half a year. We even needed permission to go to the restroom [during work time]. I only got 250 *yuan* plus 50 *yuan* allowance each month. I thought the pay was too low. The boss wanted it still lower and asked us to sign a contract. We fought with the boss together, but did not get any money and left. I cried many tears. I won't go out anymore.

Some women said that they could not get used to the different environment and cuisine elsewhere, and so came home. A twenty-one-year-old single primary school graduate from Sichuan said, "I worked in a footwear factory in Guangdong. The climate was so different, the food was so different, I couldn't stand it. I came back after three months."

Understandably, many young, unmarried women returned from the first migration episode because they were homesick, only to migrate again later:

> I worked on the production line in a Shenzhen factory. There were more than ten of us living in a room; others came from Henan, Hebei, everywhere. After several months I got really homesick, I missed my mom so much. That was my first time. My mom did not want me to go at first. My elder sister left, and I wanted to follow. Mom was afraid that others could take advantage of me, since I was young. I went to Shenzhen with my sister-in-law. I would like to go to work in the same factory in the near future, and this time I would stay longer. (an unmarried Anhui woman)

Not all migrants returned home as a result of their family situation or a failure to succeed at work or to adjust to the urban environment. Some brought skills back to the countryside or returned to attend school. A married Anhui woman came back after learning tailoring skills in a Jiangsu clothing factory. She now runs her own business in her home village: "I came back in 1993 because I could not get used to the life there. We went there together, and some of the others did not come back. I wanted to be my own boss and hire some workers to help me. I sometimes have thirty workers. I can earn more money now."

Some unmarried women returned home to continue studying in order to be better prepared for work on a second trip out later on. A sixteen-year-old Anhui woman told us, "I plan to migrate again. But now I am going to read more books to improve myself. My father taught me senior secondary school textbooks. I would like to go to vocational school to learn art. I want to work in fashion design in the future. Now I take courses at the County Normal School."

Many young women returned home in order to get married. Almost all the women in the sample married someone from their county. Surprisingly few married someone they had met while out. Interestingly, among women who migrated the first time while still single, unmarried Sichuan women were more likely than unmarried Anhui women to report "marriage" as the main reason for their return home. The variance in marriage age is lower in Sichuan; there is a clear sense that it is "time" to get married. Anhui society is a bit more open; more variation in lifestyle is tolerated, though the overwhelming proportion of women still marry before age twenty-five.

Although each of the women with whom we talked had returned home, many still planned to migrate again in the future. This was especially so for Anhui women engaged in traveling sales, who frequently returned home only to go out again. They usually went out for several months, came back home for several months to take a rest, and then went out again. They got used to this lifestyle. A woman told us that if she stayed home for too long, her parents-in-law would ask her why she did not go out to "make money."

In the survey, 49.6 percent of the returnees said that they would like to migrate again, while 15.8 percent had not made up their minds yet. Only 34.6 percent said that they would not migrate again. Of the women who said they came back to visit family members, 57 percent migrated again later, while only 38 percent of those who returned home because of "family need" migrated again. Thus, for most women migrants the possibility of migrating again stays with them even as they make their way in their rural life.

Life After Migration

The experience of migration brings changes to the individual and her family. Most women bring money home. The effects on households of this injection of money should not be discounted. When one walks around villages in either Anhui or Sichuan, it is very easy to tell which families have

Table 7.4 Family Wealth Difference by Migration Status

	Percentage Among Ever Migrated Women	Percentage Among Never Migrated Women
own at least one color TV	36.9	24.1
have a telephone	15.2	8.6
own a two-story house	48.0	39.1

DATA SOURCE: Authors' survey

somebody working outside—those with better houses. Some returning migrants even design their houses in the coastal style, which was popular where they worked. Lots of families have a color television; some have a washing machine, a motorcycle, and even a truck or car.

The survey results reveal that families with returned women migrants have more income and score higher in terms of the wealth indicators included in the survey than in families with never-migrated women (see table 7.4). Some people came back with enough money to build or buy new houses in the nearby county town (where a change in *hukou* is not required) and become "city residents," and local people admired them.

Most women did not invest their money in business, thinking it too risky.[10] Without more substantial economic development and increased investment in infrastructure, there are few investment opportunities in these rural villages. There were some business success stories: women who came back and opened a small shop, restaurant, or school. For example, a twenty-five-year-old married woman who had migrated right after graduating from secondary school now ran a snack bar near the Anhui county senior secondary school. She planned to open a larger restaurant soon. Another Anhui woman ran a workshop to train boys and girls in sewing and tailoring. After the students graduated from the workshop, she helped them find jobs in clothing factories in Jiangsu:

> Before marriage I worked in a clothing factory in Jiangsu. I stayed home after I got married. I cannot leave home, since my child is young. Two years ago I opened this training workshop in my town, so I can take care of my child while working. I had learned tailoring skills in Suzhou (a city in Jiangsu). I invested my money, bought sewing machines, and built the house. My father-in-law helped me.

Similarly, a Sichuan woman opened a kindergarten in her village after working and studying in Kunming and Chengdu. She seemed to be a good

Figure 7.3 Students in sewing class at a vocational school in Huaining county that was founded by a returned migrant woman, who also serves as an instructor. Zhenzhen Zheng

teacher, and fellow villagers were willing to pay for their children to attend her kindergarten.

However, most women returned home and took up the same life they had known before: as a farmer. As shown in table 7.5, over half of the returned migrants listed their occupation as farmer, compared to 77 percent of the women who never migrated. The second largest occupation category among returned migrants was paid employment, which differs substantially from the never-migrated group.

Although the whole family benefits from the inflow of money, women themselves are the ones most changed by the migration experience. We reported earlier that single women who had migrated showed a higher level of confidence and ease in talking to strangers than those who had not. In addition, women who had migrated reported that they had changed in fundamental ways. Many learned to imitate urban fashion, speech, and behavior, as indicated in the quotations below.

> The first feeling when I arrived in the city was that we were so rustic! The city is so busy and crowded! Our speech and dress

Table 7.5 Respondents' Current Occupation by Migration Status (column percentage)

Current Occupation	Ever Migrated	Never Migrated
farming (*wunong*)	54.7	77.5
paid job (*dagong*)	23.8	1.1
house chores (*jiawu*)	12.8	16.0
self-employed (*getihu*)	7.1	2.8
specialized (*zhuanyehu*)	.8	.9
others	.9	.15

DATA SOURCE: Authors' survey

told everybody that we were rural girls. The life in the factory was very simple at first; we did not care about the meals. Then we learned to go to the movies and buy drinks, like city girls do. At the beginning I felt humiliated wherever I went. I felt the eyes of people on me and heard them whispering: she is a *dagongmei* [working sister]. Gradually I stopped feeling that way. I went shopping and was treated just like the others. I changed also. I learned from my boss and workmates. I am careful about how I talk and behave, and my habits have changed. (a twenty-five-year-old secondary school graduate from Anhui with one daughter)

For other women, especially young women, migration marked a passage to maturity. A twenty-five-year-old primary school graduate from Anhui said, "I feel I grew up through migrating. I came to understand how hard my parents' life was, and that they did the best they could for us. I decided to come back and help them." As another summarized:

Maybe the obvious difference between never-migrated and migrated women is the style of dress. Before we dressed very simply at home. People would treat you different if you dressed like that in the city. Another difference is that we are more mature. (a twenty-one-year-old secondary school graduate from Anhui)

Others felt they had improved themselves:

I migrated because I wanted to see the world. My biggest achievement is learning a skill, but I still regret that I haven't learned more! (a twenty-year-old secondary school graduate from Anhui)

Many returned women migrants increased their standards for hygiene. In a Sichuan village, where getting fresh water is not easy, a woman said that after coming back from Guangdong, she had become used to taking baths more often than was the custom locally. She also learned to eat a healthy diet, and ate more vegetables than locals usually did. Anhui women told us that they now insist on using separate towels and washbowls, in contrast to the usual rural practice of sharing with family members. A twenty-five-year-old married secondary school graduate from Anhui told us of her use of cosmetics and her hygienic habits: "Now I use creams, I buy sanitary napkins, I care about my skin, and I brush my teeth in the morning and the evening."

The changes brought about by the urban experience affect women not only in observable ways but also in their opinions and attitudes toward issues such as marriage, divorce, and sexual/fertility behavior. Our multivariate analysis of the survey results shows that after controlling for all other differences, women who have migrated are more likely to think that couples themselves should decide whether they want to marry each other. These women are also more likely to think that divorce is acceptable in the case of a couple that does not get along,[11] and they are more likely to think that it is acceptable for a wife to refuse her husband's desire for sexual intercourse.[12] Desired fertility is lower for women who have migrated.[13]

Fertility behavior also changes in measurable ways that are good news for public officials concerned about birth rates and women's reproductive health more generally. Fewer children are born to women who have ever migrated;[14] and age of marriage and age of first birth are higher for women if they migrate before the event.[15] Furthermore, more women who migrated before marriage know about the rhythm method of contraception (*anquan qi*), more migrant women believe that contraceptives should be available to unmarried youths, and migrants' knowledge of AIDS and STDs is increased.[16] These results and those of the focus group discussions reported here strongly support the sense that the migration experience has a large positive effect on women and a positive impact on their family. However, as we will see below, migration also brings about some negative changes. In particular, it increases the level of discontent with rural life for some returned migrants.

Attitudes Toward Life in the Village

Many of the migrant women expressed dissatisfaction with rural life after returning home. They strongly felt the large contrasts between urban and rural life—developed vs. underdeveloped, advanced vs. backward, rich vs.

poor, built-up vs. desolate, fast-paced vs. slow-paced. All the good memories of the city increased their longing to go out again to what they considered the "other world." Some important differences were found between younger and older returned migrant women and, to a lesser extent, between those from Sichuan and Anhui. Younger women more often mentioned their future and career and complained about the boring life back home. They seemed to be more sensitive to urban/rural differences and sometimes expressed confusion at being caught in the middle. Older women complained less about rural life but still enjoyed reminiscing about life in the city. Some of them expressed a desire to go out again but were not sure if that would happen, since they had responsibilities to care for elderly parents-in-law and young children. It is difficult to predict whether the younger women will settle into village life as their children grow up or this generation gap will remain. Moreover, though the inequality between urban and rural China is certainly not new, the continuing gap in the standard of living between urban and rural families combined with the freedom to migrate may result in increased resentment by rural residents of urban privilege.[17]

It may be most difficult for unmarried women to fit in upon return to the village, especially when their peers have all married and settled down.[18] A twenty-seven-year-old single woman, a vocational school graduate from Sichuan, had this struggle between rural gender roles/early marriage norms and the desire for independence in mind after coming back home:

> My mother said that I should come back home finally. She did not want me to go again. So I stayed. But I still want to go. I no longer fit in with fellow villagers after coming back. Women and men are equal in the cities. In the city they pay attention to ability, but not here. I always want to be independent; I can earn enough money to make a living. But the others think that I overestimate myself.

Recall that most rural women are married by age twenty-two, so that this twenty-seven-year-old woman really does not fit in her village. The other women in her school cohort moved to other villages upon marriage, and the new wives in the village who are her age all have toddlers. Another unmarried woman from Sichuan, who worked in a Chengdu supermarket, hinted that she still hoped to find a better life outside of her village: "The difference between Chengdu and my home village is so big! It is especially apparent in the economy. Although this is my home, I don't feel comfortable here anymore. I will go back to Chengdu when my mother gets better. . . . Where I can finally settle down depends on my luck."

The inability of young women to make use of their newly acquired skills was also a source of frustration and boredom. An unmarried woman from Anhui who has tailoring skills said, "I cannot get used to the life here anymore. I want to go out again after being home for a while. The only thing I can do is help my parents on the farm. It is difficult to find a job here." An unmarried young woman from Sichuan told us, "The women my age almost all migrated out. I migrated too. I worked for three months but did not get used to life there. But I don't have anything to do now that I'm back at home. I would like to try some other place, to try a better place."

Young women also mentioned the disappointment they felt in their rural environment, lifestyle, and lack of leisure activities, as this quote from a twenty-year-old single secondary school graduate from Anhui demonstrates: "Living conditions were better there [in the city]. We could walk around after work. It is so dark here at night, we don't dare to go out." Similarly, a twenty-year-old unmarried woman from Anhui said, "I think city people have money (laugh). They have time to go shopping, it seems they basically don't work. . . . Ningbo [a city in Zhejiang Province] is so busy on the street and in the stores, lots of people. The stores here are not good, they only have a few things; there are few shoppers, and it looks empty."

Differences between Sichuan and Anhui married women emerged from the focus group discussions. In Sichuan, the married women complained about having to give up their urban lifestyles after coming back home. They dared not wear skirts, since fellow villagers would gossip.[19] They had to forget their standard Mandarin pronunciation, since using it was seen as showing off, and use only local dialect. In sum, when they came back they were expected to go back to the old way of living, and they were reluctant to do so. There were fewer such complaints in Anhui. It is easier to find many women who have had similar migration experiences in Anhui villages, who still talk and dress in an urban manner (for example, wearing earrings). Hardly any of the Anhui migrant women complained about isolation and not fitting in. We believe this is because Anhui women have been migrating for fifteen years now, migration has become nearly universal among young Anhui women, and there is more repeat migration. These three factors make rural Anhui residents more tolerant of variation and more understanding of returning migrants.

Women's lives are changed by the experience of migration in many ways. They live in houses and watch televisions purchased with money earned from migration. A few run businesses funded with money saved from work in the city. They think about their experiences as migrants with a great deal of ambivalence: the triumphs of autonomy and self-made successes mixed with memories of hard work, lack of sleep, and difficult living conditions. They view their life in the countryside through a more critical lens, often contrasting rural and urban clothing and hygiene standards. While most return to substantially the same life that they left before they migrated, they are more empowered within it by their experiences outside the village. The potential of future migration also becomes part of their own and their family's set of choices, so that even if they never go out to work again, they are changed by knowing of the possibility.

CONCLUSIONS

Using surveys of more than three thousand women, and focus group and individual interviews with at least one hundred additional women, we have explored the migration experiences of young women from rural Sichuan and Anhui provinces. We found that the experiences differed between locations and age cohorts based on the timing of migration. Anhui women started migrating in the late 1980s, while migration was very uncommon in Sichuan until much more recently. Early in the migration flow from Anhui, very young teenage girls were migrating with sisters and older relatives. The age of first migration has increased, with more girls finishing secondary school and some learning a trade before migrating. Still, the majority of young women in Anhui do migrate at least once, often before they marry, and many go out a second or third time as well. In Sichuan the age of first migration for women is older than in Anhui, and many young women marry first and then migrate.

One of the most important findings of our study is that marriage does not end migration for women in either Anhui or Sichuan. Anhui women who may first have migrated single often migrate again after marriage. Their second migration may be with their husband, but it does not have to be; many married women migrate without their husbands. In Sichuan, there may even be a preference for migrating after marriage instead of before, since the morals of married migrants are less suspect than those of unmarried women migrants.

Women's migration in China may at one time have been a signal of extreme poverty or desperation, but this is no longer the case. Now it is seen as a rite of passage by some young women, or at least a great adventure. In most cases the motive is still cash income, but often money is to be amassed for specific consumption goals, such as a new home, a bridal dowry, the bride-price for the girl's brother, or education expenses for younger siblings.

While differences in the circumstances of migration emerged across provinces in ways that we predicted ahead of time, we were somewhat surprised by the overwhelming similarity in the women's narratives about their experiences as migrants. It seems clear now that the substantial rural/urban differences faced in common by these migrants led to the recollection of their experiences as bittersweet. The factory work or service work that they do in the urban areas is at best very hard and at worst terribly exploitative; but there are the triumphs of trying something new, of being challenged, of learning new skills, of overcoming adversity, and of having more cash income than they have ever had before. They are also freed from the watching eyes of their fellow villagers and exposed to new consumer goods and new customs in the city that they sometimes feel nostalgic for upon their return home.

Their stories of migration make it clear that these rural migrants are not the docile *dagongmei* often depicted. They are active players in their own experiences, from finding employment to arguing with bosses over pay to participating in worker strikes. Within their families they discuss the costs and benefits of their migration versus their husbands' and the outcome is no longer always that women will stay at home while their husbands migrate. When someone else, like a healthy parent-in-law, is available to watch their young child, the couple may decide to migrate together, though this arrangement is viewed as more acceptable for young children than for school-age children.

Young women migrants return home when they are exhausted by the trials of the city or have met their financial goal, or when responsibilities of home call or homesickness overtakes the benefits of migration. Once returned, they usually benefit from their savings, though sometimes the money goes to other family members instead of remaining with them. Some migrants struggle to find a place for themselves upon returning. They are changed by the experience and thus no longer fit into rural society, yet they are also not accepted in urban society. But for most returned migrants the struggle is brief, with rural life the clear victor, especially for the married women, who come back to a full set of responsibilities and expectations.

Substantial differences between the women of Sichuan and Anhui have been noted in the circumstances of migration, i.e., age of migration, marital status at migration, duration, occupation, and destination. Similarly, we found some differences by location in the struggle with rural life upon return, with women in Sichuan more likely to feel censored by their community for adopting urban customs of dress or hygiene. There is also a noticeable difference by age. Upon their return, younger women were more critical of village life and more likely to expect to migrate again. Further research is needed to establish whether this generation gap will remain over time or will dissipate with age. More time must also pass before we can assess whether the increased likelihood of migration—such that it becomes an expected rite of passage for more young women—will change its impact on rural women's lives.

More time is also needed to assess the impact of migration on children's lives. The women we talked with often thought about migration in terms of their children. For many that meant a greater emphasis on education, so that their child could compete in the larger marketplace. However, for some it meant that the opportunity cost of keeping children in school was higher, and they would send their children out as soon as possible.

NOTES

1. Roberts et al. 2002.

2. Ibid.

3. The dialects of Sichuan and Anhui both belong to the northern system, the same system that *putonghua* (Mandarin) comes from. Since the accents within the system do not vary too much, there is no difficulty in communication (Hu et al. 2001:80). Most migrants had no difficulty listening to *putonghua*, but some of them mentioned communication difficulties in Guangdong (since the local dialects of Guangdong are so different from the others). None of the younger women, whether they had migrated or not, had any difficulty understanding *putonghua*. The migrants did mention that they dared not speak out for fear that their local accent would identify them as outsiders.

4. For examples of this commonly held view see Du, "Single women tend to participate in migration but married women do not" (2000:77); Jacka, "It is largely only unmarried women who leave home to work" (1997:135); Mallee, "Women tend to remain in the village after marriage" (1996:117).

5. For some parents a daughter's completion of secondary school education was not a priority, since going to secondary school cost them money, while a daughter going out to work could earn money. When asked directly, almost all parents said that they treat daughters and sons alike. However, in more subtle ways, most expressed higher expectations for their sons. All of the newly enrolled college students in the Anhui villages we visited were boys, suggesting they receive more support for their education than their sisters.

6. See Gaetano, this volume, for a discussion of historical taboos on unaccompanied women migrating.

7. Brown 2002.

8. Tsang 1996.

9. Introduction, this volume.

10. Our finding that most of the money women brought home was invested in homes rather than businesses is supported by survey research by de Brauw and Rozelle (2002).

11. Divorce is a very sensitive subject for rural women, due to unfavorable social and familial attitudes.

12. Connelly et al. 2002.

13. You and Zheng 2002.

14. Ibid.

15. Zheng et al. 2001a; Zheng 2002.

16. Xie 2001.

17. Khan and Riskin find that the gap between rural and urban has narrowed a little between 1988 and 1995 but that "China was still among the more unequal societies in developing Asia by the middle of the 1990s" (1998:246).

18. See chapters by Beynon and Murphy, this volume.

19. Most rural women wear utilitarian pants and shirts with hand-knitted sweaters when it is cold.

Rachel Murphy

8. The Impact of Labor Migration on the Well-Being and Agency of Rural Chinese Women: Cultural and Economic Contexts and the Life Course

>> Rural Chinese women at all stages of the life course are affected by the migratory process, regardless of whether they are migrants, returned migrants, or nonmigrants. Numerous young single women and some married women work in the cities, earning valuable cash income for themselves and their families. Meanwhile, girls, most married women, and especially elderly women stay in the countryside and carry out farming and domestic chores that socially and economically facilitate the migration of other family members. The movement of women in and out of nonmigrant, migrant, and returnee roles over the life course has implications for the lives of other female villagers. For example, schoolgirls in the village admire the clothes of their older migrant sisters when they return home for Spring Festival. Migrant women return to their villages to marry, rear children, and farm, often while their husbands remain in the city. Elderly women farm the land in lieu of their migrant sons and daughters-in-law and care for grandchildren or, in a few cases, venture to the city themselves.

This chapter considers the impact of migration on the well-being and agency of rural Chinese women in the Reform period, focusing mainly on returned migrants and "stayers" (that is, women who do not migrate themselves but who belong to a household in which one or more other members migrate)[1] using data from rural Jiangxi.

Following Amartya Sen's[2] theory of capabilities, a person's well-being comprises their achieved "functionings"—the "beings" and "doings" that a person values—together with their positive freedom to choose and achieve functionings. In this study I consider the functionings of spatial mobility, being educated, accruing material possessions/renovating houses, having leisure time (not being overworked), and improving the lives of family members, which are variously valued by rural Chinese women. Achieving functionings, according to Sen, requires access to resources such as money, land, labor, social networks, and information. People may need different resources to attain the same functionings depending on their personal characteristics, such as marital status, age, and health,[3] as well as on socioeconomic status and cultural context. For example, the amount of resources needed to attain a standard of "respectability" increases with the wealth of a society.[4]

Sen calls the potential to achieve a functioning a "capability" and argues that people exercise agency when they decide which capabilities to convert into functionings. Exercising agency and "choosing freely" are important because they maximize the alternatives available and, hence, the chance to achieve well-being, and they are themselves functionings integral to well-being. Sen's work on gender and households supplements the capability approach by showing that women's well-being and opportunities for exercising agency may be compromised, not only by a lack of access to resources but also by their internalization of norms about the way things are. The internalization of norms pertaining to gender, age, kinship, and class causes some women to respond to disadvantage by adapting their expectations to what seems possible, thus reproducing their subordinate social position.[5]

Women's subordinate position in the family and household[6] in rural China poses particular challenges for their exercise of agency and achievement of well-being. First, their claims on resources are undermined by cultural arrangements that make their membership in the household ambiguous. In particular, village exogamous marriage patterns mean that a woman is first a guest in her parents' home and then a guest in her husband's village. This guest status means that daughters often receive lesser investment in their education than their brothers, and wives often depend on their husbands' and in-laws' land for their livelihood.

The subordinate position of Chinese women in their households can be illuminated with reference to two concepts from Sen's work on gender and households: "cooperative conflict" and "fall-back position."[7] In the cooperative conflict model, the well-being of individuals is said to depend on their capacity to bargain for household resources, which is affected by the visibility of their contribution to the material well-being of their households. In rural China, women's labor is conceptualized as belonging to the "inner" sphere, so its perceived contribution is devalued. Women are thus less able to bargain for household resources. In addition, women in rural China lack a "fall-back position," because they are guests in their husbands' villages and depend on the family land for their livelihood. Not having a "fall-back position" outside their domestic roles leads the women to identify their needs with those of other household members, and thus maintain the status quo.

Sen's theory of capabilities and his model of cooperative conflict suggest that women who have not only access to resources but also broadened perspectives from which to reflect on their situation and consider alternatives to received norms are most able to exercise agency.[8] The value of migration for rural Chinese women, then, lies not only in its potential to increase resources for households and individual women but also in its offering broader perspectives and increased choices from which to examine and challenge gender norms and other norms that constrain their lives, for example, those involving kinship or pertaining to age.

In this chapter I use Sen's ideas as a starting point from which to assess the effect of migration on rural Chinese women in different socioeconomic circumstances and at different stages of the life course. I focus, in particular, on the impact of migration on women's workloads, the visibility and perceived value of their labor, their access to resources, and their perspectives on social norms, gender roles, and entitlements, because these are crucial to their ability to achieve functionings integral to well-being.

The chapter is based on fieldwork conducted in four villages. In the first section I describe my fieldwork and outline the basic characteristics of the economies of the villages. I then examine the gender divisions of labor in each village and how they interact with migration, before exploring the ways in which these factors influence the impact of migration on women's well-being and agency. In the final section I shift away from village-level factors to focus on how individual factors, and women's stage in the life cycle, shape the impact of migration on their well-being and agency.

CHARACTERISTICS OF THE FIELDWORK VILLAGES

The fieldwork villages are Jiaocun, Qifeng, Beihu, and Wentang, all located in Jiangxi province. Together, these four villages represent the middle range of agricultural settlements to be found in the province. Jiaocun village is in the hilly terrain of Xinbei township, in the state-designated poverty county of Yudu. Qifeng village is located in Gaocheng township, Wanzai county, and its fertile fields are interspersed among red hills. Beihu and Wentang are situated on fertile plains in northwest Jiangxi. The main agricultural activity in all four villages is double rice cropping. Per capita allocations of arable land in Jiaocun, Qifeng, Beihu, and Wentang are 0.58 *mu*, 0.6 *mu*, 0.8 *mu*, and 1.3 *mu*, respectively; for reference, the provincial average is 0.8 *mu* and the national average is 1.2 *mu*.

Reported incomes for Beihu, Qifeng, Wentang, and Jiaocun are 2,200 *yuan*, 1,800 *yuan*, 1,700 *yuan*, and 1,048 *yuan*, respectively. But caution is needed when comparing these figures. The figures incorporate migrant earnings, so there is the wider methodological problem of separating out the causes from the effects of migration. And the figures tell us little about how money from the cities is distributed between household members in the city and those in the countryside. Despite these reservations, the income figures provide a useful basis for comparing the economic standing of the villages, with Beihu, Qifeng, and Wentang ranking above the provincial average of 1,500 *yuan* and Jiaocun positioned 25 percent below it.

All four villages enjoy convenient access to transport and proximity to market towns. Moreover, most of their households have at least a black-and-white television, and in 1996–97 all the villages had at least one telephone.

The material in this chapter is drawn from interviews conducted between October 1996 and December 1997 with household members and cadres in the four fieldwork villages, and during subsequent visits in December 2000. Government officials assisted with and oversaw most of my interviewing. They selected the villages, though within the villages they selected the households by lot. The information from the interviews has been supplemented with data from Chinese-language documents, such as local government migration reports and local newspaper articles. The next section draws from the data in table 8.1 to analyze the gendered divisions of labor and patterns of migration in each village.

THE GENDERING OF MIGRATION

Migration is often perceived to be a gender-neutral economic process external to the origin area, but fieldwork in the four villages reveals that migration patterns are formed through interaction between the existing gendered divisions of labor that characterize each village, existing informal rules, and gender norms determining the intrahousehold allocation of resources as well as the gendered nature of urban labor demands. Below I

Table 8.1 Summary of Village Characteristics, 1997

Characteristic	Beihu	Wentang	Jiaocun	Qifeng
gendered division of labor	men plow	men plow	women plow, men migrate	men plow, both migrate
ethnicity	Han	Han	Hakka	mainly Han with some Hakka who have adopted the Han taboo on women plowing
main destination area	Hainan Island	Shanghai	Pearl River Delta	Pearl River Delta
migration activity	trading—garments	trading—glass decorations	factory work	factory work
main migration pattern	long-term outmigration	shuttle migration	long-term outmigration with annual returns	long-term outmigration with annual returns
volume of outmigration (migrants/ village pop.)	>1,000 out of 2,000	500 out of 2,209	600 out of 2,239	>300 out of 3,712*
as % of total population	>50%	23%	27%	~10%
female involvement in migration**	+In 50% of households, a married couple has migrated. In around 8% of households, a single daughter or son has migrated. The remainder of the households comprise either elderly couples or young married couples with children.	In 15% of households a married couple has migrated. In 35% of households a husband has migrated with the wife "shuttling" to various degrees. In around 8% of households a single daughter has migrated, and in around 12% of households a single son has migrated (to help at a relative's stall). Most of the remaining households comprise the elderly.	Over 25% of migrants are women and most of them are unmarried.	Men and women have migrated from the village in roughly equal proportion. Over 60% of the migrants are unmarried. Thirteen wives are at home alone long-term in the village, as are 9 husbands. There are a couple of instances of grandmothers migrating to the cities.
land allocation (*mu*)	0.8	1.3	0.58	0.6
agriculture after migration	much abandoned land, some hiring of labor	government support services, migrants return to farm	female mutual aid teams, ~1/6 migrants return to help in busy season	land transfers, some migrants return to help in busy season *
per capita income (*yuan*)	2,200	1,700	1,048	1,800

NOTES:

* Figure for 1996.

** It is extremely difficult to obtain accurate figures on people's involvement in migration on the basis of their gender, age, and household composition. A common lament of migration scholars is that figures for migration are like a "sponge"—full of holes. The situation is fluid, forever changing, and household members do not always classify movement as "migration" *per se*. Moreover, resource and time constraints meant that I was unable to survey every household in a village. For the most part I relied on estimates from township and village cadres. Despite the general nature of the figures and their lack of comparability, they nevertheless offer a rough overview of gendered participation in migration in each of the four villages.

+ Based on 104 households that comprise one of 8 natural villages (Yujia) in the administrative village of Beihu.

sketch the migration patterns and different effects on the gendered divisions of labor in the four villages.

In two of the villages, Beihu and Wentang, the primary migration activity is trading. Migrants from Beihu village are clothes traders on Hainan Island, and this has earned it the nickname "garment village." Migrants from Wentang run glass installation and decoration businesses in Shanghai. Trading activities from both villages are coordinated through the patriarchal family. Male family members pool money for one or more of them to set up a stall. Some men work as apprentices for male relatives until they have sufficient knowledge and savings to set up their own stalls. Young men generally start to run their own businesses shortly after marriage, operating the new stalls with their new wives. When extra labor is needed in the city, the men summon their daughters and sisters. In the case of Wentang, because travel from Shanghai requires only an overnight train journey, men and particularly married women "shuttle" periodically to help with farm tasks and the care of elderly family members. But from Beihu only long-term migration is possible because Hainan Island is three days away by bus and boat. In Wentang about 15 percent of couples migrate together; in a further 35 percent of households the husband migrates alone, with his wife shuttling to varying degrees. In contrast, in Beihu the impossibility of shuttling makes the proportion much higher, and around 50 percent of couples have left the village on a long-term basis.

Migration patterns have impact on the gendered division of labor in the origin villages by determining which and how many people are left behind. Outmigration from trading villages tends to leave few villagers at home, because many hands are needed for transporting and selling goods, managing accounts, cleaning, and cooking. This means that entire households rather than individuals leave the village. As an example, out of a total of 2,000 people registered as residents of Beihu, less than half remain in the village. In Beihu, like in many other Han Chinese villages, cultural norms designate plowing as a male task. But the severe labor shortage precipitated by migration has forced a small number of Beihu women to plow the land. Here I add the caveat that women who do not plow still carry out a substantial amount of farming: rural women's agricultural tasks generally include weeding, transplanting seedlings, growing vegetables, watering and fertilizing crops, collecting fuel, and raising small animals.

The gendered division of labor in Wentang differs from that in Beihu because, although many people have migrated (there are more than 500 migrants out of a laboring population of 1,050 and a total population of 2,209), the migration is not long-term. The "shuttling" of the married Wentang women allows them to contribute their labor to the origin village despite their involvement in trading: they move back and forth between origin and destination, performing caring and support work in both places. In Wentang as in Beihu, cultural norms designate plowing as a male task. But, despite the substantial outmigration, few women are forced to plow, because the township government has established a mechanized plowing collective and because convenient transport and the flexibility of self-employment enable male migrants to return home during the plowing season.

Although trading is the main activity among migrants from Beihu and Wentang, women, particularly single women, going to factories to work form a secondary migration stream. Beihu women work in shoes and electronics factories in Guangdong, and Wentang women work in pearl necklace factories in Zhejiang province. They are introduced to the factory through a male villager who is often a foreman, or else the young women introduce each other through their own networks. Around a third of the single women in each village migrate to the factories.

Most migrants from Jiaocun and Qifeng villages go to work in factories. In Jiaocun village, as in other parts of south Jiangxi, subethnic Hakka customs exert a strong impact on the local gendered division of labor and therefore on migration patterns. Historically, Hakka men were trained in off-farm skills, such as cotton shredding, carpentry, and metal work, and traveled to faraway places. The Hakka women performed heavy farming tasks, such as plowing, and also traded in the local marketplace.[9] Following decollectivization and the economic reforms, Hakka women assumed responsibility for all tasks on the farm, leaving the men free to use their transportable skills to find work in the cities, and later to work year round in the factories. Nowadays, out of the 720 people in Jiaocun classified as "laborers," more than 600 (90 percent) are working in Guangdong factories, though some men also load cargo at the Shanghai docks.[10] The gendered division of labor in Jiaocun, with men working off the farm and women working on the farm, is nevertheless changing as a result of migration. In recent years some Jiaocun women have found work on assembly lines and they now account for nearly one third of migrants from the village. Most are single women or younger married women without children, though some leave their children with grandparents.

In Qifeng village, social norms underpinning the gendered division of labor are being reworked in the new context of China's export-led development strategy. Women in this part of Jiangxi are said to possess "nimble fingers" and an industrious temperament; this perception existed during the late Ming dynasty, when women wove ramie cloth, and in the late

Qing when women assembled fireworks and firecrackers. Nowadays the "nimble fingers" myth makes the women particularly attractive to factory bosses, and since the early 1990s, when chain migration contacts were initially established with urban factories, Qifeng women have availed themselves of this exit opportunity from the countryside. When deciding who should migrate, couples balance considerations of urban earning potential against the need to stay in the country to carry out their respective work roles. The outcomes of these negotiations depend very much on the individual personalities and circumstances of the husband and wife. In Qifeng, ten husbands remained in the village while their wives worked in the factories and thirteen women remained on the farm while their husbands worked in the factories. There were sufficient men remaining in Qifeng village to do the plowing, so the local gender division of labor was not challenged by migration.

In sum, socioeconomic and geographic factors, cultural norms of gender, and urban labor opportunities all intertwine in constructing migration patterns and changing the divisions of labor in the fieldwork villages. In Beihu and Wentang, women participate in male-dominated migration networks, but at the same time young factory-worker daughters form a secondary migratory stream. In both trading villages, labor shortages have forced a small number of women to perform the male task of plowing, but this is less common in Wentang because labor substitutes are available. In Jiaocun village, Hakka customs designating a central role for women in heavy farm work have traditionally left the men free to work off the farm. But in recent years migration has been causing this gendered division of labor to change, with single and younger married women migrating to factories themselves. In Qifeng cultural constructions of female nimble fingers and taboos against women plowing have combined with factory introductions to produce migration streams comprising both men and women, but as yet have not led to women taking up the plow.

MIGRATION, WELL-BEING, AND AGENCY: THE IMPACT OF VILLAGE-LEVEL FACTORS

Geographical and economic factors and sociocultural gender norms combine to enhance or detract from well-being at the village level. Two key factors include the spatial mobility of women—their direct versus indirect participation in migration—and the village's migration patterns. For those women who hold the fort at home, further factors affecting well-being are the local gendered divisions of labor and access to resources such as land, labor pools, labor substitutes, and remittances.

Migration brings more benefits for women when they migrate directly than when they support the migration of other household members by staying on the farm. This is because migrating gives them more immediate control over cash income, exposure to new perspectives, freedom of movement, and the opportunity to escape some or all of their farming burden. Following Sen, it might also be argued that the location of women's work in factories outside the home increases the visibility of their labor and hence their perceived contribution to their households. Relatedly, migration gives the women a phase of life in which to experience relative freedom from village social ties and an opportunity to visibly demonstrate to other household members that they have a "fall-back position"—a way of supporting themselves—should family cooperation disband, and this increases their bargaining power.

Even though women may exercise agency by migrating, their choice of work, their use of funds, and their choices of work and life after migration are subject to constraints, shaped partially by gendered migration patterns. For example, in the trading villages of Beihu and Wentang, some single women participate in migration streams to factories, and these are secondary in two respects. First, factory work generates far less income than trading; for instance, Wentang women who were making pearl necklaces were remitting on average 2,000 *yuan* a year, approximately a third the amount of remittances from a glass decoration stall operator. Second, factory employment marks a distinct phase in a young woman's life cycle before her inevitable marriage and remigration to work at her husband's city stall. These factory daughters, like factory daughters in general, use their wages to pay for their siblings' education and to buy some items in preparation for married life. However, in trading villages they also contribute to family efforts to start a business. Factory wages are also important for bringing cash into households that lack both the funds and the male labor needed for running a stall.

Applying Sen's argument about the location and visibility of women's work and their bargaining power would suggest that women who perform domestic chores in the "inner space" of their families' stalls are worse off than their factory worker counterparts. But focusing solely on the location of work and its visibility overlooks the wider conditions in which women work and the implications of these conditions for functionings central to well-being. For example, trading women enjoy being with their families in the city and are also spared the loneliness and homesickness experienced by factory workers. Moreover, women from trading villages are able to spend most of their lives as migrants and are therefore better off than women from villages where it is customary for married men to migrate by themselves and for migrant women to return alone to the village following marriage and childbearing.

The well-being of those women who participate in migration indirectly by holding the fort at home is affected primarily by their labor burden and by their access to various economic and social resources. Although male outmigration increases the work burden of women, the extent varies according to local gendered divisions of labor. For the most part, women are happiest when customary gendered divisions of labor exclude them from both planning farming and laboring in the fields. This is reflected by the sentiments of two young natives of Guangxi province who met their Qifeng husbands while working in the city. They told me, "I am happy that women in Qifeng do not plow or do as much farming as women in my maternal home."[11] In contrast, the Hakka women of Jiaocun perform all the heavy farm and laboring tasks in their village. As an extension of Sen's thesis that women's work outside the home increases its visibility and perceived worth, it could be argued that male outmigration enhances the visibility of women's labor contribution to their households. Yet, on the other hand, the recognition that the women receive for this labor may be undermined by the fact that hard work is culturally expected of them. More pertinently, the heavy nature of their work has its own well-being implications: physical exhaustion and little leisure time.

Access to resources is a further factor affecting the well-being of women living in the village. An important resource in a rural setting is access to land for agriculture. In villages such as Jiaocun, with small per capita land allocations, the livelihoods of some women and children are adversely affected by a shortage of subsistence land; so the wives are forced to use their husbands' remittances to purchase grain. In contrast, in other villages, larger land allocations may combine with high levels of outmigration, so that elderly and married women remaining on the farm end up shouldering unmanageable burdens. As an example, in the trading villages of Beihu and Wentang many women have discontinued planting part of their early rice crop because their working lives are too busy.

In China, as elsewhere in the world, women who obtain their entitlements to land through men experience vulnerability, and in some Jiangxi villages male-dominated migration streams combine with land scarcity to exacerbate women's lack of land entitlement. Village exogamous marriage patterns are common in the four fieldwork villages, and, as already discussed, upon marriage a woman loses her land allocation in her maternal home and is allocated a new plot in her husband's village. Without inherited land, a bride has little bargaining power in her new household. In situations of extreme land shortage, as in Jiaocun, or in cases where the majority of the members of a production team votes against reallocating land to take into account demographic changes in households, as in Qifeng, a wife and her children may not be allocated any land at all. Where the husbands are working in the factory for long periods at a time, as is often the case among migrants from Jiaocun and Qifeng, the wives are farming their husband's family's land and eating their grain. Their dependence makes it difficult for them to demand a greater proportion of household resources or a reduced work burden.

Migration affects the amount of labor available within the village, influencing women's access to labor pools for help with farming and child care. There is much variety across villages in this respect because different migration patterns remove different quantities and types of labor from the village and also determine the frequency with which migrants are able to return. For example, in Beihu village, where over half the total population has left—including entire households—wives and particularly the elderly are exhausted and overworked, and they cannot hire labor to help because "whom would you hire?" When asked how they cope, the elderly women reply: "We get up early and go to bed late." In Jiaocun village, although there is a high level of outmigration, working in factories removes individuals from households rather than households from villages, so that enough married women remain at home to assist one another. Jiaocun women have formed mutual aid farming teams for coordinating assistance during the busy season, and they also help one another with looking after children and grandchildren. Additionally, overnight bus services to the destination areas enable some male factory workers to return home during the busy farming season, but the numbers of these returnees are limited because factory workers can only take leave from their jobs with the permission of their bosses. In Qifeng village, where there is no labor shortage at the village level, migrant wives and mothers have not formed mutual aid teams. The absence of such reciprocal help adversely affects the well-being of a small number of poorer older women in labor-deficient households, who are forced to exchange grain for help with plowing.

In some villages women's well-being is enhanced by the availability of affordable collective plowing services. In Songpu township, where Wentang village is located, the township government has coordinated the irrigation of land and founded a collective plowing service in response to outmigration. Wealthier Wentang families use remittances to pay for the plowing of their land, and the women shuttle back and forth to take care of supplementary farming tasks such as weeding. A similar plowing service has been established in Xinbei township, where Jiaocun village is based, but few households, certainly none in my survey, were able to afford the service.

It is somewhat obvious that women living in the more prosperous villages are better off than those living in the poorer villages, but village prosperity is not necessarily measured by average household income. The ranking of income figures in table 8.1 suggests that Beihu is the most prosperous village, but my survey of housing and possessions suggests that Wentang is the wealthiest, followed by Qifeng and then Beihu. Because most of the migrants from Beihu are traders who live on Hainan Island for extended periods, they concentrate their energies and resources on building up their urban businesses, so it is questionable how much of the urban-generated income actually benefits the people who remain in Beihu. In contrast, Wentang traders shuttle back and forth, maintaining an interest in both origin and destination, and many migrants have built new houses in the village and bought consumer goods for their families. Factory migrants from Jiaocun and Qifeng see their futures as being in the village. The low wages and poor living conditions in factories seemingly rule out the possibility of the entire household moving to the destination area. So they invest in their village lives by remitting money for building houses, life cycle celebrations, and farming.

In summary, particular combinations of cultural and economic factors at the village level combine with migration to work both for and against the well-being of women. They enjoy positive outcomes from migration when they participate directly rather than remaining on the land; when the gendered division of labor excludes them from heavy farm work; when there are labor pools and reciprocal aid networks; when labor substitutes are available and affordable; when transport and physical proximity facilitate regular return visits by migrants; and when there are larger remittances to the origin areas. This mix of factors gives women more opportunities for broadening perspectives, the greatest access to resources, and the greatest support in shouldering heavy workloads. In contrast, women tend to be disadvantaged by migration when they remain on the farm; when there is too little land to provide for their subsistence; and when labor shortages cannot be alleviated through mutual aid or labor substitutes. These women have the fewest opportunities for broadening perspectives, the least resources, and the heaviest work burdens.

MIGRATION, WELL-BEING, AND AGENCY: INDIVIDUAL AND LIFE-CYCLE FACTORS

This section explores the combinations of factors that interact with migration to bring gains and losses to women at different stages of their life cycle. While I remain mindful of the village-level factors examined above, this shift in analysis brings household- and individual-level factors into sharper focus. Broadly speaking, elderly women benefit least from migration because their health and age restrict their opportunities for earning money for themselves in urban labor markets. Their labor is instead directed toward supporting the migration of their adult children; it is invisible in the sense that their domestic caring work within the household is not seen as part of the realm of economically productive work. Younger women who have first-hand experience working in the cities and those who receive remittances directly appear to enjoy more of the positive effects of migration. As either migrants or returnees, many women benefit from the opportunity to earn income for their own use; from the increased visibility of their labor contributions to their households; and from the fact that they are able to demonstrate to other household members that they have a "fall-back position" in the form of knowledge of urban labor markets. Young married women are most constrained by the cultural expectation that they obey their husbands and sacrifice their own interests for their children, but they are also able to use their migration experience and urban earnings to bargain with their husbands. Some young girls in the countryside benefit directly from migration because remittances are used to pay for their school fees as well as to improve the quality of life in their households. The observation that migration benefits younger women more than older women is, of course, only a rough generalization.

A more nuanced understanding of the mixture of "good" and "bad" outcomes for women requires attention to the mitigating, intervening, and attenuating factors that operate at different levels. For the purposes of analytical clarity, the following discussion of how individual, household, and village-level factors interact with migration to affect the well-being of women is divided into three sections, focusing on elderly women, wives, and teenagers and girls.

Elderly Women

"Elderly woman" officially refers to a woman who is no longer classified as "labor" because she is age 65 years or older. In rural China, however, a much younger woman may be considered by other villagers as "elderly,"

Figure 8.1 Women at work in Yujia hamlet, Beihu administrative village. Rachel Murphy

especially if she has grandchildren or looks older. Because marriage and childbearing are the norm in the Chinese countryside, most women over 65 are grandmothers. Many of these women complain that norms of filial piety are changing so that it is now they who are expected to be filial to their migrant children by farming their land and caring for grandchildren. Although migration increases the workload of elderly women, the extent to which the perspectives and resources it produces offset this negative effect depends on context. Women's workload is influenced by village-level factors such as the gendered division of labor and the presence or absence of mechanized farming. The socioeconomic standing of the household also has a strong impact on the well-being of elderly women. In some households they are overworked and destitute because migration creates labor shortages and remittances do not cover subsistence costs. In other households they enjoy reduced work burdens and more resources because remittances are used to purchase labor substitutes. At the level of the individual, many elderly women improve their well-being through what Sen calls "other-regarding" categories—through taking pleasure in the well-being of other family members—so they see their extra work as worthwhile, if, for example, their sons are able to earn enough money to marry.

Other women with more assertive personalities begin to perceive that they also have some individual interests that are separate from those of their families, so they fight for a larger share of the rewards of migration. Overall, workloads followed by resources are the key variables affecting the well-being of elderly women; but at the same time the new perspectives generated by return flows of information empower some to bargain for more resources, giving them the means to reduce their workload. Here I discuss the workloads and resources available to women in both poor and wealthy households and the impact of the new perspectives generated by migration on the well-being of elderly women.

As alluded to above, the economic standing of the household is a key factor determining the impact of migration on the well-being of elderly women. In poor households that receive few remittances, elderly women *and* men rely on their own labor to support both themselves and their grandchildren. The lack of remittances may be because the adult migrant children are not successful in the city or because they are saving to build a house or develop a business of their own. For example, in Beihu village, although migrant traders can earn around 20,000 *yuan* a month, the elderly villagers receive little in the way of remittances if their migrant children are investing in their Hainan businesses. And in Qifeng, where urban earnings are often directed toward personal consumption, the only economic contribution that some elderly people receive is paid to them as rent in kind by tenants who farm the land of their migrant children. In the poorest households women's workload is particularly heavy because hiring farm labor is out of the question, so the women must help their husbands with heavy farm work in addition to carrying out their own domestic and farming tasks.

In contrast, elderly people living in more prosperous households are economically secure and actively involved in their communities. These people receive generous remittances, enabling them to withdraw either partially or completely from farm work. They either transfer their land to other households—this is possible when the land is fertile and enough labor remains in the village, as in Qifeng—or hire labor substitutes or farm the land themselves in a perfunctory manner, as in Beihu. In households that do not need to devote labor to farming, an elderly man may work locally off the farm as a village cadre, carpenter, or shop owner while his wife looks after their grandchildren. Elderly patriarchs often manage funds on behalf of their migrant adult children. Some families use remittances to build a big family house for everyone to share. Other migrants use their funds to build new houses for both themselves and their parents.

The elderly parents who benefit from remittances say that migration is good and that, although their workload has increased, life is better. In Beihu, in particular, there was a concentration of poor elderly headed households, whereas in Wentang there were more rich elderly patriarchs because of a combination of collective plowing services, fertile land, and the role of the "shuttling" pattern of migration in keeping the migrants engaged in the village community.

Both men and women benefit to some extent when remittances are used to hire labor or mechanized services for harvesting and threshing because husbands and wives carry out these tasks together. An exception, however, is Beihu, where hiring labor is virtually impossible because most laborers have left the village and there is no tractor service. Notices on village walls advise farmers that "it is a humiliation to leave the land barren," but for elderly people remaining in the village there is little choice. The shortage of labor means that many households have taken to planting ever smaller areas of the early rice, which fetches a lower price than the late crop. Studies in other parts of China similarly find that in villages with high rates of outmigration and no cooperative mechanization, the elderly and women farmers are unable to undertake some heavy work tasks, such as applying fertilizer and plowing, so land is abandoned.[12]

However, in villages where plowing is a "male" task, such as in Wentang and Qifeng, remittances used to pay for help benefit men more than women. The men gain more time for pursuing off-farm earning opportunities as well as for chatting, playing cards, and relaxing. Although hiring help with plowing and other farm tasks is widely accepted, hiring labor to help women with child care and domestic work is unthinkable. This is because domestic work is seen as caring and therefore mediated by human feeling rather than money—if a household head were to allow the hiring of help, it would be seen by others as akin to "taking a concubine." Elderly women find that caring for grandchildren is a particularly exhausting and worrying part of their domestic work. Women complained to me that their grandchildren cause them anxiety by playing in streams and ponds, and that the children have so much energy they are difficult to look after. A widow in Qifeng told me:

> I get remittances and 800 *jin* of grain from renting out the land. My sons will stay out as long as there is work. I would prefer the children to be at home, but they want to go out and see the world. My son writes that life out is not good. When my grandson drowned in the irrigation channel, my son wanted to come

back to the village. But the boss said that he was lying and deducted 800 *yuan* from his wages. I feel very sad.[13]

The exhaustion and worry of fostering grandchildren is even greater for those elderly women in poor health.

Widow-headed households are usually among the poorest and most labor-burdened in their villages. In Jiangxi province, the proportion of men to women in the sixty-five to seventy-four age cohort is roughly even, but in the seventy-five to seventy-nine age cohort there are fewer than seventy-six men to every hundred women, and in the eighty-plus age cohort the proportion of men to women continues to decline (sixty-five or fewer men to one hundred women).[14] This is not unique to China, as higher female life expectancy leads to a high proportion of widows among the elderly population in many parts of the world. In Wentang village all the women who plow are widows. And in Yujia hamlet, Beihu village, three of the four widows plow; the other women who plow are "home alone" wives.[15]

Han cultural norms in Beihu, Wentang, and Qifeng, which designate plowing as a male task, mean that the women who plow feel very much alone in their hardship. In some interviews widows cried as they talked to me about plowing, the strenuous nature of their work, going to the hills to collect ferns for fuel, caring for naughty grandchildren, and the lack of money. In contrast, in the Hakka village of Jiaocun, where women commonly plow, these women experience life as physically demanding and enduring poverty as distressing, but the fact that they must plow the land is not an added source of emotional suffering.

Cultural stereotypes of the elderly as unproductive also influence how grandmothers perceive their increased child care burden. Despite the considerable effort that elderly women devote to raising grandchildren and running their households, and despite the substantial cost to their physical and emotional health, they are often perceived as unproductive and lacking ability. Scholars writing about elderly women in other parts of the world similarly note the tendency for societies to portray elderly people as unproductive.[16] In China this lack of appreciation is reflected in criticisms of their parenting skills. According to some commentators, grandparents spoil the children, fail to educate them morally, neglect to supervise their homework, and jeopardize the "quality" of the next generation.[17] Such negative perceptions are internalized by elderly women and men themselves.[18] However, elderly women are likely to be even more deprecating of their abilities and contributions than men, because throughout their lives they have been told that they are of lesser value and have suffered systematic neglect in the allocation of household resources. This is evident in the fact that they are more likely to be illiterate than elderly men. Many elderly women described themselves to me in disparaging or dismissive terms, for example, "uneducated old woman" (*meiyou wenhua de lao taipo*) and "useless" (*meiyong*), and told me that only people without ability remain behind in the village.

Many elderly women with whom I talked in Jiangxi, like their counterparts in many other countries, interpreted their well-being exclusively in terms of their hopes for other family members. When I asked about their own personal hopes for the future, they often replied in "other-regarding" terms: "I want my son to find a wife" or "I want my son to have the money to build a house." In very poor households, the respondents would tell me, "I don't have any hopes," or else they would just smile helplessly.

There are nevertheless elderly women and couples who come to perceive that they additionally have some separate interests of their own. Migration makes some elderly women particularly aware that their interests are being overlooked, and so they protest against the lack of remittances and the unequal allocation of burdens within the family by migrating themselves. The information feedback of chain migration provides the knowledge and perspectives needed for migrating. For instance, in a different Jiangxi village a women's cadre told me of an old lady who was thin and overworked: apparently the son gave food only to his father, not to his mother. A neighbor who had worked in Nanchang city introduced the elderly woman to a family that needed a nanny. The old woman was last seen visiting her daughter in a different village, and, according to rumor, she was fatter and happier than before.[19] Several elderly people have migrated from the same village as this elderly woman, inspired by the example of others. In Qifeng there are isolated instances of grandmothers migrating to the city. Moreover, there were cases in all the fieldwork villages of grandmothers recalling their daughters-in-law from the city to take over the care of their young children. Even in Wentang, where no elderly people have migrated independently of their children, some of the older women told me that if they were younger and healthier, they would go out like their daughters have done. They lamented that it is too late for them to enjoy the new opportunities in life, not only for earning money but also for "traveling and seeing things" (*zou yi zou, kan yi kan*).

Although a few elderly who are physically strong migrate to the cities, the vast majority who are in good health use their remaining energetic years to work within the village and accumulate economic resources for themselves. One elderly woman in Qifeng, Mrs. Wu, explained to me, "We plant more peanuts and raise some turtles. We want to do a bit more work while we are able, so that we are not a burden on our children." She and her husband are quite well off and particularly determined to enjoy life, and in 1999 they even went on holiday to Guilin, a popular tourist spot. The woman told me, "Old Wu said we should go out into the world and have a look while we can," and I said, "That's a good idea."[20] Such couples take pride in their self-sufficiency.

It is thus clear that migration exerts a negative impact on the well-being of elderly women by increasing their workload, but it also has a positive impact by enabling the fulfillment of "other-regarding" aspirations and by broadening perspectives. Heavy workloads are especially serious for women living in poor households, widows, and women living in villages without access to mutual aid labor or mechanized services. Moreover, in Han villages where it is not the norm for women to plow, the emotional suffering caused by this increased workload is intensified. Despite the considerable effort elderly women expend in caring for grandchildren and farming, they tend to be viewed as unproductive and lacking ability, and many of them internalize such perceptions. Not being aware of their contribution to their households or their value as caregivers and farmers, many elderly women form aspirations only in relation to the interests of other household members. Taking pleasure in the improved well-being of family members is, nevertheless, important to their own emotional well-being. In some cases, however, return flows of ideas and resources from the city as well as the highly visible inequality in the allocation of urban savings within families cause some elderly women to perceive that they also have independent interests. Some are unable to act on this awareness, either because they are frail or because family relationships are not open to discussion and redressing imbalances, and so they lament wistfully that they are too old to migrate themselves. Others have sufficiently good health or feisty personalities to lobby for or to earn resources for themselves or to demand a reduced workload. Although it is difficult to generalize, on balance migration tends to hurt women at this stage of the life course because their workloads increase, they live separated from their children, they are perceived as unproductive, and they are not as able as other women to act on broadened perspectives.

Wives in the Village

Migration has a mixed impact on the well-being of married women. On the one hand there are the resources generated by migration and the expanded opportunities for exercising agency, while on the other hand there is an increased workload and frustration at remaining alone in the village. I explore these overlapping issues through three main themes. First, the out-migration of husbands can increase wives' work burden, depending on socioeconomic circumstances in their villages. Second, migration increases the material well-being of some married women, enabling them to live in new houses and enjoy consumer goods. Third, the women's knowledge of urban labor markets and lifestyles increases their expectations and bargaining power. This knowledge comes either from their own direct experience or via neighbors and family members. I discuss each of these effects in turn.

Although women are increasingly taking up men's farm jobs on account of migration, this should not be seen as a celebration of "equality" or progress, for they resent the heavy burden. Moreover, married women may farm, but they do not necessarily control when and what they farm. In many villages farming activities are directed by the husbands via letters from the city and when they return home for visits. The husbands decide which variety of seeds to buy and when to perform the various tasks. Often the wives are happy with this arrangement, as they do not want to incur the responsibilities that accompany increased decision making. Studies in other countries suggest that women associate their increased participation in decision making with increased potential for blame if the crops fail, and this exacerbates their mental burden.[21]

As elsewhere in the world, some rural women respond to their increased workload by establishing cooperative networks outside the family.[22] Mutual help teams have always existed in rural Jiangxi but have become increasingly important and feminized as ever more men have found work in the cities. Through these networks the women achieve material functionings, such as "obtaining a livelihood from the land," as well as those of an emotional nature, for example, "enjoying companionship and moral support." As already discussed, in Jiaocun village women have formed agricultural work teams (*banggongdui*), and after harvesting they eat and chat together and exchange information. In contrast, in Beihu the well-being of rural women is adversely affected by the absence of a social life and opportunities for reciprocal help. Although I did not encounter examples of formal financial cooperation among Jiangxi women, this has been observed to result from migration in other parts of China. For example, Kelly Tsai documents how, in parts of Fujian province that experience high levels of outmigration, women have formed credit rotation societies.[23]

The outmigration of husbands also means that wives assume responsibility for work tasks outside of agriculture, and this results in the acquisition of new skills or new areas of competence, which in turn enhances their visibility. For example, some rural financial institutions have set up electronic linkages with destination areas as a means of harnessing remittances. In Jiaocun this financial service enables wives to use newly issued bank cards to manage their township accounts. Wives in Jiaocun and Qifeng take charge of house building: managing the funds, coordinating with factories to purchase bricks and cement, and hiring labor. This occurs also in Wentang, but to a lesser extent, because men can shuttle conveniently back to the village when there are important matters that require their attention. Like their counterparts elsewhere, rural Chinese women who manage tasks that would have previously been carried out by men gain an increased awareness of their own abilities.[24] Often, their husbands also come to respect them even more for their ability and hard work. Many male migrants told me that their wives were very able: farming, budgeting, looking after children, and dealing with problems and a heavy workload in their absence. The feelings expressed by a Shanghai dock worker from Jiaocun village are not uncommon:

> My wife is very able. She looks after our son and the old people and she farms. She looks after all the things in the house and she is taking care of building the house. With me working outside, she eats much bitterness. She has been to Shanghai to visit me. But it is not possible for her to stay because there is so much work in the countryside. I am very tired. My wife is very tired. Both of us work hard for our family, and we are tired.[25]

Although wives who stay on the farm achieve valued functionings within the village, they nevertheless perceive being able "to go out" (*zou yi zou*) as a valued functioning in itself. For instance, although the train journey between Wentang and Shanghai is tiring, "shuttling" wives still enjoy the freedom of movement that it involves. Some Jiaocun wives likewise enjoy visiting their husbands in Shanghai. Women who worked in the factories before settling in the countryside to be wives and mothers said that when in the cities they had the freedom to "go out and have a look" (*zou yi zou, kan yi kan*), meaning to interact socially with other women and men in city streets, shopping or browsing the marketplace. Despite the arduous working conditions and the constraints of factory discipline, married women miss the freedom of their migrant days.[26] One Qifeng woman expressed to me her feeling of boredom and isolation:

> After having a child, it is not convenient for a woman to stay outside. There are no old people to look after the child in our

family. Plus, if the mother is not at home the child does not
study well. But life here is boring. Every day I farm and cook for
the child and myself. It's meaningless. I have no energy.[27]

This sentiment was echoed by a Jiaocun woman who told me that

Outside is more fun. But as a farm woman you must farm.
Farmers farm. What other way is there? I go round and round
in this small yard. And you can go anywhere: to England, to
Australia, to our China. I have been only to Dongwan and this
village. I have no culture, so I farm here.[28]

For wives who see the remittances raising their household's standard of
living and status in the village, material gains often compensate for increased work burdens, loneliness, and restrictions on their movement. In
Wentang, Jiaocun, and Qifeng, remittances increase overall levels of consumption needed to "participate in village life without shame," and this is
particularly evident with the rising standard of a "decent" house. For example, one Wentang woman living in a newly built house, with a video
recorder and color television, told me, "At first I did not agree to him being out, but then I saw the money and the things that it can buy. Now we
are better off than our neighbors."[29]

But women with prior experience of migration and corresponding exposure to a wider set of values, including an awareness of the functionings
enjoyed by urban women, are often dissatisfied with their lives in the village, despite increased material gains. They often express being bored,
lonely, and unhappy; describe their lives as meaningless; and refer to themselves as being without energy (*meiyou jingshen*). This is because the reality of village life prevents them from acting on their broadened perspectives and exercising agency—either because of constraining social norms
or because of inadequate resources. Often women returning to the village
live without their spouse, who remains in the city. Women in this situation
struggle against aspects of village society that they find oppressive. For example, they demand that their husbands remit all their earnings to their
care, rather than just remitting in staggered amounts in anticipation of
their needs. This behavior is more common among returnees, although
strong stay-at-home women may engage in it also. Other returned migrant women have sufficient resources saved from their earlier migration
period to set themselves up in off-farm ventures. This gives them a greater
sense of socioeconomic attainment and they are able to achieve a functioning valued by many returned migrants, that of "escaping farming."

The limitations of my data do not allow me to do more than speculate about the longer-term impact of returning to the village on the emotional well-being of women, particularly those who do not escape farming. However, studies by other scholars present possible clues. Research in Jamaica suggests that returned migrants have a much higher incidence of mental illness than nonmigrants,[30] and research in rural Sri Lanka associates return migration with higher levels of suicide.[31] Moreover, research on suicide in rural China finds, first, that death rates among women are five times higher than world averages and, second, that many of these women are educated and have exposure to the outside world.[32] The impact of migration on the well-being of returning migrant married women in rural China is a topic that demands future research.

On a more positive note, women who have migrated have demonstrated to society that they are able to earn money and that they have a "fallback position" should cooperation within the rural household break down. This is especially the case in Qifeng village, where many women have migrated. The labor contributions of married migrant women are publicized in regional newspaper reports and on county television. As an example, one news report proclaims that almost 10,000 married rural women (*dagong sao*) from Wanzai county (in which Qifeng is located) are working in coastal cities and their net annual remittances are more than 50 million *yuan*. The report praises these women as a great production army that contributes to society and the economy with sweat.[33] This visibility of their labor in turn increases their bargaining power, and they can threaten to abandon the rural household if their husband fails to remit, if their workload in the village is excessive, or if they want to transfer some of their land to another household. Nonmigrants also use the fact that migration is an option for them to bargain with household members.

Where married women migrate, as is common in Qifeng, gender roles in the household may reverse. In Qifeng, the migration of wives means that their husbands have been forced to take on the culturally unfamiliar roles of child care and cooking.[34] Some men come to appreciate the burden of housework and child care. Others who experience the double burden of farming and housework recall their wives from the city. As one man from Qifeng explained, "I no longer care about earning money, all I want is warm clothes, a full stomach, and my wife to come home and give me a rest."

Laurel Bossen shows that, although there is regional variation in the gendered divisions of labor across Chinese villages, disruptions that leave a husband without a wife are widely perceived to be detrimental to his well-being: men are believed to need the caring presence of a woman.[35]

My fieldwork concurs with this and suggests that women are therefore able to use the threat of remigrating in their interhousehold negotiations.[36] Other women return not because they have been recalled by their husbands, but because life outside is grueling and because they miss their children. In Qifeng village I met several women who had returned home following only two or three months working in Guangzhou because of both hard conditions in the cities and missing their children. Coming back under such circumstances may reinforce social perceptions that married women do not have the capacity for independence and that their place is in the home. Even so, I would argue that in villages where married women participate directly in migration, they enjoy enhanced bargaining power, freedom of movement, and greater scope for exercising agency.

Although migration might enhance the bargaining power of married women, fear of divorce is a key means for husbands to control wives' mobility. The threat of divorce is usually sufficient to recall a recalcitrant wife from Guangzhou. Divorce is legally possible, but it is largely avoided. A powerful social norm internalized by women and men alike is that once a woman has had a child with a man she must stay with him for life. Moreover, the children of divorced parents are teased mercilessly in the schoolyard. A saucy Taiwanese soap opera screened on Wanzai Television, called *People in Glass Houses*, provoked much discussion in Qifeng with its tale of extramarital affairs and divorce. Opinions aired by villagers include that it promoted unrealistic expectations of marriage and was not suitable viewing for young women. Villagers are not willing to be instrumental in the separation of a couple. A migrant in Qifeng explained that she had been approached by two women in the village who were on poor terms with their husbands and wanted her help in finding work in Guangzhou. She refused for fear of incurring the wrath of their husbands and in-laws.

Migration places stress on marriages, and this may have implications for the sexual health of women. Studies throughout the world suggest that migrant men face loneliness in the cities and physical distance from the village that enables some of them to turn to spouse substitutes. Two village doctors in Jiangxi informed me that most patients in the countryside with sexually transmitted infections are migrant factory workers, their spouses, or "little bosses" (*xiao laoban*)—owners of small businesses. They also said that the patients travel to other townships for consultation to avoid embarrassment.[37] Although information on this topic is limited, one can speculate that the well-being of some women in rural Jiangxi must be affected by the same sexual health problems faced by women in other societies with high levels of male outmigration. This may be more of a problem for the well-being of women in villages where the men migrate alone to factories (such as in Jiaocun or Qifeng) than for women in the trading villages (for example, Beihu and Wentang), who accompany their husbands to the cities. The migration patterns of villages may, therefore, produce different kinds of emotional pressures on migrants and their spouses with implications for the sexual health of married women.

In summary, migration increases married women's burdens but also produces some benefits. First, migration may increase access to money, knowledge, and other resources. This is likely in situations where women participate directly in migration, as in the trading villages, and to a lesser extent where some married women migrate to factories, as in the case of Qifeng. Women are also likely to have better access to resources in households where the husband remits on a regular basis rather than at periodic intervals in anticipation of his wife's needs. Relatedly, in Jiaocun village, the establishment of electronic banking linkages between origin and destination contributes to the well-being of women by making remittances more accessible.

Second, migration may increase the visibility of women's labor, thereby enhancing their status and improving their bargaining position. Comments by husbands suggest that the labor of women becomes more visible when they hold the fort at home. Yet I am not convinced that the heavy workloads, loneliness, and boredom endured by these women are alleviated by the increased appreciation of their husbands. On the contrary, the women who migrate with their husbands to run stalls and carry out invisible domestic chores in the city seem happier with their lot. This suggests that the nature of a woman's work and opportunities for movement could be more important for her well-being than the location and the visibility of her work.

Third, migration may enhance women's scope for exercising agency. But expanded areas of agency also involve increased responsibility, including the blame if things go wrong. Women who remain in the village are best able to exercise agency if they can draw on support networks of other women, as is common in Jiaocun village and in the trading village of Wentang, where the women shuttle to and fro.

Fourth, migration may expose women to a wider set of possibilities, strengthening their bargaining position within the household and giving them the impetus to challenge socially constructed constraints on their choices. Finally, long-term migration of a spouse may have a negative impact on women's emotional well-being, marital stability, and sexual health.

Young Women and Girls

In this section I focus on single women in their teens and early twenties. Like other women, they may incur a heavier work burden from migration but may also benefit from broadened perspectives, increased freedom, and improved access to resources. There are, nevertheless, two areas unique to women at this stage of the life cycle where migration has particular effects: educational opportunities and the selection of a marriage partner.

Girls commonly provide logistical support for the outmigration of family members, and this may affect their schooling. When one or both parents have migrated, both boys and girls help out more at home, but on account of the "fixedness" of the gendered division of labor, girls assume responsibility for a wider range of tasks including cooking, cleaning, and looking after siblings.[38] Elsewhere, I referred to school records from Wanzai county that suggest that the proportion of girls enrolled in secondary school declined between the late 1980s and mid-1990s.[39] I argued that this was the period when interactions between socioeconomic transition—(i.e., decollectivization, the introduction of the household responsibility farming system, and the migration of rural labor)—and preexisting cultural values that favor the investment of resources in sons precipitated changes in household patterns of labor and resource distribution. This suggests that girls more often than boys are withdrawn from school when the household needs more workers.

Not surprisingly, it is in the poorest households that labor shortages have the most detrimental impact on the well-being of girls. For example, I visited a poverty-stricken household in Yujia hamlet, Beihu administrative village, where an eleven-year-old girl lived with her widowed mother. Her two elder brothers had migrated and all the remittances were being saved for their marriages. Although the girl attended school, she often took days off to help her mother with a range of farm tasks, including plowing.

The decline in the proportion of girls enrolled in school is due not only to their increased involvement in household work but also to the fact that many choose to migrate for wage work. However, a teenage woman who migrates is not necessarily exercising agency in a positive sense, for example, if she also chooses to forfeit schooling. There is a perception on the part of both daughters and parents that a few years of migrant work is inevitably followed by marriage into someone else's family. So educating a girl is like allowing "fertilized water to run on someone else's garden" (*feishui wai liu*). Such a perception underpins the reluctance of some parents to invest scarce resources in the secondary school education of their daughters. For example, a girl in Qifeng informed me that her father had withdrawn her from school when she was fourteen and instructed her to make firecrackers at home until the following year, when she would be old enough to go to Guangzhou.

In the trading villages of Beihu and Wentang, daughters often migrate with their parents to help out with the stalls, while sons remain with grandparents to finish school. For instance, a man with an eighteen-year-old daughter and a twenty-year-old son explained to me:

> I went out to Hainan with my wife and daughter and we were there together for six years. We all worked together. My son did not come to Hainan at the time because he was studying. He stayed with his grandparents. We made some money, but nowadays the social conditions are not as good as before. There is extortion and crime and we have to pay higher taxes than the locals. Recently our son has taken over the running of our shop, and last month he sent a fax calling for our daughter to go out again to help.[40]

On the positive side, migration can lead to girls continuing their education. Returning siblings tell their families that study is important if a person is to progress.[41] At the same time, the school curriculum and television expose girls to new possibilities, like becoming an owner of a business, a manager, or a teacher. Both parents and daughters start to expect more for girls than early marriage, motherhood, and housework, and they see migration as a way to earn money to start a business or learn skills. Remittances provide a way for these new aspirations to be financed for both girls and boys.

Migration also creates conditions for young people, male and female, to be less accepting of parental interference in their life decisions, particularly with regard to choosing a marriage partner. In the past, young women spent most of their time in the village and had little opportunity to meet potential husbands. Even into the mid-1980s the majority of engagements in Jiangxi were organized through family and friends. Female relatives would investigate the families of possible in-laws and play an important role in facilitating the union. Many marriages are still arranged in this way, and young people returning home for Spring Festival are introduced to prospective spouses. However, in recent years, a lifestyle pattern has emerged whereby secondary school graduates go to work in the coastal cities; this enables young people to establish relationships without intermediaries. Nonetheless, parents still play an important role in marriage arrangements, and a number of young people return home to marry at a certain time because of family advice on auspicious dates. In trading villages, parents tend to influence marriage arrangements more strongly because family members and fellow villagers migrate together. Parents are usually unwilling for their daughters to marry outsiders because they will lose the young woman's care and labor. This fear is expressed through views that outsiders are dishonest and only concerned with money. Even so, some Beihu women have married Hainan men. The father of one such woman said, "What can we do? We can't tie her up and bring her back home."[42]

In sum, return flows of information generated by the migratory process broaden the perspectives of girls and young women by exposing them to a wider set of possibilities. However, the outmigration of family members also places new demands on their labor, which may adversely affect their opportunities for schooling, particularly if their households are poor.

Neither the broad category of "rural woman" nor the subcategories of "elderly woman," "married woman," and "girl" are homogenous entities. Rather, village, household, and individual factors interact with migration to affect the well-being and agency of each person in particular ways. Although migration is a mixed bag for women, it is nevertheless possible to tally a balance sheet of combinations of factors that work for and against them. These factors can be grouped in terms of women's workloads, the visibility and perceived value of their labor, their access to resources, and their perspectives on social norms, gender roles, and entitlements. These four interrelated themes emerge from the approaches to well-being and agency suggested in Sen's conceptualization of functionings and in his model of cooperative conflict. They serve as invaluable reference points for making sense of the myriad of multilevel factors that interact with migration to influence the lives of rural Chinese women. Each theme is discussed in turn.

The outmigration of family members increases the workload of women who live in the countryside across all stages of the life course. Elderly women, widows, and girls who live in poor households suffer most because of these increased workloads. This is because, even if labor substitutes are available in the village, they do not have the money to purchase them, and abandoning the land to live off remittances is not an option. Elderly women are adversely affected by migration because they must raise grandchildren and farm at the expense of their physical and emotional health, but they are not seen as productive laborers by others and may not even see themselves as such. Widows endure the greatest suffering because they are often in frail health and yet must take over heavy tasks such as plowing. In villages where there are taboos on women plowing, for example, Beihu and Wentang, these women see having to plow as a marker of their adversity. Girls in poverty-stricken households are also pulled into farming and child care, which damages their well-being because they are withdrawn from school. More positively, reciprocal aid networks operating at the village level, such as those found in Jiaocun, may alleviate the workload of some poor or disadvantaged women.

Women in middling and wealthier households who experience increased work burdens may alleviate them by paying for mechanized farming services. For example, in Wentang such farming services, organized by the township government, combine with convenient transport and a relatively short distance between origin and destination to enable the women to cooperate within spatially extended networks. In short, increased workloads are less of a problem for women from wealthier households.

The visibility of women's work and their resulting bargaining power are also affected by gendered migration patterns. Here Sen's theory of cooperative conflict and household bargaining is helpful in understanding the implications of migration for the well-being of women. For example, across the life cycle, elderly women and, to a lesser extent, girls are disadvantaged because their labor is confined to the domestic realm and so is less visible and less valued, and they are therefore less able to bargain for a share of household resources. But Sen's concept of visible labor can also be extended beyond that performed outside the domestic sphere. For example, the outmigration of married women can make their previous work in the domestic realm more visible, especially when husbands remain alone in the village, as was the case in some Qifeng households. As a further example, women with migrant husbands may gain respect when they show their capacity for managing both the household and the farm; indeed, many husbands comment on how capable their wives are.

When applying Sen's ideas to the question of how migration affects the visibility of women's labor and by extension to the question of how it affects their well-being, two further qualifications can be made. The first involves considering instances where sociocultural norms highjack the potential for the visibility of labor to translate into increased bargaining power. For example, direct participation in urban labor markets may increase the visibility of women's labor, but the potential for them to enjoy increased bargaining power may be mitigated by social norms pertaining to gender and respectability that constrain their behavior even while away from home—for example, social disapproval of divorce. As another example, in Jiaocun village, where Hakka women are historically renowned for their role in farming, being able and industrious are seen as inherent traits of Hakka women, and it would be difficult for them to act in ways that contravened these cultural expectations. The second qualification is that the nature of work and its social context may be more important for the well-being of women than the visibility of their labor. For example, women who accompany their trader husbands to city stalls are the most content despite performing invisible domestic work. They escape farm work and they enjoy the varied life of the city, the company of their family, and relative freedom of movement. It is also possible that in terms of marital stability, emotional well-being, and protection from sexually transmitted diseases, trading women are in a better position than their counterparts in villages where male migration to factories is common, because the men face less sexual loneliness and because the wives can police their husbands' behavior away from the village.

Evidence about the impact of migration on women's access to resources is mixed. Direct participation in factory work enhances their access to resources by enabling them to earn money in preparation for their future. However, when female migration to factories takes place within an environment dominated by male trading networks, there is the expectation that the women direct their wages toward helping to finance a family stall, rather than for individual benefit. Through migration women gain knowledge of urban labor markets, which is in itself a resource that assists some in bargaining within their households for extra resources and reduced work burdens. This is especially the case in Qifeng, where gendered migration patterns mean that both returned and nonmigrant women are aware that they have a "fall-back position" in the form of urban jobs. Young girls living in migrant households often benefit from the resources generated by migration through investment in their education as well as more general improvements in their households' living conditions. Elderly women seem to fare least well with respect to access to resources, particularly those living in poor households that do not receive remittances. In contrast, elderly women living in richer households are often able to relinquish farming tasks and live off remittances.

There is, of course, a difference between access to and control over resources. In households that receive remittances an elderly patriarch often controls the use of these funds. Urban wages are often controlled by the absentee husband, who decides when and how much to remit and how this money should be used. There are, however, many instances where a husband remits all his money home, entrusting his wife to manage it as she sees fit. Who controls the money depends largely on the personalities and relationship of the couple. When women are entrusted to manage the household budget and deal with finances, they acquire new areas of competence, thereby increasing their confidence. However, more responsibility means more work.

The perspectives generated through migration exert very contradictory influences on the well-being and agency of rural women. Direct participation in migration may broaden a woman's perspective on life, but on her return to the village she may be subject to social norms that undermine her claim on resources and limit her scope for exercising agency, leading to considerable personal frustration. An example is the unhappiness and frustration suffered by some returned migrant women in Qifeng and Jiaocun who, after experiencing freedom in the cities, felt trapped by the obligations of being a wife and mother in the village, especially if their husbands remained in the city. But the frustrations of married women may be much less in villages such as Wentang, where the migration pattern involves shuttling between origin and destination, thereby allowing them greater freedom of movement. Even hearing of life in the city from returned migrants affects the attitudes of nonmigrant women. This can be seen in the wistful laments of elderly women in Wentang, Beihu, and Qifeng who learn of life opportunities that are beyond their reach.

In cases where social norms constrain women and, at the same time, village or household conditions offer no way of alleviating their frustrations, the distinct interests of women and the socially constructed constraints on their choices become more visible. This leads some women to struggle against social and economic arrangements detrimental to their well-being, causing small social changes. For example, some Jiaocun women insisted that their husbands remit all their money into their care via the electronic banking service, and some women in Qifeng insisted that part of their land be transferred to other households to reduce their own farming burden. A variety of factors may contribute to married women's success in making such demands: living in a more prosperous household, threatening to migrate themselves, strong personalities, and good relationships with their husbands. Women who are younger are better able to struggle because they enjoy good health and have the "fall-back position" of being able to migrate to the city. In contrast, the relative invisibility of the labor of many elderly women and their own perceptions that they are unproductive undermine their bargaining position. On a more positive note, when broadened perspectives are accompanied by increased access to resources, women's agency is enhanced. Examples include returned women who set up businesses in the countryside and young girls who are inspired by their migrant siblings to study and who receive support from remittances to pay school fees.

Sen's theorization of well-being in his concept of functionings and in his household bargaining model is valuable in helping to conceptualize the impact of migration on the heterogeneous category of "rural woman." His emphasis on the end goals over the means (e.g., income) as the essentials of a good life has directed us to the functionings of spatial mobility, being educated, accruing material possessions, having leisure time (not being overworked), and improving lives of family members. It has also assisted us in positioning these functionings in terms of the wider physical and sociocultural environment in which individuals operate as well as in relation to the characteristics of the individuals themselves. Sen's work on cooperative conflict complements an attention to functionings by positioning women, work, and well-being within household dynamics and by highlighting the importance of social norms and perspectives for women's bargaining and agency capabilities. His approach to well-being and agency allows us to identify resources, work, and perspectives as well as individual, household, and village characteristics as central to understanding the impact of labor migration on the women involved.

ACKNOWLEDGMENTS

I am particularly grateful to the editors for their feedback on this chapter. I am also grateful to Dr. Christine Minas and Jeremy Riley for their valuable help. Most of the fieldwork for this research was made financially and logistically possible through an Australia–China Social Science Exchange Award from the Australian Academy of Social Sciences. Invaluable practical help was also provided by the Jiangxi and Shanghai Academies of Social Sciences and local officials in Wanzai, Yudu, Fengcheng, and Fengxin. I am also most grateful to the British Academy and to Jesus College, Cambridge for support.

NOTES

1. The impact of rural-to-urban labor migration on women living in the countryside is a much neglected area of research. Development agencies have frequently called for more study of this topic. See Food and Agriculture Organization 1995.

2. Sen 1983, 1991, 1992.

3. For example, an able-bodied person might need only a cow to plow, whereas a frail elderly person might need a tractor to achieve the same functioning.

4. Sen 1983, 1992:115–16. Consequently, people in poor villages may need only mud-brick houses to be "adequately sheltered," whereas people in richer villages may need brick houses.

5. Sen 1991.

6. By "household" I refer to a group of people who eat together and manage a common budget.

7. Sen 1991.

8. Kabeer 2000:30.

9. Unlike those of their Han counterparts, the feet of Hakka women were never bound, and debate continues as to whether the gendered division of labor was a cause or effect of their unbound feet. See Skinner 1997:9–10.

10. Government-organized labor export also means that large numbers of men have worked loading cargo on the Shanghai docks, but the strenuous nature of this work leads most to find factory jobs after a couple of years.

11. Conversation, March 1997.

12. Croll and Huang 1997:139.

13. Interview, January 1997.

14. *Zhongguo Wushi Nian de Jiangxi 1949–1999* 2000:42.

15. In Yujia hamlet of Beihu administrative village, there are seven households with elderly people that farm and look after children, five households that comprise only elderly farmers, and twelve households where the elderly look after children but also receive enough remittances to relinquish part or all their land.

16. Clark and Laurie 2000.

17. Meng 1997.

18. Clark and Laurie 2000.

19. Conversation, March 1997.

20. Conversation, December 2000.

21. Nelson 1992:130.

22. Gisbert et al. 1994.

23. Tsai 2000.

24. Findley and Williams 1991; Gisbert et al. 1994.

25. Interview, August 1997.

26. A slightly different example, but one that similarly shows that "being mobile" is a valued functioning, pertains to wives who have married within their villages rather than to another village. These women told me that they envy other married women who have the opportunity to *zou yi zou* to visit maternal relatives in other villages.

27. Conversation, March 1997.

28. Conversation, September 1997.

29. Interview, July 1997.

30. Hickling 1991.

31. Kearny and Miller 1987.

32. MacLeod 1998.

33. *Yichun Ribao* (*Yichun Daily*), 20 March 1997, 1.

34. The role of migration in increasing the labor burden of male nonmigrants has also been documented in Latin American countries and parts of rural Thailand. See Parnwell 1993:107.

35. Bossen 2002:200–204.

36. Murphy 2002:206.

37. Interviews, April 1997, October 2001.

38. Kabeer 1994:105–6.

39. Murphy 2002:95–97.

40. Interview, April 1997.

41. Murphy 2002:100.

42. Conversation, April 1997.

>> *Part 4*

WRITING LIVES

Tamara Jacka

9. Migrant Women's Stories

>> This part of the book includes translations of seven stories written by rural migrant women about their experiences of migration and work in the city. These were contributed to a story-writing competition with the theme "my life as a migrant worker" (*wo de dagong shengya*), organized by the journal *Rural Women Knowing All* (*Nongjianü Baishitong*). The journal is unusual, because while most Chinese media are clearly dominated by urban interests and directed primarily at an urban audience, *Rural Woman Knowing All* is directed at rural women. It is published monthly under the auspices of *Chinese Women's News* (*Zhongguo Funü Bao*) and the All China Women's Federation. The journal's editorial office also organizes a range of projects aimed at assisting rural women, for which it receives financial help from other organizations in China and overseas, including the Ford Foundation, The Global Fund for Women, and Oxfam. The chief editor, Xie Lihua, is well-known among social activists both within and outside China and has received national and international awards for her work with rural women.

Since its inception in 1993, *Rural Women Knowing All* has shown great concern for the situation of rural women working in urban areas, with nearly every issue running letters and articles devoted to this topic. In addition, in April 1996 the journal's editorial office founded what they claim is China's first club for rural migrant women, the "Migrant Women's

Club" (*Dagongmei zhi Jia*). The club now has more than three hundred members among the migrant women workers of Beijing. They meet regularly, sometimes for social occasions and sometimes for classes, for example in basic literacy, English language, and computing. The editorial office has also organized two national forums on the rights of migrant women workers, held in Beijing, with funding from Oxfam, Hong Kong.[1]

In 1998, as part of ongoing collaborative research, I suggested to Xie Lihua that the journal run a story-writing competition for rural migrant women. I would provide funding for the competition and for prizes, and they would organize the competition, judge the winning entries, and publish them. Xie Lihua and her associates agreed to the plan and the competition was launched in November 1998; it ran until the end of October 1999. Participants were asked to write approximately 1,500 words, giving a truthful account of their experiences as a migrant worker. All together, more than 300 manuscripts were received. Of these, 20 stories and one poem received prizes and were published in *Rural Women Knowing All* in 1999.

All of the stories included here were originally published in Chinese in *Rural Women Knowing All*. Zhou Rencong won first prize (500 *yuan*) for her story "Leaving Huaihua Valley," Mian Xiaohong ("Burdened Youth") was one of three people who won second prize (300 *yuan*), and Huang Zhihua ("The Law Is by My Side") was one of five people who won third prize (200 *yuan*). Li Jianying ("Working for Myself"), Cui Jingyu ("Let Bygones Be Bygones"), Pang Hui ("I Am a Cloud") and Wang Xiangfen ("Looking Back, I Am Proud") won prizes of commendation (100 *yuan*). The selection of these particular stories for republication was based on my own personal judgment of merit and interest, combined with an attempt to include stories reflecting a range of different situations and experiences.

The publication of these stories is in itself politically important, as is *Rural Women Knowing All*'s publication of other letters and stories written by rural women and rural migrants, and indeed the existence of the journal itself. By providing a forum for rural women to speak for themselves, it provides a valuable counterbalance and potential challenge to a national, and indeed international, discursive order in which subaltern voices are routinely suppressed, marginalized, silenced, or ignored.

This is not to say, however, that through these stories we can hear the "authentic" voices of the "subaltern" in China, unmediated or untainted by dominant discourses. Nor should these stories be viewed as necessarily closer to "the truth" about migrants and migration than articles in the mainstream Chinese media. The stories provide valuable information about individual migrant women's personal experiences—information that is rarely found in the mainstream media. This helps to counteract the urban elite disdain for rural migrants as faceless hordes and to encourage empathy for rural women as individual human beings with difficulties, desires, and aspirations much like "ours." At the same time, however, migrant women's representation of their own experiences and desires and the messages that they incorporate in their stories are far from being unaffected by dominant discourses. Rather, as I will try to sketch out in the remainder of this chapter, they challenge some aspects and reproduce others.

All the stories translated here, like most of those sent in for the competition, recount or at least allude to lives of hardship and struggle, both in the women's native villages and in the cities where they migrate to work. Li Jianying, for example, writes of her family's poverty, and of how, as teenagers, she and her sister went out to work in the rice paddies each spring, laboring long hours bent double, their feet cramping in the icy cold water of the paddies. Zhou Rencong writes of the pressures on young rural women to marry and alludes to the tragedies, including the suicides of women, that result from arranged marriages and the continuing expectation among villagers that once married, a woman must devote the rest of her life to serving her husband and in-laws. Pang Hui recounts how her husband, a gambler and a drunkard, beat her and the children, driving her to leave her home and children to start a new life as a migrant worker.

Mian Xiaohong and Zhou Rencong both write of the bewilderment they felt on first arriving in a large city and indicate how important initial help from a relative, fellow villager, or other contact in the city can be. Zhou Rencong gives a particularly vivid account of the initial sense of alienation in the city, the difficulty of finding work, and the struggle to survive in a strange place on meager savings.

With the exception of Wang Xiangfen, all the writers describe the jobs they found in the city as harsh, exploitative, and tiring, with very long hours of work. Huang Zhihua recounts how, in the summer she started work in a joint venture manufacturing factory in Shenzhen, she and her fellow workers labored overtime every day in hot, crowded workshops for poor wages and inadequate meals. Mian Xiaohong, in her job as a housemaid, also worked long, tiring hours, constantly anxious about performing her tasks properly. Cui Jingyu and Li Jianying, who were waitresses, both write that they worked continuously each day from before dawn until late at night. And Zhou Rencong tells of having to rush around all day in her job as a salesperson for a health care product company, and of the terrible hunger she suffered in the first month, before she received her wages.

In addition, these women write of a range of different forms of abuse, contempt, humiliation, and threats meted out to them by employers, co-workers, and others. Li Jianying, for example, writes that she and the other migrant women in the restaurant where she worked were abused by the boss, and when they tried to leave, he threatened to keep their belongings and withhold their wages. Similarly, Huang Zhihua's co-workers were afraid to complain about their working conditions for fear that they would be sacked, and Cui Jingyu *was* sacked from her job, with half a month's pay deducted for no reason. Mian Xiaohong had her first job as a housemaid terminated without notice and her belongings sent to the police station when she spent one night out at a friend's house. Later, she was again fired without notice, and when she left, the woman of the house insisted on checking her luggage to make sure that she had not stolen anything.

Sexual harassment, abuse, and exploitation figure in four out of seven of the stories. Pang Hui writes of sexual harassment from her male co-workers on the construction site as being the hardest aspect of the job.[2] And Cui Jingyu's restaurant job became unbearable when the boss put pressure on her and the other waitresses to offer sexual services as a way of attracting customers. Zhou Rencong similarly mentions that one company advertising for office workers sought to employ women who would offer sexual services to pull in customers, and she also writes of her friend turning to prostitution when her cosmetics shop went bankrupt. Huang Zhihua tells of how she was nearly persuaded to become involved in a scheme to kidnap and sell women from her home province.

Wang Xiangfen's story is unusual among those published in the competition in that she makes no explicit mention of difficulties encountered in her life as a migrant worker. However, even she alludes to the fact that many migrant women have conflicts with their employers, that the title of "outstanding housemaid" she was awarded did not come easily, and that the life of a migrant worker is full of challenges.

For all the hardships described, these stories are unlike the many articles in the mainstream press, discussed by Wanning Sun in chapter 3, in that they do not give the impression that rural women are passive, helpless victims—far from it. These women have actively resisted exploitation and abuse, defended their personal integrity, and fought for—and won—respect from others. Huang Zhihua, for example, confronted her boss about the intolerable conditions suffered by migrant workers in the factory and won not just an improvement in those conditions but also a promotion for herself. Li Jianying changed jobs several times rather than put up with insults from employers, then went to a hairdressing school and finally set up her own salon. Wang Xiangfen was awarded the title of "outstanding housemaid," and Zhou Rencong ultimately found a job as the editor of a newsletter of a well-known company and has gained national recognition as a short story writer.

Similar to the mainstream press, however, none of the stories provides any real critique of the discourses and structures that undergird migrant women's exploitation. Instead, with the exception of "I Am a Cloud," in all the stories translated here rural women's experiences of migration are depicted as a difficult journey or rite of passage, with the individual undergoing a series of struggles from which she emerges, wiser for the experience, having achieved a measure of success and personal pride or, at the least, stability. In "Burdened Youth," for example, Mian Xiaohong describes herself and the other girls setting out for Beijing as being naïve, like "newborn calves," and writes of her work as a maid in an urban household as a painful process of awakening. Wang Xiangfen concludes her story with the lines: "I'm thankful for my life as a migrant worker. It has given me the opportunity to make myself strong and it has taught me how to get on with others, and that if you try you can do anything. The long journey of the migrant worker presents even more opportunities than it does challenges."

By suggesting that it is their move to the city that makes young rural women mature, these narratives echo common urban views of rural women as naïve and simple, in comparison to their more sophisticated urban sisters. In addition, how successfully they make the transition from the countryside to the city is related, above all, to their own persistence, hard work, and ability to stand up for themselves. In the case of Huang Zhihua, success is further linked to her ability to use the law to defend her interests. In "The Law Is by My Side," she describes how she confronted her boss one day, showing him a copy of the Labor Law to demonstrate that his treatment of the women workers was illegal. The boss reacted angrily at first, but when she threatened him, he softened his stance, took her advice about improving the workers' conditions, and promoted her to the position of assistant to the deputy manager. Her story provides what is potentially an indictment of capitalist labor relations, but that indictment is weakened by the message that if you are able to work the system, you can be successful.

Much of the language in the upbeat endings of these stories is formulaic and unconvincing, and unlike the ways in which migrant women speak of their experiences in conversation. As I have discussed elsewhere, in interviews I conducted in Hangzhou in 1995, migrant women also often spoke of migration as a kind of rite of passage, but very few talked with positivity or optimism about their present and future. Rather, almost all of them voiced a high degree of uncertainty. As one woman put it, "People in Hangzhou can further themselves and think of the future—they have a good job and they go to work every day and there are lots of possibilities. But for us migrant workers it really is a matter of living from one day to the next. You can't have any aims, or think of the future."[3]

Having translated a total of thirty-five of the original manuscripts received and having scanned several more, I have no evidence that the editorial office of *Rural Women Knowing All* deliberately selected the more "positive" stories. If anything, their selection includes proportionally fewer rosy "success" stories like Wang Xiangfen's than were among the total sent in for the competition, probably because most of those stories were not very interesting and too obviously stilted to be considered good-quality writing. Nevertheless, it does seem likely that many of the participants in the competition themselves tried to make their stories more politically acceptable by tempering their accounts of difficult experiences in the past with a positive message about the present and future. This narrative structure, in which the past is criticized but the present and future are depicted with optimism, dominates post–1949 political discourse, literature, and film. And it is generally the refusal of such a narrative structure, rather than negativity *per se*, that is read as politically unacceptable. Perhaps this is why the story by Pang Hui—the only one that does not provide the reader with a way to see out of, or beyond, the tragedies and uncertainties of the author's life—received only a commendation rather than first, second, or third prize.

The dominance in these stories of the rite-of-passage narrative structure may have something to do with the nature of the story competition. In hindsight the theme, "My life as a migrant worker," combined with some basic understandings and expectations of short story narratives, probably invites reflection on the experience of being a migrant worker as a process of change and personal development, and may appear to ask for some final, balanced judgment on the experience.

Beyond this, however, rural-to-urban migration is very often, in fact, a literal rite of passage. Most migrant women are in their teens or twenties when they first leave home, and for many this is their first experience of a world beyond the village and a first step, often very consciously taken, toward adulthood. These women's difficult experiences as migrants coincide with, and indeed are very much a part of, their personal struggle for respect and identity as independent individuals.

ACKNOWLEDGMENTS

A longer version of this introduction, plus the seven stories included in chapter 10, were previously published in *Intersections: Gender, History and Culture in the Asian Context*, No. 3, http://wwwsshe.murdoch.edu.au/intersections/issue4, 2000. I am grateful to the editors of *Intersections* for permission to reprint this material, with minor revisions.

NOTES

1. For a review of the first forum, held in 1999, see Jacka 2000b.

2. For a discussion of the sexual harassment of rural migrant women, see Tang 1998. Tang argues that migrant women are more often subjected to sexual harassment than urban women because of the contempt that urbanites hold toward rural migrants, and because migrant women's insecure housing and lack of support from their employers make them more vulnerable to harassment and attack.

3. Zhou Hongxia, quoted in Jacka 1998:69.

Translated by Tamara Jacka and Song Xianlin

10. My Life as a Migrant Worker

LET BYGONES BE BYGONES / CUI JINGYU

>> The year I turned seventeen, full of dreams, I decided to go to the city to work. I wanted to make my own mark in that bustling place.

A job advertisement brought me and two other northeastern girls, Little Wu and Little Liu, to a private restaurant. Since it was the tourist season, business was booming. We started busily selling breakfast at five o'-clock every morning, by nine o'clock we began preparations for lunch, at two or three in the afternoon we finished tidying up, and then it was nearly dinnertime. In this way, we worked nonstop till ten o'clock at night. Every day we were like machines that were wound up to work. Even when we were exhausted and sore all over, the boss was still unsatisfied and gave us housework to do. Because we were outsider girls,[1] nobody told us what our rights were. Nor would anyone speak up on our behalf. We had to go on working because we had to survive.

Not long afterward, in order to compete for customers, restaurants started to employ public relations girls (in reality they were escorts).[2] The boss talked up the advantages of being a public relations girl, and thought up a scheme to invite one to "demonstrate" to us. It's true she didn't have to work as hard as we did. All she needed to do was dress up like a flower, to accompany rich customers. After a day's work, the tips she got were more than 50 or 60 *yuan*.³ But I really felt sorry for her when I saw her being kneaded like dough by the customers. Yes, everyone needs money. But no amount of money can buy back a lost soul.

We didn't want to go on working there, but the boss threatened us by withholding our pay. We were at our wits' end because we couldn't get the money that we had earned with our blood and sweat, but we had nowhere to go to seek redress. Who could help us outsiders to seek justice?

In order to get paid, we just had to swallow the insults and keep working. Under the pressure of the boss and the temptations of "Miss Dough," Little Wu and Little Liu started to give in. I implored them not to lose their integrity for some quick money. The boss learned that I was having an "adverse" effect on the group and decided to expel me, the bad apple. When settling the account, he deducted half a month's pay for no reason. I couldn't say anything to this greedy man. Who'd be willing to offend a rich and powerful local boss on behalf of a working sister from outside of town? The punishment I got scared Little Wu and Little Liu from thinking about resigning. In the end they did not escape the boss's penny-pinching. I went home full of an unutterable sense of injustice.

Later, I heard that the restaurant had been closed by the authorities. The boss was arrested and the girls were sent away. At long last I heaved a sigh, but I felt sad about Little Wu and Little Liu's misfortune. If it hadn't been for the boss's pressure and blackmail they would never have gone astray. They too were victims! When they needed justice, there was no one there to hold out a helping hand! It was lucky that the mills of God grind slowly but they grind exceedingly small, and that boss who grew fat on the blood of outsider girls was finally finished off.

That was my first experience of being a migrant worker, and a memory I never want to recall. I wish with all my heart that other working sisters will not run into similar experiences.

—Originally published in *Nongjianü Baishitong* (*Rural Women Knowing All*) 4 (1999): 32–33.

THE LAW IS BY MY SIDE / *HUANG ZHIHUA*

I am a working sister from Guizhou.⁴ I've been working in Shenzhen Special Economic Zone⁵ for eight years. I started as an ordinary worker on the factory production line. Now I'm a skilled worker in management. I owe my good fortune not only to my diligence and effort but, in even greater part, to the law, which time and again has set me on the right path.

Shenzhen is a city full of temptation. You often hear stories about the "big money" people who throw away cash like dirt. I'd think about the wages I earned with my sweat and toil each month and how there was hardly anything left after my living expenses, and I'd wonder when I would ever be able to realize my own dreams. The feeling of inequity kept welling up involuntarily and pushed me to think every minute about how to make more money. Then a middle-aged migrant woman worker from Tai'an, in Shandong province, said to me: "Come with me back to Guizhou and we'll dupe some pretty Miao girls into going to our Tai'an region. In one trip we can make thousands of bucks." Looking at her excited face, I was nearly persuaded. When I returned to the dormitory and talked to a girl from my home county about it, she was furious with me. "That is called kidnapping and selling women, and it is illegal. Don't fall into that trap." I felt I was waking from a dream. I refused the offer, and from this I came to appreciate the dangers of not understanding the law. I went specially to a bookshop and bought a copy of the *Reader on Basic Legal Knowledge for Workers and Staff.* When I had some free time I read it and explained to the other girls how to learn, apply, and abide by the law.

In the summer of 1996 I started work in a joint venture factory. In order to speed up production, the boss demanded overtime from us every day, with very low pay. In addition, the workshops were overcrowded with machines and equipment and the heat was like being inside a steamer basket. Some working sisters got so tired that they truly couldn't bear it and didn't want to do overtime. After learning this, the boss threatened to send them packing. Looking at the overworked, exhausted faces of these working sisters, I felt some responsibility to seek redress. I prepared myself to be sacked by the boss. The next day I took a copy of the Labor Law of the People's Republic of China and went to the boss's office. I showed him the relevant clauses, saying, "The workers' overtime has far exceeded the limit set by the Labor Law and, furthermore, you did not pay wages in accordance with the law."

The boss stared at me, this uninvited guest, and said to me angrily: "You're not the boss and you don't understand what it's like to be fined for failing to fulfill an order."

I said to him calmly, "I understand, but you cannot gamble with workers' health just to speed up production. Moreover, what you are doing is illegal. If the workers go to the Labor Department to complain, you will land yourself in serious trouble."

The boss softened his stance and took a conciliatory approach. "What ideas have you got to complete the production tasks without working overtime?"

I said, "There are lots of ways. For instance, you could do something to lower the temperature in the workshops and improve the working conditions of the workers. In addition, you could invest in better food and improve the workers' nutrition. Furthermore, you could pay overtime according to the Labor Law. If the workers' enthusiasm is aroused, the efficiency will most definitely double, and then you won't have to worry about not fulfilling the order, will you?"

Realizing that what I said was reasonable, the boss clapped his hands and said, "Let's do it your way."

After this incident the boss not only did not send me packing; he promoted me to the position of assistant to the deputy manager.

When I went home to see my relatives and to discuss this with the head of the village Women's Federation, she gave me a few issues of *Rural Women Knowing All* to look at. After reading them over and over, I further understood the situation with regard to the rights of working sisters. That's why I wanted to borrow a bit of space in your magazine. I hope that I can pass on to all the migrant women workers what I have learned from my personal experience: let the law be your protection on your journey in life!

—Originally published in *Nongjianü Baishitong* (*Rural Women Knowing All*) 4 (1999): 29–30.

BURDENED YOUTH[6] / MIAN XIAOHONG

In the summer of 1983, when I was sixteen, two fellow village girls and I traveled together to the distant, completely unknown, and mysterious city of Beijing.

We girls had never been away from home. Like newborn calves that do not fear the tiger, we had no fear of the unknown world. As if going to the market or going to see a film, we set off lightheartedly, without any psychological preparation. We didn't feel any sadness or regret about parting with our family and relatives. Later on, my mother said that she was hoeing in the fields at the time and she watched us leave the village, walking farther and farther along the path to the nearest township, never once looking back.

Before we left for Beijing, the county capital was the farthest I'd ever been, and I'd never even seen a train before. We walked ten *li*[7] to town to take the bus to Hefei. At Hefei we got on the train, only to discover that there were no seats left.

At midnight a kind person squeezed me onto the edge of a seat with three other people. I fell asleep as soon as I sat down. When I woke up I found myself on the floor. . . .

The train slowly drew into Beijing station. The three of us, a bit nervous and afraid, followed the tide of people out of the station.

Holding a piece of paper with an address on it, we asked directions of everyone who came along. We asked I don't know how many people and walked around in circles for I don't know how long. At dusk we eventually found the address on the paper. We knocked on the door and the person who opened was sister Zhen—just the person we were looking for to give us refuge. Seeing her was like seeing our own mother, we were so overjoyed. But sister Zhen did not smile when she saw the three of us. She didn't dare let us into the apartment and instead came out and closed the door. She took us down from the second floor to the entrance of the building. She complained about so many of us coming all at once, saying that she had written for Huazi to come, so how come Asan and I had come too? Asan and I didn't know what to say. I said I wanted a drink, so sister Zhen went back in and got a big glass of water. The three of us each had a few mouthfuls. We were so thirsty we were like the parched earth in a drought, and a few mouthfuls of water could not quench our terrible thirst. But I was too embarrassed to ask sister Zhen to get us some more water. I squatted on the ground, tears flowing down my cheeks. . . .

At the beginning of the eighties, it wasn't that common for peasants to go to the cities seeking work. When people walked down the streets and heard the familiar accent of their hometown, they would stop and chat warmly. Work was hard to find, and I remember that we looked for quite a few days without finding anything. One morning I was wandering in the gardens of the apartment complex when I saw a young mother pushing a stroller in which lay a baby, soaking up the sun. I walked up and asked in a loud voice if she needed someone to look after the baby. She was a woman of few words. Holding the baby, she packed up and asked me to carry the stroller. I followed her into the building. We went into an apartment on the fourth floor. The woman mumbled a few words with a man there. He sized me up and asked me a few questions in a stern manner. That was how I found a job. The wage was 15 *yuan* a month.[8] The wage wasn't important, the main thing was that I had somewhere to stay.

My life as a migrant worker started there. Every morning before the sun came up I went to line up for milk. Sometimes, because I was anxious, I would wake up very early and wait for daylight. At first, I had no idea how to do the work, I couldn't see what really needed to be done, so all day long

I worked without stopping, spinning around like a top. It was so tiring! When I washed the bowls I broke them, and when I cut the vegetables I cut my hand, but the most tiring thing was the stress. The child's mother was still on maternity leave, and while she was around I didn't dare to rest, even when there was nothing else left to do. Moreover, we couldn't communicate our emotions. Only when I took the child out to play did I have a chance to relax a little. It wasn't easy getting through a day. Each day dragged on and on. At home in the village I was never aware of this thing called time. I was naïve and innocent then, living without a care. Time went by like a light breeze. But now the wings of happiness had been clipped, and time was like a net that trapped me.

After one month the child's parents gave me a day off, so I went to see my friend Huazi. She persuaded me to stay for a meal, and then let me stay the night.

The next day, when I went back, no one answered the door. But it was quite clear there were people moving inside. I was so confused. I didn't understand what was going on. I knocked for a while, but no one opened the door, so I went downstairs to talk to Fat Auntie of the residents' committee[9] and tried to explain why I was crying. Fat Auntie huffed and puffed upstairs, grumbling at me, but not without sympathy: "You're so young, why do you want to leave home and do this? Is it because you have nothing to eat at home?" Hearing this made me even sadder and I couldn't stop crying.

Fat Auntie knocked on the door and called out the mother's name, and then the door opened. Fat Auntie went in, and the door shut again. After a while Fat Auntie came out and said to me, "You didn't come home last night, and that scared them. They took your things to the police station. You can go and get them back this afternoon."

That evening I took the train south. Asan didn't want to work in Beijing anymore either, so she went home with me. On the train, Asan swore she'd never come back to Beijing. I didn't say anything. But, later, Asan did go back to Beijing, and what's more, she worked there for many years before going home to get married.

From the hills of our hometown I looked down at the smoke curling up against the sunset. The red sun was like a balloon sitting on the mountains opposite, and it was so peaceful and quiet. The cowherds were riding on the backs of the cows, ambling toward the village. When I'd left the rice paddies were still like green carpet, but now everything was golden.

I returned home in a sorry plight. I didn't say a word about the wrongs that I had endured. Mom thought I would settle down and would not try to make a fuss about going to Beijing again. She didn't expect that I'd run off again to Beijing right after the harvest. This time I was too embarrassed to tell my family. Since I'd been to Beijing, my closed world had been opened, and I could not be confined again. What's more, having been to Beijing, I could never return to my original carefree, naïve, and innocent state.

The second time I came to Beijing it was much easier. It was easier to find a job looking after a child. The child, called Little Pei, was only one year old. Little Pei's parents were returned youths.[10] They were extremely good to me, and every New Year and every holiday Little Pei's mom bought presents for me. At first I couldn't believe it, thinking that she would ask me for payment. Little Pei's mom also enrolled me in a tailoring class. When they came back from work, they let me go to classes. They were accountants and they taught me how to use the abacus and how to write characters properly. During those days of looking after Little Pei I was very busy but happy and fulfilled. Little Pei's parents were my spiritual teachers. It was they who made me believe in the love and kindness of ordinary people.

After several years in Beijing, I knew the streets and alleys of the city like the back of my hand. I frequently changed employers and saw all kinds of people and all kinds of families. I was very curious and wanted to lift the veil on the mysteries of society, to see the true face of people from all walks of life.

I once cooked for a famous writer. The difference between being a cook and looking after a child lies in the fact that for the former you need to go out and buy vegetables, and when you buy vegetables you can steal a bit of money. Before this job I was like all the others from Anhui[11] who try to cheat a bit with the shopping money. We never let any chances go, even if it meant just keeping 20 cents to buy a Popsicle. But I had great respect and admiration for writers and I thought they were all saints. I felt that I couldn't let them look down on me. The first time the writer's wife tried to check the shopping bill with me, there was only one cent unaccounted for. We smiled at each other. After this she had complete faith in me and never checked the bill again. It is a great feeling to be trusted. I slowly began to understand, then, that there is such a thing as moral integrity. I appreciated my new self. Even though I left the writer's household, I never tried to cheat again, regardless of whether I was trusted or not. Because my new self was watching me, I could never do anything that would make me look down upon myself.

The reason I left the writer's household was that there was too much work. I was busy all day long, working like a machine, and I would be exhausted after a day's work. I said I wanted to leave, and the writer's wife asked me to wait until they had found someone else.

After a week the writer's wife told me that they had found a new cook and that I had to leave that day. While waiting for them to find a new cook I had worked hard like an idiot, but eventually they just sacked me, leaving me nowhere to go. The benevolent smile on the writer's wife's face made my heart turn to ice. Just as I was going, she said she wanted to check my luggage, saying that this was a regulation. Whenever someone leaves they must be checked. She was afraid I might have stolen their books. In my heart I didn't want to, but I said yes.

How I hated myself for being so weak. Why didn't I have the guts to say no! For many years I felt so sorry for myself! We girls who've left the village are poor, ignorant, and have such low self-esteem. We long for the respect of society. But if we don't stand up for ourselves, who will take us seriously? We girls who work as nannies feel this even more deeply than those who sell vegetables, work as waitresses, or work as shop assistants. We enter the most basic cells of society. The differences between city and countryside in terms of civilization and ignorance, and the differences among people in terms of beauty and ugliness are all fully exposed, directly clashing with each other. The transition from clash to harmony is a painful process of awakening.

Looking back at the past decade, the first group of country girls to enter the city as migrant workers is reminiscent of the young people who were sent to the countryside during the Cultural Revolution era. They went to the countryside from the city, whereas we went from the countryside to the city. Both groups suffered both physically and psychologically. They were swamped by the waves of politics, whereas we are swamped by the waves of the market economy. Compared with them, we are much more fortunate.

My home county, Wuwei, has already been totally transformed. In the past the road from the small township to the county capital was very narrow, and now it has become a broad highway. The thatch-roofed huts in the village have become a thing of the past. It's not a novelty to see two-storied houses appearing one after another. Peasants who've been locked away for thousands of years at long last have the opportunity to go to the outside world. Through struggle and hard work they are changing their lives. Reality has proven that we were right in having stepped forth.

—Originally published in *Nongjianü Baishitong* (*Rural Women Knowing All*) 2 (1999): 28–31.

I AM A CLOUD / PANG HUI

The year I turned eighteen I eloped with a man from another county. Later, I gave birth to three daughters. My husband was a gambler and a drunkard and boozed till he was completely legless every day. When he lost money he'd come home and beat up his wife and children. One of those awful beatings three years ago made me determined to leave him, and that's how I started my life as a migrant worker.

I don't have much education and I couldn't find any decent job. I couldn't, and I didn't want to, do those jobs where you had to sell body and soul, so all I could do was go to a construction site and cook for the workers there. Those construction workers were also migrants, living by selling their physical labor. The only thing different was that they were men. Each day I was responsible for preparing three meals for more than a hundred people. The hard work can easily be imagined, but I wasn't really afraid of hard work. What I was afraid of was lack of respect from those men. Among them, some used filthy, disgusting language with me, some made passes at me, and some made a big show of urinating in front of me. During the day it wasn't so bad, but every night, lying down in the workshed, with the wind coming in from all sides, I never dared to take off my clothes, really afraid those men would do something to me. Lying on the plank bed, I couldn't sleep, thinking about my family. I didn't want to return, but my three daughters were always on my mind. Would her dad be able to pay the school fees for the oldest girl? Had the second girl recovered from her epilepsy? And was the third one still wetting her bed? . . . Every night I would think about them for a long time before I went to sleep, and as soon as the sky grew light, I had to get up and prepare the breakfast. My wage was 150 *yuan* per month, but for someone like me who had come out to work for the first time it was quite a large sum. Four months went by, and apart from buying three packets of sanitary napkins and one bag of washing powder, which cost me 8 *yuan*, I kept the remaining 592 *yuan* in my pocket next to my skin. I hoped to use the money to pay for my older daughter's school fees and the second daughter's medicine. . . .

After four months of life as a migrant worker, I gradually got used to the environment and came to understand those men. Even though they were crude people, they were not bad. Their dirty talk was an outlet for their pent-up feelings. It wasn't easy for them to leave home and come out to work either. So I was no longer on my guard. Occasionally I would answer back when they talked dirty. Not only did they not get angry, it would make them happy. Perhaps it was because there were too few women in their lives. I often helped them to mend and wash their clothes. And they used their spare time to help me fetch the water and wash the vegetables. Eventually I won their respect through my own efforts. Once, someone found me a job painting. The pay was better than cooking, but those workers would not let me go, no matter what. They said they only wanted to eat the food I cooked. If the money was not enough, they would be willing to make it up by each taking a bit out of their pay. So I stayed working on the construction site.

In the blink of an eye it was winter and the construction site stopped work. I decided to go home. I thought that after half a year of absence my husband would have changed, but I was wrong. When I got home, carrying my cherished money that I'd earned with blood and sweat, the first thing my husband said was: "You shameless thing, how dare you come back? No old bags who go out to work ever come home intact. I'd rather be a bachelor than a cuckold. Even if we were dying of poverty, I wouldn't take the dirty money you earned. Get out!" I said to him, "My money is clean," but he wouldn't listen and pushed me out the door. I shook all over, and it wasn't the wind from the mountains that made me shiver. I secretly gave the money to my oldest daughter, who chased after me in tears, and once more took the road away from home. It was different from the last time. Having experienced life as a migrant worker, I was no longer ignorant about the outside world, my steps were no longer as hesitant, and I believed at heart: no matter what happened, I would go on living, living without complaint, regret, or shame.

I am a cloud, destined to float around in this life. I do not know where the wind will blow me next.

—Originally published in *Nongjianü Baishitong* (*Rural Women Knowing All*) 8 (1999): 28–29.

LOOKING BACK, I AM PROUD / WANG XIANGFEN

Time is a river, forever flowing.

It was September 8, 1996, when I got on the train to Beijing and started my life as a migrant worker. Two years have passed, and I have gone from being a lively junior secondary school graduate to a housemaid capable of any kind of domestic work. If someone were to ask me whether I regret my choice, I would reply "no" without hesitation.

The first time I left home to work I came across a kind family. During the day there was only Auntie and me.[12] At first, I was unsure of myself and often made mistakes, but Auntie was always very understanding.

Occasionally I missed my distant parents. I remember that every time I wrote letters home my tears flowed nonstop. When Auntie saw me she would say, "My child, everyone misses home when they first leave. At home you're the firstborn, and you have to set a good example for your younger brothers and sisters." I haven't shed any tears since then. When Auntie said that I am clever and reliable and can be trusted to do any task, I took it as a compliment on my work and it encouraged me to do even better. Auntie gradually became my good teacher and close friend. As far as my wages are concerned, she has always given me a raise before I requested. I consider that wages are the reward of labor. Good work will naturally lead to a pay raise from the employer. There should be mutual understanding and mutual respect between the employer and the housemaid. Now I feel very much at home in this family. If there is a job to be done I do it. If I have something to say I say it. Whoever is right is heeded. I'm always in a good mood.

Although I have left school, I have not left my studies behind. I feel that though it's true that it's important to work and earn money, it's even more important to learn skills and broaden one's vision. It's hard to survive without some skills in the throes of the market economy. There's no return ticket in life. I must seize the opportunity while I'm young and spend as much time as possible studying. I'm not prepared to be mediocre all my life.

My spare time is rich and colorful. Uncle works in a newspaper publishing agency and he brings home lots of newspapers every day, such as *Beijing Evening News, People's Daily,* and *China Youth Daily.* I really love reading them. I cut out the important articles, copy all the elegant phrases, and write them in my diary. I like learning English, and I bought an English–Chinese dictionary and other English textbooks for self-study. Listening to the radio and watching television are integral parts of my life. Watching the national news every day is a must for me. I cook and listen to the radio at the same time, and that way I kill two birds with one stone. On my days off, I like to take a camera to Beijing's tourist sites and go sightseeing. I'm also actively involved in the seminars run by the "Migrant Women's Club."[13] Auntie is full of praise about this, and I feel it has given me a sense of purpose and self-confidence.

In my time as a migrant worker, when people from my home county have run into difficulties and come to see me, I have always done my best to help. Many sisters don't get on well with their employers. I advise them that there are conflicts everywhere, and there's no one who is perfect in this world. You must see other people's strong points and be tolerant of their shortcomings. I also apply this strictly to myself. I've been in Beijing for two years now, and

I've hardly bought any clothes. The clothes I wear all come from Auntie's children. My parents endured all kinds of hardship to bring me up. It really wasn't easy for them. Now I send basically all the money I earn back home to pay back my parents for their kindness in bringing me up.

One's work is always rewarded. In 1997 I was awarded the title of "outstanding housemaid" by the domestic service company. And Auntie's household was awarded the title "outstanding employer." As I stood on the platform holding my gold certificate, tears of happiness poured down my cheeks. I knew myself that this honor had not come easily. I hastened to send the happy news to my parents at home, hoping they would be proud of me and understand that their distant daughter was doing well working away from home.

I'm thankful for my life as a migrant worker. It has given me the opportunity to make myself strong and it has taught me how to get on with others, and that if you try you can do anything. The long journey of the migrant worker presents even more opportunities than it does challenges. I wish all those who are working away from home more success and happiness and less unhappiness and worries. I wish that through their diligent work they will realize their dreams!

—Originally published in *Nongjianü Baishitong* (*Rural Women Knowing All*) 1 (1999): 33–34.

LEAVING HUAIHUA[14] VALLEY—A SICHUAN GIRL'S OWN ACCOUNT OF BEING A MIGRANT WORKER / ZHOU RENCONG

The name of my hometown is Huaihua Valley—such a beautiful name. But there is no place for me there.

When I opened my swollen, puckered eyes, I no longer saw the wooden firewood hut at home. This was a room about ten square meters big, with deathly pale ceiling and walls.

Where was I?

The door was pushed open, and slowly the light filtered in. A bowl of hot fish soup was placed on the chest of drawers by the bed. "Good heavens, awake at long last. You slept for two days and two nights and had everyone really worried." That was Xixi's voice.

I closed my eyes and saw the hills stretching one after another into the distance. Among the countless hills in Fushun county, southern Sichuan province, there is a place called Huaihua Valley.

From the county town to Huaihua Valley you have to walk more than two hours on a tractor path. There's no real forest or running streams, only occasionally some tractors tooting on the tractor path and some playful children chasing the tractors, breaking the endless monotony.

Even more oppressive and deadlier still than that monotony was how I felt inside.

My clash with my mother came from the so-called "important event in my life."[15] The custom of "Marry a chicken, follow a chicken; marry a dog, follow a dog" was to me like a huge black net in which all my dreams and aspirations would be swallowed up. There had been enough tragedy among the women around me, including the suicide of Auntie Yinxing, who cared for me when I was young. I had always considered myself no ordinary person. I was a girl with some ideas and some know-how, already rewarded for years of struggle with the fortune of publishing a collection of short stories called *Bamboo Walls*. In our county, which has a population of over a million, I became the only female member of the provincial writers' association.

But I was still just a twenty-four-year-old woman with rural household registration[16] in a remote mountain village. In the countryside, I should long ago have become someone's wife or mother. But I didn't want that. When my mother lost patience and gave me an ultimatum, I couldn't go along with it, but I could also no longer say no. All I could do was run away.

I ran to the top of the hill behind the house and looked back at the mud hut where I had lived for over twenty years. The whole village was unusually quiet, as if keeping silent about my escape. Only the farmers in the rice paddies were sending me off with the sound of their plaintive whistling, rising and falling.

A telephone number I got by chance became my only lifeline.

When the bus arrived at Liangjiahang station, it was three o'clock in the morning. People were hurrying along, the streetlights dragging out their shadows. Was this Chengdu? Was this how I was to enter the city?

The sky gradually lightened. I got off the bus and stood in line in front of the toilet to wash my face. There was a driver of a three-wheeled cart trying for business. I kept shaking my head. I could only shake my head, because I didn't know where I was going. When I got out of the station, the cold wind blew at me from the street. I was shivering all over. I carefully took a piece of paper from inside my clothes. On it was the telephone number that would get me in touch with Xixi. This was the only number that could connect me with this strange, big city, the only lifeline I had at that time. Xixi was a friend[17] from Zigong whom I had not seen for many years. After the call was answered, I had to wait for her to come to the phone, and I held my breath and stared fixedly at the red public telephone. Time passed, one minute after another. I couldn't wait and dialed a second time. Again I had to wait, one minute dragging like a year. After the third time, the shop owner said, "Maybe she's not up yet, or maybe she's not in Chengdu." I looked at the cyclists rushing back and forth on the road, and my mind went blank. If I couldn't get in touch with Xixi, where could I go? The fourth time I got through, she finally came to the phone. When my long-lost Xixi appeared at the entrance of the station I couldn't help feeling dizzy, and when we got to where she was living I fell down unconscious.

. . .

"It was a big thing for you to come out here. You can stay here for the time being and share what little I have," Xixi said.

Survival comes first. First you eat noodles, and then you resort to steamed buns. You eat the same thing for every meal.

This was the flat Xixi rented for 120 *yuan* per month. There was only one room, with a kitchen and toilet shared with others. Xixi said she had opened a cosmetics shop in Guanghan, but she stayed here once in a while when she came to Chengdu.

Xixi had to go to Guanghan again, so she insisted on giving me 50 *yuan* before she left.

I knew that my top priority was to find a job or, more precisely, an income as quickly as possible.

As I walked out of the little flat, it began to drizzle outside. I started taking the bus to all the different job agencies. Because I didn't know the way, I had to ask wherever I went. A few days passed, but without any result, and I was on the verge of collapse, both physically and psychologically.

In the end a health care product company agreed to "try" me. I was so excited I couldn't sleep for a whole night. I told Xixi over the phone. Xixi said that now things would be okay. My job was to sell. I had to run back and forth, and so I gritted my teeth and spent 50 *yuan* to buy a rickety old bicycle from a second-hand market in Huifu Street. Every morning I rode from Bali district to Shuinianhe.[18] Then I went to all the pharmacies in the city to stick up advertising leaflets. I asked the way as I rode along. Often I would be asking where Shuinianhe was, even when I was already there, at Chengdu Hotel.

The biggest problem was feeding myself. Running around every day, I had no way of cooking. Chengdu is the capital of cuisine, but the colorful array of restaurants and snack bars that filled the streets with wonderful smells was not for me. I ate one meal here, one meal there, before making my base at a small, nameless eatery in Shuinianhe. The cheapest noodles, with some oil and seasoning, cost three *yuan*. The main thing was that the hygiene was okay. If I got diarrhea I would have to buy medicine, and that would get me into real trouble. I became a regular customer at that small eatery. Every time I came, the boss would yell out, "One bowl of hot, sour noodle soup!" From a very early age I had had an aversion to noodles, but now I was forced to face that bowl of "hot, sour" noodles every day, because that was what was cheapest. It made me curse, but I had to swallow them. Even now, whenever I see noodles my stomach turns over.

It would be a long time before I was paid. My purse was shrinking, and I hadn't seen Xixi for a long time. It got to the stage when even noodles became a luxury for me. Then I had to go to the morning market to buy some of those big, homemade steamed buns from the peasants. Each time I bought three for one *yuan*, and that way I got a discount. I had one for breakfast, I put one in my bag for lunch, and one I left at home for dinner. I had already had stomach problems beforehand, and then, after a few days, I was completely beaten by those little steamed mounds of dough.

I woke from a dream with excruciating pain, sweat pouring down my face. The pain made me feel as if the god of death had come. Holding my stomach, I wanted to cry out for help from the woman next door who drove a three-wheeled cart, but I was so dizzy I couldn't make a sound. Suddenly my stomach turned and I vomited everything up.

The next day I struggled to get up to see a doctor. When I told her what had happened, the female doctor stared at me for an age. "When was your last period?" Suddenly I understood what she was implying. I felt so wronged and angry that I couldn't utter a word.

I was at the end of my tether. After I'd walked for a whole day without eating, my stomach started to ache again. The desire to survive made me want to eat anything I could, but I only had one *yuan* left, and if I spent it all my supplies would have run out. My lips parched, I couldn't help looking at the enticing food shops and eateries lining the streets. They looked better than heaven in my eyes. My hunger got greater and greater, but I just had to turn my head and walk away.

When I got back to Bali district, Xixi had at long last returned! One hot meal revived me. Then she had to leave again. My pride made me reluctant to open my mouth and ask her for money, but the desire to survive forced me to speak up. Xixi was really clever. She took out 50 *yuan* and gave it to me, just as I was struggling to speak. This 50 *yuan* lasted me until I got the pay from my first job as a migrant worker. No doubt that money saved my life.

Looking back at the road I traveled in search of work, it was so hard and yet so simple.[19]

I spent many days rushing around without success. I heard from the woman next door who drove a three-wheeled cart that there was a labor market at Jiuyanqiao, and there you could find a job as a nanny or a waitress. I took bus number 54 to Jiuyanqiao. I stood there for a while, but eventually I left. I definitely did not think that physical labor was second-class, but I still felt I should be able to do something different.

In the end all I could do was go to a job agency. In order to show that I had some kind of capability, I took out my book *Bamboo Walls* and the membership card from the provincial writers' association. Unexpectedly I had cold water poured on my enthusiasm. A young female attendant with heavy makeup scrutinized my "hardware" for ages and then threw at me: "If you're looking for a job, just look for a job; from now on never show these playthings. If other people see you as some bookish, annoying writer, they won't want you!"

What I saw as the crystallization of so many years of blood and tears, others saw as positively shameful. I turned cold all over. Just how much was my worthy writing really worth?[20] Of what value were the things I pursued so earnestly?

It was the Chengdu newspapers that finally got me on the right track looking for work. The large quantity of information covered by those newspapers may not all be credible, but after all it's available to everyone. It's up to oneself to weigh how credible it is and seize the opportunities provided.

One day, sitting next to the public phone and looking up at the gray sky, I wanted to cry, but no tears came. When I turned around to the newsstand, I saw the *Job News* and immediately bought a copy. I scrutinized the paper from beginning to end, but could not find even one job that would suit me. The following day I bought another copy. I found several advertisements for office workers and hastened to call them. The young lady at the other end said with a crisp, gentle, and polite voice: "Sorry, our positions have been filled." It was the same with all the others. How could it be so fast? It was only later that I learned that some so-called "information" is just a trick played by the chief editor to fill up the page. Still refusing to give up, I bought another copy on the third day. I discovered a notice for a recruitment day at the employment market on Ningxia Street. When I got there, I found this was a real employment market on a large scale. Still, it was only after going there several days in a row that I was picked by the company in Shuinianhe that sold health care products.

I promised myself I would treasure this job that had been so hard to find. Just at that time, by chance, I got to know a woman who'd come from a coastal city to Chengdu on business. After years of sinking and floating in the sea of business, she'd become what you'd call an "iron woman."[21] She didn't make a big deal out of my situation. Auntie was a woman of few words, but every word she said had an impact on me. When I asked her the telephone number of a certain company, her answer was, "Ring 114."[22] When I asked her where a certain company was, she'd say, "Look it up on the map." She actually gave me quite a few copies of the map. When Auntie was going back to her hometown, she gave me a letter and told me to open it after she'd gone. When I opened the letter, I discovered that it was a notice of enrollment for a computer training class at the Electronics University, already paid for. Through that class I acquired another practical skill and more confidence in the belief that you make your own life.

Because I lacked sales experience, I left the company that temporarily had given me shelter. Unemployed again, I rode back and forth with the map that Auntie had given me, and when one map was worn, I took out another. It was only then that I realized why Auntie had given me so many copies of the map.

I was asked to an interview by a company seeking office workers. When I found the place, I saw a few girls sitting quietly in the meeting room. The head of the office, who called himself Jiang, sat on a platform in front of us. He cast us a look and cleared his voice. "You have all been through a rigorous selection process. The company is reliant on customers, so your job is to pull in customers. How are you going to do that? You can do it any way you like. For instance, you can accompany them to go singing, dancing, and drinking." The true nature of that job became quite clear. I quietly got up and left.

I now work at a quite famous private enterprise, Sanwang Group, in Chengdu. This company is one of the top five hundred private companies in the country. I am the chief editor of the *Sanwang Group News*. I select and write articles and I also manage the literary supplement, which I love dearly. I like the vitality and the rather formal management. The company deals mainly with people from the countryside and that makes me, a country woman, happy to work as hard as I can. The wages are not bad; I could buy more than a hundred steamed buns per day, or one or two dozen bowls of hot, sour noodle soup. Some acquaintances thought I got this job by pulling strings. In reality it wasn't so. I remember standing in a crowd filling in forms, handing in my curriculum vitae, already numb from looking for jobs for so long. The person in charge of recruitment for the Sanwang Group carefully read my papers and said right away, "Come and register for work tomorrow." It took me a while to react to such a simple "recruitment." Then I was hesitant and didn't go to register for a day. Afterward, the person in charge told me that he thought highly of my "experience." Of course, he also thought highly of my membership card and my "big book," which had been disregarded by all those previous employers.

The ups and downs of looking for work made me cooler-headed without realizing it. Fate started to smile at me.

She said, "I'm actually working as an escort."

I said, "Xixi, my friend, I missed you so much that I was in tears!"

I'm deeply grateful to Xixi, even though what she said before she left shocked me and I could not accept it. She said, "In reality, I've always been an escort in a dance club. Now your situation is better, I can leave without worrying."

Xixi's eyes were full of sincerity. She said that her cosmetics shop lost a lot of money and went bankrupt and that's why she went down this path. . . . I didn't dare believe what Xixi was saying, but thinking back on two incidents, I could not help feeling very emotional.

Not long after I had gotten to Chengdu, I remembered someone from my home county, far away in Shanghai. I had heard he was doing well, so I called him, but he said, "Work is difficult to find in Shanghai too." Those few words made me feel cold all over. When I got back to the apartment, Xixi had just returned with a man who, she said, was a friend in business. The man looked me over and tried to chat me up. Xixi suddenly yelled at him: "This is my older sister, you behave yourself!" Sure enough, the man shut up.

On another occasion, Xixi rang to say that something had happened to her in Guanghan and she would not be able to return for a while. I wanted to hurry over there, but Xixi wouldn't let me. I persisted and she started yelling from the other end: "You can't come, you mustn't get involved in this business, you're different from me!"

In the end I didn't go. Afterward, she came back saying that it was just some trouble in the business, and I didn't take much notice.

This was my friend, an unremarkable girl who had done everything for me without a word. I am not making up stories here, everything is completely true. Xixi and Auntie, who gave me the chance to study computing, had done so much for me but said so little!

Writing has become a habit in my life. Looking back, the first year and a half in the city has been a prolific time for my creative writing. Literature has brought me so much loneliness, even suffering, but even more than that, it has brought me fulfillment and happiness.

City life and my job at the moment have taken me way beyond the bounds of literature. I like this type of challenge. I've devoted myself heart and soul to getting to know unfamiliar things about the economy and society, and about news and voicing opinions on politics and the like. These changes will probably make me a new person.

The thing that hasn't changed is my pursuit of literature, because it has become part of my life and way of living. Literature has been my support through all the hard times. Within the short space of a year I wrote and submitted my work nonstop. Publications like *Social Panorama*, *Short Story Writer*, *Sichuan Daily*, *Selected Short Stories*, and *Young Writers* have all published special issues of my writing. In April 1998 I was invited by *Selected Short Stories* to go to Zhengzhou to attend the second national short story conference. Nowadays, I constantly get letters from my readers. I possess such riches that others don't have; isn't this worth treasuring?

—Originally published in *Nongjianü Baishitong* (*Rural Women Knowing All*) 3 (1999): 25–30.

WORKING FOR MYSELF / LI JIANYING

I am an ordinary country woman with four years of primary school education.

The year I started out as a migrant worker I was only fifteen years old. At that time my family was very poor. To help alleviate our family's poverty, after each spring planting season my sister, who was two years older than me, and I went with other women from the village to a rice-growing area in the neighboring county to work as day laborers. We planted rice seedlings. At that time of the year, even though the weather was turning warm, the water in the rice paddy was still icy cold during the morning and the evening. Every morning as it grew light my sister and I would already be in the ice-cold, muddy water, barefooted. There was not a moment's rest from bending down to plant the seedlings, because each *mu* planted would earn another 20 *yuan*,[23] and that would be enough to buy a bag of flour. I was seduced by the meager pay, so that even though my back hurt from bending over I was never willing to stand up and stretch a little. Sometimes my feet would cramp from the cold water, but that was not enough to make me give up. At midday, we would sit on the wet bank bordering the paddy and, wiping the sweat off with our clothes, we'd gnaw the corn cakes and scallions that we'd brought from home. When we were thirsty we would run to the pump and fill ourselves up with cold water from the well.[24] In the evenings we'd be covered in mud and we'd lift our legs, heavy as lead, and hurry home unsteadily.

Even though it was exhausting, I was happy. With the 30-odd *yuan* that my sister and I earned from planting rice in our pockets, our happiness was beyond expression. Feeling very pleased with ourselves, we would fantasize about how to spend the money and how our parents would praise us. One day we worked very late. On our way home it was late at night and pitch black, so that holding out your hand you couldn't see your fingers. The other girls had all left with their bicycles. Only my sister and I were left behind because we couldn't ride bicycles. Our hearts pounded with fear. In this place in the middle of nowhere, what were we going to do if we ran into a bad person? The cawing of a crow and the sound of its flapping wings scared us so that our hair stood on end. My sister and I leaned against each other, and our feet unconsciously sped up. After a while, the voice of our younger brother came to us. It turned out that my parents, watching the sky grow dark but not being able to see my sister and me, had sent our younger brother and some other people to find us.

I planted rice seedlings every year for five years. Our family had lots of land and not enough farmhands, and also I was still very young, so my parents wouldn't let me leave home to work far away. But every year during this short month my sister and I made between 800 and 1,000 *yuan*. When I proudly handed over a pile of cash to my father, his wrinkled old face would light up with a smile.

The year I turned twenty, I started life as a real migrant worker. I went to a restaurant in Harbin to work as a waitress. Every day I got up at four o'clock in the morning and worked continuously till eleven or twelve at night when the restaurant closed. I served food, washed the dishes, looked after the guests, and cleaned the tables and chairs. I was so busy my feet hardly touched the ground, but still I was often scolded by the boss. Overwork, poor wages, and not enough sleep made all the waitresses exhausted, and we all wanted to leave. The boss didn't let us go and threatened to hold onto our belongings and our wages. This threat was really effective. As you'd expect, the other waitresses stopped asking to leave. But I couldn't stand it and lied, saying that I needed to see the doctor, and I left the restaurant with nothing. After that, I worked as a shop assistant, as a laborer in a brick factory, and I made plaster figures in a craft factory . . . all strenuous and poorly paid jobs. I could put up with low pay, but what I couldn't put up with was insults from the boss. I can do without anything except my dignity.

For the sake of my dignity I ditched one boss after another and changed from one job to another. Finally, I thought to myself, how come all the bosses I met were of the same nature? I decided to learn a skill and work for myself. In line with my level of education, I went to a beauty school to study hairdressing.

In the school I went to great pains with my study and practiced hard. Some students were a bit timid and didn't dare to make an effort. Often they hurt their customers, and once they made a mistake they didn't dare try again. I didn't worry too much about such things. Otherwise, what was the point of paying more than 1,000 *yuan* in fees and coping with just two pancakes and a glass of water for meals every day? Wasn't it in order to learn a real trade and skills, so that I could run my own business? So it was that I finished the required three months' apprenticeship in a month and a half. The principal and the teachers were all very pleased with me, saying I could set up on my own. Afterward, I ran back and forth to the trade, tax, and public health bureaus to obtain a permit and registration. Braving the hot sun, I went in search of a place to start a hairdressing salon.

The salon opened as planned. I felt so fulfilled. In less than a year I paid back all the debts my family owed. Later on, with a fellow student from the school, I ran a beauty parlor for two years.

Now I am married and have a family. Holding my one-year-old daughter, I think back on my bitter days as a migrant worker, and I think how tiring and full of hardship my life was. I can't help my bitter tears falling onto the face of my daughter, sleeping in my arms. I can't bear looking back on those years, but they've left indelible memories.

—Originally published in *Nongjianü Baishitong* (*Rural Women Knowing All*) 7 (1999): 28–29.

NOTES

1. *Wailaimei*, literally "girls who have come from outside," is a term commonly used to refer to rural migrant women. As noted elsewhere in this volume, they are also commonly referred to as *dagongmei*, working sisters or "working girls."

2. *Sanpei nü* translates literally as "women who accompany (male customers) in three ways." Such women entertain men in restaurants, bars, and nightclubs, and sometimes provide sexual services. For a detailed discussion of the lives of such women, see Tiantian Zheng, this volume.

3. One *yuan* = 10 cents (U.S.).

4. See note 1. Guizhou is a poor province in the south of China.

5. The Special Economic Zones were set up to attract foreign investment by offering foreign-funded firms, including wholly foreign-owned factories, and joint ventures tax concessions and lax labor regulations. Shenzhen Special Economic Zone, in Guangdong province, was officially opened in 1980, along with Zhuhai and Shantou Special Economic Zones. Since then, many other Special Economic Zones and "open areas" have been established across the country. They are key ar-

eas of employment for rural migrants, especially young women. The situation of rural migrant women in Shenzhen is discussed in Lee 1998 and Pun 1999.

6. A more literal translation of the title (*Chenzhong de huaji*) would be "Heavy season of flowers." This title is deliberately odd. "Season of flowers," i.e., spring, refers to youth, which is supposed to be light and happy, but here it is described as heavy.

7. One *li* = approximately 0.5 km (.31 mile).

8. This is very little. The average wage for housemaids in Beijing at that time was between 20 and 30 *yuan*.

9. *Jumin weiyuanhui* is a subgovernmental body with a jurisdiction of approximately 2,000 people, charged with maintaining harmony and order in the area. The majority of members are unemployed or retired women.

10. This term refers to urbanites who, as students during the Cultural Revolution (1966–76), were sent to the countryside but later returned to the city.

11. Anhui is a relatively poor province to the south of Beijing. The author is from Wuwei county, Anhui, a region well-known as a traditional supplier of housemaids to the capital. For a discussion of media images of Anhui housemaids see Sun, this volume.

12. I.e, her employer. "Auntie" is a term of address. For a discussion of the ways in which relations between employers and domestic maids replicate kinship relations, see Gaetano, this volume.

13. *Dagongmei zhi Jia* is a club for migrant women in Beijing, run by the editorial office of *Nongjianü Baishitong* (*Rural Women Knowing All*).

14. *Huaihua* is the flower of the Chinese scholar tree.

15. I.e., marriage.

16. The household registration system was introduced in the mid-1950s as a means of regulating the population, and in particular, of restricting rural-to-urban migration. See introduction, this volume.

17. The term used here is *laoxiang*—someone from the same region.

18. Bali district is on the outskirts of Chengdu, northeast of the city center. Shuinianhe district is southeast of the city center.

19. This section does not follow chronologically from the last. Instead, it returns us to the period before the narrator found her job with the health care product company, this time focusing on the difficulty of finding work.

20. The Chinese sentence (*wenxue jiujing zhi ji wen?*) contains a pun on the word *wen*, meaning "writing" or "literature," but also "coins."

21. *Nü qiangren*—i.e., a successful career woman.

22. I.e, inquiries.

23. One *mu* = 0.0667 hectares.

24. Most Chinese readers would consider this a potential health risk. The usual preference is to drink hot (boiled) water.

amei	阿妹	little sister
anfang	暗访	undercover
anquan	安全	safe
anquan diyi	安全第一	safety first
anquan qi	安全期	the rhythm method of contraception
banggongdui	帮工队	agricultural work team
baomu	保姆	maid; domestic worker
bi bieren di yi deng	比别人低一等	inferior to others
bianjieren	边界人	borderliners; marginalized people
chang yixie zhishi	尝一些知识	to gain knowledge
chaosheng youji dui	超生游击队	"over-quota guerrilla birth army"
chengren gaokao	成人高考	adult tertiary examination
chuantong	传统	traditional
chulai dagong	出来打工	come out to work
chunpu	纯朴	innocent; simple
chunzhen	纯真	pure, innocent
chuzhong	初中	(junior) secondary school
cong yi er zhong	从一而终	to the end
dagong	打工	to work as a wage laborer
dagong sao	打工嫂	rural migrant wife; married migrant woman
dagongmei	打工妹	working sister; migrant woman working as a waged laborer
Dagongmei zhi Jia	打工妹之家	The Migrant Women's Club
dakuan	大款	"deep-pocketed"; someone with a lot of money
daling guniang	大龄姑娘	old maid
danchun	单纯	naïve
danshen guizu	单身贵族	single aristocracy
daowei	到位	climax; orgasm
dazhuan	大专	(tertiary level) college
dei chuli guanxi	得处理关系	must manage human relations
didi daodao de nongmin	地地道道的农民	quintessential peasant
diren yideng	低人一等	low-class; demeaning; inferior

duanlian (ziji)	锻炼(自己)	to test oneself; get life experience
feishui wai liu	肥水外流	fertilized water running into someone else's garden, i.e., a girl whose parents have devoted resources to educating her, only for her to marry out
fencun	分寸	sense of propriety
fengjian	封建	feudal
Fulian	妇联	Women's Federation. See *Quanguo Funü Lianhehui.*
gaibian ziji	改变自己	to change oneself
ganqing	感情	affective ties; affection
ganshou	感受	to experience
gao qian	搞钱	to make money
gaodeng zixue gaokao	高等自学高考	tertiary-level examination for self-study students
gaozhong	高中	senior secondary school
getihu	个体户	self employed; private entrepreneur
gongping	公平	equity; justice
gongzuo zheng	工作证	work permit
guangrong	光荣	noble
guanxi	关系	relationship; social network; connections
hanxu	含蓄	reserve
hen wuliao	很无聊	bored; nothing to do
huaihua	槐花	the flower of the Chinese scholar tree
huan qin	换亲	exchange marriage (in which families exchange daughters for their sons to marry)
huanghu	恍惚	in a daze
Hui shang	徽商	merchants from Anhui
hukou	户口	household registration
hunyu zheng	婚育证	marriage and fertility permit
hutong	胡同	alley (in Beijing)
jia	家	home; family
jia ji sui ji, jia gou sui gou	嫁鸡随鸡, 嫁狗随狗	marry a chicken, follow a chicken; marry a dog, follow a dog
jian shimian, kankan chengliren de shenghuo	见世面, 看看城里人的生活	to expand one's horizons and get a glimpse of urban life

jiankang zheng	健康证	certificate of health
jianren	坚忍	steadfastness
jiao'ao	骄傲	arrogant
jiaohua	狡猾	sly
jiawu	家务	housework; chores
jiawu zheng	家务证	domestic service work permit
jiazheng fuwu	家政服务	household service
jiazheng xue	家政学	home economics
jiefang	解放	to liberate; be liberated
jieji chengfen	阶级成分	class status
jiejiu	解救	to rescue
jin	斤	unit of measurement. One jin = 0.5 kg (1.1 lbs)
jishi	纪实	eyewitness
jiuye zheng	就业证	employment permit
jizao	急躁	irritable
jumin weiyuanhui	居民委员会	residents' committee
juzhu zheng	居住证	residence permit
kaikuo yanjie	开阔眼界	to open one's eyes; broaden one's horizons
kan shimian	看世面	to see the world
kezhi	克制	restraint
kong	空	empty
kuzao	枯燥	dry
lanyin hukou	蓝印户口	"blue stamp" household registration
lao xianzhe	老闲着	nothing to do
laogong	老公	husband
laoxiang	老乡	people from the same native village, county, or, less often, province
li	里	measure of distance; half a kilometer
liange ting	练歌厅	"singing practice hall"; karaoke bar
liangqiren	两栖人	two-dwelling person; people who are attached to two places at once
liangzhi	良知	conscience
lienü	烈女	a female martyr; a woman who would rather die than have her virtue compromised
liudong renkou	流动人口	floating population
luan	乱	chaotic; unsafe
luohou	落后	backward

mami	妈咪	Madam
mei shi gan	没事干	nothing to do
meiyong	没用	useless
meiyou jingshen	没有精神	without energy
meiyou wenhua de lao taipo	没有文化的老太婆	uneducated old woman
meiyou ziji de shijian	没有自己的时间	no time to oneself
men dang hu dui	门当户对	matching bride and groom in terms of socio-economic status
mianzi	面子	face
mingongchao	民工潮	tide of migrant labor
mingyun	命运	destiny; fate
mu	亩	unit of measurement. One mu = 0.0667 hectares
nengzheng huihua	能挣会花	to be able to make money and consume
niangjia	娘家	natal home
ningzhong	凝重	dignity
nongcun ren	农村人	peasant, rural folk
nongmin	农民	peasant, farmer
nü qiangren	女强人	successful career woman
pao yewu	跑业务	to be in sales; to do business
peiqian de huo	赔钱的货	goods one loses money on; daughter
pinkun luohou	贫困落后	poor and backward
pinkun xian	贫困县	poverty county
po chuqu de shui	泼出去的水	water thrown out the door; daughter
putonghua	普通话	Mandarin Chinese
qi'an	奇案	bizarre crime
qianyi renkou	迁移人口	migrant population (*hukou* transfer)
qiaobuqi	瞧不起	to look down on
qingli	清理	street sweeps
quan pindao	全频道	"all channel (services)," i.e., a wide range of sexual services
Quanguo Funü Lianhehui	全国妇女联合会	All China Women's Federation
qucai	取材	to waste one's talent
rencai	人才	talent; skilled personnel
renjia de	人家的	member of someone else's family; daughter
rensheng dibushu	人生地不熟	stranger in a strange place
ri jiu jian renxin	日久见人心	with time one can see people's true nature

san da chabie	三大差别	"three great differences": inequalities between the city and the country-side, mental and manual labor, and workers and peasants
sanpei (nü)	三陪(女)	escort; bar hostess
sanpei xiaojie	三陪小姐	"misses accompanying (men) in three ways"; bar hostesses; escorts. See also *sanpei nü*
sanwu	三无	"three withouts": migrants without stable employ-ment, residence or identification
sao	骚	whorelike sexuality; flirta-tious
saohuang	扫黄	crackdown on prostitution
seqing peishi	色情陪侍	"erotic companies"; escort agencies
shenfen zheng	身份证	identity card
shishi zongheng	时事纵横	events and happenings
shou yueshu	受约束	to be restricted
shoujie	守节	widow chastity
shoupian	受骗	to be cheated
shunü	淑女	virtuous woman
si you	四有	to have "four qualities," i.e., to be motivated, be educated, be determined, and have goals
sixiang gongzuo	思想工作	thought work
suzhi	素质	quality (of a person)
tashi	塌实	calm
tiaochu nongmen	跳出农们	to leave the farm
tigao suzhi	提高素质	to raise the quality (of a person)
tonghang	同行	people in the same occupa-tion or trade
tongxiang	同乡	people from the same native village, county, or, less often, province. See *laoxiang*
tu	土	rustic
tuoxian	脱险	to escape from danger
tuqi	土气	rustic; boorish
tutou tunaode	土头土脑的	"dirt-head, dirt-brain"
waichu renyuan	外出人员	outgoing migrants

waichu renyuan liudong jiuye dengji ka	外出人员流动就业登记卡	employment registration card for outgoing migrants
waidiren	外地人	outsider; non-native
wailaimei	外来妹	"girls from outside"; migrant women. See *dagongmei*
weiqu	委屈	humiliated
wenhua diyun	文化底蕴	culturedness; modesty and refinement
wenming	文明	civilization; civility
wenping	文凭	diploma
wenxue jiujing zhi ji wen	文学究竟值几文	how much is "worthy writing" (literature) really worth?
"Wo de dagong shengya"	我的打工生涯	"My life as a migrant worker"
wo you shi	我有事	I have something to do
wunong	务农	agricultural work; farmer
xiadeng de gongzuo	下等的工作	low-class work
xiagang	下岗	to be laid off
xiagang nügong	下岗女工	laid off female worker
xianchang	现场	scene (of a crime)
xiandaihua	现代化	modernization; modernity
xianqi liangmu	贤妻良母	virtuous wife and good mother
xiao	小	little
xiao baomu	小保姆	little nursemaid; nanny. See also *baomu*
xiao bu ren ze daluan	小不忍则大乱	if you don't put up with a little trouble, you'll only end up with bigger trouble
xiao guniang	小姑娘	little girl
xiao laoban	小老板	"little boss"; owner of a small business
xiao pin bu xiao chang	笑贫不笑娼	people will ridicule your poverty, but not your prostitution
xiaojie	小姐	Miss; a euphemistic term for prostitute
xiaoxue	小学	primary school
xingdong	行动	operation
yaotouwu	摇头舞	shaking head dance; a strip show performed under the influence of the drug Ecstasy

yatou	丫头	rural girl
yayi	压抑	stressed and depressed
yexi	夜袭	night raid
yimin	移民	migrant; immigrant
yinsi	隐私	hidden self; private matters
you baofu	有抱负	to have goals
you ganqing	有感情	to have feelings; be affectionate
you lixiang	有理想	to have ideals; be motivated
you wenhua	有文化	to be educated
you zhiqi	有志气	to be determined
yu shijie jiegui	与世界接轨	linking tracks with the rest of the world
yuan	元	the Chinese monetary unit; *Renminbi*
yuanwang	冤枉	wronged
zanzhu zheng	暂住证	temporary residence permit
zhanxian ziwo	展现自我	to express oneself
zhao ge hao zhangfu	找个好丈夫	to find a better husband
zhao qian	找钱	to look for money
zhao renao	找热闹	to look for excitement
zhencao	贞操	virginity; chastity
zhengyi	正义	justice
zhongzhuan	中专	technical degree
zhuang chun	装纯	to fake purity
zhuanyehu	转业户	specialized household
zili	自立	independent
zili kouliang chengzhen hukou	自立口粮城镇户口	self-supplied food grain *hukou*
ziqiang	自强	strong
zisi	自私	selfish
zixin	自信	self-confident
zizhong	自重	self-respect
zizun	自尊	(self) dignity
zou yitian, suan yitian	走一天, 算一天	to live one day at a time
zou yi zou, kan yi kan	走一走, 看一看	to go out and have a look
zuotai xiaojie	坐台小姐	"women who sit on the stage" ("stage" refers to the sofa in a private karaoke room found in karaoke bars); bar hostesses' form of self-address

REFERENCES

Abu-Lughod, Janet. 1975. "Comments: The end of the age of innocence in migration theory." In Helen I. Safa and Brian M. DuToit, eds., *Migration and Urbanization*, 201–6. The Hague: Mouton.

Abu-Lughod, Lila. 1990. "The romance of resistance: Tracing transformations of power through Bedouin women." *American Ethnologist* 17 (1): 41–55.

The American Embassy in China. 2002. "*Hukou* reform targets urban-rural divide." 1 March. http://www.usembassy-china.org.cn/econ/hukou.html.

Anagnost, Ann. 1994. "The politicized body." In Angela Zito and Tani E. Barlow, eds., *Body, Subject, and Power in China*, 131–56. Chicago: University of Chicago Press.

———. 1995. "A surfeit of bodies: Population and the rationality of the state in post–Mao China." In Faye D. Ginsburg and Rayna Rapp, eds., *Conceiving the New World Order: The Global Politics of Reproduction*, 22–41. Berkeley: University of California Press.

———. 1997. *National Past-times: Narrative, Representation, and Power in Modern China*. Durham, NC: Duke University Press.

An Chunying. 1996. "Zaojiaren budeyi (The pressure to marry early)." *Nongjianü Baishitong* (Rural Women Knowing All) (September):22.

Anderson, Bridget. 2000. *Doing the Dirty Work? The Global Politics of Domestic Labour*. London: ZED Books.

Andors, Phyllis. 1988. "Women and work in Shenzhen." *Bulletin of Concerned Asian Scholars* 20 (3): 22–41.

Anhui Province Women's Federation's Legal Consultation Office. 1998. "Hong Zhaodi shijian fasheng yihou (After the Hong Zhaodi incident)." *Anhui Fuyun* (Anhui Women's Movement) 259 (July–August): 20–21.

Asia Monitor Resource Centre, *China Labour Bulletin*, the Hong Kong Christian Industrial Committee and Human Rights in China, eds. 1999. "Many words, not enough action." *Human Rights in China* (spring):38–69.

Bai Jianfeng. 1998. "'Saohuang' qianwan buneng shouruan (Pornography crackdown must be resolute)." *Renmin Ribao* (People's Daily), 8 January, 1.

Bakhtin, Michael. 1981. "Forms of time and of the chronotope in the novel." In Michael Holquist, ed.; Caryl Emerson and Michael Holquist, trans., *The Dialogic Imagination: Four Essays*, 84–258. Austin: University of Texas Press.

Barlow, Tani E. 1994a. "Theorizing woman: *Funü, guojia, jiating* (Woman, state, family)." In Angela Zito and Tani E. Barlow, eds., *Body, Subject, Power in China*, 253–89. Chicago: University of Chicago Press.

———. 1994b. "Politics and protocols of *funü*: (Un)making national women." In Christina K. Gilmartin and Gail Hershatter, eds., *Engendering China*, 339–59. Cambridge: Harvard University Press.

———. 1997. "Woman at the close of the Maoist era in the polemics of Li Xiaojiang and her associates." In Lisa Lowe and David Lloyd, eds., *The Politics of Culture in the Shadow of Capital*, 506–13. Durham, NC: Duke University Press.

Baudrillard, Jean. 1997 (1981). *Simulacrum and Simulation*. Ann Arbor: University of Michigan Press.

"Beijing cuts red tape for staff of foreign enterprises." *China News Digest*, 16 June 2002. http://www.cnd.org/Global/02/06/16/020616–92.html.

Beijing Laodongju (Beijing Labor Bureau). 1995. *Waidi Laijing Renyuan Bidu* (Mandatory Reading for Migrant Service Workers in the Capital). Beijing: Industrial and Commercial Press.

———. 1999. *Waidi Jinjing Wugong Renyuan Bidu* (Mandatory Reading for Migrant Service Workers in the Capital). Beijing: Industrial and Commercial Press.

Beijing Wailai Renkou Pucha Bangongshi (Beijing Migrant Census Office), eds. 1998. *1997 Beijingshi Wailai Renkou Pucha Ziliao* (1997 Beijing Migrant Population Census). Beijing: China Commercial Press.

Bilsborrow, Richard E. and the UN Secretariat. 1993. "Internal female migration and development: An overview." In *Internal Migration of Women in Developing Countries: Proceedings of the UN Expert Meeting on the Feminization of Internal Migration* (Aguascalientes, Mexico, 22–25 October 1991), 1–17. New York: Department for Economic and Social Information and Policy Analysis, United Nations.

Bordo, Susan. 1993. *Unbearable Weight: Feminism, Western Culture, and the Body*. Berkeley: University of California Press.

Bossen, Laurel. 1994. "Zhongguo nongcun funü: Shenmo yuanyin shi tamen liu zai nongtianli (Gender and Chinese peasant women: What caused them to stay in the field)?" In Li Xiaojiang, Zhu Hong, and Dong Xiuyu, eds., *Xingbie yu Zhongguo* (Gender and China), 128–54. Beijing: Sanlian Shudian.

———. 2002. *Chinese Women and Rural Development*. Boulder, CO: Rowman and Littlefield.

Bourdieu, Pierre. 1984. *Distinction: A Social Critique of the Judgments of Taste*. Cambridge: Harvard University Press.

Brown, Phil. 2002. "Dowry, brideprice and household bargaining in rural China." Working paper.

Brownell, Susan. 1995. *Training the Body for China*. Chicago: University of Chicago Press.

Buijs, Gina, ed. 1993. *Migrant Women: Crossing Boundaries and Changing Identities*. Oxford, Providence: Berg.

Butler, Judith. 1993. *Bodies That Matter: On the Discursive Limits of "Sex."* New York: Routledge.

Cai Fang. 1997. "Qianyi juece zhong de jiating jiaose he xingbie tezheng (The role of family and gender characteristics in migration decision making)." *Renkou Yanjiu* (Population Research) 21 (2): 7–12.

Chan, Anita. 2002. "The culture of survival: Lives of migrant workers through the prism of private letters." In Perry Link, Richard P. Madsen, and Paul G. Pickowicz, eds., *Popular China: Unofficial Culture in a Globalizing Society*, 163–88. Boulder, CO: Rowman and Littlefield.

Chan, Kam Wing. 1994. "Urbanization and rural-urban migration in China since 1982: A new baseline." *Modern China* 20 (3) (July): 243–81.

———. 1996. "Post–Mao China: A two-class urban society in the making." *International Journal of Urban and Regional Research* 20 (1): 134–50.

———. 1999. "Internal migration in China: A dualistic approach." In Frank N. Pieke and Hein Mallee, eds., *Internal and International Migration: Chinese Perspectives*, 49–71. Surrey: Curzon Press.

Chan, Kam Wing and Li Zhang. 1999. "The *hukou* system and rural-urban migration in China: Processes and changes." *China Quarterly* 160:818–55.

Chant, Sylvia. 1992. "Conclusion: Toward a framework for the analysis of gender-selective migration." In Sylvia Chant and Sarah Radcliffe, eds., *Gender and Migration in Developing Countries*, 197–205. New York: Belhaven Press.

Chant, Sylvia and Sarah Radcliffe. 1992. "Migration and development: The importance of gender." In Sylvia Chant and Sarah Radcliffe, eds., *Gender and Migration in Developing Countries*, 1–29. New York: Belhaven Press.

Chen Yintao. 1997. "Dagongmei de hunlianguan ji qi kunrao (Rural working women's attitudes toward love and marriage and their dilemmas)." *Renkou Yanjiu* (Population Research) 21 (2): 39–44.

———. 1999. "Marriage attitudes and problems among migrant women workers: Survey results in Guangdong." In N. Chiang and C. Sung, eds., *Population, Urban and Regional Development in China*, 181–92. Taipei: China Studies Program, Population Studies Center, National Taiwan University.

Cheng Naishan. 1999. "Ni jiang pinwei ma (Do you care about taste)?" *Xin Zhou Kan* (New Weekly) 7 (July 1): 52–56.

Chiang, Nora. 1999. "Research on the floating population in China: Female migrant workers in Guangdong's township-village enterprises." In Nora Chiang and Cathy Sung, eds., *Population, Urban and Regional Development in China*, 163–80. Taipei: Population Studies Center, National Taiwan University.

China Population Information and Research Center. 1997. *China Population Data Sheet*. Beijing.

Chu Nü. 2001. "Chengshi nüren (City women)." *Dongbei zhi Chuang* (The Window to the Northeast) 17:19.

Clark, C. Fiona and Nina Laurie. 2000. "Gender, age and exclusion: A challenge to community organisations in Lima, Peru." In Caroline Sweetman, ed., *Gender and Lifecycles*, 80–88. Oxford: Oxfam.

Clarke, M. Kamari, ed. 1999. "To reclaim Yoruba traditions is to reclaim the gods of Africa: Reflections on the uses of ethnography and history in Yoruba revivalism." In Rae Anderson, Sally Cole, and Heather Howard, eds., *Feminist Lives, Texts and Practice in Anthropology*, 229–42. New York: Broadview Press.

Cohen, Myron L. 1993. "Cultural and political inventions in modern China: The case of the Chinese 'peasant.'" *Daedalus* 122 (2): 151–70.

Connelly, Rachel, Kenneth D. Roberts, Zhenzhen Zheng, and Zhenming Xie. 2002. "The impact of migration on the status of women in rural China."

Paper presented at 2002 Association of Asian Studies Meeting, Washington, D.C., April.

Constable, Nicole. 1997. *Maid to Order in Hong Kong: Stories of Filipina Workers.* Ithaca: Cornell University Press.

Cook, James. 1996. "Penetration and neocolonialism: The Shen Chong rape case and the anti-American student movement of 1946–47." *Republican China* 22 (1): 65–97.

Croll, Elisabeth J. 1986. "Domestic service in China." *Economic and Political Weekly* 21 (6) (February 8): 256–60.

———. 1994. *From Heaven to Earth: Images and Experiences of Development in China.* London: Routledge.

Croll, Elizabeth and Huang Ping. 1997. "Migration for and against agriculture in eight Chinese villages." *The China Quarterly* 149 (March): 128–46.

Dagongmei zhi Jia Jianbao (Migrant Women's Club Newsletter) 6, January 2000.

Dai Chengjiao. 1996. "Youyou wu nian jian (Five long years)." *Nongjianü Baishitong* (Rural Women Knowing All) (August):18–20.

Davin, Delia. 1997. "Migration, women and gender issues in contemporary China." In T. Sharping, ed., *Floating Population and Migration in China,* 297–314. Hamburg: Institut für Asienkunde.

———. 1998. "Gender and migration in China." In F. Christiansen and J. Zhang, eds., *Village Inc.: Chinese Rural Society in the 1990s,* 230–40. Surrey: Curzon Press.

———. 1999. *Internal Migration in Contemporary China.* London: Macmillan; New York: St. Martin's Press.

Davin, Delia and Mahmood Messkoub. 1994. *Migration in China: Results from the 1990 Census.* Leeds: East Asia Papers 24.

de Brauw, Alan and Scott Rozelle. 2002. "Migration and investment in rural China." Paper presented at the 2002 Association of Asian Studies Meeting, Washington, D.C., April.

Dorgan, Michael. 2000. "Thousands each year are sold into forced marriages, slavery." *San Jose Mercury-News,* 19 April, 19.

Du Ying. 2000. "Rural labor migration in contemporary China: An analysis of its features and the macro context." In L. A. West and Y. Zhao, eds., *Rural Labor Flows in China,* 67–100. Berkeley: Institute of East Asian Studies, University of California Press.

Duara, Prasenjit. 2001. "The regime of authenticity: Timelessness, gender, and national history in modern China." In Kai-wing Chow and Kevin Michael Doak, eds., *Constructing Nationhood in Modern East Asia,* 359–85. Ann Arbor: University of Michigan Press.

Dutton, Michael. 1998. *Streetlife China.* Cambridge: Cambridge University Press.

Eckholm, Erik. 1999. "For China's rural migrants, an education wall." *New York Times International,* 12 December.

Ellen, Roy. 1988. "Fetishism." *Man* 23 (2): 213–35.

Elson, Diane and Ruth Pearson. 1984. "The subordination of women and the internationalisation of factory production." In Kate Young, Carol Walkowitz, and Roslyn McCullogh, eds., *Of Marriage and the Market: Wo-*

men's Subordination Internationally and Its Lessons, 18–40. London: Routledge and Kegan Paul.

Entwisle, Barbara and Feinan Chen. 2002. "Work patterns following a birth in urban and rural China: A longitudinal study." *European Journal of Population* 18 (2) (June): 99–119.

Evans, Harriet. 2000. "Marketing femininity: Images of the modern Chinese woman." In Timothy B. Weston and Lionel M. Jensen, eds., *China Beyond the Headlines*, 217–44. Boulder, CO: Rowman and Littlefield.

Fan, C. Cindy. 1996. "Economic opportunities and internal migration: A case study of Guangdong province, China." *Professional Geographer* 48 (1): 28–45.

———. 1999. "Migration in a socialist transitional economy: Heterogeneity, socioeconomic and spatial characteristics of migrants in China and Guangdong province." *International Migration Review* 33 (4): 954–87.

———. 2000. "Migration and gender in China." In Chung-Ming Lau and Jianfa Shen, eds., *China Review 2000*, 423–54. Hong Kong: The Chinese University Press.

———. 2001. "Migration and labor market returns in urban China: Results from a recent survey in Guangzhou." *Environment and Planning* A 33 (3): 479–508.

———. 2002. "The elite, the natives, and the outsiders: Migration and labor market segmentation in urban China." *Annals of the Association of American Geographers* 92 (1): 103–24.

———. 2003a. "The transitional state, rural-urban migration and gender division of labor in China." *International Journal of Urban and Regional Research* 27 (1): 24–47.

———. 2003b. "The state, the migrant labor regime, and maiden workers in China." Manuscript.

Fan, C. Cindy, and Ling Li. 2002. "Marriage and migration in transitional China: A field study of Gaozhou, Western Guangdong." *Environment and Planning* A 34 (4): 619–38.

Fan, C. Cindy and Youqin Huang. 1998. "Waves of rural brides: Female marriage migration in China." *Annals of the Association of American Geographers* 88 (2): 227–51.

Farrer, James. 1999. "Uncivil society: Dancing in Shanghai in the 1990s." In Deborah Davis, ed., *The Consumer Revolution in Contemporary China*, 226–49 Berkeley: University of California Press.

Feng Xiaoshuang. 1997. "The costs and benefits of rural-urban migration: A report on an inquiry conducted among rural women employed in the service, retail, and other trades in Beijing." *Social Sciences in China* 18 (4) (winter): 52–65.

Feuerwerker, Yi-tsi Mei. 1998. *Ideology, Power, Text. Self-Representation and the Peasant "Other" in Modern Chinese Literature*. Stanford: Stanford University Press.

Findley, Sally and Williams, L. 1991. "Women who go and women who stay: Reflections of family migration processes in a changing world." Population and Labor Policies Programme Working Paper, 176. Geneva: International Labor Organisation.

Finnane, Antonia. 1996. "What should Chinese women wear?" *Modern China* 22 (2) (April): 99–131.

Fitzgerald, John. 1996. *Awakening China: Politics, Culture and Class in the Nationalist Revolution.* Stanford: Stanford University Press.

Food and Agriculture Organization. 1995. "Module IV: Gender, Migration, Farming Systems and Land Tenure." Rome: Population Programme Service, November. http://www.undp.org/popin/faomod/mod4.html.

Foucault, Michel. 1978. *History of Sexuality.* Vol. I. New York: Random House.

Gan Ri. 1958. "Bi qin bi jian bubi chi chuan (Compare who is more frugal and do not compare the quality of eating or dress)." *Dalian Ribao* (Dalian Daily), 7 February, 1.

Gao Jieqiong. 2000. "Zhongshi fahui gonghui nüzhigong zuzhi zuoyong (Stress the role of the trade union's women's organization)." *Anhui Fuyun* (Anhui Women's Movement) 7–8: 15–16.

Gao Zhihua. 1999. "Wo neng gaibian shenmo (What can I change)?" *Nongjianü Baishitong* (Rural Women Knowing All) (December):22–23.

Gaonkar, Dilip Parameshwar. 1999. "On alternative modernities." *Public Culture* 11 (1): 1–18.

Gisbert, Maria Elena, Michael Painter, and Mery Quiton. 1994. "Gender issues associated with labour migration and dependence on off-farm income in rural Bolivia." *Human Organisation* 53:110–22.

Gladney, Dru. 1994. "Representing nationality in China: Prefiguring majority/minority identities." *Journal of Asian Studies* 53 (1): 92–123.

Goldstein, Sidney and Alice Goldstein. 1991. "Permanent and temporary migration differentials in China." Honolulu: East-West Population Institute. Papers of the East-West Population Institute, 117.

Goldstein, Sidney, Zai Liang, and Alice Goldstein. 2000. "Migration, gender, and labor force in Hubei Province, 1985–1990." In Barbara Entwisle and Gail E. Henderson, eds., *Re-Drawing Boundaries: Work, Households, and Gender in China*, 214–30. Berkeley: University of California Press.

Gong Weibin. 1998. *Laodongli Waichu Jiuye yu Nongcun Shehui Bianqian* (Labor Migration and Village Social Change). Beijing: Cultural Relics Press, 1998.

Gransow, Bettina. 2000. "Global forces and working girls in the Pearl River Delta." Paper presented at the workshop, The Internationalization of China, Harvard University Asia Center, 24–27 August.

Greenhalgh, Susan. 1985. "Sexual stratification: The other side of growth with equity in East Asia." *Population and Development Review* 11 (2): 265–414.

———. 1986. "Shifts in China's population policy, 1984–1986: Views from the central, provincial and local levels." *Population and Development Review* 12 (3): 491–515.

Gu Qiuping. 2000. "Guoji mingcheng li women hai you duo yuan (How remote is the internationally famous city from us)?" *Dalian Ribao* (Dalian Daily), 25 May, C1.

Gu Yaode. 1991. "Dui bianyuan diqu nüxing renkou yongru Zhejiang qianjian (A rudimentary perspective on the women marriage migrants from remote areas)." *Renkou yu Jingji* (Population and Economics) 64 (1): 33–36.

"*Guanyu Shanghaishi juzhu zheng* (Regarding Shanghai's residence permit),"
   downloaded 17 June 2002. http://www.21cnhr.com/egov/jzzfaq.asp.

Hall, Stuart. 1996. "Who Needs Identity?" In Stuart Hall and Paul du Gay, eds.,
   Questions of Cultural Identity, 1–17. London: Sage.

———. 1997. "The spectacle of the other." In Stuart Hall, ed., *Representation:
   Cultural Representations and Signifying Practices*, 223–90. London: Sage.

Hartley, John. 1992. *The Politics of Pictures*. London: Routledge.

———. 1999. *Uses of Television*. London: Routledge.

He Shuqing, and Shi Jian. 2000. "Zhongguo chengshi shi da baibi (The ten de-
   fects of Chinese cities." *Xin Zhou Kan* (New Weekly) 6 (March 15): 12–16.

Hickling, F. W. 1991. "Double jeopardy: Psychopathology of black mentally ill
   returned migrants to Jamaica." *International Journal of Social Psychiatry* 37
   (2) (summer): 80–89.

Hirsch, Eric. 2001. "When was modernity in Melanesia?" *Social Anthropology* 9
   (2): 131–46.

Hondagneu-Sotelo, Pierrette. 1994. *Gendered Transitions: Mexican Experiences of
   Immigration*. Berkeley: University of California Press.

Honig, Emily. 1986. *Sisters and Strangers: Women in the Shanghai Cotton Mills,
   1919–1949*. Stanford: Stanford University Press.

———. 1992. *Creating Chinese Ethnicity: Subei People in Shanghai, 1850–1980*.
   New Haven: Yale University Press, 1992.

Horizon Research Co., State Statistical Bureau, China Entrepreneurial Research
   Group, eds. 1997. *Guancha Zhongguo* (Investigating China). Beijing: Commercial Press.

"Household registration system plays vital role, says minister." *South China
   Morning Post*, 26 February 2002.

Hoy, Caroline. 1999. "Issues in the fertility of temporary migrants in Beijing." In
   Frank N. Pieke and Hein Mallee, eds., *Internal and International Migration: Chinese Perspectives*, 134–55. Surrey: Curzon Press.

Hu, Hsien Chin. 1944. "The Chinese concept of face." *American Anthropologist*
   46:45–64.

Hu Zhaoliang et al. 2001. *Cultural Geography of China*. Beijing: Peking University
   Press.

Huang Xiyi. 1999. "Divided gender, divided women: State policy and the labour
   market." In Jackie West, Zhao Minghua, Chang Xiangqun, and Cheng
   Yuan, eds., *Women of China: Economic and Social Transformation*, 90–107.
   London: Macmillan.

Huang, Youqin. 2001. "Gender, *hukou*, and the occupational attainment of female
   migrants in China (1985–1990)." *Environment and Planning* A 33 (2):
   257–79.

Huangshan Lai de Guniang (The Girl from Yellow Mountain). Changchun:
   Changchun Film Studio, 1984.

Hughes, Helen. 1968. *News and the Human Interest Story*. New York: Greenwood
   Press.

Hugo, Graeme. 1993. "Migrant women in developing countries." In *Internal
   Migration of Women in Developing Countries*, 46–76. New York: United
   Nations.

Human Rights in China. 2002. "Institutionalized exclusion: The tenuous legal status of internal migrants in China's major cities." 6 November. http://www.hric.org.

Jacka, Tamara. 1997. *Women's Work in Rural China: Change and Continuity in an Era of Reform.* New York: Cambridge University Press.

———. 1998. "Working sisters answer back: The representation and self-representation of women in China's floating population." *China Information* 13 (1): 43–75.

———. 2000a. "The centrality of outsiders: *Wailaimei* and the politics of modernity, capitalism and identity in contemporary China." Paper presented at the workshop, Women, Modernity and Opportunity in Twentieth-Century China, Sydney, April.

———. 2000b. "Other Chinas/China's others: A report on the First National Forum on the Protection of the Rights of Rural Migrant Women Workers, Beijing, June 1999." *New Formations* 40 (spring): 128–37.

Jian Ping. 2001. "Caifang shouji: Jingyan Dalian (Interview memoirs: Experiencing Dalian)." *Xin Zhou Kan* (New Weekly) 10:44.

Jiang Hong. 1996. "Chenzhong de tanxi (A deep sigh)." *Shehui* (Society) 3:26–27.

Judd, Ellen R. 1989. "Niangjia: Chinese women and their natal families." *Journal of Asian Studies* 48 (3): 525–44.

———. 1994. *Gender and Power in Rural North China.* Stanford: Stanford University Press.

———. 2002. *The Chinese Women's Movement Between the State and Market.* Stanford: Stanford University Press.

Kabeer, Naila. 1994. *Reversed Realities: Gender Hierarchies in Development Thought.* London: Verso.

———. 2000. "Resources, agency, achievements: Reflections on the measurement of women's empowerment." In Shahra Razavi, ed., *Gendered Poverty and Well-Being,* 27–56. Oxford: Blackwells.

Kearny, Robert N. and Barbara Diane Miller. 1987. *Internal Migration in Sri Lanka and Its Social Consequences.* London: Westview.

Khan, Azizur Rahman and Carl Riskin. 1998. "Income and inequality in China: Composition, distribution and growth of household income, 1988 to 1995." *China Quarterly* 154 (June): 221–53.

Kipnis, Andrew. 1995. "Within and against peasantness: Backwardness and filiality in rural China." *Society for the Comparative Study of Society and History* 37:110–35.

———. 1997. *Producing Guanxi: Sentiment, Self, and Subculture in a North China Village.* Durham, NC: Duke University Press.

Ku, Fong. 1999. "Migrant schools: Basic education not yet universal." *Chinabrief* 11 (3): 1–15.

Kung, Lydia. 1981. "Perceptions of work among factory women." In E. Ahern and Hill Gates, eds., *Anthropology of Taiwanese Society,* 184–211. Stanford: Stanford University Press.

———. 1983. *Factory Women in Taiwan.* Ann Arbor: University of Michigan Press.

———. 1994. *Factory Women in Taiwan.* New York: Columbia University Press.

Kutsche, Paul. 1994. *Voices of Migrants: Rural-Urban Migration in Costa Rica.* Florida: University Press of Florida.

Lan Daju. 1997. "An investigative report on the migrant population of Caitang village, Xiamen Special Economic Zone." In Gregory Eliyu Guldin, ed., *Farewell to Peasant China: Rural Urbanization and Social Change in the Late Twentieth Century*, 248–64. Armonk, N.Y.: M. E. Sharpe.

Lavely, William. 1991. "Marriage and mobility under rural collectivization." In R. Watson and P. Buckley Ebrey, eds., *Marriage and Inequality in Chinese Society*, 286–312. Berkeley: University of California Press.

———. 2001. "First Impressions of the 2000 Census of China." 4 November. http://www.csde.washington.edu/pubs/wps/01–13.pdf, 1–22.

Lee, Ching Kwan. 1995. "Engendering the worlds of labor: Women workers, labor markets, and production politics in the South China economic miracle." *American Sociological Review* 60:378–97.

———. 1998. *Gender and the South China Miracle: Two Worlds of Factory Women.* Berkeley: University of California Press.

Lee, Minja. 2001. "Regional discrimination against female migrants in Chinese cities." Paper presented at the International Forum on Rural Labor Mobility in China, Beijing, 3–5 July.

Lee, Sing and Arthur Kleinman. 2000. "Suicide as resistance in Chinese society." In Elizabeth Perry and Mark Selden, eds., *Chinese Society: Change, Conflict and Resistance*, 221–40. London and New York: Routledge.

Li Jianyong and Li Tao, eds. 1999. *Chengshi Li Ni You Duo Yuan—Jingcheng Dagong Baishitong* (How Remote Is the City—A Handbook for Migrant Workers Entering the City). Shanghai: Shanghai Kexue Puji Chubanshe.

Li Mengbai and Hu Xin. 1991. *Liudong Renkou dui Dachengshi Fazhan de Yingxiang ji Duice* (The Influence of the Floating Population on the Development of Large Cities and Countermeasures). Beijing: Jingji Ribao Chubanshe.

Li Min. 1999. "Shi shang zazhi zhi da bing (The ten ills of fashion magazines)." *Xin Zhou Kan* (New Weekly) 7: 43–45.

Li Shuang. 1998. *Xiaofei de Xianjing: Dangqian Zhongguo Xiaofei Wenti* (Consumption Trap: Contemporary Chinese Consumption Problems). Zhuhai: Zhuhai Publishing House.

Li Shuzhuo. 1994. "Bashi niandai Zhongguo nüxing renkou qianyi de xuanzexing tantao (A discussion of characteristics of female migration in China in the 1980s)." *Funü Yanjiu Luncong* (A Collection of Women's Research) 10 (2): 26–28.

Li, Xiaoping. 2000. "'Focus (*Jiaodian Fangtan*)' and the changes in the Chinese television industry." *Journal of Contemporary China* 11 (30): 17–34.

Li Yixin and Zhang Huaping. 1994. "Nongcun zaohun zaoyu wenti ji dei jiejue (Urgent need to resolve problem of early marriage and childbirth in rural areas)." *Renkou Yanjiu* (Population Research) 18 (4): 60–61.

Liechty, Mark. 1995. "Media, markets and modernization." In Vered Amit-Talai and Helena Wulff, eds., *Youth Cultures: A Cross-Cultural Perspective*, 166–201. London, New York: Routledge.

Lin Yanping. 1999. "Qi cheng bei guaimai funü bu yuan hui jia (Seventy percent of trafficked women refuse to return home)." *Nanfang Ribao* (Southern Daily), 4 October.

Liu Dalin. 1995. *Zhongguo Dangdai Xing Wenhua: Zhongguo Wan Li "Xing Wenming" Diaocha Baogao* (Sex Culture in China: A Report on the 10,000 Survey Cases). Shanghai: Sanlian Shudian Press.

Liu Li. 1998. "Liaoxi yuan an (A case of injustice in western Liaoning)." *Zhi Yin* (Bosom Friend) 10:33–35.

Liu Wei and Li Wenhua. 2000. "Zou jin wailaimei (Looking closely at rural-to-urban female migrants)." *Shehui* (Society) 180 (2): 32–40.

Liu Wenzhang and Yang Sheng. 2000. "Shuishang leyuan le zai hechu (Where is the fun bit in the fun park)?" *Xin An Evening News*, 17 July, 1.

Liu, Xin. 2000. *In One's Own Shadow: An Ethnographic Account of the Condition of Post-Reform Rural China*. Berkeley: University of California Press.

Liu Yida. 1998. "Jingcheng baomu (Beijing maids)." In *Cang Sheng Fan Jing* (Common Circumstances), 106–28. "Eyes of Beijing" Series. Beijing: China Society Press.

Lu Shaoqing. 1999. "China's rural women in internal migration." Working paper.

Lu Yuegang and Luo Jianglie, eds. 2000. *Bengbao Jingri Chuji* (The Target of Today's Paper). Guangzhou: Nanfang Daily Press.

Luo Xi. 2001. "Shunü de moyan (The appearance of a fair lady)." *Nüzi Shijie* (Women's World) 3:42–43.

Ma Jianqing. 1995. "Chengxiang wenhua de pengzhuang (The clash of urban and rural cultures)." *Qingnian Yanjiu* (Youth Research) 8:14–16.

Ma, Lawrence J.C. and Biao Xiang. 1998. "Native place, migration and the emergence of peasant enclaves in Beijing." *China Quarterly* 155:546–81.

Ma Zhongdong. 2001. "Urban labour-force experience as a determinant of rural occupational change: Evidence from recent urban-rural migration in China." *Environment and Planning* A 33:237–55.

MacLeod, Lijia. 1998. "The Dying Fields." *Far Eastern Economic Review*, 23 April:62–63.

Mai Zi. 1996. "Nar bushuyu women (That place does not belong to us)." *Nongjianü Baishitong* (Rural Women Knowing All) (June):32.

Mallee, Hein. 1996. "In defense of migration: Recent Chinese studies on rural population mobility." *China Information* 10 (3/4): 108–40.

———. 2000. "Agricultural labor and rural population mobility: Some observations." In Loraine A. West and Yaohui Zhao, *Rural Labor Flows in China*, 34–59. Berkeley: Institute of East Asian Studies, University of California Press.

Mann, Susan. 1997. *Precious Records: Women in China's Long Eighteenth Century*. Stanford: Stanford University Press.

Massey, Douglas S. and Felipe G. España. 1987. "The social process of international migration." *Science* 237 (4816) (August): 733–38.

McClintock, Anne. 1995. *Imperial Leather*. New York: Routledge.

McDowell, Linda. 1999. *Gender, Identity and Place*. Minneapolis: University of Minnesota Press.

"Meng gai xing le (Awake from a dream)!" *Nongjianü Baishitong* (Rural Women Knowing All) (July):34.

Meng Xianfan. 1995. *Gaige Dachao Zhong de Zhongguo Nüxing* (Chinese Women in the Tide of Reform). Beijing: China Social Sciences Press.

Meng Zhaopu. 1997. "Nongcun gedai jiaoyu yousi (Troubled thoughts on reeducation by the older generation in the countryside)." *Nongmin Wenzhai* (Farmers' Digest) 4:43.

Miao Qingqing. 1996. "Shibasui wo bujiaren (I will not marry at eighteen)." *Nongjianü Baishitong* (Rural Women Knowing All) (September):15.

Miller, Daniel. 1994. *Modernity: An Ethnographic Approach*. Oxford: Berg.

Mills, Mary Beth. 1999. *Thai Women in the Global Labor Force: Consuming Desires, Contested Selves*. New Brunswick: Rutgers University Press.

Moore, Henrietta. 1994. *A Passion for Difference*. Bloomington: Indiana University Press.

"Muji shengcheng 'saohuang' (Eyewitness to Hefei's crackdown on prostitution)." 2000. *Xin An Evening News*, 30 July:15.

Mulvey, Laura. 1975. "Visual pleasure and narrative cinema." *Screen* 16 (3): 6–18.

Murphy, Rachel. 2002. *How Migrant Labor Is Changing Rural China*. New York: Cambridge University Press.

Nakano Glenn, Evelyn. 1986. *Issei, Nissei, Warbride: Three Generations of Japanese American Women in Domestic Service*. Philadelphia: Temple University Press.

Neale, Sean. 1997. "Masculinity as spectacle." In Stuart Hall, ed., *Representation: Cultural Representations and Signifying Practices*, 331–33. London: Sage.

Nelson, Nici. 1992. "The women who have left and those who have stayed behind: Rural-urban migration in central and western Kenya." In Sylvia Chant and Sarah Radcliffe, eds., *Gender and Migration in Developing Countries*, 109–38. New York: Belhaven Press.

Nongyebu nongcun jingji yanjiu zhongxin (NNJYZ) (Research Center for the Rural Economy, Ministry of Agriculture). 1995. *Zhongguo Nongcun Laodongli Liudong: Ge'an Fangtan Ziliao* (Labor Migration in China: Accounts of Individual Interviews). Beijing: Ministry of Agriculture.

Ong, Aihwa. 1988. "Colonialism and modernity: Feminist re-presentations of women in non-western societies." *Inscriptions* 3/4:79–93.

———. 1999. *Flexible Citizenship: The Cultural Logics of Transnationality*. Durham, NC: Duke University Press.

Ortner, Sherry B. 1998. "Identities: The hidden life of class." *Journal of Anthropological Research* 54 (1): 1–17.

Ozyegin, Gul. 2001. *Untidy Gender in Turkey's Domestic Service*. Philadelphia: Temple University Press.

Parker, Andrew, Mary Russo, et al. 1992. "Introduction." In Andrew Parker et al., *Nationalisms and Sexualities*, 1–18. New York: Routledge,.

Parnwell, Michael. 1993. *Population Movements and the Third World*. London: Routledge.

The Peasant-Worker Migration Project Group. 1996. "The migration of peasant-workers into the Pearl River Delta Region." *Social Sciences in China* 17 (3): 54–62.

Pedraza, Sylvia. 1991. "Women and migration: The social consequences of gender." *Annual Review of Sociology* 17:303–25.

Phongpaichet, Pasuk. 1993. "The labour market aspects of female migration to Bangkok." In *Internal Migration of Women in Developing Countries*, 178–94. New York: United Nations.

Pieke, Frank. 1999. "Chinese migration compared." In Frank N. Pieke and Hein Mallee, eds., *Internal and International Migration: Chinese Perspectives*, 1–26. London: Curzon Press.

Pred, Allan, and Michael John Watts. 1992. *Reworking Modernity: Capitalisms and Symbolic Discontent*. New Brunswick: Rutgers University Press.

Pruitt, Ida. 1967 (1945). *A Daughter of Han: The Autobiography of a Chinese Working Woman*. Stanford: Stanford University Press.

Pryor, Robin. 1975. *The Motivation of Migration*. Canberra: Australian National University.

Pun Ngai. 1999. "Becoming *dagongmei* (working girls): The politics of identity and difference in reform China." *The China Journal* 42:1–18.

Research Center for Rural Economics. *Synthesis for the Sixth Session of the Forum on China's Rural Labor Mobility Studies*. December 1999.

Riley, Nancy E. and Robert W. Gardner. 1993. "Migration decisions: The role of gender." In *Internal Migration of Women in Developing Countries: Proceedings of the UN Expert Meeting on the Feminization of Internal Migration* (Aguascalientes, Mexico, 22–25 October 1991), 195–206. New York: Department for Economic and Social Information and Policy Analysis, United Nations.

Roberts, Kenneth. 1997. "China's 'tidal wave' of migrant labor: What can we learn from Mexican undocumented migration to the United States?" *International Migration Review* 31 (2): 249–93.

———. 2000. "Rural labor migration, women's status, and fertility in China." Paper presented at the conference on rural labor mobility in China, Beijing, June:1–20.

———. 2002. "Female labor migrants to Shanghai: Temporary 'floaters' or potential settlers?" *International Migration Review* 36 (2): 492–519.

Roberts, Kenneth D., Rachel Connelly, Zhenzhen Zheng, and Zhenming Xie. 2002. "Patterns of temporary migration of rural women in China." Paper presented at 2002 Annual Meeting of Population Association of America, Atlanta, May.

Robison, Richard and David S.G. Goodman. 1996. "The new rich in Asia: Economic development, social status and political consciousness." In Richard Robison and David S.G. Goodman, eds., *The New Rich in Asia: Mobile Phones, McDonald's and Middle-Class Revolution*, 1–16. London: Routledge.

Rodenburg, Janet. 1993. "Emancipation or subordination? Consequences of female migration for migrants and their families." In *Internal Migration of Women in Developing Countries: Proceedings of the UN Expert Meeting on the Feminization of Internal Migration* (Aguascalientes, Mexico, 22–25 October 1991), 273–89. New York: Department for Economic and Social Information and Policy Analysis, United Nations.

Rofel, Lisa. 1999. *Other Modernities: Gendered Yearnings in China After Socialism*. Berkeley: University of California Press.

Rollins, Judith. 1985. *Between Women: Domestics and Their Employers.* Philadelphia: Temple University Press.

Romero, Mary. 1992. *Maid in the USA.* New York: Routledge.

Rosenthal, Elisabeth. 1999. "In China, school fees keep many children away." *The New York Times*, 2 November.

———. 2001a. "College entrance in China: 'No' to the handicapped." *The New York Times*, 15 May, A3.

———. 2001b. "Harsh Chinese reality feeds a black market in women." *The New York Times*, 25 June.

Rowe, David. 1999. *Sport, Culture and the Media.* Buckingham, England: Open University Press.

Rowland, D. T. 1994. "Family characteristics of the migrants." In L. Day and Ma Xia, eds., *Migration and Urbanization in China*, 129–53. Armonk, N.Y., London: M. E. Sharpe.

Rozelle, Scott, Li Guo, Minggao Shen, Amelia Hughart, and John Giles. 1999. "Leaving China's farms: Survey results of new paths and remaining hurdles to rural migration." *China Quarterly* 58 (June): 367–93.

Rural Women Knowing All (magazine attached to *China Women's News*), ed. 1999. *Shoujie Quanguo Dagongmei Quanyi Wenti Yantaohui* (The Collected Works of the First National Forum on Issues About Women Migrant Workers' Rights and Interests, 16–18 June, Beijing).

Rural Women Knowing All Project Committee, ed. 2000. *Zhongguo Nongcun Funü Qinggan Zishu* (Testimonies About Romance by Rural Chinese Women). Guiyang: Guizhou People's Press.

Salaff, Janet W. 1981. *Working Daughters of Hong Kong: Filial Piety or Power in the Family?* Cambridge: Cambridge University Press.

———. 1995. *Working Daughters of Hong Kong: Filial Piety or Power in the Family?* New York: Columbia University Press.

Scharping, Thomas. 1997. "Studying migration in contemporary China: Models and methods, issues and evidence." In Thomas Scharping, ed., *Floating Population and Migration in China: The Impact of Economic Reforms*, 9–55. Hamburg: Institut fur Asienkunde.

———. 1999. "Selectivity, migration reasons and backward linkages of rural-urban migrants: A sample survey of migrants to Foshan and Shenzhen in comparative perspective." In Frank N. Pieke and Hein Mallee, eds., *Internal and International Migration: Chinese Perspectives*, 73–102. Surrey: Curzon Press.

Scharping, Thomas and Sun Huaiyang, eds. 1997. *Migration in China's Guangdong Province: Major Results of a 1993 Sample Survey on Migrants and Floating Population in Shenzhen and Foshan.* Hamburg: Institut fur Asienkunde.

Schein, Louisa. 1994. "The consumption of color and the politics of white skin in post–Mao China." *Social Text* 41 (winter): 141–64.

———. 1999. "The consumption of color: The politics of white skin in post–Mao China." In Micaela Di Leonardo and Roger N. Lancaster, eds., *The Gender/Sexuality Reader: Culture, History, Political Economy*, 471–84. New York: Routledge.

———. 2000. *Minority Rules: The Miao and the Feminine in China's Cultural Policies.* Durham, NC: Duke University Press.

Scott, Joan. 1992. "Experience." In Judith Butler and Joan Scott, eds., *Feminists Theorize the Political*, 22–40. New York and London: Routledge.

Sen, Amartya. 1983. "Poor, relatively speaking." *Oxford Economic Papers* 35:153–69.

———. 1991."Gender and co-operative conflicts." In Irene Tinker, ed., *Persistent Inequalities: Women and World Development*, 123–49. Oxford: Oxford University Press.

———. 1992. *Inequality Re-Examined*. Oxford: Clarendon Press.

Shen Ping. 1999. "Guxi gangke baoyang miaoling nü: xiangxia 'jin wu' nan cang 'jin si que' (Elderly Hong Kong gentleman keeps a young mistress: A palace cannot hide the 'caged canary')." *Nanfang Ribao* (Southern Weekly), August 6.

Short, Susan E. and Zhai Fengying. 1998. "Looking locally at China's one child policy." *Studies in Family Planning* 29 (4): 373–87.

Short, Susan E., Feinian Chen, Barbara Entwisle, and Zhai Fengying. 2002. "Maternal work and time spent in child care in China: A multimethod approach." *Population and Development Review* 28 (1): 31–57.

Skinner, G. William. 1997. "Introduction." In Sow Theng Leong, *Migration and Ethnicity in Chinese History: Hakkas, Pengmin and Their Neighbours*, 1–18. Ed. Tim Wright. Stanford: Stanford University Press.

Smart, Josephine. 1999. "The global economy and south China development in post–1978 China: Relevance and limitations of the flexible accumulation approach." *Urban Anthropology* 28 (3–4): 407–45.

Smith, Arthur H. 1894. *Chinese Characteristics*. New York, Chicago, Toronto: Fleming H. Revell Company.

Solinger, Dorothy. 1995. "The floating population in the cities: Chances for assimilation?" In D. Davis et al., eds., *Urban Spaces in Contemporary China*, 113–39. Washington, DC: Woodrow Wilson Center Press.

———. 1999. *Contesting Citizenship in Urban China: Peasant Migrants, the State, and the Logic of the Market*. Berkeley: University of California Press.

Song, Lina. 1999. "The role of women in labour migration: A case study in northern China." In Jackie West, Zhao Minghua, Chang Xiangqun, and Cheng Yuan, eds., *Women of China: Economic and Social Transformation*, 69–89. London: Macmillan.

Song Meiya. 1996. "Lu zai hefang?—miandui hunjia shao kunhuo (Where is the right path?—facing up to the perplexities of marriage)." *Nongjianü Baishitong* (Rural Women Knowing All) (April):9–11.

Song Zhongzheng. 2000. *Dushi Xin Dangan* (New Urban Case Files). Guangzhou: Luyou Publishing House.

Stallybrass, Peter and Allon White. 1986. *The Politics and Poetics of Transgression*. London: Methuen.

Stockman, Norman. 2000. *Understanding Chinese Society*. Cambridge: Polity Press.

Sun Baili. 2000. "Dagongzhe de fuqi fang (Migrant couples' bedroom)." *Southern Weekend*, 26 October, 16.

Sun Hongmei. 1996. "Ge'an you diandian denghuo (There is some hope in the city)." *Nongjianü Baishitong* (Rural Women Knowing All) (March):28–29.

Sun, Wanning. 2000. "Discourse of poverty: Weakness, potential and provincial identity in Anhui." In John Fitzgerald, ed., *Rethinking China's Provinces*, 153–78. London: Routledge.

———. 2002. *Leaving China: Media, Migration, and Transnational Imagination.* Boulder, CO: Rowman and Littlefield.

The Survey of Occupational Mobility and Migration: A Research Co-operation Between Fafo and the National Research Center for Science and Technology for Development, Beijing. Presentation to the Network for Asia-Pacific Studies, Sunvolden, 5–7 June, 2000. http://www.fafo.no/ais/eastasia/labourmobility/labourmobilityprelim.pdf.

Tam, Siumi Maria. 2000. "Modernization from a grassroots perspective: Women workers in Shekou industrial zone." In S. Li and W. Tang, eds., *China's Regions, Polity, and Economy: A Study of Spatial Transformation in the Post-Reform Era*, 371–90. Hong Kong: The Chinese University Press.

Tan Lin and Christina Gilmartin. 1998. "Lun woguo hunyin qianyi de taishi he tedian (The situation and characteristics of marriage migration in China)." *Nanfang Renkou* (Southern Population) 50 (2): 41–45.

———. 2001. "Fleeing poverty: Rural women, expanding marriage markets, and strategies for social mobility in contemporary China." In Esther Nganling Chow, ed., *Transforming Gender and Development in East Asia*, 203–16. New York: Routledge.

Tan Shen. 1996. "Zhongguo nongcun laodongli liudong de xingbie chayi (Gender differences in the migration of the rural labor force)." Paper presented at the International Conference on Rural Labor Migration, Beijing, China, 1996.

———. 1998a. "Gender differences in the migration of rural labor." *Social Sciences in China* (spring):70–76.

———. 1998b. "Zhujiang sanjiaozhou wailai dagongmei de xianzhuang yu fazhan (The current conditions and future of working sisters in the Pearl River Delta)." In Jin Yihong and Liu Bohong, eds., *Sheji zhi Jiao de Zhongguo Funü yu Fazhan* (Chinese Women and Development into the Twenty-first Century), 117–31. Nanjing: Nanjing Daxue Chubanshe.

———. 2000. "The relationship between foreign enterprises, local governments, and women migrant workers in the Pearl River Delta." In Loraine A. West and Yaohui Zhao, eds., *Rural Labor Flows in China*, 292–309. Berkeley: Institute of East Asian Studies, University of California Press.

Tan Shen, Li Yinhe, and Feng Xiaoshuang. 1996. "Hechu qishen (Where to stay)?" *Zhongguo Funü Bao* (China Women's News), 26 June, 26.

Tang Can. 1998. "Sexual harassment: The dual status of and discrimination against female migrant workers in urban areas." *Social Sciences in China* 19 (3) (autumn): 64–71.

Tang Can and Feng Xiaoshuang. 1996. "Lao baomu yu xiao baomu: Liang bei ren de shidai xinhen: Anhui Wuweixian diaocha sanji (Old maids and young maids: The travails of two generations: An account of an investigation in Wuwei County, Anhui)." *Dong Fang* (Orient) (June):49–54.

Teng Wei. 2000. "Yingxiong yinqu chu zhongcan jieji de ziwo shuxie (Where the hero disappears: The self-writing of the middle-class)." In Dai Jinhua, ed.,

Shuxie Wenhua Yingxiong (Writing Cultural Heroes), 292–324. Nanjing: Jiangsu People's Press.

Tian Hua. 1991. "Xinan nongcun funü: Dongqian hunpei taishi tanxi (Preliminary analysis of the trends of the eastward female marriage migration from southwestern villages)." *Nanfang Renkou* (Southern Population) 21 (1): 39–42.

Tian Jiaoshou Jia de Ershiba ge Baomu (Professor Tian's Household and Their Twenty-eight Maids). Shanghai: Shanghai Film Studio, 1999.

Tong Xing. 1995. *Kaifang Dachao xia de Shenghuo Fangshi* (Lifestyles in the Tide of Opening). Beijing: China Youth Publishing House.

Tong Yuying. 2001. "Dui wailai dagongmei shenghuo zhuangtai de fenxi yu sikao (Analysis and reflection on the lifestyles of *dagongmei*)." *Xibei Renkou* (Northwest Population) 2 (84): 48–50.

Tsai, Kellee S. 2000. "Banquet banking: Gender and rotating savings and credit associations in South China." *China Quarterly* 115 (summer): 201–25.

Tsang, Mun. 1996. "Financial reform of basic education in China." *Economics of Education Review* 15 (4): 423–44.

Wang Feng. 2000. "Gendered migration and the migration of genders in contemporary China." In B. Entwisle and G. Henderson, eds., *Re-Drawing Boundaries: Work, Households, and Gender in China*, 231–42. Berkeley: University of California Press.

Wang Feng and Zuo Xuejin. 1997. "Socialist dualism and the migration process in China: The case of Shanghai." Paper presented at the workshop, Rural Labor Migration in 1990s China, University of California, Irvine, 26 April.

Wang Jianmin and Hu Qi. 1996. *Zhongguo Liudong Renkou* (China's Floating Population). Shanghai: Shanghai University of Finance and Economics Press.

Wang Jinling. 1992. "Zhejiang nongmin yidi lianyin xin tedian (New characteristics of interprovincial marriage migrants into Zhejiang rural areas)." *Shehuixue Yanjiu* (Sociological Research) 40 (4): 92–95.

———. 1994. "New characteristics of marriages between Zhejiang farmers and women from outside the province." *Social Sciences in China* 15 (2): 59–64.

Wang Jinling and Guo Hong. 1993. *Yue Chu Hunyin Quan* (Beyond the Bounds of the Marriage Circle). Lijiang: Lijiang Publishing House.

Wang Shaoguang. 1995. "The politics of private time: Changing leisure patterns in urban China." In D. Davis et al., eds., *Urban Spaces in Contemporary China*, 149–73. Washington, DC: Woodrow Wilson Center Press.

Wang Xia. 1999. "Qiantan shengchanli yu funü hunyin guan (A brief discussion of the issue of productivity and women's attitude toward marriage)." *Anhui Fuyun* (Anhui Women's Movement) 273:18.

Wang Xuetai. 1999. *Youmin Wenhua yu Zhongguo Shehui* (Drifters' Culture and Chinese Society). Beijing: Xueyuan Publishing House.

Wang Zheng. 2000. "Gender, employment, and women's resistance." In Elizabeth J. Perry and Mark Selden, eds., *Chinese Society: Change, Conflict, and Resistance*, 62–82. London: Routledge.

Wei Chunlong. 1996. "Luoye ying guidao hechu (Where should falling leaves return to)?" *Nongjianü Baishitong* (Rural Women Knowing All) (September):32.

Wen Yue and Ma Zhong. 1991. "Zoujin dushi de nongjia nü (Rural migrant women entering the city)." In Ji Fang and Luo Zhan, eds., *Jingtou Zai Yanshen* (The Extending Focus), 221–26. Chengdu: Sichuan Nationalities Publishing House.

West, Loraine A. 2000. "Introduction." In Loraine A. West and Zhao Yaohui, eds., *Rural Labor Flows in China*, 1–13. Berkeley: Institute of East Asian Studies, University of California Press.

Williams, Raymond. 1973. *The Country and the City*. London: Chatto and Windus.

Winckler, Edwin A. 2002. "Chinese reproductive policy at the turn of the century." *Population and Development Review* 28 (3): 379–418.

Wolf, Diane. 1992. *Factory Daughters: Gender, Household Dynamics, and Rural Industrialization in Java*. Berkeley: University of California Press.

"Women zheli ershisi xiaoshi yingye (Here, we are open 24 hours a day)." *Xin An Evening News*, 22 July 2002, 1.

Wong, Linda and Wai-po Huen. 1998. "Reforming the household registration system: A preliminary glimpse of the blue chop household registration system in Shanghai and Shenzhen." *International Migration Review* 32 (4): 974–94.

Woon, Yuen-fong. 2000. "Filial or rebellious daughters? *Dagongmei* in the Pearl River Delta Region, South China, in the 1990s." *Asian and Pacific Migration Journal* 9 (2): 137–69.

Xiang Biao. 1999. "'Zhejiang village' in Beijing: Creating a visible nonstate place through migration and marketized traditional networks." In Frank N. Pieke and Hein Mallee, eds., *Internal and International Migration: Chinese Perspectives*, 215–50. London: Curzon Press.

"Xiao chengshi liugei wode . . . (Small city life has given me . . .)." *Nongjianü Baishitong* (Rural Women Knowing All) (March 1996):30–31.

Xiao Lingxia. 1996. "Huijiaqu (I'm going home)." *Nongjianü Baishitong* (Rural Women Knowing All) (February):26–27.

Xie Zhengming. 2001. "Effect of migration on rural women's family planning and reproductive health." *China Population Today* 3–4:7–11.

Xin Meng. 2000. "Regional wage gap, information flow, and rural-urban migration." In Loraine A. West and Yaohui Zhao, eds., *Rural Labor Flows in China*, 251–77. Berkeley: Institute of East Asian Studies, University of California Press.

Xin Yang. 1999. "Yingzhe zhengwu de taiyang (Welcoming the sun at high noon)." *Nongjianü Baishitong* (Rural Women Knowing All) (May):30–31.

Xu Feng. 2000. *Women Migrant Workers in China's Economic Reform*. New York: St. Martin's Press.

Xu Jian. 1999. "Body, discourse, and the cultural politics of contemporary Chinese Qigong." *The Journal of Asian Studies* 58 (4): 961–91.

Xu Nan. 1996. "Liudong nüxing maiyin de chengyin yu zhili duice (Migrant women in the sex trade: Reasons and regulations)." In Gao Fumin, ed., *Funü yu Shehui Fazhan* (Women and Social Development), 264–68. Hefei: Anhui Renmin Chubanshe (Anhui People's Press).

Xu Yanxiu. 1996. "Women de weizhi zai nali (Where is our place)?" *Nongjianü Baishitong* (Rural Women Knowing All) (June):33.

Yan, Yunxiang. 1997. "McDonald's in Beijing: The localization of Americana." In James Watson, ed., *Golden Arches East: McDonald's in East Asia*, 39–76. Stanford: Stanford University Press.

Yang Laisheng, Hong Renlong, and Yu Shenguan. 1999. "Jiangsu nongcun wailainü de hunyu guanli yu jiaoyu (A study on the marriage and fertility management and education of rural-to-urban female migrants)." *Renkou Yanjiu* (Population Research) 118 (4): 77–80.

Yang, Martin C. 1946. *A Chinese Village: Taitou, Shantung Province*. New York: Columbia University Press.

Yang, Mayfair. 1994. *Gifts, Favors, and Banquets*. Ithaca: Cornell University Press.

Yang, Quanhe and Fei Guo. 1996. "Occupational attainments of rural to urban temporary economic migrants in China, 1985–1990." *International Migration Review* 30 (3): 771–87.

Yang Xiaozheng and Guan Weilian. 1999. "Fenghuang huanchao chuang xin ye (The phoenix returns to her nest and builds a new career)." *Anhui Fuyun* (Anhui Women's Movement) 267:24.

Yang, Xiushi. 2000. "Interconnections among gender, work, and migration: Evidence from Zhejiang province." In Barbara Entwisle and Gail E. Henderson, eds., *Re-Drawing Boundaries: Work, Households, and Gender in China*, 197–213. Berkeley: University of California Press.

Yang, Xiushi, and Fei Guo. 1999. "Gender differences in determinants of temporary labor migration in China: A multilevel analysis." *International Migration Review* 33 (4): 929–53.

Yang Yunyan. 1992. "Wo guo renkou hunyin qianyi de hongguan liuxiang chuxi (A macroscopic study of the trend of China's marriage migration)." *Nanfang Renkou* (Southern Population) 28 (4): 39–42.

You Danzhen and Zheng Zhenzhen. 2002. "Nongcun waichu funü de shengyu yiyuan fenxi (Fertility desire of returned migrant women in rural China)." *Shehuixue Yanjiu* (Sociological Research) 6:52–62.

You Zhenglin. 1992. "Nongcun funü yuanjia xianxiang yanjiu (Research on rural women marrying far away)." *Shehuixue Yanjiu* (Sociological Research) 41 (5): 105–14.

Yu, Sam Wai Kam, and Ruby Chui Man Chau. 1997. "The sexual division of care in mainland China and Hong Kong." *International Journal of Urban and Regional Research* 21 (4): 607–19.

Yuan, Victor and Wong Xin. 1999. "Migrant construction teams in Beijing." In Frank N. Pieke and Hein Mallee, eds., *Internal and International Migration: Chinese Perspectives*, 103–18. London: Curzon Press.

Zhang Haibing. 2001. *Singapore and Dalian*. Shenyang: Liaoning People's Press.

Zhang, Heather Xiaoquan. 1999a. "Female migration and urban labour markets in Tianjin." *Development and Change* 30:21–41.

———. 1999b. "Understanding changes in women's status in the context of the recent rural reform." In Jackie West, Zhao Minhu, Chang Xiangqun, and Cheng Yuan, eds., *Women of China: Economic and Social Transformation*, 45–66. London: Macmillan.

Zhang Hesheng. 1994. *Hunyin Daliudong: Wailiu Funü Hunyin Diaocha Jishi* (The Great Marriage Migration: A Survey of Female Marriage Migrants). Shenyang: Liaoning People's Press.

——. 1995. "Kuashengqu lianyin kuodahua chengyin yu yinxiang fenxi (The cause and influence of transprovincial marriage)." *Shehuixue Yanjiu* (Sociological Research) 59 (5): 91–96.

Zhang Li. 2000. "The interplay of gender, space, and work in China's floating population." In Barbara Entwisle and Gail E. Henderson, eds., *Re-Drawing Boundaries: Work, Households, and Gender in China*, 171–96. Berkeley: University of California Press.

——. 2001a. *Strangers in the City: Reconfigurations of Space, Power, and Social Networks Within China's Floating Population*. Stanford: Stanford University Press.

——. 2001b. "Contesting crime, order, and migrant spaces in Beijing." In Nancy N. Chen, Constance D. Clark, Suzanne Z. Gottschang, and Lyn Jeffery, eds., *China Urban: Ethnographies of Contemporary Culture*, 201–22. Durham, NC: Duke University Press.

Zhang Mei. 1996. "Women buyuan zaojia (We're not willing to marry early)." *Nongjianü Baishitong* (Rural Women Knowing All) (March):15.

Zhang Zhenhua. 1990. "Nongcun funü hunqian sheji de falü wenti (Legislative issues related to female marriage migrants in rural China)." *Renkou Yanjiu* (Population Research) 64 (5): 60–62.

Zhao Bin. 1999. "Mouthpiece or money-spinner?: The double life of Chinese television in the late 1990s." *International Journal of Cultural Studies* 2 (3): 291–306.

Zhao Shukai. 2000. "Organizational characteristics of rural labor mobility in China." In Loraine A. West and Yaohui Zhao, eds., *Rural Labor Flows in China*, 231–50. Berkeley: Institute of East Asian Studies, University of California Press.

Zhao, Yuezhi. 1998. *Media, Market, and Democracy in China*. Urbana: University of Illinois Press.

——. 2000. "From commercialisation to conglomeration: The transformation of the Chinese press within the orbit of the party state." *Journal of Communication* (spring):3–24.

——. 2002. "The rich, the laid-off, and the criminal in tabloid tales: Read all about it!" In Perry Link, Richard P. Madsen, and Paul G. Pickowicz, eds., *Popular China: Unofficial Culture in a Globalizing Society*, 111–35. Boulder, CO: Rowman and Littlefield.

Zhao Zhongling. 1996. "Jiejie qu Beijing le (Elder sister has gone to Beijing)." *Nongjianü Baishitong* (Rural Women Knowing All) (February):27.

Zhen, Zhang. 2000. "Mediating time: The 'rice bowl of youth' in fin de siècle urban China." *Public Culture* 12 (1) (winter): 93–113.

Zheng Zhenzhen. 1999. "Xiangcheng qianyi yu nongcun funü de fazhan (Rural-urban migration and rural women's development)." Paper presented at the 50th Anniversary Theoretical Symposium of All-China Women's Federation, December, 289–93.

————. 2002. "Waichu jingli dui nongcun funü chuhun nianling de yingxiang (Migration and age at first marriage of rural women)." *Zhongguo Renkou Kexue* (Chinese Journal of Population Science) 2:61–65.

Zheng, Zhenzhen, Rachel Connelly, Kenneth D. Roberts, Zhenming Xie, and Baochang Gu. 2001a. "Event history analysis on women's age at first migration and age at first marriage in four counties of China." Paper presented at 2001 Joint Statistical Meetings, Atlanta, August.

Zheng, Zhenzhen, Yun Zhou, Lixin Zheng, Dongxia Zhao, Chaohua Lou, and Shuangling Zhao. 2001b. "Sexual behavior and contraceptive use among unmarried young women migrant workers in five cities in China." *Reproductive Health Matters* 9 (17): 118–27.

Zhongguo Di Er Jie Dushi Nühai Fushi Fengcai Dasai Dalian Sai Qu (Dalian's Second Women's Fashion Contest). Dalian: Di Er Jie Zhongguo Dushi Nühai Fushi Fengcai Dasai Dalian Saiqu Zuzhi Weiyuanhui (Committee for Dalian's Women's Fashion Contest), 2001.

Zhongguo Wushi Nian de Jiangxi 1949–1999 (Jiangxi of Fifty Years 1949–1999). 2000. Beijing: China Statistical Press.

Zhou Chengwei. 2001. "Dagongmei cong duoluo de heidong zhong fenqi (Migrant working women rise up from the abyss)." *Aiqing, Hunyin, Jiating* (Love, Marriage, Family) 5:8–10.

Zhou Daming. 1997. "Investigation and analysis of 'migrant odd-job workers' in Guangzhou." In Gregory Eliyu Guldin, ed., *Farewell to Peasant China: Rural Urbanization and Social Change in the Late Twentieth Century*, 227–47. Armonk, N.Y.: M. E. Sharpe.

————. 1998. "Zhongguo nongmingong de liudong: Nongmingong shurudi yu shuchudi bijiao (Migration of peasants in China: Comparison of origins and destinations)." In Zhongshan University Anthropology Department, ed., *Waichu Wugong Diaocha Yanjiu Wenji* (Collection of Papers on Surveys of Peasant Outmigration), 3–23. Guangzhou: Zhongshan University Anthropology Department.

Zhou, Kate Xiao. 1996. *How the Farmers Changed China: Power of the People*. Boulder, CO: Westview Press.

Zhou Xiaohong. 1998. *Chuantong yu Bianqian: Jiangzhe Nongmin de Chanbian* (Tradition and Change: The Social Psychology of Peasants in Jiangsu and Zhejiang Provinces and Its Recent Changes). Beijing: Sanlian Bookstore.

CONTRIBUTORS

LOUISE BEYNON completed a Ph.D. in social anthropology at the School of Oriental and African Studies that analyzed changes in contemporary urban society in China through a comparison of the lives of young rural migrant women and urban unemployed women in Chengdu, Sichuan. She has received a British Academy–funded postdoctoral fellowship to research urban poverty and new forms of social organization in contemporary China.

RACHEL CONNELLY is professor of economics at Bowdoin College. She received her Ph.D. in economics from the University of Michigan in 1985, writing a dissertation on immigrant wages in the United States. Since then she has published a number of papers on the economics of women's employment, fertility, and child care demand using data from both the United States and Brazil. More recently, her Chinese-focused research looks at the effect of migration on women's lives and the social determinants of educational attainment.

C. CINDY FAN is professor of geography and past chair of the Asian American Studies Interdepartmental Program at UCLA. She has a Ph.D. in geography from Ohio State University. Her research interests focus on regional development, migration, and gender in China. She has published in *Annals of the Association of American Geographers, Professional Geographer, International Journal of Urban and Regional Research, International Migration Review, Environment and Planning A, Regional Studies, Urban Geography, Geographical Analysis,* and other refereed journals and books. Her work on regional development and internal migration in China has received the support of three research grants from the National Science Foundation and an award from the Luce Foundation.

ARIANNE M. GAETANO is a doctoral candidate in the Department of Anthropology at the University of Southern California writing a dissertation on "Engendering Post–Mao Modernity: Rural Migrant Women Crafting and Contesting Identity." Her six years in China included time spent teaching, translating, studying, and conducting research.

TAMARA JACKA is fellow in the Gender Relations Centre, Research School of Pacific and Asian Studies at the Australian National University. She has a Ph.D. in Asian Studies from the University of Adelaide (1994) and has published several articles relating to women's work in rural and urban China, women in rural-to-urban migration in China, and the politics and epistemology of cross-cultural research. She is the author of *Women's Work in Rural China: Change and Continuity in an Era of Reform* (Cambridge University Press, 1997), and is currently working on a book about the experiences of rural migrant women in Beijing.

BINBIN LOU is an associate researcher at the China Population Information and Research Center in Beijing. Her most recent research is related to women's status, family planning, and migration in rural China. She is the author of "Evaluate international cooperation projects from a gender perspective," *China Population Today* (2002); "The development of a reproductive health care system in rural China," *Population Research* (1999); "Family, marriage, and fertility of Zang women in Tibet," *Population Science of China* (1996); and "The study of rural migration in China," in *Collection of Research Papers of 1992 Fertility Sampling Survey in China* (China Population Publishing House, 1996).

RACHEL MURPHY obtained her Ph.D. in the Faculty of Social and Political Sciences, Cambridge University. Since October 2000 she has been a British Academy Postdoctoral Research Fellow in Development Studies at Jesus College, Cambridge, where she has coordinated and taught a course, "Population, Politics and Culture." Her publications include *How Migrant Labor Is Changing Rural China* (New York: Cambridge University Press, 2002) and "Turning Chinese peasants into modern farmers: Population quality discourse, demographic transition, and primary education," *China Quarterly* (in press, 2003). She is currently writing a book on population quality and the state in rural China and is co-convenor of a British Academy Networks project on "Chinese Experiences of the State and Cultural Citizenship."

KENNETH D. ROBERTS holds the Cullen Chair in Economics at Southwestern University. His research interests are broadly in economic development, focusing upon Latin America and East Asia, and more narrowly upon agrarian change and demographic processes, especially migration, in Mexico and China. His published articles on these topics appear in *Population and Development Review*, *International Migration Review*, *China Economic Review*, and other journals and edited books.

SUSAN E. SHORT is assistant professor of sociology and faculty associate director of the Population Studies and Training Center at Brown University. She specializes in family sociology, social demography, and social inequality. Recent publications include "Maternal work and time spent in childcare in China: A multimethod approach," *Population and Development Review* (2002); "China's one-child policy and the care of children: An analysis of qualitative and quantitative data," *Social Forces* (2001); and "Birth planning and sterilization in China," *Population Studies* (2000). Currently, she is completing research, funded by a three-year award from the National Institute of Health, on the consequences of China's one-child policy for children's well-being.

WANNING SUN is a lecturer in media and communication at Curtin University of Technology in western Australia. She is a native of Anhui province and has an ongoing interest in gendered mobility and social change in China, and in Anhui in particular. She is a Foundation Fellow at the Research Center for Provincial China (University of New South Wales–University of Technology Sydney). Her recent work appears in *Rethinking China's Provinces* (ed. John Fitzgerald, Routledge, 2002). She is the author of *Leaving China: Media, Migration, and Transnational Imagination* (Rowman and Littlefield, 2002).

LIN TAN is director of the Women's Studies Institute of China of the All-China Women's Federation, Beijing. She received her Ph.D. in demography from Xi'an Jiaotong University in 1990. She was professor of social demography at Nankai University, Tianjin, from June 1990 until March 2003. From 2000 to 2001 she was a Fulbright Scholar at Brown University. She has published widely on gender and migration, particularly on marriage migration; gender inequality in the labor market; and women's health issues in China. Her current research focuses on the effects of globalization on Chinese women's employment, health, and family life.

TIANTIAN ZHENG has an M.A in English linguistics and literature from Dalian University of Foreign Language, an M.A in Women's Studies from the University of Northern Iowa, and a Ph.D. in anthropology from Yale University. She is currently assistant professor of anthropology at State University of New York at Cortland.

ZHENZHEN ZHENG is a researcher at the Institute of Population and Labor Economics at the Chinese Academy of Social Sciences (CASS), Beijing. She received her Ph.D. in demography from Peking University. Her recent publications include "Migration and age at first marriage of rural women," *Chinese Journal of Population Science* (2002); "Sexual behavior and contraceptive use among unmarried young female migratory workers in 5 cities of China," *Population Science of China* (2001); and "Socio-demographic influences on first birth intervals in China, 1980–1992," *Journal of Biosocial Science* (2000).